www.wadsworth.com

wadsworth.com is the World Wide Web site
for Wadsworth and is your direct
source to dozens of online resources.

At *wadsworth.com* you can find out about
supplements, demonstration software, and
student resources. You can also send e-mail to
many of our authors and preview new publications
and exciting new technologies.

wadsworth.com
Changing the way the world learns®

ANTHOLOGY OF ASIAN SCRIPTURES

Robert E. Van Voorst

Western Theological Seminary

Wadsworth
Thomson Learning

Australia • Canada • Mexico • Singapore • Spain • United Kingdom • United States

Religion Editor: Peter Adams
Assistant Editor: Kerri Abdinoor
Editorial Assistant: Mindy Newfarmer/
  Mark Andrews
Marketing Manager: Dave Garrison
Print Buyer: Mary Noel
Permissions Editor: Robert Kauser
Production Service: Matrix Productions

Copy Editor: Vicki Nelson
Cover Designer: Annabelle Ison
Cover painting: Meryon (1960–1961) by Franz Kline. Tate
  Gallery, London. © 2000 The Franz Kline Estate/Artists
  Rights Society (ARS), New York
Compositor: G & S Typesetters
Printer/Binder: Webcom

Printed in Canada

1 2 3 4 5 6 04 03 02 01 00

For more information, contact
Wadsworth/Thomson Learning
10 Davis Drive
Belmont, CA 94002-3098
USA
www.wadsworth.com

International Headquarters
Thomson Learning
290 Harbor Drive, 2nd Floor
Stamford, CT 06902-7477
USA

UK/Europe/Middle East
Thomson Learning
Berkshire House
168-173 High Holborn
London WC1V 7AA
United Kingdom

Asia
Thomson Learning
60 Albert Street #15-01
Albert Complex
Singapore 189969

Canada
Nelson/Thomson Learning
1120 Birchmount Road
Scarborough, Ontario M1K 5G4
Canada

Library of Congress Cataloging-in-Publication Data
Anthology of Asian scriptures / Robert E. Van Voorst.
    p.   cm.
  Includes index.
  ISBN 0-534-51246-1
  1. Sacred books.   2. Asia—Religion.   I. Van Voorst, Robert E.

BL1010.V36 2000
291.8'2'095—dc21

99-050349

To Mary, my wife
and Richard and Nicholas, our sons
In gratitude for all the happiness you have given me

Contents

Preface   xiii
Acknowledgments   xv

CHAPTER ONE
Asian Scriptures Among the World's Religions   1

    A Brief History of Scripture Scholarship,   2
    The Nature and Definition of Scripture,   4
    The Uses of Scripture,   9
    Advantages and Disadvantages,   11
    Asian Scriptures and Modern Scholarship,   14
    Scriptures and the World Wide Web,   15
    The Plan of This Book,   16
    A Guide to Pronunciation,   17
    Suggestions on How to Read Scriptures,   18

    Glossary,   20
    Questions for Study and Discussion,   20
    Suggestions for Further Reading,   21

CHAPTER TWO
Hinduism   23

    Introduction   23
    Overview of Structure,   23
    Origin and Development,   26
    Use,   28

    Teaching   30
    Aditi and the Birth of the Gods (*Rig-Veda* 10.72),   30
    The Creation Hymn (*Rig-Veda* 10.129),   30
    Creation from Brahman (*Brihad-Aranyaka Upanishad* 1.4.1–7),   31
    The God Indra (*Rig-Veda* 2.12),   32
    The God Shiva (*Shvetashvatara Upanishad* 3.1–13),   33
    "That You Are" (*Chandogya Upanishad* 6.1–2, 9–11),   34
    The Goddess as Kali (*Markandeya Purana, Devi-Mahatmya* 7.1–25),   35

Organization 36
The Creation of the Caste System (*Rig-Veda* 10.90), 36
The Four Castes (*Institutes of Vishnu* 2.1–17), 37

Ethics 38
Sin and Forgiveness (*Rig-Veda* 7.86), 38
The Three *Das* (*Brihadaranyaka Upanishad* 5.2), 39
The Way of Asceticism (*Mundaka Upanishad* 2.1–3, 5–8, 10–13), 39
Stages of Life for a Twice-Born Man (*Laws of Manu* 2.69–74, 191–201; 3.1–19;
    6.1–9, 33–49), 40
The Life of Women (*Laws of Manu* 3.55–60; 5.147–165), 43

Ritual and Meditation 44
The Gayatri Mantra (*Rig-Veda* 3.62.10), 44
Hymn to Agni (*Rig-Veda* 1.1), 45
The Meaning of the Agnihotra Sacrifice (*Agni-Brahmana* 1.1–19), 45
The *Puja* of a Yogin (*Agni Purana*), 46
Soma (*Rig-Veda* 8.48), 47
Marriage (*Rig-Veda* 10.85.20–47), 48
Cremation (*Rig-Veda* 10.16), 50
Charms and Spells (*Atharva-Veda* 6.20; 7.70; 6.9; 3.16), 50
Chanting of *Om* (*Chandogya Upanishad* 1.1.1–10), 51
The Practice of Yoga (*Shvetashvatara Upanishad* 2.8–15), 52

Appendix 1: Selections from the *Bhagavad-Gita*, 53
Appendix 2: Mohandas Gandhi on the *Bhagavad-Gita* 63
Appendix 3: Two Tamil Poets, Appar and Tukaram, 64
Appendix 4: Poems of Mira, a Hindi Female Saint, 66

Glossary, 66
Questions for Study and Discussion, 67
Suggestions for Further Reading, 67

CHAPTER THREE
Buddhism 71

Introduction 71
Overview of Structure, 71
Origin and Development, 75
Use, 76

History 77
The Past Lives of Gotama Buddha (*Jataka* 190), 77
The Life of Gotama Buddha (Selections from the *Buddhacarita*), 79
The Death of Gotama Buddha (*Mahaparinibbana Sutta* 6.1-14, 31–35,
    45–48), 84

The Life of Milarepa (*The Life of Milarepa* 2.7), 86

Teaching 88
The Sermon on the Four Noble Truths (*Dhammacakkappavattana Sutta* 1–8), 88
The *Skandhas* and the Chain of Causation (*Buddhacarita* 16.1, 28–50), 89
The Essence of Buddhism (*Heart Sutra*), 90
A Tibetan Commentary on the *Heart Sutra* (*Jewel Light Illuminating the Meaning*), 91
A Description of Nirvana (*Milinda-panha* 4.8.65–66), 92
A Mahayana View of the Buddha (*Saddharma-pundarika Sutra* 2.36; 10.1), 93
Poems of Early Nuns (*Therigatha*), 95

Ethics 96
Conduct of the Monk (*Dhammapada* 25.360–382), 96
Admonition to Laity (*Cullavagga, Dhammikasutta* 18–29), 97
Wisdom of the Buddha (*Dhammapada* 1–20, 157–166), 98
The Bodhisattva Ideal (*Mahavastu*), 100

Organization 101
Founding of the Order (*Mahavagga* 1.6.10, 11–16, 27–30, 32, 34, 37), 101
The Rules of Defeat (*Patimokkha, Parajika Dhamma* 1–4), 102
Rules Requiring Formal Meetings (*Patimokkha, Samghadisesa Dhamma* 1–13), 103
The Order of Nuns (*Cullavagga* 10.1.1–6), 105

Ritual and Meditation 107
The Relics of the Buddha (*Mahaparinibbana Sutta* 6.58–60), 107
Mindfulness in Meditation (*Majjhima-Nikaya, Satipatthanasutta* 10.1–9), 107
The Merit of Making Images (*Taisho Shinshu Daizokyo*, 16, no. 694), 110
Scripture to Guide the Soul After Death (*Bardo Thodol* 1.1–2), 112

Glossary, 113
Questions for Study and Discussion, 114
Suggestions for Further Reading, 115

CHAPTER FOUR
Jainism 117

Introduction 117
Overview of Structure, 117
Origin, Development, and Use, 118

History 119
The Life of Mahavira (*Acaranga Sutra* 2.15.6–9, 14, 16–20, 22–25, 27), 119

Teaching 122

The World Is Uncreated (*Mahapurana* 4.16–31, 38–40), 122

The Causes of Sin (*Acaranga Sutra* 1.1–2), 123

Can Women Achieve Liberation? (*Strinirvana-pariccheda* 2, 4; *Sutraprabrita* 1.22–26), 124

The World Is Full of Suffering (*Uttaradhyayana Sutra* 19.61–67, 71, 74), 125

The Road to Final Deliverance (*Uttaradhyayana Sutra* 28), 125

Organization 127

The Five Great Vows (*Acaranga Sutra* 2.15i–v), 127

Ethics 128

Ahimsa (*Sutrakritanga* 1.7.1–9), 128

Rules for Monastic Life (*Uttaradhyayana Sutra* 35), 129

The True Monk (*Uttaradhyayana Sutra* 15.1–16), 130

Stories from Jaina Scriptures and Commentary (*Avasyakasutra* 1.484.11–485.13; 2.200.11–201.12; *Mulasuddhiprakarana*, 179–180), 131

Glossary, 134
Questions for Study and Discussion, 134
Suggestions for Further Reading, 134

CHAPTER FIVE

Sikhism 137

Introduction 137

Overview of Structure, 137

Origin and Development, 138

Use, 139

Teaching 140

Selections from the *Japji* (1–3, 5–6, 9–10, 12–13, 15, 17–18, 20–22, 25, 28–29, 33, 37–Epilogue), 140

Remembering God (*Gauri Sukhmani*, Mahala 5), 145

Creation of the World (*Asa Ki Var*, Mahala 1), 146

Dancing for Krishna (*Rag Gurji*, Mahala 3), 147

The Hindu Thread (*Asa Ki Var*, Mahala 1), 147

Ethics 148

Truth Is the Basis of Conduct (*Hymns of Guru Nanak*), 148

Prayer for Forgiveness (*Rag Bihagra*, Mahala 5), 149

Against the Use of Wine (*Rag Bihagra*, Mahala 1), 149

Ritual 150

Hymn for the Installation of the *Guru Granth* (*Rag Devgandhari*, Mahala 5), 150

A Marriage Hymn (*Rag Asa*, Mahala 5), 150

Organization 151
The Guru (*Rag Gauri,* Mahala 3),   151
God's Power in the Sikh Community (*Rag Gauri,* Mahala 5),   152

Appendix: Selections from the *Dasam Granth* 152
A. Guru Gobind Singh's Story (*Vichitar Natak,* 6),   152
B. God as the Holy Sword (*Vichitar Natak,* 1),   153

Glossary,   154
Questions for Study and Discussion,   155
Suggestions for Further Reading,   155

CHAPTER SIX
Zoroastrianism 157

Introduction 157
Overview of Structure,   157
Origin and Development,   158
Use,   159

History 160
The Call of Zarathushtra (*Yasna* 29),   160
A Hymn of Praise to Zarathushtra (*Yasht* 24:87b–94),   161

Teaching 162
Hymn to Ahura and the Purifying Fire (*Yasna* 36),   162
Hymn to Ahura Mazda the Creator (*Yasna* 37:1–5),   163
The Doctrine of Dualism (*Yasna* 30),   163

Ethics 164
Personal Virtues (*Denkard* 6.23, 24),   164
Six Ritual Obligations (*Sad Dar* 6.1–7),   165

Ritual 165
The Place of the *Gathas* (*Yasna* 55:1–3),   165
The Zoroastrian Confession (*Yasna* 12),   166
The Four Great Prayers (From the *Yasna*),   167
Disposal of the Dead (*Vendidad, Fargard* 6, section 5, 44–51),   167

Glossary,   168
Questions for Study and Discussion,   168
Suggestions for Further Reading,   168

CHAPTER SEVEN
Confucianism 171

Introduction 171
Overview of Structure,   171

Origin and Development,   173
Use,   174

History   175
The Character of Confucius (*Analects* 2.4; 7.1–9, 19–24; 10.1–4, 8–12),   175

Ethics   177
The Virtues of the Superior Man (*Analects* 1.1–4, 6–9, 14; 15.17–23),   177
Benevolence (*Analects* 4.1–6),   178
The Actions of Filiality (*Classic of Rites,* 10.1, 4, 7, 10–11, 13–15),   179
The Attitude of Filiality (*Analects* 2.5–8; 4.18–21; 13.18),   180
Propriety (*Analects* 3.3–4, 8–9, 12–15, 17–19),   181
The Way (*Analects* 16.2),   182
The Love of Learning (*Analects* 17.8–9, 12),   183
Early Debate over the Goodness of Human Nature (*Mencius* 6.1.1–4, 6),   183
The Basis of Good Government (*The Great Learning* 1–7; 9.1, 3–9),   185
The Ruler as Example to the People (*Analects* 2.18–20; 12.11, 17, 19;
    13.4–6),   187
Confidence and Prosperity in Government (*Mencius* 4.3, 9; 1.6.20–24),   188

Ritual   189
Divination (*Classic of Changes* 1, 47, 54),   189
Songs for Sacrifice (*Classic of Poetry, Shang* 1; *Kau* 7; *Minor Odes* 10.1, 3; 5),   190
Music and Morality (*Classic of Rites* 17.2.10–11, 15–18, 20–21),   193

Appendix: Later Developments of Early Themes,   194
Later Debate over Human Nature (*Xunzi* 3.150–151; *Fuyan* 3.1a–b),   194
Attack on Buddhism (*Ch'ang-li hsien-sheng wen-chi* 39.2b-42),   195
Advice for Reading Texts (*Conversations of Master Chu* 4.37–39, 41),   196
Neoconfucian Ethics (Chang Tsai, *The Western Inscription*),   197

Glossary,   198
Questions for Study and Discussion,   198
Suggestions for Further Reading,   199

CHAPTER EIGHT
Taoism   **201**

Introduction   201
Overview of Structure,   201
Origin, Development, and Use,   202

Teaching   203
The Nature of the Tao (*Tao Te Ching,* 1, 6, 25, 34; *Chuang-tzu* 29),   203
The World (*Tao Te Ching* 7, 42, 52),   205
The Domain of Nothingness (*Chuang-tzu,* book 7),   206

Ethics   206
Nonaction (*Chuang-tzu*, book 7),   206
Individual Life in Harmony with the Tao (*Tao Te Ching* 16, 22, 33, 44),   206
The Superior Man (*Chuang-tzu*, book 12),   208
Government (*Tao Te Ching* 3, 18, 57, 64),   209
Great and Small Rulers (*Chuang-tzu*, book 1),   210
On Death (*Chuang-tzu*, book 18),   210
Reward and Retribution (*T'ai-Shang*, book 1),   211

Ritual   212
Methods of Prolonging Life (*Pao-p'u-tzu* 15.6b–7a; 19.6b–7a),   212
The Life and Ascension of Shen Xi (*Shenxian zhuan, Daozang jinghua* 5.11),   214
The Relationship of Taoism to Confucianism (*Pao-p'u Tzu* 7.5a),   215

Appendix: A Complete Taoist Scripture
(*The True Scripture of the Great Emperor*),   216

Glossary,   219
Questions for Study and Discussion,   220
Suggestions for Further Reading,   220

CHAPTER NINE
Shinto   223

Introduction   223
The *Kojiki*,   223
The *Nihongi*,   224

Selections from the *Kojiki* and the *Nihongi*   224
Preface to the *Kojiki*,   224
The Creation of Japan (*Kojiki*, chapters 1–5, 11, 33),   227
The Shrine at Ise (*Nihongi*, chapter 5),   230
Emperor Yuryaku and the Story of the Woman Akawi-ko (*Kojiki*,
    chapter 154),   231

Selections from the *Norito*
Festival of the Gates (*Norito*),   232
Ritual Prayer for Forgiveness and Purification of Government Officials (*Norito*),   233

Glossary,   234
Questions for Study and Discussion,   234
Suggestions for Further Reading,   234

Index   236

Preface

The major living religions of Asia have all expressed their teachings and practices in writing. Over the course of time, some of these writings gained unique standing in their traditions and became scriptures. As scriptures, they continue to influence the course of their religions. To read these scriptures, therefore, is to encounter world religions from Asia in a meaningful way.

This book is designed to facilitate this encounter for the general reader and especially for the student of Asian religion. Its pages contain many of the most notable and instructive scriptures of Hinduism, Buddhism, Jainism, Sikhism, Zoroastrianism, Confucianism, Taoism, and Shinto. The collection began with my efforts to gather the most important passages of world scripture for my students, organize them in a way helpful for teaching and learning, and include the full set of pedagogical aids that students have come to expect. This anthology not only presents scripture readings, but also sets them in the context of their application in the traditions themselves, taking into account recent scholarship on the role of scriptures in religion. Moreover, it does this in one volume and in one format. Designed to be used as a secondary textbook, the anthology has an organization that is easily adaptable to a range of primary textbooks and most of the current methods of teaching comparative religion.

Anthology of Asian Scriptures is organized as follows: The first chapter examines the general phenomenon of scripture in the world's religions, its nature, use, and place in modern scholarship. Chapter 1 also introduces the reader to the art of reading scripture with practical suggestions, a pronunciation guide for foreign words, and other aids.

Each subsequent chapter presents the scripture of a single religion and is organized as follows: Three or four vignettes about scripture and its usage draw the reader's interest and imagination. Then an introduction sets the context by explaining the overall structure, origin, development, and use of the scripture in its religion. The first grouping of scripture passages concerns the history of the religion, especially the founder (if any) and early history of the tradition. The second grouping covers main doctrinal teachings, including Divine or Ultimate Reality, creation and the environment, human nature, and human fulfillment. The third grouping deals with ethical systems, both personal and social; topics such as war and peace, justice, and the role of women will be anthologized as fully as possible here. The fourth grouping focuses on organization, both the ways that religion orders itself and seeks to order its wider culture. The fifth grouping includes worship, devotion, ritual, and meditation. Each chapter has full pedagogical aids, including introductions to each passage, tables listing scripture canons, full annotations to explain difficult items in the readings (placed at the bottom of the page for easy access), questions for study and discussion, a glossary with pronunciations, and suggestions for further reading.

The translations used here have been selected for their accuracy and readability. I have been fortunate to receive permission to reprint many of the finest and most current English translations of many world scriptures. Where it has not been possible to get permission, or where recent English translations are incomplete or too technical for undergraduate students, I have relied on a few older translations that have proven their worth over time and are now in the public domain. I have edited these to update vocabulary, spelling, and occasionally syntax, removing the peculiarities of the English in which these translations were done. But I have endeavored to let the "voice" of both text and translator come through.

The scriptures presented here come from the religions commonly understood to be the major living world religions indigenous to Asia. Although Islam is widely spread through Asia, it has been excluded from this book because it is not indigenous to Asia (the "Far East," at least).

My hope is that this book will stimulate its readers to explore the religions of Asia more deeply.

Acknowledgments

I would like to thank here the many people who have helped me in the writing of this book, and its predecessor volume, *Anthology of World Scriptures* (3rd ed.). Lycoming College, where I was privileged to teach for ten years, assisted the writing of this book with two summer research grants. The faculty and staff of Lycoming College's Snowden Library helped me in the large task of gathering materials, by acquisition, interlibrary loan, and Internet. Some research was carried out at the Bodleian Library of the University of Oxford, England, while I was on sabbatical leave there in 1997. My student assistant at Lycoming College, Daven Oskvig, assisted in the compilation of these readings. My son Richard helped with the computer processing. Not least in importance, my students in ten classes at Lycoming and in one at Bucknell University used earlier drafts and editions of this book and contributed many helpful suggestions that found their way into this book.

The editorial staff at Wadsworth have been fine partners in developing and producing this book. While they all have done excellent work for me, I especially want to thank my editor Peter Adams, Merrill Peterson of Matrix Productions, and my copyeditor Vicki Nelson.

Scholars at other institutions offered detailed, insightful critiques at many points along the way. For reviewing most of this book as it appeared in the first three editions of my *Anthology of World Scriptures,* I thank Vivodh J. Z. Anand, Montclair State University; Paul Bernadicou, University of San Francisco; James Cook, Oakland Community College, Orchard Ridge; Marianne Ferguson, Buffalo State College; Etta Hesselink, University of Michigan; Roger Keller, Brigham Young University; William K. Mahony, Davidson College; Michael McKale, Saint Francis College; Vivian-Lee Nyitray, University of California at Riverside; Christopher Queen, Harvard University; Stephen J. Reno, Southern Oregon State College; Philip Riley, Santa Clara University; Roger L. Schmidt, San Bernardino Valley College; Philip Schmitz, Eastern Michigan University; Daniel Sheridan, Loyola University of New Orleans; Robert Smith, Trenton State College; Donald Swearer, Swarthmore College; James Whitehill, Stephens College; Boyd Wilson, Hope College; and Glenn Yocum, Whittier College. For their careful, helpful review of the current book, I thank Anne Birdwhistell, Richard Stockton College of New Jersey, Anne Monius, University of Virginia; Vivian-Lee Nyitray, University of California at Riverside; and Gail Hinich Sutherland, Louisiana State University.

Though all these made this a better book, any errors that remain are mine alone. I would be most grateful if those of you who use this book and my website on scripture would send me your comments and suggestions for improving them. You can reach me by post at 101 East 13th Street, Holland, MI 49423, or by e-mail at bob.vanvoorst@westernsem.org.

CHAPTER ONE

Asian Scriptures Among the World's Religions

❖ In an Indian city, Hindu priests and Sanskrit-language scholars call a news conference to criticize a song, "Shanti," on the latest album by the American pop singer Madonna. Unlike most religious critiques of rock music, which focus on an argued lack of moral values, the Hindus' criticisms focus on Madonna's pronunciation of that ancient divine name. Reflecting Hindu spoken use of scripture, the priests and scholars state that the spiritual power of this name is not effective unless it is pronounced correctly.

❖ In London, a Sikh family gathers at their dining room table for devotional reading of the *Adi Granth*. The adult family members take turns in reading, and everyone pays reverent attention to the words. This daily event is one of the main building blocks of faith and family solidarity among observant Sikhs.

❖ In New York City, the government of Taiwan takes out a large, expensive advertisement on the op-ed page of the *New York Times*. It argues that Taiwan is an orderly, virtuous, and industrious society because it is founded on the principles of Confucius' *Analects* and *Great Learning*. Therefore, Taiwan is an excellent partner in international trade.

❖ In Maharagama, Sri Lanka, several Buddhist monks work at computer keyboards. They are keying in the complete text of the Pali version of the Buddhist collection of scriptures. After three years at their task, the scriptures are to be published on the World Wide Web and then will be available in a fully searchable CD ROM. The monks and the private patrons funding this project see it as yet another phase in the preservation of Buddhist scripture from 2,500 years ago.

The influence of Asian scripture is felt throughout the world in ways both extraordinary and commonplace. The scriptures of Asian religions have a continuing profound impact on life and culture in Asia and the wider world. This anthology introduces the reader to these scriptures and encourages a deep encounter with them in all their variety. Scriptures of Asia are so vast in number—Max Müller's *Sacred Books of the East*[1] series had fifty volumes when it was finished in 1910, and its coverage of Asian scripture was still far from complete—that some sort of sampling is necessary for all but the most expert specialist. An anthology is by its very nature a selection; it includes some key passages, but unhappily many more must be left out. The best that can be hoped

---

[1] F. Max Müller, gen. ed., *The Sacred Books of the East,* 50 vols. (Oxford: Oxford University Press, 1879–1910; reprinted in 1969 in India, with some volumes still in print).

for is that the anthology selects excerpts from each tradition that faithfully reflect the history and continuing life of the tradition. These selections offer the reader the possibility of a meaningful insight into Asian religions.

This introductory chapter is organized into several sections. "A Brief History of Scripture Scholarship" outlines the main periods of the study of world scriptures. "The Nature and Definition of Scripture" discusses the term *scripture* as a comprehensive generic label suitable to religious scholarship, followed by a consideration of the varied functions of scripture in "The Uses of Scripture." "Advantages and Disadvantages" deals with the important question of the strengths and weaknesses of this approach. "World Scriptures and Modern Scholarship" discusses the impact of Western academic study on how we understand Asian scriptures. "Scriptures on the World Wide Web" examines how students can best use the growing number of Asian scriptures on the Internet. "The Plan of This Book" explains how the scripture selections are organized, and "A Guide to Pronunciation" provides some general rules for saying aloud the proper nouns in the readings. Finally, "Suggestions on How to Read Scriptures" gives helpful hints on the process of reading scriptures for fuller comprehension.

A BRIEF HISTORY
OF SCRIPTURE SCHOLARSHIP

The scholarly study of world scripture[2] in the last hundred years has passed through three distinct stages that have strongly influenced how we read scriptures.[3] Near the middle of the nineteenth century, European scholars began a vast enterprise of making critically reliable translations of Asian scriptures, with a special focus on the little-translated sacred literature of Asia. Their concern was to translate individual texts, an important and necessary first step, not to examine the general religious phenomenon of scripture. They treated scripture as a mine out of which to dig the history and doctrine of religions, with little regard for the ways scripture functioned in religious communities. Müller's *Sacred Books of the East* is the most prominent result of this movement.[4]

---

[2] By "world scriptures" I mean scriptures of the major religions of the world, not necessarily scriptures that are spread *throughout* the world.

[3] For an excellent comprehensive discussion of the history of the academic study of world religions, with some detailed comments on scripture study, see E. Sharpe, *Comparative Religion: A History*, 2d ed. (LaSalle, IL: Open Court Press, 1987). Perhaps the best succinct presentation of this topic is by S. Cain, "History of the Study of Religion," in M. Eliade, ed., *Encyclopedia of Religion* (New York: Macmillan, 1987), vol. 14, pp. 64–83.

[4] A continuing manifestation of this first stage are the popular anthologies of world scriptures that have been published almost continually for many years. To cite only a few examples, Robert Ballou's *The Bible of the World* (New York: Viking, 1939) and its abridgment in *World Bible* (Viking Portable Library; New York: Viking, 1944) have remained in print continually, although unrevised. The Unification Church has published *World Scripture: A Comparative Anthology of Sacred Texts*, ed. Andrew Wilson (New York: Paragon House, 1991). And Philip Novak has edited *The World's Wisdom: Sacred Texts of the World's Religions* (San Francisco: Harper San Francisco, 1994). Popular anthologies, like the first scholarly stage of study, use world scriptures as a mine for enlightenment with little attention to how scripture functions in world religious communities.

The second stage in the study of scriptures was dominated by the academic movement customarily known by its German name, *Religionswissenschaft*. This name is usually understood as "history of religion" but means more accurately "science of religion." This school, which continues to exert a strong influence today, analyzes the historical development of each religion. Perhaps in reaction to the earlier methodological reliance on scriptures, scholars like Joachim Wach and Mircea Eliade relied on the study of other, nontextual elements of religion, such as ritual, myth, symbols, and the like. Scripture was largely neglected at this stage. Such a magisterial treatment of comparative religion as Gerardus van der Leeuw's *Religion in Essence and Manifestation*[5] contains only a spare discussion of scripture as a universal religious phenomenon. Moreover, as social scientific methods increasingly entered the field of religious scholarship, researchers turned away from literary sources from the past in favor of the study of present-day living communities of faith.[6]

Although this second stage is still very influential, a third stage is emerging in which scholars of religious studies are rediscovering the value of scripture. The overreliance on scripture characteristic of the first stage and the neglect of scripture in the second stage are being balanced as researchers increasingly view scripture as an important aspect of religion. One new element here is that scripture is correctly seen as one religious phenomenon among many and therefore not to be isolated from the others. Another new element is an emphasis on the actual ways in which scripture is viewed and used in world religions. To understand scripture, according to this view, we must know not just the text, but also how it comes alive in the total life of the religion.

Recent research in comparative religion gives evidence of this emerging third stage. Large-scale studies of comparative religion such as Geo Widengren's *Religionsphänomenologie* [Phenomenology of Religion][7] and Friedrich Heiler's *Erscheinungsformen und Wesen der Religion* [Manifestations and Essence of Religion][8] both deal extensively with the nature and use of scripture among the world's religions. Ninian Smart's recent *Sacred Texts of the World*[9] uses scripture to approach several different religious phenomena in each world religion. Four recent books deal with scripture and its role in religion: *The Holy Book in Comparative Perspective,* by Frederick Denny and Roderick Taylor;[10] *Sacred Word and Sacred Text,* by Harold Coward;[11] *Rethinking Scripture: Essays from a Comparative Perspective,* by Miriam Levering;[12] *Sacred Texts and*

---

[5] Gerardus van der Leeuw, *Religion in Essence and Manifestation* (London: Allen & Unwin, 1938); German original, 1933. One short chapter, 64, deals almost exclusively with Western scripture.

[6] For example, the widely used *Reader in Comparative Religion: An Anthropological Approach,* ed. W. A. Lessa and E. Z. Vogt, 4th ed. (New York: Harper & Row, 1979), has excellent readings in all the basic topics in the cultural-anthropological study of religion—symbol, myth, ritual, shamanism, magic—but not one essay on scripture and its uses.

[7] Geo Widengren, *Religionsphänomenologie* (Berlin: de Gruyter, 1969).

[8] Friedrich Heiler, *Erscheinungsformen und Wesen der Religion,* 2d ed. (Stuttgart: Kohlhammer, 1979).

[9] Ninian Smart, *Sacred Texts of the World* (London: Macmillan, 1982).

[10] F. M. Denny and R. L. Taylor, eds., *The Holy Book in Comparative Perspective* (Charleston: University of South Carolina Press, 1985).

[11] Harold Coward, *Sacred Word and Sacred Text* (Maryknoll, NY: Orbis, 1988).

[12] Miriam Levering, ed., *Rethinking Scripture: Essays from a Comparative Perspective* (Albany: State University of New York Press, 1989); contains two programmatic essays by Smith, an essay on the oral character of

Authority, by Jacob Neusner;[13] and, most important, *What Is Scripture? A Comparative Approach,* by Wilfred Cantwell Smith.[14] As a result of this research, the comparative study of scripture is today one of the leading features in the study of religion.

Smith, of Harvard University, and some of his former doctoral students have had a strong influence on current scripture study. They argue for scripture study centered on the actual reception and use of scriptures. The work of William Graham on the oral dimensions of scripture has been especially influential.[15] A measure of the strength of this stage is that it is now appearing in textbooks, where several works are notable: T. W. Hall, R. B. Pilgrim, and R. R. Cavanagh, *Religion: An Introduction;*[16] Kenneth Kramer, *World Scriptures: An Introduction to Comparative Religion;*[17] Roger Schmidt, *Exploring Religion;*[18] Jean Holm and John Bowker, *Sacred Writings;*[19] Richard Viladesau and Mark Massa, *World Religions: A Sourcebook for Students of Christian Theology;*[20] and most recently, Ian Markham, *A World Religions Reader.*[21] Asian religions typically receive extensive treatment in these books. As a representative of this third stage of scripture study, the present work offers a wide range of scripture selections from the world religions originating in Asia, with introductions and annotations to set the readings in the context of their actual usage.

THE NATURE AND DEFINITION OF SCRIPTURE

At first glance, defining our term seems easy enough. Scripture is the holy writing, the sacred text of a religion. All religions seem to have scriptures, and all appear to use them in the same way. As a phenomenon among religions, scripture seems on the surface to be a constant. But on closer examination these simple notions vanish. Books of world religions that are traditionally regarded as scriptures vary in several important aspects. The content of this anthology will bear out this variety, but it would be well to sketch in some of it here.

---

world scriptures by W. Graham, and chapter-length treatments by others of Buddhism, Hinduism, Jainism, and Judaism.

[13] J. Neusner, ed., *Sacred Texts and Authority* (Cleveland: Pilgrim, 1998).

[14] Wilfred Cantwell Smith, *What Is Scripture? A Comparative Approach* (Philadelphia: Augsburg Fortress, 1993).

[15] See especially William Graham's *Beyond the Written Word: Oral Aspects of Scripture in the History of Religion* (Cambridge: Cambridge University Press, 1983).

[16] T. W. Hall, R. B. Pilgrim, and R. R. Cavanagh, *Religion: An Introduction* (San Francisco: Harper & Row, 1985). This book contains a finely nuanced chapter on scripture as one of the varieties of religious expression on pp. 108–124.

[17] Kenneth Kramer, *World Scriptures: An Introduction to Comparative Religion* (New York: Paulist, 1986). Kramer approaches scripture by means of narrative.

[18] Roger Schmidt, *Exploring Religion,* 2d ed. (Belmont, CA: Wadsworth, 1988). Schmidt has a chapter-length treatment of world scripture.

[19] Jean Holm and John Bower, *Sacred Writings* (Themes in Religious Studies Series; London: Pinter, 1994).

[20] Richard Viladesau and Mark Massa, *World Religions: A Sourcebook for the Student of Christian Theology* (New York: Paulist, 1994). As its subtitle indicates, this book is intended for those who study world religions from within a Christian perspective.

[21] Ian S. Markham, ed., *A World Religions Reader* (Oxford: Blackwell, 1996).

The first variation among scriptures is in literary form, or **genre**. Scripture as a general category implies that all scriptures look alike in literary form and content. Persons who come from religious traditions with scriptures naturally tend to assume that the sacred texts of other religions look and function exactly like theirs. Scripture, however, has a literary variety as numerous as the religions and cultures from which it comes. Some scriptures, especially of those Asian faiths that consider salvation a release from historical existence, have few narratives or none at all. Some scriptures have their vision of a moral life enshrined in law codes, some feature more loosely bound moral precepts, and still others do not seem concerned about ethics. Poetry is the leading literary form of some scriptures; others feature prose. Some scriptural books (the Hindu *Upanishads*) have metaphysical philosophy, others (the Confucian *Analects*) moral philosophy, but many have no explicit philosophy at all. Some scriptures (the Hindu *Vedas*) contain directions and songs for sacrifice, whereas others (the *Analects*) have no prescriptions for rites and ceremonies. We also find myth, legend, prophecy, sermons, love poems, divination, and magic, among many other such genres, in the scriptures of the world.

Even this cursory overview of the sacred literature shows that scriptures do not entail a fixed literary form, because almost every type of form can be found in them. Therefore, we cannot open a book, browse through its contents, and pronounce it scriptural. Scripture is primarily a relational, not a literary, phenomenon. "The sacrality or holiness of a book is not an *a priori* attribute but one that is realized historically in the life of communities who respond to it as something sacred or holy."[22] Communities shape and receive scripture, and scripture shapes the life of faith. The relation between scripture and religion is reciprocal and dynamic.

The second variation among scriptures has to do with their *number* within any one religion, which can range from one book to an entire library. Like the *Quran*, scriptures can be one unified book of moderate size under two covers. Like the Jewish and Christian scriptures, they can be many different short books collected into one scripture corpus, usually of a larger size. In Asian religions, canons tend to be much larger. They can be different books ranging in number from the many Hindu texts, to the dozen or so Confucian texts (depending on how the Classics are numbered), and to the more than 1,000 texts found in Taoism and in some forms of Mahayana Buddhism.

The third variation in scripture lies in *function*. In some religions, scripture is so central—or so it may look to the outsider—that the life of the believer seems virtually dictated by scripture. Zoroastrianism is properly called "a religion of the book" because of the high place and powerful function their scriptures have. Asian religions often have a more informal relationship to their scripture than do Western religions; devotees consult Asian scriptures often for general guidance and inspiration.

The varying oral and textual dimensions of scripture also lead to differences in function. Some religions—as, for example, Hinduism—view the spoken word of scripture as primary. Hindus regard the *Vedas* essentially as speech rather than as printed word and see the written text as inferior to the "oral text." In other religions, the power and function of the book seem to depend upon its written, textual nature. A later section

---

[22] W. A. Graham, "Scripture," *Encyclopedia of Religion*, vol. 13, p. 134.

of this chapter will deal more fully with the topic of the uses of scripture, but enough has been said here to suggest that they function in different ways.

Given all this variety, is it possible to define scripture in a way that can take variety into account and yet serve as a valid conceptual category for all Asian religions? Although some scholars answer in the negative,[23] most would argue that a comprehensive definition of scripture is possible and necessary. Despite its inherent ambiguities and difficulties, scholars commonly accept and use this term generically. The definition we will use here is this: **Scripture** *is the writing accepted by and used in a religious community as especially sacred and authoritative.* We can follow up on this definition by looking more closely at its key words and its implications. In what follows we will discuss both the formal and functional aspects of scriptures—what they are and how they are used.

First, all scripture is a *writing*. Scripture exercises much of its authority as a book, and we encounter it as such. Some scholars argue that **oral tradition** is "scriptural."[24] Although oral and written traditions do have some similar characteristics and functions, strictly speaking "oral scripture" is a contradiction in terms—all scripture is by definition written. The scripture of every religion, however, does have continuing, significant oral and aural dimensions.[25] Speaking and hearing the scriptural words are essential to the meaning and function of scripture. Most scriptures originated in oral tradition and stayed in oral tradition for several generations before being put down in writing. Although the writing down of scripture obscures its oral dimensions, the orality of the text is still embedded in the writing, waiting to be drawn out by faithful vocalizing of the words. Scripture comes most fully alive when believers read it aloud and hear it in worship. Most believers, even those in highly literate cultures, hear scripture in worship more often and more meaningfully than they read it privately. In this book, as in any book, we encounter scriptures as texts. The reader must always remember that these texts are also meant to be spoken and heard.

The second element of our definition is that scriptures are *especially sacred*. They have special religious significance in pointing to ultimate reality and truth. Sacredness should not be seen simply as of divine origin, or even as the "wholly other," Rudolf Otto's influential conception of sacredness that suits Western religions but not many Asian faiths. For example, the sacred *Tao* ("Way") witnessed by the *Tao Te Ching* is not wholly other but is hidden in the universe and the self, waiting to be discovered and "tuned into." Moreover, only a few books among world scriptures explicitly claim sacrality for themselves, with the *Adi Granth* of Sikhism the most notable example.

---

[23] In *Rethinking Scripture,* for example, the essays by Coburn and Folkert reject "scripture" for "the Word" and "canon," respectively. But the other authors keep scripture as a conceptual category, and it is the dominant category in the volume as a whole, as the title implies.

[24] See, e.g., Schmidt, *Exploring Religion,* p. 208: "Broadly conceived, *scripture* refers to oral as well as written traditions that a people regard as sacred. Each religious community has a scripture, a body of sacred oral or written traditions."

[25] We will consider this topic more fully later in this chapter, but it is important enough to merit a preliminary statement here. See especially Graham, *Beyond the Written Word.* For a general treatment of orality, see W. Ong, *Orality and Literacy* (New York: Routledge, Chapman and Hall, 1982), and J. Goody, *The Interface Between the Written and the Oral* (Cambridge: Cambridge University Press, 1982).

Most scriptures receive their sacred status only after they have been written, circulated, and widely accepted as reflecting the faith in some special sense. Again, the relational aspect of all scripture comes to the fore. Writings become scripture as they are recognized, received, and used as authoritative in a religious community.

Another mark of special holiness is use in ritual. When believers read books aloud in worship, when they speak their words to carry out sacrifice, and especially when they venerate books during worship, we have a sure indication that these books are especially sacred. (Secondary religious literature as described earlier rarely makes its way into worship.) Different types of veneration are practiced in Zoroastrianism and Sikhism. Even in everyday life, scripture enjoys special respect: Buddhist scriptures for monastic use are still handwritten on palm leaves.

The third element of our definition is the authority of scripture. Just as sacredness is an aspect of all scripture, scripture is also *especially authoritative* for its communities. Among all written texts, scripture is always the most authoritative and is often the court of final appeal in religious matters. The range of this authority and the way it is exercised varies depending on the nature of the religion and the content of its scriptures. In Asian religions, scripture is often not authoritative in the same way as scripture in the Western, Abrahamic traditions. Yet Asian scriptures often express the heart of their faith, the way of salvation. The *Lotus Sutra* in Japanese Nichiren Buddhism is a prominent example of a book with a limited theme and purpose that has great standing in the sect because it addresses what is perceived as the heart of the religion. Moreover, "at least four of the six South Asian or Far Eastern fundamentalist-like movements . . . do in fact privilege a sacred text and presume to draw certain fundamentals—beliefs and behaviors—from it." [26] The authority of scripture for most followers of a given religion is paradoxically acknowledged even when some occasionally reject it. For example, some Hindu Brahmins burn their *Veda* books when they become ascetics. For the sake of greater enlightenment, some Zen Buddhist monks make disparaging comments about the Buddha (e.g., "That old degenerate!") and his scriptural teachings.

Scriptures are generally authoritative for their communities alone, who accept them as expressing the heart of the religion. One exception is in Chinese religion, where some older Classics like the *I Ching* are used to some degree as scripture by both Confucians and Taoists. More typically among Asia's religions, to receive one's texts as scripture is automatically to devalue the texts of others. For example, Confucian scriptures like the *Analects* are generally not read as scripture (but rather as cultural) by Taoists. As the *Tao Te Ching* cuttingly remarks, "When the great way [*Tao*] falls into disuse, there are benevolence and rectitude [the chief Confucian virtues of the *Analects*]." [27]

The authority of scripture comes with a special class of scholars who are the guardians of scripture and recognized experts in its interpretation. In Buddhism, monks with special training and ability teach the sacred writings to other monks and inquiring laypeople. The Confucian scholar is the master of the Classics and teaches them to others.

---

[26] M. E. Marty and R. S. Appleby, eds., *Fundamentalisms Observed* (Chicago: University of Chicago Press, 1991), p. 820.
[27] *Tao Te Ching* 18:1.

In virtually every faith, therefore, the authority of its scripture is mediated largely by those recognized as its official interpreters. **Commentary** has a large role in the history of many religions and regulates how scriptures are received and used, especially at the official level. As John Henderson states, "Commentaries and commentarial modes of thinking dominated the intellectual history of most premodern civilizations. . . . Until the seventeenth century in Europe, and even later in China, India, and the Near East, thought, especially within high intellectual traditions, was primarily exegetical in character and expression."[28] Moreover, only quite recently in the sweep of human history have books appeared and mass literacy become possible. This is another reason for having a special class to read, comment on, and relate sacred books to a religious community. Of course, the uses of scriptures at the level of the ordinary follower of a religion will at times be quite different from this official interpretation.

Two other features of scripture not directly related to our definition should be stated here. First, scriptures of each religion are often heterogeneous but are nonetheless *seen as a unity* by their communities. This is also the case with Asian religions, as in Hinduism's distinction between Vedic scripture, which is called Shruti ("what is heard" from the beginning) and the post-Vedic Smirti ("what is remembered"). All of it is the scripture of Hinduism, and believers see it as speaking essentially the same message. In China, the principle holds even in reverse: the secondary scriptures are the earlier Classics, and Confucians see the later *Analects* and Taoists the *Tao Te Ching* as one with earlier tradition.

A second main feature of scripture is that it has *a degree of closure*. This closure is often called a **canon,** a list or collection of books recognized as scriptural.[29] This canon is absolutely fixed in Zoroastrianism and Sikhism. All the scriptures of these religions have long ago been officially identified, and nothing can now be added or subtracted from their canons. With Hinduism, Buddhism, Jainism, Confucianism, and Taoism, however, the situation is quite different. First, their sacred literature is vast, and the problems in defining a canon for a religion like Taoism, which has 1,200 sacred texts, are enormous. Second, the process of producing scripture has not officially ended. Where new books can be added, as Taoists added one at the beginning of the twentieth century, a closed canon cannot exist.

How can a religion relate to its scriptures when they are so vast that no one person or group can know them all, let alone be expert in them all? In traditions with large canons, certain books, such as the *Tao Te Ching,* are basic for almost everyone. Also, different groups in a religion attach themselves to a few select scriptures that reflect their particular interests. In Taoism, as L. G. Thompson explains, "the practitioner or priest would usually be an adherent to one of the several major 'schools' or traditions of Taoism, and would specialize in those texts relevant to his school's interests."[30] This tendency to choose one's own books from among the total corpus of scripture results

---

[28] J. B. Henderson, *Scripture, Canon, Commentary: A Comparison of Confucian and Western Exegesis* (Princeton: Princeton University Press, 1991), p. 3.

[29] For a general discussion of the idea of canon, see the article under that heading by G. T. Sheppard in *Encyclopedia of Religion,* vol. 3, pp. 62–68.

[30] "Taoism: Classic and Canon," in Denny and Taylor, *Holy Book,* p. 205.

in a "canon within the canon." Most commonly it occurs in religions with very large numbers of books, but it also can be found in religions with smaller canons. In sum, scripture canons can be either completely closed or open to development and change. No matter how readily they can be altered, canonical texts are still viewed and treated as scripture.

THE USES OF SCRIPTURE

When scripture is set in the full context of the everyday life of its religion, its uses become plain. How believers use scripture shows its status and role in a religion. The following chapters of this book will outline the varied uses of scripture in each religion. In this section, we will discuss some basic dimensions of the comparative study of scripture usage.

First, scripture is a source for establishing and defending key doctrines. Scriptures can be used doctrinally because they typically contain the key teachings of the faith and because believers usually see them as continuing the voice of the founders. They have primary importance as statements of the deep truths of the universe and the right way to live in it. These teachings can assume different forms: God(s) and humanity; human imperfections and salvation; beginnings and ends of the individual and the cosmos; the moral life and how to achieve it. When scripture is used to establish doctrine, this is most often done by its official interpreters—monks, priests, scholars, and the like. Sometimes it is done by formal debate in councils or assemblies, sometimes within the confines of a monastery or temple. Defending doctrine occurs less often at the popular level, but even here scripture can function authoritatively. An appeal to a passage of holy writ is often the final word in any argument about religion.

Second, scripture is also prominently used in public worship. Worshippers often display and read it aloud. Although this is characteristic especially of the so-called Western "religions of the book," it is also significant in religions such as Hinduism and Buddhism that are not so book oriented. The worship that goes on in a Buddhist monastery, for example, prominently features the scriptures. Monks read them, chant them, meditate on them, and walk around them in solemn procession. Even when the book is not prominent in worship, its content often permeates the ceremonies of most scripturalizing religions. Prayers, sacrifices, and hymns come from and echo the language of scripture. Many lyrics of the music of worship are drawn from the scriptural text. Hymns and chants, with their emotional power, are significant vehicles for use of scripture in most religious traditions in the East.

Perhaps the place and function of scripture are never so prominent as when worshippers formally venerate it. Almost every religion in the world with scripture pays it ritual respect in some way. Hindus speak the words of the *Veda* with great care. These words are the center of holiness in worship, though the *Veda* book is usually not to be seen. In certain Taoist and Confucian temples, the location of the scripture collection is itself holy. **Bibliolatry** [bib-lee-AHL-ah-tree] results when believers give excessive veneration to their scriptures or become absolutely dependent on them.

A third typical use of scripture is in meditation and devotion. This is usually private and individual, but it can also occur in group settings, as when Buddhist monks meditate in session on sutra passages or on mantras drawn from scripture. Sometimes they meditate on the words and other times "look through" the words to find the truth "behind" them. The conclusions of many Hindu scriptures specify a blessing on those who listen or read faithfully. In meditation and devotion, the scriptures teach the truth of the religion and promote the growth of the reader into the fullness of the faith.

All these uses of scripture can be described as primarily *cognitive,* understanding and thinking in some way about the words and their meaning. Another important dimension of the usage of scripture, one often overlooked, is *noncognitive* usage. Here the words are used in a variety of ways without any attempt to understand their meaning rationally.

A first noncognitive type of usage occurs when scriptures are used in a language that cannot be understood by the follower of the faith. This is especially the case when a religion like Hinduism or Islam holds that its scriptures are so essentially bound to their original language that they cannot be translated and retain their sacred nature.

A second noncognitive use of scripture is decorative and **iconic.** Many Hindus cannot read their sacred literature, but images and pictures of the gods and their stories are all around them. One cannot live in any Muslim area without encountering Quranic verses everywhere. They are displayed on private houses and public buildings, often in a stylized calligraphy that is a mainstay of art in Muslim lands. These word decorations are not meant to be read so much as to be felt, thereby exercising their holy presence for the blessing of the community. In these and other usages of scripture as icons, the appeal is more to the imagination and emotion than to the mind.

A third noncognitive application mixes religion and magic. The power of scripture is such that it can bring blessing and keep away evil; it has an objective, supernatural power quite by itself. We have already spoken of scripture as used in charms or talismans, a manifestation of the magical power of scripture. The mere possession of a holy book also has power to bless and ward off evil. It is sometimes put in the bed of a sick person to bring them back to health. In many religions, those who can afford it will often buy one for possession in the home. Often family genealogical records will be written into the front of this scripture in the home.

Perhaps the most striking popular use of scripture is **bibliomancy** [BIB-lee-oh-mansee], the use of holy books to foresee the future and guide one's response to it. Many religions feature the informal practice of opening a scripture book at random and reading the first passage that meets the eye. This passage, it is thought, has special power to direct the believer through an uncertain or difficult situation in life or just through the difficulties of the new day. Some Taoists read the *I Ching* philosophically, but more use it in divination. Its many hexagrams and their fortune-telling interpretations are selected by a special procedure with sticks. All these forms of bibliomancy assume that a supernatural guidance is exercised in and through the book for the blessing of the believer.

The usages described here have been categorized in other ways (beyond cognitive and noncognitive) by scholars of religion. Perhaps the most helpful is that of Sam D. Gill, who proposed that uses of scripture are "informative" and "performative." "Informative" means imparting information in various ways, such as in doctrine and history. "Performative" *does* something, as for example when scripture is used to make sacrifice, to make the laws of a religious or civil community, or to bless and curse.[31] In both its informative and performative aspects, scripture is also used for transformation. This transformative power is a result of its sacrality and authority. Scriptures come from a sacred source and are themselves sacred. This sacred quality generally entails some power to make holy those who read or listen to them.

The transformative power of scripture occurs in both an individual and communal way—for example, to gain insight on personal or group problems and find the resources to solve them. Not all religions consider their scriptures to be divinely inspired, but all hold them to be inspiring and transformative in some way. This transformative power can be based on cognition, in which believers directly encounter the scriptures and experience their life-changing meaning. It can also happen just as often in non-cognitive ways, as described earlier.

ADVANTAGES AND DISADVANTAGES

The study of Asian religions through their sacred scriptures has both advantages and disadvantages. We need to be aware of the limitations of this method and work from strengths to ameliorate the weaknesses as much as possible.

The first disadvantage is that scriptures are *not universal.* Some religions do not have them—if a culture has no writing, it obviously can have no scripture. Of course, not having a scripture does not invalidate a religion. The religions and cultures of non-literate peoples do have oral traditions that function prominently in storytelling and in rituals that enact myths. A religion based on oral traditions is every bit as living and real for its followers as a religion that produces and uses scripture.

Second, as we saw earlier, the reception and use of scripture is *not uniform* across religions. Religions regard their scriptures in different ways, and scriptures function differently in each religion. Students of Asian religions must take note of these variations and learn to look at each religion's scriptures in a fresh way. Readers of scripture who come from a "religion of the book" must especially try to lay aside their preconceptions. Protestant Christians, for example, must beware of assuming that certain qualities of scripture and its function to which they are accustomed (e.g., that scripture is best absorbed by individual silent reading and meditation) will be true of every religion's scripture. The more we genuinely encounter Asian scriptures in their full range of reception and use, the less likely we will be to inject our own bias into the scriptures of others. Then "scripture" itself will become a fuller, more useful category.

A third disadvantage is that we must *read translations,* which cannot fully capture the literary characteristics or meaning of the original. An old Italian proverb says, "Translators are traitors," and all scriptures are betrayed in some way by translation. Among Brahmanic Hindus, the oral power of the *Vedas* in their Sanskrit language is such that it would be unthinkable to translate them into another language for use in worship. Brahmins use them in that ancient language even though they often do not

---

[31] Gill, "Nonliterate Traditions and Holy Books: Toward a New Model," in Denny and Taylor, *Holy Book,* p. 234.

fully understand the words. As we read in translation, we must remember that some of the original meaning and resonance of the words is thereby lost.

A fourth disadvantage is that scriptures tend to *reflect only the patriarchal and elite perspectives* of their traditions. They come from times and cultures that are more or less patriarchal, where the voices of women are muted and filtered.[32] Scriptures strongly tend to embody official and elite ideas. Comparatively little of popular religion can be found in them. This book will offer some coverage of social justice and the role of women, but the perspective through which these scriptures are filtered is necessarily that of the elite male.[33]

Finally, and perhaps most seriously, we *lack the living context* of scripture when we encounter only its textual form. Scripture, which for almost all traditions comes from ancient times, comes alive as it is appropriated in the life of religious communities. Despite growing religious pluralism, many North American readers of scripture do not have access to these communities. They cannot visit a mosque, see the ritual of a Hindu home or temple, or live for a time in a Buddhist monastery. They cannot directly see the broad ways that scripture is reflected in religious life, or the more specific ways it is used in worship, devotion, or law. What can be reproduced in a book like this is primarily the written text itself. The uses of scripture can be outlined here, but a printed book will inevitably emphasize the written, textual aspects of scripture over the oral and living.

These disadvantages might seem strong enough to cause the reader to give up the encounter with Asian scriptures. The advantages of studying religions through their scripture are compelling, however. By working from the strengths of this approach, the reader can overcome the weaknesses to some extent and use scripture appropriately to enter the world of other religions.

The first advantage of this approach is that scripture is *widespread* among religions. Even though it is not fully universal, each "major" (to use a traditional but rather prejudicial term) living religion has a scripture. Scriptures naturally vary in form, content, and usage, but they are usually present in a religion. As we have seen, recent researchers emphasize that they form a distinct and important element in the life of most religions. The tendency to "scripturalize," to make and use scriptures, is strong among religions. Indeed, almost every contemporary religion that is based in a literate culture produces and uses scriptures of some sort.[34]

Second, scriptures tend to be *comprehensive* for their faiths. Matters that a religion considers of great importance for its life are generally written down for the continu-

---

[32] See the introductory section of Serinity Young, ed., *An Anthology of Sacred Texts by and about Women* (New York: Crossroad, 1993), for a good treatment of this issue.

[33] An excellent new series edited by Donald S. Lopez, Jr., "Princeton Readings in Religions," seeks to rectify this male-elite perspective with anthologies that draw on more popular writings and anthropological field reports. Its first volume, *Religions of India in Practice* (Princeton, N.J.: Princeton University Press, 1995), deals with Hinduism, Sikhism, Islam, and Jainism. The second volume is *Buddhism in Practice* (1995), the third is *Religions of China in Practice* (1996); the fourth is *Religions of Tibet in Practice* (1997). Other volumes are planned for the religions of Japan, Islam, Africa, Judaism, and Christianity.

[34] Only Shinto does not treat its holy books as scripture in the full sense. Thus Shinto is "the exception that proves the rule" that religions based in literate cultures produce and use scriptures.

ing community. "The sacred writings provide not only the essence of each particular religious tradition, but also the archetypal experiences which stir in the depths of all human lives . . . —death, trust, anxiety, wonder, loyalty to a cause greater than oneself, fascination, healing, fulfillment, peace."[35] Of course, what religions view as important does vary, and scriptures reflect this variety. What each religion considers of paramount importance will be strongly reflected in its scriptures. They offer comprehensive insight into the key characteristics of their faiths.

Third, scriptures are *authoritative* for their religions. Because they are believed to come from God or the gods, an enlightened teacher, or a wise sage, and because they bear witness to an ultimate reality, the truth contained in scriptures is recognized and lived out by believers. To read a scripture is to discover what is of primary value in religions. And because scriptures are authoritative, they typically reflect the distinctive main aspects of each tradition. As one commentator has noted, "Despite the variety of attitudes to scriptural works [in Asian religions], there is a continuing tendency to find in a sacred text . . . the primary source for true doctrine, correct ritual, [and] appropriate conduct."[36]

The fourth advantage of studying scriptures lies in their *ancient* character. They or the oral tradition on which they are based arise soon after the beginning of a religion and often signal important stages in its early development. Chinese religions call their oldest scriptures the "Classics," and in a sense all scriptures are classic treatments of their religious tradition. Moreover, where a religion has a founder(s), scriptures usually give deep insight into the life of the founder(s) from the perspective of later followers. The ancient, classical character of scriptures thus makes them valuable as a primary source for the history of religions.

Furthermore, because the religions of the world have so richly influenced and been influenced by their cultures, scriptures are among the most important literary sources for the understanding of world cultures. Though scriptures are indeed ancient and important, it is erroneous to argue, as does Charles Braden, that religion is somehow "founded on" scriptures.[37] Rather, as T. W. Hall puts it so well, "Historical investigations show that the religious communities existed prior to the writing of their scripture . . . religions produced scripture and scripture did not produce religion."[38]

Fifth, scriptures are *accessible* in translation to English-language readers. Many, if not most, of the important religious books of Asia have been translated into English, and many of those that have not are now being translated. Sometimes the translations of a certain scripture are few, but others can boast a virtual riot of English versions. The *Tao Te Ching*, for example, had more than thirty English versions in print in 1999. Although no translation can convey the full meaning and feeling of the original, a good translation can suggest it.

Finally, scriptures as literary texts are *open to critical analysis*. Both the specialist scholar and the beginning reader can analyze them directly or, better yet, enter a

---

[35] Leonard J. Biallas, "Teaching World Religions Through Their Scriptures," *Horizons* 17 (1990) 80.

[36] K. Yates et al., *The Religious World: Communities of Faith,* 2d ed. (New York: Macmillan, 1988), p. 3.

[37] Charles Braden, *The Scriptures of Mankind: An Introduction* (New York: Macmillan, 1952), p. 8.

[38] Hall et al., *Religion: An Introduction,* p. 109.

conversation with them. Although most religious texts will range from mildly strange to completely baffling for those who come from other cultures and religious traditions, the same intellectual and scholarly skills used to read any other text can be put to use on Asian scriptures. With some effort, the North American reader can understand scriptures and use them as a pathway into other faiths.

ASIAN SCRIPTURES AND MODERN SCHOLARSHIP

The earlier discussion of critical analysis of scripture leads us to an important but often neglected topic. How does the modern academic study of scripture influence how Asian religions use scriptures and how we read them?

Historical and critical literary scholarship is largely Western and European in origin, stemming from various methods of interpreting literature developed in the Renaissance. Textual criticism methodically judges manuscripts to find the likely original reading; grammatical criticism analyzes the content and style of the wording of a work in its original language; literary criticism studies genres. Most important is historical criticism, which probes the developmental genesis of works from the past, their original meaning and authenticity.[39]

The effort to collect, edit, and publish the literature of Asian religions is also a Western academic enterprise. It had its roots in the eighteenth century, when the first copies of Chinese and Indian scripture made their way to Europe and were greeted with great interest, even enthusiasm, in some circles. A part of this enthusiasm was an Enlightenment hope that these scriptures might be a religious or philosophical alternative to what some saw as the hide-bound clericalism of Christianity. The *Vedas,* for example, were at first viewed as religious expressions from near the dawn of time, pristine and unspoiled by priestcraft. Gradually Europeans realized that they reflect a priestly system as traditional as that of Christianity, and even older. By the middle of the nineteenth century, as we saw, a more mature, scholarly interest in world scripture blossomed into a systematic effort to publish reliable translations of scriptures. The editing and publishing of sacred texts continue today, especially with religions that have large canons. The methods used to edit, translate, publish, and interpret these scriptures draw generally from the Western tradition.

With scholarship in comparative religion coming from a background that was largely Protestant Christian in orientation, over the last century an inevitable "Protestant bias" has crept into the way scholarship has looked at the scriptures of other faiths.[40] Certain mainstream Protestant ideas about the nature of scripture colored the study of the scriptures of other religions that only today are being identified and corrected. They can be listed serially: a preoccupation with textuality to the exclusion of orality, from the Protestant emphasis on the scripture as *written;* an individualistic orientation that

---

[39] See the essay "Modern Approaches to Biblical Study" in the *New Oxford Annotated Bible* (New York: Oxford, 1990) for a brief discussion of how these and other methods are applied to the study of the Hebrew Scriptures and the New Testament.

[40] M. Levering, in her introduction to *Rethinking Scripture* (Albany: State University of New York Press, 1989), pp. 3–5, has some good comments on this Protestant bias.

assumes that scriptures are to be read mainly by the individual, from Protestant ideas of "the priesthood of all believers" and universal literacy; the notion that scriptures are widely authoritative over every aspect of religious life, from the Protestant assertion that the scriptures are the sole authority in the Christian faith; and the assumption that scriptures are best understood by academically recognized methods of study.

Of course, this bias is not shared by the religions of the world, as we can see as we reflect comparatively on each of these assumptions. In some religions, such as Hinduism, the oral dimension dominates the written. Most religions do not share the Protestant notion that scriptures are meant to be read by the individual; rather, their adherents speak and hear their scriptures in groups, usually in worship and ritual. Indeed, it comes as a striking realization for modern North Americans that most followers of many religions throughout history (and even today!) cannot read, and therefore cannot read their sacred texts. For the typical follower of most faiths, texts must be *spoken* (often from memory) and *heard*.

We examined earlier the next Protestant assumption, that scriptures seek to regulate every aspect of religious life, and we concluded that they seek to regulate the center of religious life as their religion conceives that center. For most religions of the world, the Western academic approach to scripture goes against the grain of faith and is consequently viewed as alien. Other literature may be studied critically, but to study scripture historically and critically is to question its sacredness because such study employs the same methods used to study other nonsacred literature. Each religion has some systematic study of its sacred texts, but such study usually remains devotional, meditative, and interpretive. Noncritical and unthreatening, it does not question the received beliefs about the origin and standing of the text.

When we read scriptures, then, we must always remember that the way we read is fully conditioned by our cultural background and academic enterprise. Those who read from a religious background must always try to keep their own viewpoint identified and in check. Those with no religious commitments must try to suspend any doubts they may have about religion and scriptures. We read scriptures as *outsiders*, in an objective, scholarly, noncommittal way. This is altogether necessary as a first step in coming to grips with scriptures. A second step, more difficult than the first but equally necessary, is to read them as much as possible as *insiders*, with the eyes, minds, and hearts of those for whom these scriptures are much more than the object of scholarship.[41]

SCRIPTURES AND THE WORLD WIDE WEB

The last five years have seen an explosive growth in the World Wide Web, the linked computer system on the Internet. Much information about religion can be found on the Web; it seems to be one of the leading topics of discussion and inquiry. As a part of this interest in religion, many sites on the Web feature scriptures in translation or sometimes in the original.

---

[41] See the excellent remarks by Eric Sharpe in *Encyclopedia of Religion*, vol. 14, p. 85, on "imaginative sympathy" in reading scripture as "insiders." See also Ross N. Reat, "Insiders and Outsiders in the Study of Religious Traditions," *Journal of the American Academy of Religion* 51 (1983), pp. 459–75.

Several positive features of this new opportunity to encounter scriptures can be adduced. The access is almost always free. The amount of scripture on the Web is growing rapidly, and may someday encompass most world scriptures. The Internet is an appealing way for most young, computer-oriented students (but not always their professors!) to encounter scriptures. It presents different ways of studying and learning, for example, the ability to search a text electronically. Finally, but not least, when students encounter a religion site sponsored by its followers, they encounter it a bit more "from within."

The drawbacks of studying world scriptures on the Web are also significant. Some sites are not well constructed; they may have poor layout, little eye appeal, out-of-date links, or suffer from other technical deficiencies. While Internet coverage of Asian scripture is growing, it is still largely incomplete. The translations used are usually older, public-domain works that are out of date. When religions post their writings for missionary and/or public relations purposes, the "spin" put on them may not agree with the current academic consensus on that religion. Most significantly, these "electronic publications" are subject to little or no scholarly control, such as peer review before publication, so their quality varies greatly. Some sites are excellent, some average, and some are poor.

The result of this mixed situation is that many students need help in finding, using and especially analyzing critically these Web-based scripture sites. The few books on this topic are of some value, especially Patrick Durusau's *High Places in Cyberspace*,[42] with its updates available online at http://scholar.cc.emory.edu/scripts/highplaces.html. For readers of the current book and readers of my *Anthology of World Scriptures*, I have designed a special website to further their use of the Web in religious studies. It has links to short, helpful essays on using the Internet in an academically appropriate way. It also has links to sites that my students and I have found useful in the study of scriptures. This listing cannot pretend to be comprehensive, but it does offer a starting place to "surf" and learn. Its address is: http://religion.wadsworth.com/relinks.html.

THE PLAN OF THIS BOOK

This book contains excerpts of Asian scriptures in the following order of religions: Hinduism, Buddhism, Jainism, Sikhism, Zoroastrianism, Confucianism, Taoism, and Shinto.[43] (While Islam, and to a lesser degree Christianity, has numerous followers in Asia, they are not indigenous to the Far East, and so will not be treated here.[44]) This progression keeps the religions of India, China, and Japan together, usually in their family groups. Moreover, the reader can see the relationships among religions and

---

[42] Patrick Durusau, *High Places in Cyberspace* 2d ed. (Atlanta: Scholars, 1998).

[43] Strictly speaking, Shinto does not have "scripture" as this term is understood in modern scholarship. However, since the ancient sacred writings of Japan are very instructive for understanding Shinto, we will anthologize them briefly here.

[44] For a treatment of Christian and Islamic scriptures, see my *Anthology of World Scriptures,* 3d ed. (Belmont, CA: Wadsworth, 1999).

scriptures more easily when related bodies of texts are dealt with in succession. This is true to a significant degree with Hinduism, Buddhism, and Jainism, and to a lesser degree with Confucianism and Taoism.

Each chapter is structured as follows. An introduction outlines the scriptures included, setting them in the context of the whole religion by examining briefly their name(s), structure, origin and growth, and use. The first grouping of scripture passages deals with the history of the religion. If the faith has a founder, special attention will be given to him or her; any subsequent history of the religion that scripture reflects will also be excerpted. Second are passages covering the main doctrinal teaching of the religion. These topics include Divine or Ultimate Reality, creation and the environment, the nature of humanity, and achieving human fulfillment (salvation, release, harmony, etc.). Third are passages about the moral/ethical structure of the scriptures: good, evil, and the authentic human life. Personal morality is probably more widely treated in scriptures, but social ethics are also prominent. Such topics as war and peace, violence and nonviolence, tolerance and intolerance of people of other faiths, the status of women, and a just society will be represented as fully as possible. Fourth are passages about the organization of the religion, either in its internal organization (e.g., monks and laity in Buddhism) or in its attempts to organize its wider culture (e.g., the Hindu caste system in India). Last are passages about religious worship, ritual, devotion and meditation. Of course, some religions will have more in some of these categories than others, but most do fit into them without significant distortion. Where they do not fully fit, this format will be adapted as necessary to do justice to the particular nature of the texts.

The predominant rationale for this organization is *pedagogical*. It is meant to further the learning of the reader, especially students being introduced to the religions of Asia. North American readers are familiar with the categories used here, and both teachers and students of world religions will recognize them as a standard paradigm for research and teaching in religion. Moreover, they are categories that seem to "fit" scriptures themselves. But why not discard any attempt to use categories of organization and simply provide one or two longer excerpts from each religion's body of scripture? What Paul Muller-Ortega says about Hinduism is true of many religions: "It is not possible to put a single sacred text in the hands of students and expect the reading of that one text to allow students to encompass the tradition. . . . Thus, the preferred method of exposing students to the enormity of the Hindu sacred literature has been by means of anthologies."[45]

A GUIDE TO PRONUNCIATION

The languages in which the scriptures of this book are written include, among others, Sanskrit, Pali, and Chinese. These languages have scripts very different from our alphabet. Many translations from these languages use a system of diacritical marks to

---

[45] Paul Muller-Ortega, "Exploring Textbooks: Introductions to Hinduism," in B. R. Gaventa, ed., *Critical Review of Books in Religion,* 1988 (Atlanta: Scholars Press, 1989), p. 71.

translate proper nouns, especially on the consonants in personal names. For example, in Hinduism one often finds the names Kṛṣṇa or Śiva. These marks serve to indicate their rather exact pronunciation.

This method, though fully appropriate for scholars, is confusing for most beginning readers. Therefore, this book uses a simplified method of translation with no diacritical symbols or marks. Here each word is spelled in a way that permits the reader to pronounce proper nouns directly and more easily. Instead of Kṛṣṇa, the reader will see the more pronounceable Krishna; Śiva becomes Shiva. The pronunciation that results is *approximate,* but accurate enough to be appropriate for beginning readers of Asian scriptures. Of course, students should follow the lead of their teachers in pronouncing these words.

Pronouncing foreign-language words correctly is challenging, and here the student needs some specific guidance. In what follows we will proceed religion by religion, beginning with the easiest to pronounce. In this section, we will deal only with the rules that come into play in this anthology.

Hinduism and Buddhism

Sanskrit is the main language of Hindu scripture and much of Buddhist scripture. Buddhism also employs the Pali language, which is closely related to Sanskrit. Sanskrit itself is an Indo-European language and as such is pronounced in much the same way as modern European languages. The main exceptions are as follows: *c* is pronounced "ch," as in *chair. g* is usually hard, as the first (not second) *g* in *garage. h* is pronounced separately from the preceding consonant, as the second *h* in *hothouse,* not the *h* in *think.* The vowels are much the same as in German or Spanish, except that a short *a* (found in an unstressed syllable) is vocalized as "u" in *but.*

Taoism and Confucianism

The Chinese language presents the most challenge to English speakers. A tonal language, Chinese contains sounds that are difficult to capture in other languages. Chinese words are given here in the Wade-Giles system, which despite the newer and generally more accurate *pinyin* system is still the choice in most scholarly literature and the one students will find in most other books. (Because it is becoming more common, we will note the *pinyin* spelling in the glossaries.) Consonants, especially when not immediately followed by an apostrophe, are as follows: *j* = *r*, as for example the Chinese word for "humaneness," *jen*, is pronounced *ren. k* = *g*, as for example the goddess Kwan ("Gwan") Yin. *p*, especially at the beginning of a word, is pronounced *b. ch* is pronounced *j*, as in the word for "classic scripture," Ching ("Jing"). *t* is pronounced *d*, as in Tao ("Dow").

SUGGESTIONS ON HOW TO READ SCRIPTURES

Those who are reading Asian scriptures for the first time often feel they are entering a strange new world. Sometimes one's preconceived notion of what reading a given scripture will be like turns out to be quite wrong. Students of Asian religion are especially susceptible to the difficulties of reading scripture. Their textbooks usually try to make scriptures easier to encounter by simplifying and summarizing the contents. To encounter scriptures more directly and in their original form is a harder process. As Mortimer Adler and Charles Van Doren once wrote, "The problem of reading the Holy Book . . . is the most difficult problem in the field of reading."[46] In the end, however, it is more profitable for readers to wrestle as directly as possible with the texts. Of course, an anthology such as this does not present world scriptures in their totality but serves as a bridge to the full scripture text.

Each reader must ultimately find an individually suitable method for reading scriptures. But these suggestions drawn from my experience and the experience of others may be helpful.

1.   Use your knowledge of religion to set these readings in a fuller context. Try to relate scriptures as fully as possible to the life of the religions from which they come. For example, when you are reading a passage about ritual, visualize how the ritual is carried out.

2.   Read the introductions to each chapter before you turn to the passages. They will provide an important background for understanding the passages.

3.   Next, take a few moments to skim the selections. Having a general feel for "the lay of the land" will help you when you begin to read in detail.

4.   Read the scripture passages with the same intellectual skills as you would any other text, religious or nonreligious. Remember their holy status in their religions, but don't be intimidated by it.

5.   Mark the text as you read. Research on reading shows that students who mark the text, underlining or highlighting as few as three or four items per page, understand and remember more than readers who do not mark their text. Marking the text helps to make it your own.

6.   Pay attention to literary genre. The form and content of any literary passage will reflect its genre. Read with a feeling for the differences among myth, poetry, narrative, law, and other literary forms.

7.   Make a "personal glossary" of unfamiliar terms and names as you go along. You can do this quite easily by circling them in the text and writing them in the bottom margin. (Use circles or other type of marking that will distinguish them from other marked material.) Then you can go back later to make a short note of their meaning, also in the margin. The unfamiliarity and difficulty of so many words, both technical terms and personal names, is a large obstacle for many students of Asian religions. With a little extra effort, you can minimize this difficulty.

8.   Be careful to pronounce the proper nouns correctly. Take an extra moment to sound them out and make them familiar. If necessary, use the pronunciation guide in this chapter and the glossary at the back of each chapter.

9.   Read each selection repeatedly until you are familiar with it and can identify any problems you have in understanding it. View these problems as opportunities, not roadblocks, to achieving greater understanding.

---

[46] Mortimer Adler and Charles Van Doren, *How to Read a Book* (New York: Simon & Schuster, 1940), p. 288.

10.   Read the selections aloud as much as possible. This may feel embarrassing at first because you are not accustomed to it. Listen to the sounds of the words, and try to get a sense of the oral dimensions of the text. You cannot reproduce the feeling of the original language, but reading aloud will at least remind you that the text does have an oral dimension.

11.   Put yourself, as well as you can, inside the faith of the scripture. What could these writings mean to you if you were among those who first heard them? What could they mean to you today if you were a typical follower of that faith? By using your knowledge and imagination, you can participate in the unique use of scripture in each religion and become—partially and temporarily—an "insider."[47]

12.   Memorize short, selected passages as a way of internalizing scriptures.

13.   If you wish to explore the scriptures more fully, begin by comparing the translations found here with other translations. Next, you can study other books and commentaries about the scriptures, many of which can be found in the "Suggestions for Further Reading" section of each chapter.

14.   As time permits, read other scriptures besides those passages anthologized here. Best of all, read entire texts of scripture.

GLOSSARY

bibliolatry [bib-lee-AHL-ah-tree] excessive veneration of a scripture book.

bibliomancy [BIB-lee-oh-man-see] the use of scripture to foresee future events and guide one's control of them.

canon a more or less fixed collection of books regarded as scriptural.

commentary a book written to explain another book, often passage by passage. Many religions possess commentaries on their scriptures.

genre a type of literary form, such as poetry, proverb, narrative history, philosophical meditation, and so on.

icon a holy picture. Metaphorically, scripture is an icon when it is revered as a sacred object apart from its contents.

narrative the telling of an event or series of events in story form.

oral tradition the passing down, usually through many generations, of myths, narratives, poems, and the like by word of mouth.

scripture texts that a religion holds to be especially sacred and authoritative.

QUESTIONS FOR STUDY AND DISCUSSION

1.   "Scripture is more a Western concept than an Asian concept." To what extent do you agree or disagree with this common statement?

---

[47] "By an act of historical imagination we can actually participate up to a certain point in the aspirations and devotions of other times and places. Yet this truly is only up to a certain point, for the curtain is suddenly lowered and we realize with a shock just how far way those places and times really are. That experience has been called 'the paradox of understanding'." Jaroslav Pelikan, *On Searching the Scriptures—Your Own or Someone Else's* (New York: Quality Paperback Book Club, 1992).

2.   What special problems and opportunities are posed by having a very large scripture canon, such as in Taoism or Buddhism?

3.   What uses of scripture seem most important and/or interesting to you? Why?

4.   What disadvantages are posed by the ancient character of scriptures? Can these be overcome? If so, how?

5.   How can you best become an "insider" in the study of Asian religions?

6.   Reflect on Mohandas Ghandhi's teaching on studying others' scriptures: "One should read others' scriptures with respect and reverence even to be enriched in one's own religious convictions."

7.   What other advantages and disadvantages to using the Internet in religious studies occur to you, besides the ones given here?

SUGGESTIONS FOR FURTHER READING

L. J. Biallas, "Teaching World Religions Through their Scriptures," *Horizons* (Villanova University) 17 (1990): 76–91. Especially useful to teachers, but students can profit from it as well; centers on narrative forms.

H. Coward, *Sacred Word and Sacred Text: Scripture in World Religions.* Maryknoll, NY: Orbis, 1988. Sound, chapter-length treatments (especially of orality) of scripture in Christianity, Islam, Hinduism, Sikhism, and Buddhism, with a conclusion on "Scripture and the Future of Religions."

F. M. Denny and R. L. Taylor, eds., *The Holy Book in Comparative Perspective.* Columbia, SC: University of South Carolina Press, 1985. After an introduction by the editors, this volume features up-to-date treatments of the scriptures of nine major religions. Also included is an essay by S. D. Gill, "Nonliterate Traditions and Holy Books: Toward a New Model."

W. A. Graham, "Scripture." In M. Eliade, ed., *The Encyclopedia of Religion,* vol. 13, pp. 133–145. New York: Macmillan, 1987. This lucid article is the best short survey of its topic.

T. W. Hall, R. B. Pilgrim, and R. R. Cavanagh, *Religion: An Introduction.* San Francisco: Harper & Row, 1985. A particularly good discussion of scripture as a form of religious expression is found on pp. 108–124.

M. Levering, ed., *Rethinking Scripture: Essays from a Comparative Perspective.* Albany: State University of New York Press, 1989. Begins with two excellent essays by W. C. Smith, "The Study of Religion and the Study of the Bible," and "Scripture as Form and Concept: Their Emergence in the Western World." There are chapters on Buddhist scripture by Levering, on Hinduism by T. B. Coburn, and on Jainism by K. W. Folkert. W. A. Graham also has an essay, "Scripture as Spoken Word."

W. C. Smith, *What Is Scripture? A Comparative Approach.* Minneapolis, MN: Fortress, 1993. A full survey of its topic by the most influential researcher on world scriptures.

S. Young, *An Anthology of Sacred Texts By and About Women.* New York: Crossroad, 1993. A comprehensive selection of scriptures and other important religious writings from Judaism, Christianity, Islam, Hinduism, Buddhism, Confucianism, Taoism, ancient European and Near Eastern religions, shamanism and tribal religions, and new religions of modern times.

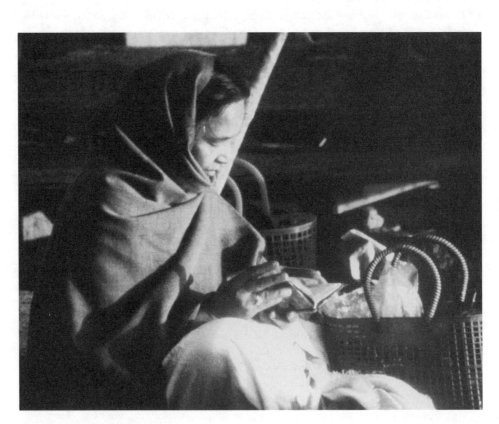

Reading Hindu Scripture
A Hindu woman in Banaras, India reads the *Bhagavad Gita* devotionally. Credit: Photo by Diana Eck, from the Image Bank of the Center for the Study of World Religions, Harvard University. Photo courtesy Diana Eck.

CHAPTER TWO

Hinduism

❖ After the monsoon season, people all over northern India gather outside their cities and villages to celebrate Rama-Lilas, a dramatic reading and reenactment of the *Ramayana,* the epic Hindu scripture. At its decisive point, wood and straw effigies of the demon Ravana are made and stuffed with fireworks. When night falls, the fireworks are set off and the demon is destroyed. Rama and the forces of good have prevailed.

❖ Just before dawn breaks in India, a householder rises and purifies himself with water. He then stirs back to life the embers of the sacred household fire while chanting sacred verses. Raising his arms to the rising sun, he recites a prayer to the sun-god from the most ancient scripture, the *Rig-Veda.* This ritual, called the Agnihotra, has been performed continually in India for more than three thousand years.

❖ In Hardwar, India, people gather in what is billed as the "world's largest religious festival." Ten million people have gathered in 1998 at this site on the upper Ganges River. According to Hindu scriptures, bathing during this festival is the supreme act of worship. Much of the other activity on this site is scripture oriented: holy men read scripture aloud, chant their mantras, and teach them to the pilgrims.

❖ At another popular pilgrimage site, people gather at a booth to hear a holy man recite the *Bhagavad-Gita.* Even though the *Gita* is familiar to them, they are still attracted to its telling. Of special interest is the end of the text, which promises them a blessing. The person who listens in true faith will win release from suffering and rebirth.

INTRODUCTION

Hinduism is one of the oldest of world religions, and certainly the most internally diverse. It encompasses many gods and features many paths to salvation. The scriptures of Hinduism mirror this diversity. Vast in size, varied in usage, and profound in influence, many scriptures have been chanted, heard, taught, and repeated for three thousand years. Generalizations about Hindu scriptures are thus especially difficult; almost every statement has exceptions. Still, the main lines of these scriptures can be reliably traced, and they provide good doors into the many-roomed mansion of Hinduism.

Overview of Structure

Hindus have not given any single comprehensive name to their scriptures. They divide its overall structure into two classes, Shruti [SHROO-tee] and Smriti [SMRIH-tee] (see Table 2.1). **Shruti,** "what is heard," is the primary revelation. It has no human or divine author but captures the cosmic sounds of truth heard by the ancient seers or **rishis** [REE-shees]. The seers then began a process of oral transmission and use through priestly families that has continued until today. Shruti consists of the four Vedas [VAY-duhs], the Brahmanas [BRAH-muh-nuhs], the Aranyakas [ah-RUN-yah-kuhs], and the Upanishads [oo-PAH-nee-shahds]. The canon of Shruti has been basically fixed for almost two thousand years, and all of Hinduism is in some sense based on it.

Smriti, "what is remembered," designates all other scripture. The role of Smriti is to bring out the meaning of Shruti and apply it to later ages. Hindus do not consider Smriti revelatory in itself, but only as it is grounded in Shruti. The Smriti literature is vast in size and scope. It ranges from myths and legends of the *Puranas,* epics like the *Mahabharata* and the *Ramayana,* and law codes like the *Laws of Manu* and the *Institutes of Vishnu.* These scriptures have been widely translated from their original Sanskrit into the other languages of the Indian subcontinent, and the canon of Smriti is still open. Because of its more popular and ever-developing nature, Smriti scripture has had, despite its officially secondary status to Shruti, a strong influence on Hindu religion and Indian culture.

We turn now to a fuller treatment of the structure of Hindu scripture. Its development over time and its customary use, both very important in understanding Hindu scripture, will be dealt with more fully later in the chapter. But some mention of applications will be made in this section because an understanding of the meaning of Hindu scripture is impossible without it. We will follow the literature in the rough order of its chronological development.

In the Shruti category, the four *Vedas* ("books of knowledge") are the foundation of Hindu scripture. They are gathered into **samhitas** [SAHM-hee-tuhs], or "collections." The *Rig-* ("hymn") *Veda samhita* has 1,028 hymns divided into ten books. Each hymn is addressed to a single god or goddess. Indra, the sky god and king of gods, and Agni, the god of fire, are most prominent in the *Rig-Veda.* Soma, the god of the hallucinogenic drug from a plant (perhaps a mushroom) consumed during a main sacrifice, is also prominent. When a god is extolled in a hymn, the hymn praises that god above other deities and ascribes key functions to the god, a form of worship called *henotheism.* For example, the *Rig-Veda* ascribes the creation of the world to almost all the individual gods. Readers of the *Rig-Veda* will note a fairly common sequence in each hymn: It begins with the invocation of a deity; it then makes requests of that deity and offers praises by recounting her or his deeds in myth; it finishes with a brief restatement of the worshippers' request.

The other *Vedas* follow up on the *Rig-Veda.* The *Yajur-Veda* is a collection of mostly prose sacrificial formulas *(yajus)* used by the presiding priest in a sacrifice. The *Sama-Veda* is a collection of songs and melodies *(saman)* used in sacrifice, with most of the words taken from the *Rig-Veda.* The *Rig-, Yajur-* and *Sama-Veda* are together known in Hinduism as the "threefold Veda." The *Atharva-Veda* differs remarkably from the others, containing mostly spells, curses, and charms in 731 hymns divided into twenty books. It reflects the everyday religious life of the common person, just as the threefold Veda reflects the religious life of the priestly group.

The next part of Shruti to emerge is the *Brahmanas,* "Brahmin books" that are manuals for sacrifice. They describe ancient Vedic sacrifice in great and fascinating detail and are organized to correspond to the four *Veda samhitas.* They present sacrifice

Table 2.1
Hindu Scriptures

	Name	*Translation/Content*	*Size*
Shruti	*Veda-samhitas:*		
	Rig-Veda	Hymn *Veda*	1,028 hymns in 10 books
	Yajur-Veda	Formula *Veda*	
	Sama-Veda	Song *Veda*	1,549 mantras
	Atharva-Veda	Spell *Veda*	731 hymns in twenty books
	Brahmanas	Brahmin Books	Correspond to each *Veda*
	Aranyakas	Forest Books	
	Upanishads	Sittings near a Teacher	123 total; 13 principal
Smriti	*Puranas*	Legends	18 books
	Mahabharata	Great Story of the Bharatas	18 books
	Ramayana	Story of Rama	50,000 lines in 7 books
	Manusmriti	Laws of Manu	12 books
	Vishnusmriti	Institutes of Vishnu	100 chapters
	Tantras	Weavings	Uncertain number of books

—and especially ritual utterance, the powerful sacrificial word correctly spoken—as the power that strengthens the gods, keeps the universe intact, and brings blessing to the sacrificer. The soma sacrifice is the most prominent. A development of the *Brahmanas* is the **Aranyakas,** "Forest Books" containing philosophical speculations on sacrifice, especially the sacrificial fire. Reflections on the New Year festival are also prominent. These speculations were considered unsuitable for open knowledge and so were done in the privacy of the forest. Some *Aranyakas* have been incorporated into the *Upanishads.*

The **Upanishads** ("sittings near a teacher") form the final part of Shruti. One hundred twenty-three *Upanishads* have survived, but only thirteen have been the most influential in Hindu history. The *Upanishads* are philosophical monologues on the nature of cosmic reality and sometimes feature debates between opposing teachers. Their emphasis is on self-denial as a way to find religious truth, the way of asceticism. The ritualism of the *Vedas* and especially the *Brahmanas* is downplayed and even attacked. The *Upanishads* are concerned to find the One, the absolute spiritual reality that lies in and behind all the visible elements and beings of this physical world. As the conclusion of Shruti and the Vedic scripture collection, they are also called the *Vedanta* ("end of the *Veda*").

We begin describing the Smriti with the two main epics, the *Mahabharata* and the *Ramayana.* The *Ramayana,* or "Story of Rama," is traditionally attributed to the poet Valkimi and was written in the third century B.C.E. Prince Rama was exiled from his kingdom and his wife Sita was kidnapped by the demon Ravana, but Rama was restored to his kingdom and his wife with the help of the monkey god. The *Mahabharata* is "The Great [Story] of the Bharatas," an early Indian dynasty. The longest epic in the world, it is four times longer than the Christian *Bible*. Its basic story involves the feud and eventual war between two sides of King Bharata's family. The *Mahabharata* is a vast repository of Indian myths and legends, and the famous *Bhagavad-Gita* is a small part of this larger epic. Both the *Mahabharata* and the *Ramayana* share a common body of myth and folklore.

Puranas

The *Puranas,* traditionally eighteen in number, are also concerned with myth, lore, and legend. Like the epics (and Smriti in general), they are addressed to the common person. Emerging about 400 to 1000 C.E., they stress devotion to a specific divinity as the way to release. Thus some speak of Shiva, some of Vishnu, and some of Shakti, the three main devotional movements of Hinduism. By far the most popular, and influential for medieval and early modern Indian popular literature and painting, is the *Bhagavata-Purana*. This tenth-century work provides background on the Krishna of the *Bhagavad-Gita,* especially his youth among the cowherders of his village and his romantic adventures with the cowherd women.

Tantras are "looms, weavings" that mirror the Hinduism of medieval India. They deal with beliefs, rituals, and yogic meditation in a popular way. Each of the three main devotional movements mentioned earlier have their own official collections of *tantras*. These *tantras* tell the exploits of their own gods and bring their powers to the devotee by ritual and yoga.

The final type of Smriti to be considered here is the manual of dharma, or law code. Law here is broadly conceived in its social and personal dimensions: it encompasses caste, life stages, diet, government, and other matters. The most important dharma manual is the *Laws of Manu,* composed around 200 C.E. in twelve books. The main concern of *Manu* is the codification and operation of the four-caste system, and its influence on Hindu life has been profound. Indeed, the two things that are most often said to define a practicing Hindu are acceptance of the *Veda* and following caste duty.

Origin and Development

The long history of Hindu scripture parallels to a large degree the history of the religion as a whole. We here will briefly survey how it began, the process of its growth, and how it took its present form. One general principle of Hindu scripture should be kept in mind as we begin this section: The literature grows by association. Earlier works, no matter how sacred, invite and attract later works with related themes and styles, which in turn attract still further sacred literature.

The four *Vedas* have their origin in ritual. Sacrifice itself seems to have come first, as even the earliest *Vedas* presuppose an established sacrifice. Then the songs, melodies, and formal directions for their performance were drawn up soon after the Aryan invasion of India. As mentioned, the *Rig-Veda* contains songs for sacrifice. It began about 2000 B.C.E. The oldest hymns deal with the gods of the Indo-Aryans: the sky god Dyaus Pitar, whom the Greeks knew as Zeus, and the earth goddess Prithivi Mater. In the next stage, these old gods receded, and new gods arose: Indra the new sky god, Agni the god of fire, Soma the god of drugged sacrifice. The final hymns written down are found in the present *Rig-Veda* books 1 and 10, which move from polytheistic nature gods to the kind of cosmic speculations that search for the oneness of all being. The final form of the *Rig-Veda* was reached about 1200 B.C.E.

The *Sama-Veda* was composed after the *Rig-Veda* was complete. It has lines from the *Rig-Veda,* chanted to fixed melodies. The melodies are not captured in the written text but are passed on from singing priest to his disciples. The proper lyrics and music were essential to the success of the rite. The *Yajur-Veda* contains directions for sacrifice and also comes after the *Rig-Veda* was established. The *Atharva-Veda* with its magical spells gives a glimpse into the more popular levels of ancient Hinduism. They are not addressed to the great gods, but to the gods and spirits that control everyday life, its cycles and challenges. The first seven books are the earliest, whereas books 8 through 12 are later and contain cosmological speculations similar to book 10 of the *Rig-Veda* and the later *Upanishads.*

The four *Vedas* were orally composed and handed down orally for thousands of years. To put them in a book would have seemed absurd, even sacrilegious, because they were in essence a spoken and heard revelation (Shruti) and their power was in their spokenness. As a student, each young Brahmin is educated in one of the four *Vedas* and becomes an expert in the use of that *Veda* in sacrifice.

The *Brahmanas* mark the high point of Hindu ritualism. The power of the priesthood steadily grew in Vedic times (2000–1000 B.C.E.), and the focus of the *Brahmanas* is on sacrifice itself, not on the gods. Sacrifice is the power that generates the cosmos and keeps it going. The main group of the *Brahmanas* deals with the *Yajur-Veda* and the ritual process. Sacrifices using soma are prominent, as is the horse sacrifice, which took great expense and an entire year to enact. The *Aranyakas* mark the beginning of a departure from Vedic ritualism. Mixed and disjointed in content, these reflections may have been developed by marginalized Brahmins or members of the warrior caste.

The *Upanishads,* the last of the *Vedas,* are close in style to the *Aranyakas,* from which they are often generically indistinguishable. Most were written from the eighth to the fourth centuries B.C.E. The so-called "Principal *Upanishads*" number about thirteen and are the only *Upanishads* accepted by all Hindus. Some with special devotion to a particular deity date from the beginnings of the common era all the way to the sixteenth century C.E. and are accepted only by certain Hindu sects as interest in ritual fades and philosophy/renunciation advances. The oldest of these are the *Chandogya* and *Brihad-Aranyaka Upanishads.*

The *Upanishads,* like most Shruti, are not uniform or systematic, but diverse collections of philosophical materials from different teachers over the centuries. The "world-affirming" Vedic religion that originally sought salvation in this world has become a "world-negating" religion that seeks release from the world. These *Upanishads* present the way of knowledge, the search for the eternal One called **Brahman** [BRAH-muhn] as it relates to the eternal Self or **Atman** [AHT-muhn] at the hidden center of every human. They are the beginnings of Hindu philosophy, which has continued and been influential until today, although it has been an option for only a tiny minority of Hindus of any period.

Unlike the Shruti, the epics of Smriti have very little interest in ritual, and deal with broad religious and cultural topics. The *Mahabharata* was finished by 400 C.E., the *Ramayana* by 200 B.C.E. Both epics have many layers of development: (1) myths of the gods, coming from earliest Hinduism; (2) the central plot of the epic itself; (3) a large bloc of material on religious duty and law. The insertion of this last layer into the epic is typically Indian: to pause at key points in the narrative for a religious discussion. The most famous such insertion is the *Bhagavad-Gita* [BAH-gah-vahd GEE-tuh] in the *Mahabharata,* which today is reckoned a book in itself. These discussions are precursors of the law books, to which we now turn.

The law codes are called ***Dharma-Shastras*** [DAHR-muh SHAS-truhs], "writings on duty." In the schools in which the *Vedas* and *Brahmanas* were studied, books on duty began to be compiled. These developed into more comprehensive and systematic books that formed the basis of Hindu law. The laws of *Manu* was written perhaps about 200 C.E. as a full code for all Hindu society, for every caste, occupation, and stage of life. Like the law books of most religions and civilizations, *Manu* and the other law codes were developed by commentary as the centuries passed, and thus their influence was perpetuated. How deep this influence may have been is unknown, because *Manu* (again like most law codes) gives prescriptions for an ideal society. Real Hindu life no doubt fell short of this ideal.

The ancient stories of the *Puranas* number eighteen important ones. Their themes are creation, re-creation, origins of the gods and sages, eras of common history, and dynastic histories. Some, like the *Upanishads,* are sectarian, appealing to devotees of only one god. They fall into three main categories as they promote the gods Vishnu, Shiva, and others. The most important *Purana* is the *Bhagavata-Purana,* composed about 400–1000 C.E. This *Purana* is based on and furthers the book for which it is named, the *Bhagavad-Gita.*

Tantras, books of mystical teachings, spells, and directions for rituals, arose as a popular supplement to Vedic religion. While acknowledging the truth and authority of the *Vedas,* the *tantras* go beyond them to provide updated rituals. They perfect the use of specific techniques for the body and the mind. Tantrism is widespread in Hindu religion, but the devotional cult of the goddess Shakti has a special attachment to it. The Shaktic *tantras* occasionally feature "left-handed" tantrism, which most Westerners wrongly associate with tantrism as a whole: esoteric practices, magic, and sexual practices. The *tantras* were written in the period 500–1800 C.E.

Use

Hindu scriptures have a wide variety of uses, some of which have already been mentioned. In what follows, we will trace these uses briefly, with a special focus on orality.

The *Vedas* have been used for ritual by the Brahmin priests. The threefold *Veda* has always been the text of this religious aristocracy, never of the people as a whole. From the first, the *sound* of these scriptures was more important than their *content.* Traditionalist Hindus believe that the sounds of the *Veda* were the sounds that the sages heard reverberating from the creation of the universe and that they will be the same sounds used again at the next cycle of re-creation. These sounds were passed on orally from guru to student for thousands of years. Gurus taught their students every element of correct oral usage of the *Veda,* including correct enunciation, poetic meter, volume, pitch, and so on. Those Brahmins who excelled in *Veda* memorization and ritual enactment were known as **pandits.** The *Rig-Veda* itself often ends its hymns with a request to the deity that the sacrificers might "speak as men of power" during the rites. Hindus do not study the content of the *Vedas,* as for example in meditation or doctrinal instruction. Much of the ancient Vedic form of the Sanskrit language has been lost, and much of its meaning is not recoverable. During the last two thousand years, accordingly, Brahmins often do not understand what they are saying as the *Vedas* are chanted in the rituals. This is not important; only the correct sounds matter. To-day only a few Brahmin families keep up a ritually correct form of the ancient Vedic sacrifices. However, all domestic rituals are done with Vedic formulas. By speaking and concentrating on the **mantra** [MAHN-truh], the believer taps into the cosmic power of creative speech.

The *Upanishads* became the texts of the philosophers, especially of the Vedanta school of Hindu philosophy. By reflecting on the meaning of this scripture in a life of strict renunciation, the sage will be set free from desire and rebirth. In the last hundred years, a neo-Vedantic school has arisen, influenced by Western (especially Christian) religious ideas such as theism, ethics, and tolerance among religions. This school represents a break from traditional Vedanta.

Law codes are used for the ordering of society. They especially reflect the Brahmin caste and its view of Hindu life. How closely these books were followed and enforced in ancient times cannot now be determined, but their broadest aspects have certainly kept much authority. Of all Hindu scripture the epics have been the best known and most loved. The *Bhagavad-Gita,* because of the way it affirms and integrates many main aspects of Hinduism, has been acceptable and influential among most Hindus. For its promotion of one way as the best, however, it remains the special text of the Vishnu-Krishna devotional movement.

For most of Hindu history, the primacy of these works has been in their oral, not their written, form. For example, the *Veda-samhitas* were largely composed and collected probably before writing was known in India. The *Upanishads* were not fully written down until 1656 C.E., and then only at the command of the non-Hindu Sultan Dara Shakoh, a translation of these oral works into Persian. Since then, the *Upanishads* have been translated by Hindus into the other main Indian languages; the original Sanskrit was written down as well.

The Hindu tradition has even regarded writing itself as a polluting medium compared with the sanctity of the spoken word. Now, however, orality is fading, and it is common to see even holy men reading aloud from books instead of "reading" from their memory. Still, the "sound" of the scriptures will continue to be important, as sound is their very essence.

Comparing a typical Hindu attitude toward scripture with Western attitudes, Daniel Gold remarks, "The idea of Vedic authority known to traditional Hindus is much more diffuse and abstract than the idea of a closed biblical canon known to the West. Christians, for example, variously interpret a revealed text to which most people have access and of which they can make some literal sense. For Hindus, by contrast, a reverence for scriptural authority can often mean simply that they think that what they do somehow comes from the Vedas, texts which in their antiquity are very rarely used or understood anymore. . . . They exist now primarily as words of power incorporated into newer rites."[1]

---

[1] D. Gold, "Organized Hinduisms," in M. E. Marty and R. S. Appleby, *Fundamentalisms Observed* (Chicago: University of Chicago Press, 1991), pp. 542–543.

To sum up: Hindus' use of scripture depends on their class and occupation and on the particular type of Hinduism (philosophical, devotional, etc.) they follow. All Hindus have a strong, if vague, reverence for the threefold *Veda*, a feeling for the structure of society as reflected in the law codes, and, in devotional Hinduism, a strong feeling for the literature of one's single chosen god or goddess.

TEACHING

Aditi and the Birth of the Gods *

This hymn presents several different and seemingly contradictory explanations of the creation of the world. It was spoken by the lord of sacred speech; it came from nonexistence; the mother goddess gave birth to it; it was formed from the mutual births of Aditi and Daksa; it was formed from Martanda. These and other various explanations still exist among Hindus today.[2]

Let us now speak with wonder of the births of the gods, so that someone may see them when the hymns are chanted in this later age. The lord of sacred speech, like a smith, fanned them together. In the earliest age of the gods, existence was born from non-existence. In the first age of the gods, existence was born from non-existence. After this the quarters of the sky were born from her who crouched with legs spread. The earth was born from her who crouched with legs spread, and from the earth the quarters of the sky were born. From Aditi, Daksa was born, and from Daksa Aditi was born. [5] For Aditi was born as your daughter, O Daksa, and after her were born the blessed gods, the kinsmen of immortality. When you gods took your places there in the water with your hands joined,[3] a thick cloud of mist arose from you like dust from dancers. When you gods like magicians caused the worlds to swell, you drew forth the sun that was hidden in the ocean. Eight sons are there of Aditi, who were born of her body. With seven she went forth among the gods, but she threw Martanda, the sun, aside. With seven sons Aditi went forth into the earliest age. But she bore Martanda so that he would in turn beget offspring[4] and then soon die.

---

* *Rig-Veda* 10.72

[2] All selections from the *Rig-Veda* are reprinted from *The Rig Veda, An Anthology,* by Wendy Doniger O'Flaherty (London: Penguin, 1981). Copyright 1981 by Wendy Doniger O'Flaherty. Used by permission.

---

[3] *hands joined:* the typical Indian posture of greeting and respect.

[4] *offspring:* humanity, that begets its own offspring and dies.

The Creation Hymn **

This account of the origin of the universe is philosophical rather than mythological and similar to the treatment of creation in the Upanishads. *Questioning and puzzling, it stirs up the listener to reflection. "That one" is the impersonal creator by whom the gods themselves are created. This hymn has been most influential among Hindus.*

There was neither non-existence nor existence then; there was neither the realm of space nor the sky which is beyond. What stirred? Where? In

---

** *Rig-Veda* 10.129

whose protection? Was there water, bottomlessly deep? There was neither death nor immortality then. There was no distinguishing sign of night nor of day. That one breathed, windless, by its own impulse. Other than that there was nothing beyond. Darkness was hidden by darkness in the beginning; with no distinguishing sign, all this was water. The life force that was covered with emptiness, that one arose through the power of heat. Desire came upon that one in the beginning; that was the first seed of mind. Poets seeking in their heart with wisdom found the bond of existence in non-existence. [5] Their cord[5]

was extended across. Was there below? Was there above? There were seed-placers; there were powers. There was impulse beneath; there was giving-forth above. Who really knows? Who will here proclaim it? Where was it produced? From where is this creation? The gods came afterwards, with the creation of this universe. Who then knows where it has arisen? Where this creation has arisen—perhaps it formed itself, or perhaps it did not—the one[6] who looks down on it, in the highest heaven, only he knows—or perhaps he does not know.

---

[5] *cord:* the bond of existence, extending across the universe.

[6] *the one:* Prajapati, the high god.

Creation from Brahman*

This selection from an important Upanishad *presents a philosophical reflection on the origin of the world. It traces creation to Brahman, the world soul that is the All in and behind the world. The cosmic Person* (purusha) *identified with the world soul is neither male nor female, despite the references to the Person as "he."*[7]

In the beginning this world was Soul alone, in the shape of a Person. He looked around and saw nothing but himself. He first said, "This is I." Therefore, he became I by name. Therefore even now, if a man is asked he first says, "This is I," and then pronounces his other name. Before [*purva*] all this he burnt down [*ush*] all evils; therefore he was a Person [*purusha*]. Truly he who knows this burns down everyone who tries to be before him.

He feared, and therefore anyone who is lonely fears. He thought, "As there is nothing but myself, why should I fear?" Then his fear passed

away. For what should he have feared? But he felt no delight. Therefore a man who is lonely feels no delight. He longed for a second person. As he was as large as a man and woman together, he made his Self to fall in two, and there came husband and wife. Therefore Yajnavalkya said: "We two are thus like half a shell." Therefore the void that was there [in the male] is filled by the wife. He had sexual intercourse with her, and humans were born.

She thought, "How can he have sexual intercourse with me, after having produced me from himself? I shall hide myself." She then became a cow. But he became a bull and had sex with her, and therefore cows were born. Then she became a mare, and he a stallion; then he a male ass, and she a female ass. He had sex with her [in both forms], and therefore one-hoofed animals were born. He became a she-goat, she a he-goat; he became a ewe, she a ram. He had sex with her, and therefore goats and sheep were born. In this way he created everything that exists in pairs, down to the ants. [5] He knew this: "I indeed am this creation, for I created all this." Therefore he became the creation, and he who knows this lives in this his creation.

---

* *Brihad-Aranyaka Upanishad* 1.4.1–7

[7] This and all other selections from the *Upanishads* are taken, with editing, from Max Müller, trans., *The Upanishads, Sacred Books of the East*, vols. 1 and 15 (Oxford: Oxford University Press, 1878, 1884).

Next he thus produced fire by rubbing. From the mouth, as from the fire-hole,[8] and from the hands he created fire. Therefore both the mouth and the hands are hairless inside, for the fire-hole is without hair inside.

People say, "Sacrifice to this god or that god." But each god is his manifestation, for he is all gods.

Whatever is moist he created from semen; this is Soma. So this universe is really either food or eaters of food. Soma is food, Agni the eater. This is the highest creation of Brahman, when he

created the gods from his better part, and when he who was then mortal created the immortals. Therefore it was the highest creation. He who knows this lives in this highest creation. . . .

He cannot be seen, for when breathing he is called breath. When speaking, he is called speech; when seeing, eye; when hearing, ear; when thinking, mind. All these are only the names of his acts. He who worships him as the one or the other, does not know him. . . . Let men worship him as Soul [Atman], for in the Soul all these are one. This Soul is the footprint of everything, for through it one knows everything. As one can find again by footprints what was lost, he who knows this finds glory and praise.

---

[8] *fire-hole:* Sanskrit *yoni,* the circular religious image of the human vagina symbolizing the female cosmic creative power.

The God Indra*

Indra is the sky god, the king of the gods. This hymn extols Indra's accomplishments over several opposing gods and for promoting the welfare of the people. It seeks to defend the importance of Indra against those who ignore him or even deny his existence (verse 5). This defense evidently did not succeed, because in post-Vedic Hinduism Indra has largely disappeared.

The god who had insight the moment he was born, the first who protected the gods with his power of thought, before whose hot breath the two world-halves tremble at the greatness of his manly powers—he, my people, is Indra. He who made fast the tottering earth, who made still the quaking mountains, who measured out and extended the expanse of the air, who propped up the sky—he, my people, is Indra. He who killed the serpent and loosed the seven rivers, who drove out the cows that had been pent up by Vala,[9] who gave birth to fire between two stones, the winner of booty in combats—he, my people, is Indra. He by whom all these changes were

rung, who drove the race of Dasas[10] down into obscurity, who took away the flourishing wealth of the enemy as a winning gambler takes the stake—he, my people, is Indra. [5] He about whom they ask, "Where is he?," or they say of him, the terrible one, "He does not exist," he who diminishes the flourishing wealth of the enemy as gambling does—believe in him! He, my people, is Indra. He who encourages the weary and the sick, and the poor priest who is in need, who helps the man who harnesses the stones to press Soma, he who has lips fine for drinking— he, my people, is Indra.

He under whose command are horses and cows and villages and all chariots, who gave birth to the sun and the dawn and led out the waters, he, my people, is Indra. He who is invoked by both of two armies, enemies locked in combat, on this side and that side, he who is even invoked separately by each of two men standing on the very same chariot, he, my people, is Indra. He without whom people do not conquer, he whom they call on for help when they are fighting, who

---

* *Rig-Veda* 2.12
[9] *Vala:* Indra's demonic enemy, who penned up the cows.

[10] *Dasas:* literally, "slaves," enemies of the Aryans whom they subjugated; called in verse 10 "Dasyus."

became the image of everything, who shakes the unshakable—he, my people, is Indra. [10] He who killed with his weapon all those who had committed a great sin, even when they did not know it, he who does not pardon the arrogant man for his arrogance, who is the slayer of the Dasyus, he, my people, is Indra. He who in the fortieth autumn discovered Sambara living in the mountains, who killed the violent serpent, the Danu, as he lay there, he, my people, is Indra. He, the mighty bull who with his seven reins let loose the seven rivers to flow, who with his thunderbolt in his hand hurled down Rauhina as he was climbing up to the sky, he, my people, is Indra. Even the sky and the earth bow low before him, and the mountains are terrified of his hot breath. He who is known as the Soma-drinker, with the thunderbolt in his hand, with the thunderbolt in his palm, he, my people, is Indra. He who helps with his favor the one who presses and the one who cooks,[11] the praiser and the preparer, he for whom prayer is nourishment, for whom Soma is the special gift, he, my people, is Indra. [15] You who furiously grasp the prize for the one who presses and the one who cooks, you are truly real. Let us be dear to you, Indra, all our days, and let us speak as men of power in the sacrificial gathering.

---

[11] *presses . . . cooks:* in preparation of the soma.

The God Shiva*

Although one of the main branches of devotional Hinduism is Shaivism, Shiva does not have a text to celebrate him as Krishna does in the Bhagavad-Gita. *This late Upanishadic hymn identifies the Vedic god Rudra and the Cosmic Person with Shiva. It is used today by the worshippers of Shiva to express his praise. This hymn shows how the worship of one god characteristic of devotional Hinduism is related to the wider Hindu traditions with many gods.*

The snarer rules alone by his powers, rules all the worlds by his powers. He is the same, while things arise and exist. They who know this are immortal. There is only one Rudra. They do not allow a second; he rules all the worlds by his powers. He stands behind all persons. Having created all worlds, he, the protector, rolls it up at the end of time. This god has his eyes, his face, his arms, and his feet in every place. When producing heaven and earth, he forges them together with his arms and his wings. He is the creator and supporter of the gods. Rudra is the great seer, the lord of all, who formerly gave birth to Hiranyagarbha. May he endow us with good thoughts.

[5] O Rudra, dweller in the mountains, look upon us with your most blessed form that is auspicious, not terrible, and reveals no evil! O lord of the mountains, make lucky that arrow that you hold in your hand to shoot. Do not hurt man or beast!

Beyond this is the High Brahman, the vast, hidden in the bodies of all creatures. He alone envelopes everything, as the Lord. Those who know this become immortal. I know that great Person [*purusha*] of sunlike luster beyond the darkness. A man who truly knows him passes over death; there is no other path to go.

This whole universe is filled by this Person, to whom there is nothing superior, from whom there is nothing different, than whom there is nothing smaller or larger. This Person stands alone, fixed like a tree in the sky. [10] That which is beyond this world is without form and without suffering. They who know this become immortal, but others suffer pain.

The Blessed One exists in the faces, the heads, the necks of all. He dwells in the cave of the heart of all beings. He is all-pervading, and therefore he is the omnipresent Shiva. That Person is the great lord. He is the mover of existence. He possesses the purest power reaching everything.

---

* *Shvetashvatara Upanishad* 3.1–13

He is light; he is undecaying. The Person, not larger than a thumb, always dwelling in the heart of man, is perceived by the heart, the thought,

"That You Are"*

In this reading, the Oneness that exists in and beyond the world is developed in a dialogue between a son and his father. Popularly known as "The Education of Svetaketu," this story points to the cosmic Self as the inner essence of all that is.

Om.[12] There lived once Svetaketu Aruneya, the grandson of Aruna. To him his father, Uddalaka, the son of Aruna, said: "Svetaketu, go to school. For there is none belonging to our race, who, not having studied the Veda, is, so to speak, a Brahmana by birth only."

Having begun his apprenticeship with a teacher when he was twelve years of age, Svetaketu returned to his father when he was twenty-four, having then studied all the Vedas. But he was conceited, considering himself well-read and stern.

His father said to him: "Svetaketu, as you are so conceited, considering yourself so well-read, and so stern, my dear, have you ever asked for that instruction by which we hear what cannot be heard? Have you asked for that by which we perceive what cannot be perceived, by which we know what cannot be known?"

"What is that instruction, sir?" he asked.

The father replied: "My dear, as by one clod of clay all that is made of clay is known, the difference being only a name, arising from speech, but the truth being that all is clay. As, my dear, by one nugget of gold all that is made of gold is known, the difference being only a name, arising from speech, but the truth being that all is gold. As, my dear, by one pair of nail scissors all that is made of iron is known, the difference being only a name, arising from speech, but the truth being that all is iron—thus, my dear, is that instruction."

* *Chandogya Upanishad* 6.1–2, 9–11
[12] *Om:* a lesson is often begun with this cosmic sound.

and the mind. Those who know this become immortal.

The son said: "Surely those venerable men, my teachers, did not know that. For if they had known it, why should they not have told it me? Sir, tell me that." "Be it so," said the father.

"In the beginning, my dear, there was that only which is, one thing only, without a second. It thought, May I be many, may I grow forth. It sent forth fire. That fire thought, May I be many, may I grow forth. It sent forth water. Therefore whenever anybody anywhere is hot and perspires, water is produced on him from fire alone.

"Water thought, may I be many, may I grow forth. It sent forth earth (food). Therefore whenever it rains anywhere, most food is then produced. From water alone is eatable food produced. . . .

[9] "As the bees, my son, make honey by collecting the juices of distant trees, and reduce the juice into one form, and as these juices have no discrimination, so that they might say, I am the juice of this tree or that, in the same manner, my son, all these creatures, when they have become merged in the True (either in deep sleep or in death), know not that they are merged in the True. Whatever these creatures are here, whether a lion, or a wolf, or a boar, or a worm, or a fly, or a gnat, or a mosquito, that they become again and again. Now that which is that subtle essence, in it all that exists has its self. It is the True. It is the Self, and that, Svetaketu, you are."

"Please, Sir, inform me still more," said the son.

"Be it so, my child," the father replied.

"These rivers, my son, run, the eastern like the Ganges, toward the east, the western like the Sindhu, toward the west. They go from sea to sea, that is, the clouds lift up the water from the sea to the sky, and send it back as rain to the sea. They become indeed sea. And as those rivers, when they are in the sea, do not know, I am this or that river, in the same manner, my son, all these creatures, when they have come back from the True, know not that they have come back from the True. Whatever these creatures are here, whether a lion, or a wolf, or a boar, or a worm, or a midge, or a gnat, or a mosquito, that they become again and again.

"That which is that subtle essence, in it all that exists has its self. It is the True. It is the Self, and that, Svetaketu, you are."

"Please, Sir, inform me still more," said the son.

"Be it so, my child," the father replied.

"If someone were to strike at the root of this large tree here, it would bleed, but live. If he were to strike at its stem, it would bleed, but live. If he were to strike at its top, it would bleed, but live. Pervaded by the living Self that tree stands firm, drinking in its nourishment and rejoicing; but if the life (the living Self) leaves one of its branches, that branch withers; if it leaves a second, that branch withers; if it leaves a third, that branch withers. If it leaves the whole tree, the whole tree withers.

"In exactly the same manner, my son, know this. This body indeed withers and dies when the living Self has left it; the living Self dies not.

"That subtle essence is the self of all that exists. It is the True. It is the Self, and that, Svetaketu, you are."

The Goddess as Kali*

The Devi-Mahatmya, *or "The Greatness of the Goddess," is a leading medieval* Purana. *Popular since its oral origins among goddess devotees, it is now the best-known and most often recited goddess text in modern India. The goddess has many names and forms; here she fights a fearsome battle in her form as Kali, the goddess of destruction.*[13]

Directed in this fashion . . . the demons,
    arranged as a fourfold army
With Canda and Munda at their head, went
    forth with upraised weapons.

Then they saw the Goddess, smiling slightly,
    mounted
On her lion on the great golden peak of the
    highest mountain.

Having seen her, they made ready in their
    efforts to abduct her,
While others approached her with swords
    drawn and bows bent.

Ambika then uttered a great wrathful cry
    against them,
And her face became black as ink in anger.

[5] From the knitted brows of her forehead's
    surface immediately
Came forth Kali, with her dreadful face,
    carrying sword and noose.

She carried a strange skull-topped staff, and
    wore a garland of human heads.
She was shrouded in a tiger skin, and looked
    utterly gruesome with her emaciated skin,

Her widely gaping mouth, terrifying with its
    lolling tongue,
With sunken, reddened eyes and a mouth that
    filled the directions with roars.

She fell upon the great Asuras in that army,
    slaying them immediately.
She then devoured the forces of the enemies of
    the gods.

Attacking both the front and rear guard, having
    seized the elephants
Together with their riders and bells, she hurled
    them into her mouth with a single hand.

[10] Likewise having flung the cavalry with its
    horses and the chariots with their charioteers

---

* *Markandeya Purana, Devi-Mahatmya 7.1–25*
[13] From Tomas B. Coburn, *Encountering the Goddess: A Translation of the Devi-Mahatmya and a Study of its Interpretation* (Albany, NY: State University of New York Press, 1991), pp. 60–62. Copyright, 1991 State University of New York Press. Used by permission.

Into her mouth, she brutally pulverized them
     with her teeth.

She seized one by the hair, and another by the
     throat.
Having attacked one with her foot, she crushed
     another against her breast.

The weapons and missiles that were hurled by
     the demons
She seized with her mouth, and crunched them
     to bits with her teeth.

The army of all those mighty and distinguished
     demons
She destroyed: she devoured some, and thrashed
     the others.

Some were sliced by her sword, others pounded
     with her skull-topped staff.
Just in this way did the Asuras meet their
     destruction, ground up by the edges of her
     fangs.

[15] Immediately upon seeing the entire army
     of the Asuras slain,
Canda rushed at the incredibly fearsome Kali.

The great Asura enveloped the dread-eyed
     female with a horrendous great shower of
     arrows,
And Munda did the same with discuses hurled
     by the thousand.

This stream of discuses entering her mouth
Resembled a multitude of suns entering into
     the middle of a black cloud.

Then Kali, her ugly teeth gleaming within her
     dreadful mouth,
Angrily cackled with terrible sounds.

Mounting her great lion, the Goddess ran at
     Canda,
And having seized him by the hair, she cut off
     his head with her sword.

[20] On seeing Canda slain, Munda rushed at
     her.
She caused him to fall to the ground, wrathfully
     smitten with her sword.

On seeing Canda slain, and also Munda,
     What was left of the assaulted army was
     overcome with fear, and fled in all directions.

Picking up the heads of Canda and Munda,
     Kali Approached Candika and spoke words
     mixed with loud and cruel laughter:

"Here, as a present from me to you, are Canda
     and Munda, two beasts
Slain in the sacrifice of battle. Now you yourself
     can slay Shumbha and Nishumbha!" . . .

Seeing the two great Asuras brought there,
The beautiful Candika spoke these playful
     words to Kali:

"Because you have seized Canda and Munda
     and brought them here,
You will henceforth be known in the world as
     the Goddess 'Camundi.'"

ORGANIZATION

The Creation of the Caste System*

One of the many creation hymns of the Rig, *this
poem presents the cosmic Man (Sanskrit* purusha)
*as the one through whose sacrifice the gods fashioned
the universe. The making of humanity is presented*

*in terms of the caste system, its first appearance in
Hindu literature and the foundation of its later
authority. Much of the caste system is undergoing a
liberalizing change in modern India, especially in
the cities. But it is still important and pervasive as a
general social structure and cultural inheritance.*

* Rig-Veda 10.90

The Man has a thousand heads, a thousand eyes, a thousand feet. He pervaded the earth on all sides and extended beyond it as far as ten fingers. It is the Man who is all this, whatever has been and whatever is to be. He is the ruler of immortality, when he grows beyond everything through food. This is his greatness, and the Man is yet more than this. All creatures are a quarter of him; three quarters are what is immortal in heaven. With three quarters the Man rose upwards, and one quarter of him remains here.

From this he spread out in all directions, into that which eats and that which does not eat. [5] From him Viraj[14] was born, and from Viraj came the Man. When he was born, he ranged beyond the earth behind and before. When the gods spread the sacrifice with the Man as the offering, spring was the clarified butter, summer was the fuel, autumn was the oblation.[15] They anointed the Man, the sacrifice born at the beginning, upon the sacred grass. With him the gods, Sadhyas,[16] and sages sacrificed. From that sacrifice in which everything was offered, the melted fat was collected. He made it into those beasts who live in the air, in the forest, and in villages. From that

---

[14] *Viraj:* the female counterpart of the man.
[15] *oblation:* what is sacrificed.
[16] *Sadhyas:* saints, called in the last verse of this hymn "the ancient gods."

sacrifice in which everything was offered, the verses and chants were born, the meters were born from it, and from it the formulas were born.[17] [10] Horses were born from it, and those other animals that have two rows of teeth; cows were born from it, and from it goats and sheep were born.

When they divided the Man, into how many parts did they apportion him? What do they call his mouth, his two arms and thighs and feet? His mouth became the Brahmin; his arms were made into the Warrior, his thighs the People, and from his feet the Servants were born. The moon was born from his mind; from his eye the sun was born. Indra and Agni came from his mouth, and from his vital breath the Wind was born. From his navel the middle realm of space arose; from his head the sky evolved. From his two feet came the earth, and the quarters of the sky from his ear. Thus they set the worlds in order. [15] There were seven enclosing-sticks for him, and thrice seven fuel-sticks, when the gods, spreading the sacrifice, bound the Man as the sacrificial beast. With the sacrifice the gods sacrificed to the sacrifice. These were the first ritual laws. These very powers reached the dome of the sky where dwell the Sadhyas, the ancient gods.

---

[17] *verses, chants, meters, formulas:* the *Vedas.*

The Four Castes*

This passage contains a short description of the main structure of the caste system. The duties and means of livelihood of each caste are indicated. The end of this passage gives the moral duties binding on everyone of whatever caste, gender, or stage of life. These general rules are growing more important in contemporary Hinduism as the caste system fades.[18]

---

* *Institutes of Vishnu 2.1–17*
[18] Taken, with editing, from Julius Jolly, trans., *The Institutes of Vishnu, Sacred Books of the East,* vol. 7 (Oxford: Oxford University Press, 1880).

Brahmins, Kshatriyas, Vaishyas, and Shudras are the four castes. The first three of these are called twice-born. They must perform with mantras[19] the whole number of ceremonies, which begin with impregnation and end with the ceremony of burning the dead body. Their duties are as follows. [5] A Brahmin teaches the Veda. A Kshatriya has constant practice in arms. A Vaishya tends cattle. A Shudra serves the twice-born. All

---

[19] *mantras:* sacred words or syllables chanted to create and acquire cosmic spiritual power.

the twice-born are to sacrifice and study the Veda. [10] Their modes of livelihood are as follows. A Brahmin sacrifices for others and receives alms. A Kshatriya protects the world. A Vaishya engages in farming, keeps cows, trades, lends money at interest, and grows seeds. A Shudra engages in all branches of crafts. In times of distress, each caste may follow the occupation of that below it in rank. Duties common to all castes are patience, truthfulness, restraint, purity, liberality, self-control, not to kill, obedience toward one's gurus, visiting places of pilgrimage, sympathy, straightforwardness, freedom from covetousness, reverence toward gods and Brahmins,[20] and freedom from anger.

---

[20] *reverence towards . . . Brahmins:* as sacrificers, the Brahmins preserve the order of the universe, and other castes are to honor them. India has seen an almost continuous struggle between the priestly caste and the warrior-ruler caste.

ETHICS

Sin and Forgiveness*

The god Varuna protects the cosmic order and punishes those humans who violate it by misdeeds. This passage presents the heartfelt pleas of the worshipper to Varuna to reveal his unknown sin to him and pardon it.

The generations have become wise by the power of him who has propped apart the two world-halves even though they are so vast. He has pushed away the dome of the sky to make it high and wide; he has set the sun on its double journey and spread out the earth. I ask my own heart, "When shall I be close to Varuna? Will he enjoy my offering and not be provoked to anger? When shall I see his mercy and rejoice?" I ask myself what that transgression was, Varuna, for I wish to understand. I turn to the wise to ask them. The poets have told me the very same thing: "Varuna has been provoked to anger against you."

O Varuna, what was the terrible crime for which you wish to destroy your friend who praises you? Proclaim it to me so that I may hasten to prostrate myself before you and be free from sin, for you are hard to deceive and are ruled by yourself alone. [5] Free us from the harmful deeds of our fathers, and from those that we have committed with our own bodies. O king, free Vasistha[21] like a thief who has stolen cattle, like a calf set free from a rope. The mischief was not done by my own free will, Varuna; wine, anger, dice, or carelessness led me astray. The older shares in the mistake of the younger. Even sleep does not avert evil. As a slave serves a generous master, so would I serve the furious god and be free from sin. The noble god[22] gave understanding to those who did not understand; being yet wiser, he speeds the clever man to wealth. O Varuna, you who are ruled by yourself alone, let this praise lodge in your very heart. Let it go well for us always with your blessings.

---

[21] *Vasistha:* a wise man who, according to myth, broke into Varuna's house; he was tied up but then freed when he praised Varuna.

[22] *the noble god:* Varuna.

---

* *Rig-Veda* 7.86

The Three *Das**

The main virtues of Hinduism are often put in their most elemental for as the three das: damyata restraint, self-control; datta, generosity; and da-yadhvam, compassion. These are said to be commanded from the beginning.

The threefold offspring of Prajapati—gods, men, and demons—lived as students of sacred knowledge with their father Prajapati.

Having lived the life of a student of sacred knowledge, the gods said: "Speak to us, sir." Prajapati spoke to them this syllable, "Da. Do you understand this?" "We did understand," they

said. "You said to us, 'Control yourselves (damyata).'" "Om!" he replied. "You did understand."

Then they said to him again, "Speak to us, sir." He spoke to them this syllable, "Da. Do you understand this?" "We did understand," they said. "You said to us, 'Give (datta).'" "Om!" he said. "You did understand."

So then the demons said to him, "Speak to us, sir." He said this syllable to them, "Da. Do you understand?" "We understand," they said. "You said to us, 'Be compassionate (dayadhvam).'" "Om!" he said. "You did understand."

The divine voice of the thunder repeats, "Da! Da! Da! Control yourself, give, be compassionate." One should practice this same triad: self-control, giving, compassion.

*(Brihadaranyaka Upanisad 5.2)

The Way of Asceticism**

This reading presents all the ancient practices of Hinduism as necessary. But they are "unsafe boats," and those who trust in them to accomplish release are "fools" and "ignorant." The only effective way of release is the way of knowledge based on renunciation and asceticism. This belief has been a guiding principle for ascetics and holy men from Upanishadic times until today.

This is the truth: the sacrificial works that the poets saw in the hymns [of the Veda] have been performed in many ways in the Vedic age. Practice them diligently, you lovers of truth! This is your path that leads to the world of good works!

When the fire is lighted and the flame flickers, let a man offer his oblations between the two portions of melted butter, as an offering with faith. A man's Agnihotra sacrifice destroys his seven worlds if it is not followed by the new-moon and full-moon sacrifices, by the four-months' sacrifices, and by the harvest sacrifice. It destroys his

seven worlds if it is unattended by guests, not offered at all, done without the ceremony to all the gods, or not offered according to the rules. . . .

[5] If a man performs his sacred works when these flames are shining, and the sacrificial offerings follow at the right time, they lead him as sunrays to where the one Lord of the gods dwells. "Come here, come here!", the brilliant offerings say to him. They carry the sacrificer on the rays of the sun, while they utter pleasant speech and praise him: "This is your holy Brahma-world, gained by your good works."

But those boats, the eighteen sacrifices,[23] are truly frail. Fools who praise this as the highest good are subjected again and again to old age and death. Fools dwelling in darkness, wise in their own conceit and puffed up with vain knowledge, go round and round staggering back and forth, like blind men led by the blind. . . . [10] Considering sacrifice and good works as the best, these fools know no higher good. Having

** *Mundaka Upanishad* 2.1–3, 5–8, 10–13

[23] *eighteen sacrifices:* Vedic rituals.

enjoyed their reward in the height of heaven, gained by good works, they come back again to this world or a lower one. But those who practice penance and faith in the forest, who are tranquil, wise and live on alms, depart free from passion through the sun to where that immortal Person dwells, whose nature is imperishable.

Let a Brahmin, after he has examined all these worlds that are gained by works, acquire freedom from all desires. Nothing that is eternal can be gained by what is not eternal. To understand this, let him take fuel in his hand[24] and approach a Guru who is learned and dwells entirely in Brahman. The wise teacher truly tells that knowledge of Brahman through which he knows the eternal and true Person. He tells a pupil who has approached him respectfully, whose thoughts are not troubled by any desires and who has obtained perfect peace.

---

[24] *fuel in hand:* a sign of studentship.

Stages of Life for a Twice-Born Man*

The first stage of Hindu life is that of the student, who lives and studies with his guru (private teacher). The first passage gives the rules for the student's relationship with his teacher, especially the respect owed to one's teacher. The second stage is that of the householder, when the young man, his studies complete, must marry and father children. Here the rules for whom to marry are presented. The third stage is that of retirement into the forest, and Manu relates the style of life and religious aims of this stage. The fourth stage presented is that of the ascetic who renounces all typical life to find release from rebirth. These laws on the stages of life reflect the situation of about 200 C.E., when Manu was written. Some differ from present practice, notably that asceticism no longer requires a prior retirement stage but can be entered by an adult male at any time. The system presented here is idealized— only a minority of Hindus in the past and present have carried them out fully. Nonetheless, they continue to be influential.[25]

[2.69, the stage of studentship] Having performed the rite of initiation,[26] the teacher must first instruct the pupil in the rules of personal purification, conduct, fire-worship, and twilight devotions. [70] A student who is about to begin the study of the Veda shall receive instruction after he has sipped water according to the sacred law, has made the *Brahmangali,*[27] has put on clean clothing, and has brought his sexual organs under due control. At the beginning and at the end of a lesson in the Veda he must always clasp both the feet of his teacher. He must study by joining hands; that is called the Brahmangali [joining the palms for the sake of the Veda]. With crossed hands he must clasp the feet of the teacher, and touch the left foot with his left hand, the right foot with his right hand. The teacher, always unwearied, must say to him who is about to begin studying, "Recite!" He shall stop when the teacher says: "Let a stoppage take place!" Let him always pronounce the syllable "Om" at the beginning and at the end of a lesson in the Veda. Unless the syllable "Om" precedes, the lesson will slip away from him, and unless it follows it will fade away. . . .

[191] Both when ordered by his teacher, and without a command, a student shall always exert himself in studying [the Veda], and in doing what is serviceable to his teacher. Controlling his body,

---

* *Laws of Manu* 2.69–74, 191–201; 3.1–19; 6.1–9, 33–49
[25] Selections from *Manu* are taken, with editing, from G. Buhler, trans, *The Laws of Manu, Sacred Books of the East,* vol. 25 (Oxford University Press, 1886).
[26] *rite of initiation:* the acceptance of a male into full membership in the Hindu community.

[27] *Brahmangali:* the traditional Indian gesture of greeting and respect, explained more fully in the next verse.

his speech, his organs of sense, and his mind, let him stand with joined hands, looking at the face of his teacher. Let him always keep his right arm uncovered, behave decently, and keep the rest of his body well covered. When he is addressed with the words, "Be seated," he shall sit down, facing his teacher. In the presence of his teacher let him always eat less [than the teacher], and wear less valuable clothing and ornaments. Let him rise earlier and go to bed later. [195] Let him not answer or talk with his teacher while reclining on a bed, or while sitting, or eating, or standing, or with an averted face. Let him talk standing up, if his teacher is seated, advancing toward him when he stands, going to meet him if he advances, and running after him when he runs. . . . When his teacher is near, let his bed or seat be low; but within sight of his teacher he shall not sit carelessly at ease. Let him not pronounce the name of his teacher without adding an honorific title, even when talking about him behind his back. Let him not mimic his gait, speech, or conduct. [200] Wherever people justly criticize or falsely defame his teacher, he must cover his ears or depart to another place. By criticizing his teacher, even though justly, he will become in his next birth an ass. By falsely defaming him, he will become a dog. He who lives on his teacher's belongings will become a worm, and he who is envious of his merit will become a larger insect.

[3.1, The stage of the householder] The vow of studying the three Vedas under a teacher must be kept for thirty-six years, or for half that time, or for a quarter, or until the student has perfectly learned them. A student who has studied in due order the three Vedas, or two, or even only one, without breaking the rules of studentship, shall enter the order of householders. He who is famous for the strict performance of his duties and has received his heritage, the Veda, from his father, shall be honored. He will sit on a couch and be adorned with a garland, with the present of a cow and honey-mixture.

With the permission of his teacher, having bathed and performed according to the rule the ritual for returning home, a twice-born man shall marry a wife of equal caste who is endowed with auspicious bodily marks. [5] A young woman who is neither a Sapinda[28] on the mother's side nor belongs to the same family on the father's side is recommended to twice-born men for marriage and conjugal union. In connecting himself with a wife, let him carefully avoid the ten following types of families, even if they are great, or rich in cattle, horses, sheep, grain, or other property. He must avoid a family that neglects the sacred rites, one in which no male children are born, one in which the Veda is not studied, one that has thick hair on the body, those that are subject to hemorrhoids, tuberculosis, weakness of digestion, epilepsy, or white and black leprosy. Let him not marry a young woman with reddish hair, nor one who has a redundant body part, nor one who is sickly, nor one either with no hair on the body or too much hair. Let him not marry one who is too talkative or has red eyes. Let him not marry one named after a constellation, a tree, or a river, nor one bearing the name of a low caste, or of a mountain, nor one named after a bird, a snake, or a slave, nor one whose name inspires terror. [10] Let him wed a female free from bodily defects and who has an agreeable name. She must have the graceful gait of a swan or of an elephant, moderate hair on the body and on the head, small teeth, and soft limbs.

For the first marriage of twice-born men, wives of equal caste are recommended. But for those who because of desire marry another woman, the following females are approved. They are chosen according to the order of the castes. It is declared that a Shudra woman alone can be the wife of a Shudra, she and one of his own caste the wives of a Vaisya, those two and one of his own caste the wives of a Kshatriya, those three and one of his own caste the wives of a Brahmin. A Shudra woman is not mentioned even in any ancient story as the first wife of a Brahmin or of a

---

[28] *Sapinda*: a close relative; literally, a sharer in the funeral feast, an obligation usually considered to go back six generations.

Kshatriya, though they lived in the greatest distress. [15] Twice-born men who foolishly marry wives of the low caste soon degrade their families and their children to the state of Shudras. According to Atri and to Gautama the son of Utathya,[29] he who weds a Shudra woman becomes an outcast. According to Saunaka, he becomes an outcaste on the birth of a son, and according to Bhrigu when he has a male child from a Shudra female. A Brahmin who takes a Shudra wife to his bed will sink into hell. If he begets a child by her, he will lose the rank of a Brahmin. The spirits of deceased ancestors and the gods will not eat the offerings of a man who performs the rites in honor of the gods, of the manes, and of guests with a Shudra wife's assistance. Such a man will not go to heaven. For him who drinks the moisture of a Shudra's lips, who is tainted by her breath, and who begets a son on her, no way of forgiveness is prescribed.

[6.1, The Stage of Retirement] A twice-born Snataka,[30] who has lived according to the law of householders, taking a firm resolution and keeping his organs in subjection, may dwell in the forest. He must duly observe the rules given below. When a householder sees his skin wrinkled, and his hair white, and the sons of his sons, then he may depart to the forest. Abandoning all food raised by cultivation, and all his belongings, he may depart into the forest. He may either commit his wife to his sons or be accompanied by her.[31] Taking with him the sacred fire and the implements required for domestic sacrifices, he may go forth from the village into the forest and reside there, controlling his senses. [5] Let him offer those five great sacrifices according to the rule, with various kinds of pure food fit for ascetics, or with herbs, roots, and fruit. Let him

wear a skin or a tattered garment; let him bathe in the evening or in the morning. Let him always wear his hair in braids, with the hair on his body, his beard, and his nails uncut. Let him perform the Bali-offering with the kind of food he eats, and give alms according to his ability. Let him honor those who come to his hermitage to give him alms of water, roots, and fruit. Let him always be industrious in privately reciting the Veda. Let him be patient in hardships, friendly toward all, collected in mind, always liberal and never a receiver of gifts, and compassionate toward all living creatures. Let him offer, according to the law, the Agnihotra with three sacred fires, and never omit the new-moon and full-moon sacrifices at the proper time. . . .

[6.33, The stage of asceticism] Having passed the third part of his natural term of life in the forest, a man may live as an ascetic during the fourth part of his existence. First he must abandon all attachment to worldly objects. He who . . . offers sacrifices and subdues his senses, busies himself with giving alms and offerings of food, and becomes an ascetic gains bliss after death. [35] When he has paid the three debts,[32] let him apply his mind to the attainment of final liberation. He who seeks it without having paid his debts sinks downwards. Having studied the Vedas according to the rule, having fathered sons according to the sacred law, and having offered sacrifices according to his ability, he may direct his mind to the attainment of final liberation. A twice-born man who seeks final liberation sinks downward if he has not studied the Vedas, fathered sons, and offered sacrifices. Having performed the Ishti, sacred to the Lord of creatures, in which he gives all his property as the sacrificial fee, having reposited the sacred fires in himself, a Brahmin may depart from his house as an ascetic. Worlds, radiant in brilliancy, become his who recites the texts regarding Brahman and departs from his house

---

[29] *Gautama:* not Gautama Buddha.

[30] *Snataka:* a Brahmin who has completed his studentship.

[31] *accompanied by her:* Note in the next passage that if the husband chooses the way of ascetic renunciation, the wife cannot accompany him. She is in a difficult situation: her husband, having renounced his old life, no longer belongs to her, but she still belongs to him.

---

[32] *the three debts:* the three obligations discussed in the next verses: study, having sons, sacrifice. These are similar to the modern Hindu expression "the three debts": to the gods, to the guru, to be a father.

as an ascetic, after giving a promise of safety to all created beings.[33] [40] For that twice-born man who causes not even the smallest danger to created beings, there will be no danger from anything after he is freed from his body.

Departing from his house fully provided with the means of purification, let him wander about absolutely silent. He must care nothing for enjoyments that may be offered to him. Let him always wander about alone to attain final liberation. The solitary man, who neither forsakes nor is forsaken, gains his desired result. He shall neither possess a fire nor a dwelling. He may go to a village for his food. He shall be indifferent to everything, firm of purpose, meditating and concentrating his mind on Brahman. The marks of one who has attained liberation are a broken pot instead of an alms-bowl, the roots of trees for a dwelling, coarse wornout garments, life in solitude and indifference toward everything. [45] Let him not desire to die, let him not desire to

live. Let him wait for his appointed time as a servant waits for the payment of his wages. Let him put down his foot purified by his sight,[34] let him drink water purified by straining with a cloth, let him utter speech purified by truth, let him keep his heart pure. Let him patiently bear hard words, let him not insult anybody. Let him not become anybody's enemy for the sake of this perishable body. Against an angry man let him not show anger, let him bless when he is cursed, and let him not utter false speech. . . . He shall delight in matters of the Soul, sit in the postures prescribed by the Yoga, be independent of external help, entirely abstain from sensual enjoyments, and have himself for his only companion. He shall live in this world, but desire only the bliss of final liberation.

---

[33] *safety to all created beings:* the vow of *ahimsa,* nonviolence to all creatures.

[34] *put down his foot purified by his sight:* i.e., in a place on the ground with no visible living beings on it; so too he must *drink water purified* of living creatures. This requirement, which follows up on the ascetic's "promise of safety to all created beings" (verse 39), will become more important in Jainism.

The Life of Women*

The first passage is often quoted as an example of a positive Hindu attitude to women. It gives some indication of the respected place of Hindu women in the home (in the context of a strongly patriarchal society, of course). Much of this passage has as its background the participation of the wife in all the sacred rites of the home. The second passage contains rules for the whole life of women, emphasizing respect and obedience to husbands during their life. After her husband's death, she must not remarry and must live an ascetic life.

[3.55] Women must be honored and adorned by their fathers, brothers, husbands, and brothers-in-law, who desire their own welfare. Where

women are honored, there the gods are pleased. Where they are not honored, no sacred rite yields rewards. Where the female relations live in grief, the family soon perishes completely. But the family where they are not unhappy always prospers. Female relations pronounce a curse on houses where they are not honored; these houses perish completely, as if destroyed by magic. Men who seek their own welfare should always honor women on holidays and festivals with gifts of jewelry, clothes, and dainty food. [60] In a family where the husband is pleased with his wife and the wife with her husband, happiness will certainly be lasting.

[5.147] Nothing must be done independently by a girl, by a young woman, or by an old woman, even in her own house. In childhood a female must be subject to her father, in youth to her

---

* *Laws of Manu* 3.55–60; 5.147–165

husband, and when her husband is dead to her sons. A woman must never be independent. She must not seek to separate herself from her father, husband, or sons. By leaving them she would make both her own and her husband's families contemptible.

[150] She must always be cheerful, clever in household affairs, careful in cleaning her utensils, and economical in expenditure. She shall obey the man to whom her father may give her . . . as long as he lives. When he is dead, she must not insult his memory. For the sake of getting good fortune for brides, the recitation of benedictory texts and the sacrifice to the Lord of creatures are used at weddings; but the betrothal by the father or guardian is the cause of the husband's dominion over his wife. The husband who wedded her with sacred texts always gives happiness to his wife, both in season and out of season, in this world and in the next. Although he may be destitute of virtue, or seek pleasure elsewhere, or lacking good qualities, yet a husband must be constantly worshipped as a god by a faithful wife. [155] No sacrifice, no vow, no fast must be performed by women apart from their husbands. If a wife obeys her husband, she will for that reason alone be exalted in heaven.[35]

A faithful wife who desires to dwell after death with her husband must never do anything that might displease him, whether he is alive or dead. She may emaciate her body by living on pure flowers, roots, and fruit; but she must never even mention the name of another man after her husband has died. Until death let her be patient in hardships, self-controlled, and chaste. Let her strive to fulfil that most excellent duty that is prescribed for wives who have one husband only. Many thousands of Brahmins who were chaste from their youth have gone to heaven without continuing their race. [160] A virtuous wife who after the death of her husband constantly remains chaste reaches heaven although she has no son, just like those chaste men. But a woman who desires to have offspring violates her duty toward her [deceased] husband. She brings disgrace on herself in this world, and loses her place with her husband in heaven. Offspring begotten by another man is not considered lawful, offspring begotten on another man's wife does not belong to the begetter, nor is a second husband anywhere allowed for virtuous women.[36] She who lives with a man of higher caste, forsaking her own husband who belongs to a lower one, will become contemptible in this world, and is called a remarried woman. By violating her duty toward her husband a wife is disgraced in this world. After death she enters the womb of a jackal, and is tormented by diseases as the punishment of her sin. [165] She who controls her thoughts, words, and deeds, and never slights her husband will reside after death with him in heaven. She is called a virtuous wife.

---

[35] *heaven:* as elsewhere in Hinduism, usually a temporary reward before reincarnation.

[36] *anywhere allowed . . . women:* no ancient stories or laws permit it.

RITUAL AND MEDITATION

The Gayatri Mantra*

The name of this short prayer means "the savior of the singer." Considered the single most important prayer-formula of Hinduism, pious believers re-

---

* *Rig-Veda* 3.62.10

peat it at least three times a day. On its literal level, this verse is a simple prayer to the sun god Savitar for blessing. On its deeper level, it expresses and applies the power that the god himself holds. Given to a young man at his initiation with the sa-

cred thread, it helps to produce his rebirth. Believers in other Hindu deities have adapted it for their use from early times through today.

May we attain to the excellent glory of Savitar the god; so may he stimulate our prayers.

Hymn to Agni*

Agni is the god of fire, especially the sacrificial fire, and he is the priest among the gods (verse 1). This first hymn of the Rig-Veda *seeks to please Agni by praises and invoke his blessings. Like many other hymns of the* Rig, *it uses both the second person (e.g., "To you, Agni . . .") and the third person ("Agni earned the prayers . . ."), but all of it is addressed to Agni.*

I pray to Agni, the household priest who is the god of the sacrifice, the one who chants and invokes and brings most treasure. Agni earned the prayers of the ancient sages, and of those of the present, too; he will bring the gods here. Through Agni one may win wealth, and growth from day to day, glorious and most abounding in heroic sons. Agni, only the sacrificial ritual that you encompass on all sides goes to the gods. [5] Agni, the priest with the sharp sight of a poet, the true and most brilliant, the god will come with the gods. Whatever good you wish to do for the one who worships you, Agni, through you, O Angiras,[37] that comes true. To you, Agni, who shine upon darkness, we come day after day, bringing our thoughts and homage. [We come t]o you, the king over sacrifices, the shining guardian of the Order, growing in your own house. Be easy for us to reach, like a father to his son. Abide with us, Agni, for our happiness.

_____

* *Rig-Veda* 1.1

[37] *Angiras:* messenger to the gods and the father of an ancient family of priests.

The Meaning of the Agnihotra Sacrifice**

This Brahmana *follows up on the previous reading. It is a good example of the Brahmanic exposition and development of the sacrificial rite. The ritual expounded here is the* Agnihotra, *the daily household sacrifice to Agni. The god Prajapati is the precursor of Brahman.*[38]

Prajapati alone existed here in the beginning. He considered, "How may I be reproduced?" He toiled and performed acts of penance. He generated Agni from his mouth. Because he generated him from his mouth, therefore Agni is a consumer of food. Truly, he who knows Agni to be a consumer of food becomes himself a consumer of food.

He thus generated him first of the gods; and therefore [he is called] Agni, for *agni* [they say] is the same as *agri.* He, being generated, went forth as the first; for of him who goes first, they say that he goes at the head. Such, then, is the origin and nature of that Agni.

Prajapati then considered, "In Agni I have generated a food-eater for myself. But there is no other food here but myself, whom Agni certainly would not eat." Then this earth had been made

_____

** *Agni-Brahmana* 1.1–19

[38] Taken, with editing, from Julius Eggeling, trans., *The Satapatha-Brahmana,* part 1, *Sacred Books of the East,* vol. 12 (Oxford: Oxford University Press, 1882).

quite bald; there were neither plants nor trees. This, then, weighed on his mind.

Then Agni turned toward him with open mouth. Prajapati was terrified, and his own greatness departed from him. Now his own greatness is his speech; his speech departed from him. He desired an offering in himself and rubbed his hands; and because he rubbed his hands, palms are hairless. He then obtained either a butter-offering or a milk-offering; but they are both [acceptable because they are] made of milk.

[5] But this offering did not satisfy him, because it had hairs mixed with it. He poured it away into the fire, saying, "Drink, while burning!" From it plants sprang; hence their name "plants." He rubbed his hands a second time, and by that obtained another offering, either a butter-offering or a milk-offering. . . .

This offering then satisfied him. He hesitated: "Shall I offer it up? Or shall I not offer it up?" he thought. His own greatness said to him, "Offer it up!" Prajapati was aware that it was his own [*sva*] greatness that had spoken [*aha*] to him; and offered it up with the word *svaha!* This is why offerings are made with *svaha!* Then that burning one, the sun, rose; and then that blowing one, the wind, sprang up. Then Agni turned away.

Prajapati, having performed offering, reproduced himself, and saved himself from Agni as he was about to devour him. Truly whoever, knowing this, offers the agnihotra reproduces himself by offspring even as Prajapati reproduced himself. He saves himself from Agni, death, when he is about to devour him.

And when he dies, and when they place him on the fire, then he is born again out of the fire, and the fire only consumes his body. Even as he is born from his father and mother, so is he born from the fire. But he who does not offer the agnihotra does not come into life at all. Therefore the agnihotra must be offered.

The *Puja* of a Yogin*

Puja *is the worship of a god, including ritual actions such as invoking and praising the god, care for the image of the deity, and offering it food. This reading describes* puja *to several gods offered by yogic means, with these ritual actions by ordinary worshippers also included.*

I will now describe the mode of puja by performing which the sages attain all objects of life. After washing his head, rinsing his mouth and controlling his speech, one should sit well-protected in a svastika posture, padma posture or any other sitting position, with his face directed towards the east. He should then meditate in the middle of his navel on the mantra Yam, smoke colored and identical with the terrific wind, and purify all the impurities of the body. Then meditating on the mantra Kshoum, the ocean of light, situate in the lotus heart, he should, with flames going up, down and in contrary directions, burn down all impurities. He should then meditate on the mantra Van of the shape of the moon in the sky. And then the intelligent worshipper should sprinkle his own body extending from the lotus heart with nectarine drops passing through the generative organ and other tubes.

Having purified the ingredients of worship he should assign them. He should then purify his hand and the implements. First, he should assign, beginning with the thumb of the right hand, the fingers of the two hands to the principal limbs. Then with the sixty-two mantras he should assign the twelve limbs to the body namely heart, head, tuft of hair on head, skin, two eyes, belly, back, arms, thighs, knee-joints and feet. Then having offered hand postures and recited his name one hundred and eight times he should meditate on and adore Vishnu. Having placed a water-jar on his left and articles of wor-

* *Agni Purana*

ship on his right he should wash them with implements and then place flowers and scents. Having recited eight times the adorable light of Omnipresence and consciousness he should take up water in his palm with the mantra Phat and then meditate on Hari. With his face directed towards the south-east direction presided over by Agni he should pray for virtue, knowledge, disassociation from worldly objects and lordly powers. He should cast off his sins and physical impurities in the Yoga postures beginning with the East. In the tortoise posture he should adore Ananta [Vishnu], Yama, the sun and other luminous bodies. Having first meditated on them in his heart, invoked them and adored them in the circle he should again place offerings, water for washing the feet and for rinsing the mouth. Then by means of the knowledge of the art of worshipping the lotus-eyed deity [Vishnu] he should place water for bathing, clotad, ornaments, scents, flowers, incense, lamps and edibles.

He should first adore the limbs at the gate in the east and then Brahma. He should then assign the discus and club to the southern quarter and the conch-shell and bow to the corner presided over by the moon. He should then assign arrows and the quiver to the left and right side of the deity. He should assign leather fence and prosperity to the left and nourishment to the right. With mantras he should worship the garland of wild-flowers, the mystic mark *Srivasta* [Vishnu] and the *kaustava* gem and all the deities of the quarters in the outside—all these paraphernalia and attendants of Vishnu. Either partially or wholly he should recite the mantras for adoring limbs, and adore them, circumambulate them and then offer offerings. He should meditate in his mind 'I am Brahma, Hari' and should utter the world 'come' and the words 'forgive me.' Those who seek salvation should thus perform *puja* with the mantra of eight letters.

Soma*

Soma is here, as elsewhere in the Vedas, *at once a plant, a drink, and a god. To judge from this hymn, it had an effect that was hallucinogenic. The term* soma *is still used today, but it refers not to a hallucinogenic drug but to a fruit drink made of wild rhubarb. Other religions have words spoken during ritual intoxication. Few, however, are as evocative as this hymn's "We have drunk the Soma; we have become immortal; we have gone to the light; we have found the gods."*

I have tasted the sweet drink of life, knowing that it inspires good thoughts and joyous expansiveness to the extreme, that all the gods and mortals seek it together, calling it honey. When you penetrate inside, you will know no limits, and you will avert the wrath of the gods. Enjoying Indra's

friendship, O drop of Soma, bring riches as a docile cow brings the yoke. We have drunk the Soma; we have become immortal; we have gone to the light; we have found the gods. What can hatred and the malice of a mortal do to us now, O immortal one? When we have drunk you, O drop of Soma, be good to our heart, kind as a father to his son, thoughtful as a friend to a friend. Far-famed Soma, stretch out our lifespan so that we may live.

[5] The glorious drops that I have drunk set me free in wide space. You have bound me together in my limbs as thongs bind a chariot. Let the drops protect me from the foot that stumbles and keep lameness away from me. Inflame me like a fire kindled by friction; make us see far; make us richer, better. For when I am intoxicated with you, Soma, I think myself rich. Draw near and make us thrive. We would enjoy you, pressed with a fervent heart, like riches from a father.

---

* *Rig-Veda* 8.48

King Soma, stretch out our lifespans as the sun stretches the spring days. King Soma, have mercy on us for our well-being. Know that we are devoted to your laws. Passion and fury are stirred up. O drop of Soma, do not hand us over to the pleasure of the enemy. For you, Soma, are the guardian of our body; watching over men, you have settled down in every limb.

If we break your laws, O god, have mercy on us like a good friend, to make us better. [10] Let me join closely with my compassionate friend so that he will not injure me when I have drunk him. O lord of bay horses, for the Soma that is lodged in us I approach Indra to stretch out our lifespan. Weaknesses and diseases have gone; the forces of darkness have fled in terror. Soma has climbed up in us, expanding. We have come to the place where they stretch out lifespans. The drop that we have drunk has entered our hearts, an immortal inside mortals. O fathers, let us serve that Soma with the oblations and abide in his mercy and kindness. Uniting in agreement with the fathers, O drop of Soma, you have extended yourself through sky and earth. Let us serve him with an oblation; let us be masters of riches. You protecting gods, speak out for us. Do not let sleep or harmful speech seize us. Let us, always dear to Soma, speak as men of power in the sacrificial gathering. [15] Soma, you give us the force of life on every side. Enter into us, finding the sunlight, watching over men. O drop of Soma, summon your helpers and protect us before and after.

Marriage*

The first part of this hymn, not given here, recounts the myth of the marriage of Surya the goddess. The part printed here contains the incantations and blessings still spoken at weddings to bring good and repel evil. The bride is compared to Surya, and the wedding of the humans is set in parallel with divine marriage. The words are designed to bring good fortune: that the wife continue to have beauty and passion, and so be loved by her husband; that both have a long life together; that the marriage produce many sons. The careful reader can discern several different ritual actions of the marriage. First comes leaving the site of the wedding, then traveling to the couple's home, then consummation of marriage, and finally the anointing of the couple. Verses from this hymn are still a part of observant, traditional Hindu weddings.

Mount the world of immortality, O Surya, that is adorned with red flowers and made of fragrant wood, carved with many forms and painted with gold, rolling smoothly on its fine wheels. Prepare an exquisite wedding voyage for your husband.

"Go away from here! For this woman has a husband." Thus I implore Visvavasu [39] with words of praise as I bow to him. "Look for another girl who is ripe and still lives in her father's house. That is your birthright; find it. Go away from here, Visvavasu, we implore you as we bow. Look for another girl, willing and ready. Leave the wife to unite with her husband." May the roads be straight and thornless on which our friends go courting. May Aryaman and Bhaga united lead us together. O Gods, may the united household be easy to manage. I free you from Varuna's snare, with which the gentle Savitr bound you. In the seat of the Law, in the world of good action, I place you unharmed with your husband. [25] I free her from here, but not from there. [40] I have bound her firmly there, so that through the grace of Indra she will have fine sons and be fortunate in her husband's love. Let Pusan lead you from here, taking you by the hand; let the Asvins carry you in their chariot. Go home to be mistress of

* *Rig-Veda* 10.85.20–47

[39] *Visvavasu:* a demigod who possesses virgins.
[40] *here:* her father's house; *there:* her new house with her husband.

the house with the right to speak commands to the gathered people. May happiness be fated for you here through your children. Watch over this house as mistress of the house.

Mingle your body with that of your husband, and even when you are gray with age you will have the right to speak to the gathered people. The purple and red appears, a magic spirit; the stain is imprinted.[41] Her family prospers, and her husband is bound in the bonds. Throw away the gown, and distribute wealth to the priests. It becomes a magic spirit walking on feet, and like the wife it draws near the husband. [30] The body becomes ugly and sinisterly pale if the husband with evil desire covers his sexual limb with his wife's robe. The diseases that come from her own people and follow the glorious bridal procession, may the gods who receive sacrifices lead them back whence they have come. Let no highwaymen, lying in ambush, fall upon the wedding couple. Let the two of them on good paths avoid the dangerous path. Let all demonic powers run away. This bride has auspicious signs; come and look at her. Wish her the good fortune of her husband's love, and depart, each to your own house. It burns, it bites, it has claws, it is as dangerous as poison to eat.[42] Only the priest who knows the Surya hymn is able to receive the bridal gown. [35] Cutting, carving, and chopping into pieces—see the colors of Surya, which the priest alone purifies.

I [the husband] take your hand for good fortune, so that with me as your husband you will attain a ripe old age. Bhaga, Aryaman, Savitr, Purandhi—the gods have given you to me to be mistress of the house. Pusan, rouse her to be most eager to please, the woman in whom men sow their seed, so that she will spread her thighs in her desire for us and we,[43] in our desire, will plant our penis in her. To you first of all they led Surya, circling with the bridal procession. Give her back to her husbands, Agni, now as a wife with progeny. Agni has given the wife back again, together with long life and beauty. Let her have a long lifespan, and let her husband live for a hundred autumns. [40] Soma first possessed her, and the Gandharva possessed her second. Agni was your third husband, and the fourth was the son of a man. Soma gave her to the Gandharva, and the Gandharva gave her to Agni. Agni gave me wealth and sons—and her.

Stay here and do not separate. Enjoy your whole lifespan playing with sons and grandsons and rejoicing in your own home. Let Prajapati create progeny for us; let Aryaman anoint us into old age. Free from evil signs, enter the world of your husband. Be good luck for our two-legged creatures and good luck for our four-legged creatures. Have no evil eye; do not be a husband-killer.[44] Be friendly to animals, good-tempered and glowing with beauty. Bringing forth strong sons, prosper as one beloved of the gods and eager to please. Be good luck for our two-legged creatures and good luck for our four-legged creatures. [45] Generous Indra, give this woman fine sons and the good fortune of her husband's love. Place ten sons in her and make her husband the eleventh.[45] Be an empress over your husband's father, an empress over your husband's mother; be an empress over your husband's sister and an empress over your husband's brothers. Let all the gods and the waters together anoint our two hearts together. Let Matarisvan[46] together with the Creator and with her who shows the way join the two of us together.

---

[41] *The purple and red appears . . . imprinted:* In the consummation of the marriage, the bride bleeds on her wedding robe as her hymen is ruptured. The resulting stain becomes a magic spirit with power to curse and destroy the marriage. The procedure for dealing with the robe is given at the end of this paragraph.

[42] *it:* the spirit arising from the stained robe.

[43] *us, we:* the husband, and the gods who are said to have spiritually possessed the wife before her marriage.

[44] *Have no evil eye . . . husband-killer:* a charm against any evil possibly residing in the wife that may threaten her husband.

[45] *her husband the eleventh:* a common Hindu idea is that the husband is the last son of the wife, perhaps signifying the care given to the husband by his wife.

[46] *Matarisvan:* an assistant of Agni.

Cremation*

Agni is petitioned here to bring a good burning to the body of the dead, strikingly called in sacrificial imagery "a good cooking." The proper funeral ritual enables the dead man to go to his fathers. No mention is made here of heaven or hell, transmigration or reincarnation, important in later Hinduism through today.

Do not burn him entirely, Agni, or engulf him in your flames. Do not consume his skin or his flesh. When you have cooked him perfectly, O knower of creatures, only then send him forth to the fathers. When you cook him perfectly, O knower of creatures, then give him over to the fathers. When he goes on the path that leads away the breath of life, then he will be led by the will of the gods. [To the dead man:] May your eye go to the sun, your life's breath to the wind. Go to the sky or to earth, as is your nature; or go to the waters, if that is your fate. Take root in the plants with your limbs. [To Agni:] The goat is your share; burn him with your heat. Let your brilliant light and flame burn him. With your gentle forms, O knower of creatures, carry this man to the world of those who have done good deeds. [5] Set him free again to go to the fathers, Agni, when he has been offered as an oblation in you and wanders with the sacrificial drink. Let him reach his own descendants, dressing himself in a lifespan. O knower of creatures, let him join with a body. [To the dead man:] Whatever the black

* *Rig-Veda* 10.16

bird has pecked out of you, or the ant, the snake, or even a beast of prey, may Agni who eats all things make it whole, and Soma who has entered the Brahmins. Gird yourself with the limbs of the cow as an armor against Agni, and cover yourself with fat and suet, so that he will not embrace you with his impetuous heat in his passionate desire to burn you up.

[To Agni:] O Agni, do not overturn this cup that is dear to the gods and to those who love Soma, fit for the gods to drink from, a cup in which the immortal gods carouse. I send the flesh-eating fire far away. Let him go to those whose king is Yama, carrying away all impurities. But let that other, the knower of creatures, come here and carry the oblation to the gods, since he knows the way in advance. [10] The flesh-eating fire has entered your house, though he sees there the other, the knower of creatures; I take that god away to the sacrifice of the fathers. Let him carry the heated drink to the farthest dwelling-place. Agni who carries away the corpse, who gives sacrifice to the fathers who are strengthened by truth—let him proclaim the oblation to the gods and to the fathers. [To the new fire:] Joyously would we put you in place, joyously would we kindle you. Joyously carry the joyous fathers here to eat the oblation. Now, Agni, quench and revive the very one you have burnt up. Let Kiyamba, Pakadurva, and Vyalkasa plants grow in this place. O cool one, bringer of coolness; O fresh one, bringer of freshness; unite with the female frog. Delight and inspire this, O Agni.

Charms and Spells**

The first of these incantations is a charm against fever, the second a spell to frustrate the sacrifice of an enemy, the third a charm to induce the sexual passion of a woman (perhaps a wife who comes by an arranged marriage), the fourth a spell for suc-

** *Atharva-Veda* 6.20, 7.70, 6.9, 3.16

cess in business. Note that the main point of the charm is often repeated to increase its power. Ritual actions that accompany the saying of these spells are occasionally suggested in the words.[47]

[47] Taken, with editing, from Maurice Bloomfield, trans., *Hymns of the Atharva-Veda, Sacred Books of the East,* vol. 42 (Oxford: Oxford University Press, 1897).

[6.20, against fever] As if from this Agni [fire], that burns and flashes, the fever comes. Let him pass away like a babbling drunkard! Let him, the impious one, search out another person, not ourselves! Reverence be to the fever with the burning weapon![48] Reverence be to Rudra, reverence to the fever, reverence to the luminous king Varuna! Reverence to heaven, reverence to earth, reverence to the plants! To you that burns through, and turns all bodies yellow . . . to the fever produced by the forest, I render honor.

[7.70, for frustration of sacrifice] Whenever that person over there in his thought and with his speech offers sacrifice accompanied by offerings and benedictions, may Nirriti the goddess of destruction ally herself with death and strike his offering before it takes effect! May the sorcerers Nirriti and Rakshas mar his true work with error![49] May the gods, despatched by Indra, churn up his sacrificial butter! May that which he offers not succeed! . . . I tie back both your arms, I shut your mouth. With the fury of Agni, I have destroyed your sacrifice.

[6.9, for love] Desire my body, my feet, my eyes, my thighs! As you lust after me, your eyes and your hair shall be hot with love! I make you cling to my arm, cling to my heart, so that you shall be in my power and shall come to my wish! The cows, the mothers of the sacrificial butter who lick their young, in whose heart love is planted, shall make this woman love me!

[3.16, for success in business] I urge Indra the merchant, come to us and be our forerunner. Ward off the unpaying one, the cutting beast, and let masterful Indra be a bringer of wealth to me. O Gods! That money with which, desiring more money, I conduct my business, let that multiply and never decrease. O Agni, with this sacrifice frustrate those who would ruin my profit.

---

[48] *Reverence:* the spell uses flattering praise, as well as insults, to drive the fever away.

[49] *mar . . . with error:* if an error of word or deed is made in the sacrificial ceremony, it is not effective. Such a belief is common to many religions with well-developed sacrificial systems.

Chanting of *Om**

The udgitha, *or "loud chant," is the important* **Om** *(OHM) in the Vedic ritual. Members of the various Hindu schools differ on whether Om is Brahman itself or a near verbal expression of Brahman. But for all Hindus it is the most sacred of sounds, the mantra that contains all other mantras, all the* Vedas, *all the meaning of the universe. Those who chant it with full knowledge will be freed from* karma.

Let a man meditate on the syllable *Om*, called the *udgitha;* for the *udgitha* is sung, beginning with *Om*. The full account of *Om* is this.

The essence of all beings is the earth, the essence of the earth is water, the essence of water the plants, the essence of plants man, the essence of man speech, the essence of speech the *Rig-veda*, the essence of the *Rig-veda* the *Sama-veda*, the essence of the *Sama-veda* the *udgitha*, *Om*. The *udgitha* is the best of all essences, the highest, deserving the highest place, the eighth.

What then is the *Rig?* What is the *Saman?* What is the *udgitha?* This is the question. [5] The *Rig* is speech, *Saman* is breath, the *udgitha* is the syllable *Om*. Now speech and breath, or *Rig* and *Saman*, form one couple. That couple is joined in the syllable *Om*. When two people come together, they fulfil each other's desire. Thus he who knowing this meditates on the syllable *Om*, the *udgitha*, becomes a fulfiller of desires.

That syllable is a syllable of permission, for whenever we permit anything, we say *Om*, yes.

---

*Chandogya Upanishad 1.1.1–10

Now permission is gratification. He who knows this and meditates on the syllable *Om* becomes a gratifier of desires.

By that syllable proceeds the threefold knowledge (of the three *Vedas*). When the Adhvaryu priest gives an order, he says *Om.* When the Hotri priest recites, he says *Om.* When the Udgatri priest sings, he says *Om,* all for the glory of that syllable. The threefold knowledge and threefold sacrifice proceed by the greatness of that syllable and by its essence. [10] Therefore it seems that both he who knows this [the true meaning of *Om*], and he who does not, perform the same sacrifice. But this is not so, for knowledge and ignorance are different. The sacrifice that a man performs with knowledge, faith, and the *Upanishad* is more powerful. This is the full account of the syllable *Om.*

The Practice of Yoga*

Yoga is a physical discipline to promote knowledge that the individual soul and the world soul are one. This passage relates some of the main components of yogic meditation.[50]

Holding his body steady with the three [upper parts][51] erect,
And causing the senses with the mind to enter the heart,
A wise man with the Brahma-boat will cross over
All the fear-bringing streams.

Compressing his breathings here in the body, and having his movements checked,
One should breathe through his nostrils with diminished breath.
Like that chariot yoked with vicious horses,
His mind the wise man should restrain undistractedly.

[10] In a clean level spot, free from pebbles, fire, and gravel,
By the sound of water and other propinquities
Favorable to thought, not offensive to the eye,
In a hidden retreat protected from the wind, one should practice Yoga.

Fog, smoke, sun, fire, wind,
Fire-flies, lightning, a crystal, a moon—
These are the preliminary appearances,
Which produce the manifestation of Brahma in Yoga.

When the fivefold quality of Yoga has been produced,
Arising from earth, water, fire, air, and space,
No sickness, no old age, no death has he
Who has obtained a body made out of the fire of Yoga.

Lightness, healthiness, steadiness,
Clearness of countenance and pleasantness of voice,
Sweetness of odor, and scanty excretions—
These, they say, are the first stage in the progress of Yoga.

Even as a mirror stained by dust
Shines brilliantly when it has been cleansed,
So the embodied one, on seeing the nature of the Soul,
Becomes unitary, his end attained, from sorrow freed.

[15] When with the nature of the self, as with a lamp,
A practiser of Yoga beholds here the nature of Brahma,
Unborn, steadfast, from every nature free—
By knowing God one is released from all fetters!

---

* *Shvetashvatara Upanishad* 2.8–15
[50] Max Müller, trans., *The Upanishads,* part 2, *Sacred Books of the East,* vol. 15 (Oxford: Oxford University Press, 1884), pp. 241–243.
[51] *the three [upper parts]:* head, neck, and torso.

APPENDIX I: SELECTIONS FROM THE *BHAGAVAD-GITA*

The most famous and influential text of Hinduism is section 6 of the *Mahabharata* epic known as the Bhagavad-Gita (Song of the Lord). The *Gita* is especially important for an understanding of the devotional Hinduism that has flourished from about 400 C.E. until today. The background of the *Gita* is the rivalry between the Kaurava brothers and the Pandava brothers for the rule of India. In a game of dice, the leader of the Pandavas loses their claim to the throne. For thirteen years the Pandavas are forced into exile. This results in civil war as the Pandavas return to seize rule. As preparation for war begins, Krishna becomes a charioteer for Arjuna.

But just as the battle is about to begin, Arjuna is appalled at the fratricide that will surely result. Moreover, he is afraid that this great evil will harm his own soul now and, by implication, in its later incarnations. His charioteer, the god Krishna, teaches Arjuna the divine truth that enables him to overcome his doubtings. This teaching forms the content of the *Gita*. First, and most immediately for the plot of the *Mahabharata,* Krishna teaches Arjuna that he must do his caste duty and fight. Arjuna knows that his warfare will not harm the souls of the slain. Second, the several ways to salvation given in the long history of Hinduism —sacrifice (the Vedic path), meditation (Upanishadic and ascetic path), and action (the way of caste duty)—are each only effective if done in a spirit of complete detachment. The *Gita* teaches full involvement in life coupled with inner restraint and indifference. Third, the best way is devotion to Krishna, whom the *Gita* portrays as the "base of Brahman," yet filled with love for his devotees. In this way, the *Gita* is typically Hindu— it acknowledges and affirms all Hindu ways to the truth, but affirms its own way as the best.

The *Gita* contains 7,000 verses grouped into eighteen chapters. It has no plot, only the setting just outlined that poses the religious problem. Most chapters begin with Arjuna's question, which typically deals with the meaning of previous teachings in the *Gita;* a lengthy answer from Krishna follows. Many chapters end with a call for devotion to Krishna. Much of the content of the *Gita* is repetitious; the key teachings are returned to again and again and examined from different perspectives. The following excerpts attempt to reduce this repetition and present the essence of the *Gita*'s argument. A short paragraph introduces and summarizes the content of each of the selections given here.[52]

[1.20–47] Chapter I provides the narrative setting and the religious problem of the Gita. *King Dhritarashtra's charioteer, Sanjaya, tells the king what happened before the battle that took place to decide the fate of his kingdom. As Prince Arjuna came onto the battlefield, he was overcome by the horrors of the impending fratricidal war. He expresses his misgivings to his charioteer, Krishna, saying that war will lead to the ruin of the kingdom, its families, and its entire social system. He prefers death to fighting such a war. Then he drops his weapons, waiting for his death at the hands of the enemy.*

Arjuna, his war flag a rampant monkey,
saw Dhritarashtra's sons assembled
as weapons were ready to clash,
and he lifted his bow.

He told his charioteer:
"Krishna,
halt my chariot
between the armies!

Far enough for me to see
these men who lust for war,
ready to fight with me
in the strain of battle.

I see men gathered here,
eager to fight,

---

[52] From *Bhagavad-Gita*, by Barbara Stoler Miller, translation copyright 1986 by Barbara Stoler Miller. Used by permission of Bantam Books, a division of Bantam Doubleday Dell Publishing Group, Inc.

bent on serving the folly
of Dhritarashtra's son."

When Arjuna had spoken,
Krishna halted
their splendid chariot
between the armies.

[25] Facing Bhishma and Drona
and all the great kings,
he said, "Arjuna, see
the Kuru men assembled here!"

Arjuna saw them standing there:
fathers, grandfathers, teachers,
uncles, brothers, sons,
grandsons, and friends.

He surveyed his elders
and companions in both armies,
all his kinsmen
assembled together.

Dejected, filled with strange pity,
he said this:
"Krishna, I see my kinsmen
gathered here, wanting war.

My limbs sink,
my mouth is parched,
my body trembles,
the hair bristles on my flesh.

[30] The magic bow slips
from my hand, my skin burns,
I cannot stand still,
my mind reels.

I see omens of chaos,
Krishna; I see no good
in killing my kinsmen
in battle.

Krishna, I seek no victory,
or kingship or pleasures.
What use to us are kingship,
delights, or life itself?

We sought kingship, delights,
and pleasures for the sake of those
assembled to abandon their lives
and fortunes in battle.

They are teachers, fathers, sons,
and grandfathers, uncles, grandsons,
fathers and brothers of wives,
and other men of our family.

[35] I do not want to kill them
even if I am killed, Krishna;
not for kingship of all three worlds,
much less for the earth!

What joy is there for us, Krishna,
in killing Dhritarashtra's sons?
Evil will haunt us if we kill them,
though their bows are drawn to kill.

Honor forbids us to kill
our cousins, Dhritarashtra's sons;
how can we know happiness
if we kill our own kinsmen?

The greed that distorts their reason
blinds them to the sin they commit
in ruining the family, blinds them
to the crime of betraying friends.

How can we ignore the wisdom
of turning from this evil
when we see the sin
of family destruction, Krishna?

[40] When the family is ruined,
the timeless laws of family duty
perish; and when duty is lost,
chaos overwhelms the family.

In overwhelming chaos, Krishna,
women of the family are corrupted;
and when women are corrupted,
disorder is born in society.

This discord drags the violators
and the family itself to hell;
for ancestors fall when rites
of offering rice and water lapse.

The sins of men who violate
the family create disorder in society
that undermines the constant laws
of caste and family duty.

Krishna, we have heard
that a place in hell

is reserved for men
who undermine family duties.

[45] I lament the great sin
we commit when our greed
for kingship and pleasures
drives us to kill our kinsmen.

If Dhritarashtra's armed sons
kill me in battle when I am unarmed
and offer no resistance,
it will be my reward."

Saying this in the time of war,
Arjuna slumped into the chariot
and laid down his bow and arrows,
his mind tormented by grief.

*[2:1–7, 11–27, 31–38, 47–48] In chapter 2,
Krishna rebukes Arjuna and urges him to fight.
Krishna advances several arguments: (1) the soul
is immortal, and all else is impermanent; therefore
the battle has no real eternal significance; (2) Arjuna, a Kshatriya (warrior) must do his caste-
duty and fight; (3) he must fight in a contempla-
tive, detached manner; (4) yoga (discipline) is the
way to such detachment. Verse 38 is the key: "Impartial to joy and suffering, gain and loss, victory
and defeat, arm yourself for the battle, lest you fall
into evil."*

Sanjaya:

Arjuna sat dejected,
filled with pity,
his sad eyes blurred by tears.
Krishna gave him counsel.

Lord Krishna:

Why this cowardice
in time of crisis, Arjuna?
The coward is ignoble, shameful,
foreign to the ways of heaven.

Don't yield to impotence!
It is unnatural in you!
Banish this petty weakness from your heart.
Rise to the fight, Arjuna!

Arjuna:

Krishna, how can I fight
against Bhishma and Drona
with arrows
when they deserve my worship?

[5] It is better in this world
to beg for scraps of food
than to eat meals
smeared with the blood
of elders I killed
at the height of their power
while their goals
were still desires.

We don't know which weight
is worse to bear—
our conquering them
or their conquering us.
We will not want to live
if we kill
the sons of Dhritarashtra
assembled before us.

The flaw of pity
blights my very being;
conflicting sacred duties
confound my reason.
I ask you to tell me
decisively—Which is better?
I am your pupil.
Teach me what I seek! . . .

Lord Krishna:

[11] You grieve for those beyond grief,
and you speak words of insight;
but learned men do not grieve
for the dead or the living.

Never have I not existed,
nor you, nor these kings;
and never in the future
shall we cease to exist.

Just as the embodied self
enters childhood, youth, and old age,
so does it enter another body;
this does not confound a steadfast man.

Contacts with matter make us feel
heat and cold, pleasure and pain.
Arjuna, you must learn to endure
fleeting things—they come and go!

[15] When these cannot torment a man,
when suffering and joy are equal
for him and he has courage,
he is fit for immortality.

Nothing of nonbeing comes to be,
nor does being cease to exist;
the boundary between these two
is seen by men who see reality.

Indestructible is the presence
that pervades all this;
no one can destroy
this unchanging reality.

Our bodies are known to end,
but the embodied self is enduring,
indestructible, and immeasurable;
therefore, Arjuna, fight the battle!

He who thinks this self a killer
and he who thinks it killed,
both fail to understand;
it does not kill, nor is it killed.

[20] It is not born,
it does not die;
having been,
it will never not be;
unborn, enduring,
constant, and primordial,
it is not killed
when the body is killed.

Arjuna, when a man knows the self
to be indestructible, enduring, unborn,
unchanging, how does he kill
or cause anyone to kill?

As a man discards
worn-out clothes
to put on new
and different ones,
so the embodied self discards

its worn-out bodies
to take on other new ones.

Weapons do not cut it,
fire does not burn it,
waters do not wet it,
wind does not wither it.

It cannot be cut or burned;
it cannot be wet or withered;
it is enduring, all-pervasive,
fixed, immovable, and timeless.

[25] It is called unmanifest,
inconceivable, and immutable;
since you know that to be so,
you should not grieve!

If you think of its birth
and death as ever-recurring,
then too, Great Warrior,
you have no cause to grieve!

Death is certain for anyone born,
and birth is certain for the dead;
since the cycle is inevitable,
you have no cause to grieve! . . .

[31] Look to your own duty;
do not tremble before it;
nothing is better for a warrior
than a battle of sacred duty.

The doors of heaven open
for warriors who rejoice
to have a battle like this
thrust on them by chance.

If you fail to wage this war
of sacred duty,
you will abandon your own duty
and fame only to gain evil.

People will tell
of your undying shame,
and for a man of honor
shame is worse than death.

[35] The great chariot warriors will think
you deserted in fear of battle;

you will be despised
by those who held you in esteem.

Your enemies will slander you,
scorning your skill
in so many unspeakable ways—
could any suffering be worse?

If you are killed, you win heaven;
if you triumph, you enjoy the earth;
therefore, Arjuna, stand up
and resolve to fight the battle!

Impartial to joy and suffering,
gain and loss, victory and defeat,
arm yourself for the battle,
lest you fall into evil. . . .

[47] Be intent on action,
not on the fruits of action;
avoid attraction to the fruits
and attachment to inaction!

Perform actions, firm in discipline,
relinquishing attachment;
be impartial to failure and success—
this equanimity is called discipline.

*[4:1–15] In chapter 4 Krishna tells Arjuna of his
many incarnations. The* Gita *itself does not explicitly state that Krishna is an incarnation of Vishnu,
but the Vaishnavites of later devotional Hinduism
saw this relationship and developed it fully.*

Lord Krishna:

I taught this undying discipline
to the shining sun, first of mortals,
who told it to Manu, the progenitor of man;
Manu told it to the solar king Ikshvaku.

Royal sages knew this discipline,
which the tradition handed down;
but over the course of time
it has decayed, Arjuna.

This is the ancient discipline
that I have taught to you today;
you are my devotee and my friend,
and this is the deepest mystery.

Arjuna:

Your birth followed the birth
of the sun;
how can I comprehend that you taught it
in the beginning?

Lord Krishna:

[5] I have passed through many births
and so have you;
I know them all,
but you do not, Arjuna.

Though myself unborn, undying,
the lord of creatures, I fashion nature,
which is mine, and I come into being
through my own magic.

Whenever sacred duty decays
and chaos prevails,
then, I create
myself, Arjuna.

To protect men of virtue
and destroy men who do evil,
to set the standard of sacred duty,
I appear in age after age.

He who really knows my divine
birth and my action, escapes rebirth
when he abandons the body—
and he comes to me, Arjuna.

[10] Free from attraction, fear, and anger,
filled with me, dependent on me,
purified by the fire of knowledge,
many come into my presence.

As they seek refuge in me,
I devote myself to them;
Arjuna, men retrace
my path in every way.

Desiring success in their actions,
men sacrifice here to the gods;
in the world of man
success comes quickly from action.

I created mankind in four classes,
different in their qualities and actions;

though unchanging, I am the agent of this,
the actor who never acts!

I desire no fruit of actions,
and actions do not defile me;
one who knows this about me
is not bound by actions.

[15] Knowing this, even ancient seekers
of freedom performed action—
do as these seers
did in ancient times.

*[9:16–28] Chapter 9 tells how the universe was
spun out of Krishna's body. Next come the attributes of God (Krishna), service of different (Hindu)
gods, and a critique of Vedic religion. At the end,
devotion to Krishna is emphasized as the part that,
in contrast to the Vedic cult, is open to all.*

Lord Krishna:

I am the rite, the sacrifice,
the libation for the dead, the healing herb,
the sacred hymn, the clarified butter,
the fire, the oblation.

I am the universal father,
mother, granter of all, grandfather,
object of knowledge, purifier,
holy syllable *Om*, threefold sacred lore.

I am the way, sustainer, lord,
witness, shelter, refuge, friend,
source, dissolution, stability,
treasure, and unchanging seed.

I am heat that withholds
and sends down the rains;
I am immortality and death;
both being and nonbeing am I.

[20] Men learned in sacred lore,
Soma drinkers, their sins absolved,
worship me with sacrifices,
seeking to win heaven.

Reaching the holy world of Indra,
king of the gods,
they savor the heavenly delights
of the gods in the celestial sphere.

When they have long enjoyed
the world of heaven
and their merit is exhausted,
they enter the mortal world;
following the duties
ordained in sacred lore,
desiring desires,
they obtain what is transient.

Men who worship me,
thinking solely of me,
always disciplined,
win the reward I secure.

When devoted men sacrifice
to other deities with faith,
they sacrifice to me, Arjuna,
however aberrant the rites.

I am the enjoyer
and the lord of all sacrifices;
they do not know me in reality,
and so they fail.

[25] Votaries of the gods go to the gods,
ancestor-worshippers go to the ancestors,
those who propitiate ghosts go to them,
and my worshippers go to me.

The leaf or flower or fruit or water
that he offers with devotion,
I take from the man of self-restraint
in response to his devotion.

Whatever you do—what you take,
what you offer, what you give,
what penances you perform—
do as an offering to me, Arjuna!

You will be freed from the bonds of action,
from the fruit of fortune and misfortune;
armed with the discipline of renunciation,
your self liberated, you will join me.

*[11:1–20, 50–55] In chapter 11, after Arjuna
asks to see Krishna's divine form, Krishna shows
him all his divine forms at once. Arjuna is filled
with awe and praises Krishna. Krishna then returns to his human form. The praise of Krishna ex-*

presses the kind of attachment to one god that is characteristic of devotional Hinduism.

Arjuna:

To favor me you revealed
the deepest mystery of the self,
and by your words
my delusion is dispelled.

I heard from you in detail
how creatures come to be and die,
Krishna, and about the self
in its immutable greatness.

Just as you have described
yourself, I wish to see your form
in all its majesty,
Krishna, Supreme among Men.

If you think I can see it,
reveal to me
your immutable self,
Krishna, Lord of Discipline.

Lord Krishna:

[5] Arjuna, see my forms
in hundreds and thousands;
diverse, divine,
of many colors and shapes.

See the sun gods, gods of light,
howling storm gods, twin gods of dawn,
and gods of wind, Arjuna,
wondrous forms not seen before.

Arjuna, see all the universe,
animate and inanimate,
and whatever else you wish to see;
all stands here as one in my body.

But you cannot see me
with your own eye;
I will give you a divine eye to see
the majesty or my discipline.

Sanjaya:

O King, saying this, Krishna,
the great lord of discipline,

revealed to Arjuna
the true majesty of his form.

[10] It was a multiform, wondrous vision,
with countless mouths and eyes
and celestial ornaments,
brandishing many divine weapons.

Everywhere was boundless divinity
containing all astonishing things,
wearing divine garlands and garments,
annointed with divine perfume.

If the light of a thousand suns
were to rise in the sky at once,
it would be like the light
of that great spirit.

Arjuna saw all the universe
in its many ways and parts,
standing as one in the body
of the god of gods.

Then filled with amazement,
his hair bristling on his flesh,
Arjuna bowed his head to the god,
joined his hands in homage, and spoke.

Arjuna:

[15] I see the gods
in your body, O God,
and hordes
of varied creatures:

Brahma, the cosmic creator,
on his lotus throne,
all the seers
and celestial serpents.

I see your boundless form
everywhere,
the countless arms,
bellies, mouths, and eyes;
Lord of All,
I see no end,
or middle or beginning
to your totality.

I see you blazing
through the fiery rays

of your crown, mace, and discus,
hard to behold
in the burning light
of fire and sun
that surrounds
your measureless presence.

You are to be known
as supreme eternity,
the deepest treasure
of all that is,
the immutable guardian
of enduring sacred duty;
I think you are
man's timeless spirit.

I see no beginning
or middle or end to you;
only boundless strength
in your endless arms,
the moon and sun in your eyes,
your mouths of consuming flames,
your own brilliance
scorching this universe.

[20] You alone
fill the space
between heaven and earth
and all the directions;
seeing this awesome,
terrible form of yours,
Great Soul,
the three worlds
tremble. . . .

Sanjaya:

[50] Saying this to Arjuna,
Krishna once more
revealed
his intimate form;
resuming his gentle body,
the great spirit
let the terrified hero
regain his breath.

Arjuna:

Seeing your gentle human form,
Krishna, I recover

my own nature,
and my reason is restored.

Lord Krishna:

This form you have seen
is rarely revealed;
the gods are constantly craving
for a vision of this form.

Not through sacred lore,
penances, charity, or sacrificial rites
can I be seen in the form
that you saw me.

By devotion alone
can I, as I really am,
be known and seen
and entered into, Arjuna.

[55] Acting only for me, intent on me,
free from attachment,
hostile to no creature, Arjuna,
a man of devotion comes to me.

*[16:1–11, 21–24] Chapter 16 is a summary of
general morality suitable for all twice-born Hindus. It first describes the person "born to inherit a
godly destiny," who quickly escapes the process of rebirth. Then it tells of "human devils," who are eter-
nally recycling through rebirth.*

Lord Krishna:

Fearlessness, purity, determination
in the discipline of knowledge,
charity, self-control, sacrifice,
study of sacred lore, penance, honesty;

Nonviolence, truth, absence of anger,
disengagement, peace, loyalty,
compassion for creatures, lack of greed,
gentleness, modesty, reliability;

Brilliance, patience, resolve,
clarity, absence of envy and of pride;
these characterize a man
born with divine traits.

Hypocrisy, arrogance, vanity,
anger, harshness, ignorance;

these characterize a man
born with demonic traits.

[5] The divine traits lead to freedom,
the demonic lead to bondage;
do not despair, Arjuna;
you were born with the divine.

All creatures in the world
are either divine or demonic;
I described the divine at length;
hear what I say of the demonic.

Demonic men cannot comprehend
activity and rest;
there exists no clarity,
no morality, no truth in them.

They say that the world
has no truth, no basis, no god,
that no power of mutual dependence
is its cause, but only desire.

Mired in this view, lost to themselves
with their meager understanding,
these fiends contrive terrible acts
to destroy the world.

[10] Subject to insatiable desire,
drunk with hypocrisy and pride,
holding false notions from delusion,
they act with impure vows.

In their certainty that life
consists in sating their desires,
they suffer immeasurable anxiety
that ends only with death. . . .

[21] The three gates of hell
that destroy the self
are desire, anger, and greed;
one must relinquish all three.

Released through these three gates
of darkness, Arjuna,
a man elevates the self
and ascends to the highest way.

If he rejects norms of tradition
and lives to fulfill his desires,
he does not reach perfection
or happiness or the highest way.

Let tradition be your standard
in judging what to do or avoid;
knowing the norms of tradition,
perform your action here.

*[18:1–9, 41–49, 60–73] In the eighteenth and
last chapter of the* Gita, *the topics of renunciation
and the three constituents of nature are treated for
the last time. Krishna summarizes the duties of the
castes and stresses the importance of doing one's
caste duty in a spirit of detachment. Then comes a
short summary of the teaching of the whole book
and a description of the merits obtained by reading it. Arjuna is convinced by Krishna and sur-
renders himself in obedience.*

Arjuna:

Krishna, I want to know
the real essence
of both renunciation
and relinquishment.

Lord Krishna:

Giving up actions based on desire,
the poets know as "renunciation";
relinquishing all fruit of action,
learned men call "relinquishment."

Some wise men say all action
is flawed and must be relinquished;
others say action in sacrifice, charity,
and penance must not be relinquished.

Arjuna, hear my decision
about relinquishment;
it is rightly declared
to be of three kinds.

[5] Action in sacrifice, charity,
and penance is to be performed,
not relinquished—for wise men,
they are acts of sanctity.

But even these actions
should be done by relinquishing to me
attachment and the fruit of action—
this is my decisive idea.

Renunciation of prescribed action
is inappropriate;
relinquished in delusion,
it becomes a way of dark inertia.

When one passionately relinquishes
difficult action from fear
of bodily harm, he cannot win
the fruit of relinquishment.

But if one performs prescribed action
because it must be done,
relinquishing attachment and the fruit,
his relinquishment is a lucid act. . . .

[41] The actions of priests, warriors,
commoners, and servants
are apportioned by qualities
born of their intrinsic being.

Tranquility, control, penance,
purity, patience and honesty,
knowledge, judgment, and piety
are intrinsic to the action of a priest.

Heroism, fiery energy, resolve,
skill, refusal to retreat in battle,
charity, and majesty in conduct
are intrinsic to the action of a warrior.

Farming, herding cattle, and commerce
are intrinsic to the action of a commoner;
action that is essentially service
is intrinsic to the servant.

[45] Each one achieves success
by focusing on his own action;
hear how one finds success
by focusing on his own action.

By his own action a man finds success,
worshipping the source
of all creatures' activity,
the presence pervading all that is.

Better to do one's own duty imperfectly
than to do another man's well;
doing action intrinsic to his being,
a man avoids guilt.

Arjuna, a man should not relinquish
action he is born to, even if it is flawed;

all undertakings are marred by a flaw,
as fire is obscured by smoke.

His understanding everywhere detached,
the self mastered, longing gone,
one finds through renunciation
the supreme success beyond action. . . .

[60] You are bound by your own action,
intrinsic to your being, Arjuna;
even against your will you must do
what delusion now makes you refuse.

Arjuna, the lord resides
in the heart of all creatures,
making them reel magically,
as if a machine moved them.

With your whole being, Arjuna,
take refuge in him alone—
from his grace you will attain
the eternal place that is peace.

This knowledge I have taught
is more arcane than any mystery—
consider it completely,
then act as you choose.

Listen to my profound words,
the deepest mystery of all,
for you are precious to me
and I tell you for your good.

[65] Keep your mind on me,
be my devotee, sacrificing, bow to me—
you will come to me, I promise,
for you are dear to me.

Relinquishing all sacred duties to me,
make me your only refuge;
do not grieve,
for I shall free you from all evils.

You must not speak of this
to one who is without penance and devotion,
or who does not wish to hear,
or who finds fault with me.

When he shares this deepest mystery
with others devoted to me,
giving me his total devotion,
a man will come to me without doubt.

No mortal can perform
service for me that I value more,
and no other man on earth
will be more dear to me than he is.

[70] I judge the man who studies
our dialogue on sacred duty
to offer me sacrifice
through sacrifice in knowledge.

If he listens in faith,
finding no fault, a man is free
and will attain the cherished worlds
of those who act in virtue.

Arjuna, have you listened
with your full powers of reason?
Has the delusion of ignorance
now been destroyed?

Arjuna:

Krishna, my delusion is destroyed,
and by your grace I have regained memory;
I stand here, my doubt dispelled,
ready to act on your words.

APPENDIX 2: MOHANDAS GANDHI ON THE *BHAGAVAD-GITA*

The Bhagavad Gita *has inspired many generations of Hindu leaders, including Mohandas Gandhi, the leader of Indian independence. Gandhi called it "a dictionary for life." Here is his reflection on the meaning of the* Gita.[53]

Even in 1888–9, when I first became acquainted with the Gita, I felt that it was not an historical work, but that, under the guise of physical warfare, it described the duel that perpetually went on in the hearts of mankind, and that physical warfare was brought in merely to make the description of the internal duel more alluring. This preliminary intuition became more confirmed on a closer study of religion and the Gita. A study of the Mahabharata gave it added confirmation. I do not regard the Mahabharata as an historical work in the accepted sense. . . . The persons therein described may be historical, but the author of the Mahabharata has used them merely to drive home his religious theme.

The author of the Mahabharata has not established the necessity of physical warfare; on the contrary he has proved its futility. He has made the victors shed tears of sorrow and repentance, and has left them nothing but a legacy of miseries.

In this great work the Gita is the crown. Its second chapter, instead of teaching the rules of physical warfare, tells us how a perfected man is to be known. In the characteristics of the perfected man of the Gita I do not see any to correspond to physical warfare. Its whole design is inconsistent with the rules of conduct governing the relations between warring parties.

Krishna of the Gita is perfection and right knowledge personified; but the picture is imaginary. That does not mean that Krishna, the adored of his people, never lived. But perfection is imagined. The idea of a perfect incarnation is an aftergrowth.

In Hinduism, incarnation is ascribed to one who has performed some extraordinary service of mankind. All embodied life is in reality an incarnation of God, but it is not usual to consider every living being an incarnation. Future generations pay this homage to one who in his own generation, has been extraordinarily religious in his conduct. I can see nothing wrong in this procedure. It takes nothing from God's greatness, and there is no violence done to Truth. There is

---

[53] From M. K. Gandhi, *The Gospel of Selfless Action or the Gita According to Gandhi* (Ahmedabad: Navagivan Publishing, 1946), 123–31.

an Urdu saying which means, 'Adam is not God but he is a spark of the Divine.' And therefore he who is the most religiously behaved has most of the divine spark in him. It is in accordance with this train of thought, that Krishna enjoys, in Hinduism, the status of the most perfect incarnation.

This belief in incarnation is a testimony of man's lofty spiritual ambition. Man is not at peace with himself till he has become like unto God. The endeavor to reach this state is the supreme, the only ambition worth having. And this is self-realization. This self-realization is the subject of the Gita, as it is of all scriptures. But its author surely did not write it to establish that doctrine. The object of the Gita appears to me to be that of showing the most excellent way to attain self-realization. That which is to be found, more or less clearly, spread out here and there in Hindu religious books, has been brought out in the clearest possible language in the Gita even at the risk of repetition.

The Gita is not an aphoristic work; it is a great religious poem. The deeper you dive into it, the richer the meanings you get. It being meant for the people at large, there is pleasing repetition. With every age the important words will carry new and expanding meanings. But its central teaching will never vary. The seeker is at liberty to extract from this treasure any meaning he likes so as to enable him to enforce in his life the central teaching.

Nor is the Gita a collection of do's and don'ts. What is lawful for one may be unlawful for another. What may be permissible at one time, or in one place, may not be so at another time, and in another place. Desire for fruit is the only universal prohibition. Desirelessness is obligatory.

The Gita has sung the praises of Knowledge, but it is beyond the mere intellect; it is essentially addressed to the heart and capable of being understood by the heart. Therefore the Gita is not for those who have no faith.

APPENDIX 3: TWO TAMIL POETS, APPAR AND TUKARAM

Much of the Sanskrit foundation of Hinduism was creatively adapted for the myriad of languages in India. These adaptations preserved and extended the basic ideas of the ancient scriptural sources. The first two poems of this appendix will sample the Tamil (south-Indian) religious poetry of Appar (seventh century), the best-known of the "Shaivite saints" whose writings are given a scriptural func- *tion, if not formal status.[54] The last two poems are by Tukaram (seventeenth century), the greatest Maharashtrian poet. These poems reflect popular* bhakti *tradition, and many of them are recited in the humblest households in India.*

---

[54] Taken from K. Kingsbury and G. E. Phillips, *Hymns of the Tamil Shaivite Saints* (Calcutta: Association Press, 1921), pp. 47–51.

Confession of Sin

Evil, all evil, my race, evil my qualities all,
Great am I only in sin, evil is even my good.
Evil my innermost self, foolish, avoiding the
    pure,
Beast am I not, yet the ways of the beast I can
    never forsake.

I can exhort with strong words, telling men
    what they should hate.
Yet can I never give gifts, only to beg them I
    know.
Ah! wretched man that I am, why did I come
    to birth?

The Presence of God

No man holds sway over us,
Nor death nor hell fear we;
No tremblings, griefs of mind,
No pains nor cringings see.
Joy, day by day, unchanged
Is ours, for we are His,
His ever, who does reign,
Our Shankara,[55] in bliss.
Here to His feet we've come,
Feet as plucked flow'rets fair;
See how His ears divine
Ring and white conch-shell wear.

He is ever hard to find, but He lives in the
    thought of the good;
He is innermost secret of Scripture, inscrutable,
    unknowable;
He is holy and milk and the shining light.
He is the king of the Devas,
Immanent in Vishnu, in Brahma, in flame and
    in wind,
Yet in the mighty sounding sea and in the
    mountains.
He is the great One who chooses Shiva's par-
    adise for his own.
If there be days when my tongue is dumb and
    speaks not of him,
Let no such days be counted in the record of
    my life.

---

[55] *Shankara:* Shiva.

[Tukaram:] Waiting[56]

With head on hand before my door,
    I sit and wait in vain.
Along the road to Pandhari
    My heart and eyes I strain.

When shall I look upon my Lord?
    When shall I see him come?
Of all the passing days and hours
    I count the heavy sum.

With watching long my eyelids throb,
    My limbs with sore distress,

But my impatient heart forgets
    My body's weariness.

Sleep is no longer sweet to me;
    I care not for my bed;
Forgotten are my house and home,
    All thirst and hunger fled.

Says Tuka,[57] Blest shall be the day—
    Ah, soon may it betide!—
When one shall come from Pandhari
    To summon back the bride.

---

[56] Taken from N. Macnicol, *Psalms of the Maratha Saints* (Calcutta: Association Press, 1920), p. 58.

[57] *Tuka:* The poet Tukaram himself.

The Burden of the Past[58]

I have been harassed by the world.
I have dwelled in my mother's womb and I
    must enter the gate of the womb eight
    million times.

I was born a needy beggar and my life is passed
    under a stranger's power.
I am bound fast in the meshes of my past and
    its later influence continues with me,
It puts forth its power and whirls me along.
My stomach is empty and never at rest.
I have no fixed course or home or village.

---

[58] From J. N. Fraser and K. B. Marathe, *The Poems of Tukaram* (Madras: Christian Literature Society, 1909), pp. 114–115.

I have no power, O God, to end my wanderings;
My soul dances about like rice in a frying pan.
Ages have passed in this way and I do not know
    how many more await me.
I cannot end my course, for it begins again;
Only the ending of the world can set me free.
Who will finish this suffering of mine?
Who will take my burden on himself?
Your name will carry me over the sea of this
    world,

You run to the help of the distressed.
Now run to me, Narayana,[59] to me, poor and
    wretched as I am.
Consider neither my merits nor my faults.
Tukaram implores your mercy.

_____

[59] *Narayana:* Vishnu.

APPENDIX 4: POEMS OF MIRA, A HINDI FEMALE SAINT

Here are two Hindi-language poems by the most famous female saint, the sixteenth-century poet Mirabai (Mira for short). The themes of her poetry are typical of the other bhakti *saints.*

[4] O Hari! You are the support of my life!
I have no other refuge but you
In all three worlds.
I have searched the whole universe for you,
Nothing pleases me but you.
Mira says, "O Lord, I am your slave.
Do not forget me."

[63] Without Hari, behold my wretched
    condition.

They say that you are my protector
And I your servant.
I have practised remembrance of your name
In my heart, day and night.
Again and again I call upon you,
In grievous affliction.
This world is a threatening sea,
Surrounding me on every side.
My boat has broken;
Hoist the sail quickly
Before it sinks.
This forlorn one waits anxiously for her Lord;
Grant her your nearness.
Your servant Mira repeats, "Ram, Ram!"
I take refuge in you alone.

GLOSSARY

Aranyakas (ah-RUN-yah-kuhs) "Forest Books," containing a philosophical treatment of sacrifice.

Atman (AHT-muhn) the individual self or soul.

Bhagavad-Gita (BAH-gah-vahd GEE-tuh) "The Song of the Lord," the story of Arjuna and Krishna from the *Mahabharata*.

Brahman (BRAH-muhn) the ultimate, absolute reality of the cosmos; the world soul.

Brahmanas (BRAH-muh-nuhs) Vedic expositions of sacrifice.

Dharma-Shastras (DAHR-muh SHAS-truhs) writings on personal and social duties.

henotheism the worship of one god as most important among other gods, without denying their existence.

mantra (MAHN-truh) a short sacred formula used in prayer or meditation.

Om (or **Aum**) (OHM) a syllable symbolizing the fundamental hidden reality of the universe.

pandit Brahmins who specialize in Vedic memorization and ritual enactment. (Compare our word *pundit.*)

rishis (REE-shees) "seers" who heard the sounds of the four *Vedas* and collected them into the Veda *samhitas.*

samhitas (SAHM-hee-tuhs) "collections" of the four *Vedas.*

Shruti (SHROO-tee) "what was heard" by the ancients, the *Vedas;* the first level of scripture, considered of cosmic, not human, authorship.

Smriti (SMRIH-tee) "what was remembered" about divine revelation; the second level of scripture.

Upanishads (oo-PAH-nee-shahds) "Sittings near a Teacher"; philosophical collections forming the end of the *Veda.*

Vedas (VAY-duhs) the body of Shruti, consisting of the four *Vedas,* the *Brahmanas,* the *Aranyakas,* and the principal *Upanishads.*

QUESTIONS FOR STUDY AND DISCUSSION

1.   To what degree, if any, can the *Vedas* be described as reflecting a "nature-worship" religion?

2.   Compare the use and effects of soma to the modern use of drugs among those who argue that it brings a "higher consciousness." What might the similarities and differences be?

3.   In what ways did the *Upanishads* both differ from and agree with earlier Vedic literature? Do you agree with those scholars who argue that the differences between the earlier *Vedas* and later writings (including the *Upanishads*) justify calling the first stage "Vedic religion" and only the second stage "Hinduism"?

4.   How does the variety of usages of Hindu scripture in the past and present mirror the variety of Hindu religion?

5.   If you were to become a Hindu, which caste would you like to belong to? Which sex? Why?

6.   How would you characterize the role of women in Hinduism? Are the texts given here reflective of what you see as their actual conditions in India?

7.   In what ways and for what reasons does the *Bhagavad-Gita* (Appendix 1) present the path of devotion as the best form of Hinduism?

8.   How does the *Bhagavad-Gita* present and answer the problem of war? What is your critique of its answer? To what degree may its answer be applicable to peoples of other cultures and other religions?

9.   How do the later devotional songs (Appendix 2) carry forth and develop the traditions of devotional Hinduism?

SUGGESTIONS FOR FURTHER READING

Primary Readings

The most complete and accessible translations of Hindu scripture remain the several volumes in Max Müller, ed., *Sacred Books of the East* (Oxford: Oxford University Press, 1879–1910). For more recent translations, begin with the following works.

Thomas B. Coburn, *Encountering the Goddess: A Translation of the* Devi-Mahatmya *and a Study of its Interpretation*. Albany, NY: State University of New York Press, 1991. A translation and study of the best-known goddess text in modern India.

Ainslie T. Embree, ed., *The Hindu Tradition*. Readings in Oriental Thought Series. New York: Vintage Books, 1972. Selections ranging from the earliest times to modern times, with excellent introductions.

John S. Hawley and Mark Juergensmeyer, *Songs of the Saints of India*. New York: Oxford University Press, 1988. An excellent introduction to saint-poetry.

Robert E. Hume, *The Thirteen Principal Upanishads,* 2d ed. Oxford: Oxford University Press, 1983. Perhaps the best translation of the most important *Upanishads*.

Donald S. Lopez, Jr., *Religions of India in Practice*. Princeton: Princeton University Press, 1995. Contains primary documents, many never translated before, of more recent Hindu literature that has scriptural use. See especially the section "Songs of Devotion and Praise," which treats devotional poetry.

Wendy Doniger O'Flaherty, *The* Rig Veda: *An Anthology*. London: Penguin, 1981. A selection of 108 hymns, with excellent translations and full annotations.

Wendy Doniger O'Flaherty, ed., *Textual Sources for the Study of Hinduism*. Totowa, N.J.: Barnes & Noble, 1988. A selection of readings from both Shruti and *Smriti*.

Patrick Olivelle, Samnyasa Upanishads: *Hindu Scriptures on Asceticism and Renunciation*. New York: Oxford University Press, 1992. Full introduction, fresh translation, and notes for those *Upanishads* that deal with the "stage" of renunciation.

Barbara Stoller Miller, *The* Bhagavad-Gita: *Krishna's Counsel in Time of War*. New York: Columbia University Press, 1986. The most readable recent translation of the *Gita,* and one that suggests its power and beauty.

S. Radhakrishnan, *The Principal* Upanishads. New York: Harper, 1953. Translation and notes by an influential Hindu thinker whose neo-Vedantist perspective colors some of the commentary.

R. C. Zaehner, *The* Bhagavad-Gita. London: Oxford University Press, 1969. The English translation, while powerful, is stilted; excellent introduction and commentary.

Secondary Readings

A. L. Basham, *The Origins and Development of Classical Hinduism,* ed. K. Zysk. New York: Oxford University Press, 1989. An insightful and concise treatment of Hindu scriptures in the context of a survey of the stages of Hinduism.

Harold Coward, "Scripture in Hinduism," in *Sacred Word and Sacred Text*. Maryknoll, NY: Orbis, 1988. A survey of the Hindu scriptures with special attention to orality.

Thomas J. Hopkins, *The Hindu Religious Tradition*. Belmont, CA: Wadsworth, 1971. This brief introductory textbook is noted for a fine analysis of Hindu scripture.

Robert C. Lester, "Hinduism: Veda and Sacred Texts." In F. M. Denny and R. L. Taylor, *The Holy Book in Comparative Perspective*. Charleston: University of South Carolina Press, 1985, pp. 126–147. A good treatment of the relationship of Vedic texts and other Hindu scriptures, especially the Smriti.

Thomas B. Coburn, " 'Scripture' in India: Towards a Typology of the Word in Hindu Life," in M. Levering, ed., *Rethinking Scripture*. Albany: State University of New York Press, 1989, pp. 102–128; also published in *Journal of the American Academy of Religion* 52 (1984):

435–459. Argues that "scripture" is an ill-fitting label for Hinduism and proposes instead a "typology of the word."

Katherine K. Young, "[Women in] Hinduism," in Arvind Sharma, ed., *Women in World Religions*. Albany: State University of New York Press, 1987, pp. 59–103. This concise but fairly comprehensive survey of its topic has good references to the content and usage of Hindu sacred writings.

Krishna Sivaraman, ed., *Hindu Spirituality:* Vedas *through Vedanta*. New York: Crossroad, 1989. A treatment by mostly Indian scholars of the continuing significance of Vedic and Upanishadic traditions for contemporary Hinduism.

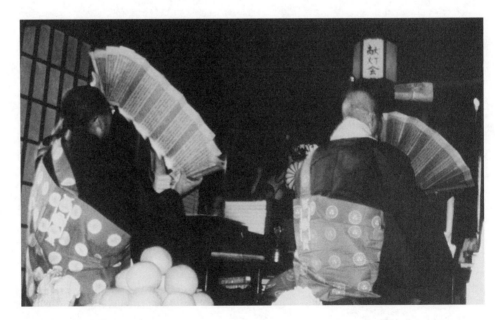

Chanting Buddhist Scripture
Japanese Buddhist monks chant scriptures at a Buddhist altar. Credit: Michel Strickmann, from the Image Bank of the Center for the Study of World Religions, Harvard University. Used by permission of Mr. and Mrs. Leo Strickmann.

CHAPTER THREE

Buddhism

❖ In a Chinese convent, Buddhist nuns gather daily to read scripture. A low hum fills the reading room as they all recite together. They are "making merit," doing a deed that will wear away karma. This merit will enable them to be reborn after death into a better existence, eventually to achieve Nirvana and be reborn no more.

❖ In Washington, D.C., a new "Dharma Wheel Cutting Karma" has been turning since 1997 in the Asian section of the Library of Congress. The wheel contains 208 repetitions of 42 Tibetan scriptures, which otherwise fill 15 Tibetan volumes. The spiritual power generated by the constant electrical turning of the wheel is said to generate compassion, prevent natural disasters, and promote peace in the world.

❖ In Tokyo, worshippers from the Nichiren sect of Buddhism gather in their temple. A steady chant goes up: "Hail to the Lotus Sutra." Like all followers of Nichiren, they constantly recite this formula of devotion to a leading scripture to bring blessing on themselves and ultimately unite with the eternal spirit of the Buddha.

INTRODUCTION

The Buddhist religion is based on the life and teaching of the Indian sage Siddhartha Gotama (ca. 536–476 B.C.E.), the Enlightened One or **Buddha** [BUHD-ha]. It believes that persons can overcome the misery of the world and reach their own Buddha status by a process of mental and moral purification. Buddhism has spread virtually throughout Asia. With this growth has come a wide diversity within Buddhism that is mirrored in its scriptures. The Buddhist canon has three main forms, hundreds of scriptural texts, and many different types of usage. This assemblage of scriptures provides a fascinating overview of the early history of the Buddhist tradition and insight into the contemporary life of Buddhists everywhere.

Overview of Structure

The scriptures of Theravada (south Asian) Buddhism are known as the **Tipitaka**[1] [tih-pee-TAH-kuh], or Three Baskets (see Table 3.1). Tradition says that the early disciples of Buddha wrote his words on palm-leaf manuscripts and collected them into three baskets (*pitakas*). The term *pitaka* as a division of scripture does not occur in the scriptures themselves, but it seems to have arisen around 300 B.C.E. and is now universal among Buddhists. The three *pitakas* are **Vinaya** [vih-NIGH-yuh] Pitaka ("Discipline Basket"), the **Sutta** [SUH-tuh] Pitaka ("Discourse Basket"), and the

---

[1] Sanskrit *Tripitaka*. Throughout this chapter, we will generally use the Pali-language forms of key Buddhist words, with the Sanskrit equivalents, where necessary, in parentheses. The titles of scripture books will reflect their language of origin, generally Pali.

Table 3.1
The Pali Canon: The Tipitaka (Three Baskets)

Name	Translation	Content/Size
Vinaya Pitaka (Discipline Basket):		
1. *Sutta-vibhanga*	Division of Rules	Monastic rules stated and expanded
a. *Mahavibhanga*	Great Division	227 rules for monks
b. *Bhikkuni-vibhanga*	Division about Nuns	Rules for nuns
2. *Khandhaka*	Sections	
a. *Mahavagga*	Great Group	Main rules
b. *Cullavagga*	Small Group	Miscellaneous rules
3. *Parivara*	Accessory	Summaries of rules
Sutta Pitaka (Discourse Basket):		
1. *Digha-nikaya*	Collection of Long Discourses	34 suttas
2. *Majjhima-nikaya*	Collection of Medium Discourses	152 suttas
3. *Samyutta-nikaya*	Collection of Corrected Discourses	56 groups of suttas
4. *Anguttara-nikaya*	Collection of Item-More Discourses	2308 suttas
5. *Khuddaka-nikaya*	Collection of Little Texts	
a. *Khuddaka-patha*	Little Readings	A meditation book
b. *Dhammapada*	Verses on Teaching	26 chapters
c. *Udana*	Utterances	80 utterances
d. *Itivuttaka*	Thus-saids	112 suttas
e. *Sutta-nipata*	Sutta Collection	71 suttas
f. *Vimana-vatthu*	Tales of Heavenly Mansions	85 poems
g. *Peta-vatthu*	Tales of Ghosts	Rebirth as ghosts
h. *Thera-Gatha*	Verses of Elder Men	Poems from earliest monks
i. *Theri-Gatha*	Verses of Elder Women	Poems from early nuns
j. *Jataka*	Lives	550 past lives of Gotama
k. *Nidessa*	Exposition	2 commentaries
l. *Patisambhida-magga*	Way of Analysis	Doctrinal exposition
m. *Apadana*	Stories	Saints' past lives
n. *Buddhavamsa*	Lineage of the Buddhas	Stories of 24 pre-Gotama Buddhas
o. *Cariya-pitaka*	Basket of Perfections	35 tales from *Jataka*
Abhidhamma Pitaka ("Special Teaching Basket"):		
1. *Dhamma-sangani*	Enumeration of Dhammas	
2. *Vibhanga*	Distinctions	
3. *Dhastu-Kadha*	Discussions of Elements	
4. *Puggala-pannatti*	Designation of Persons	
5. *Yamaka*	The Pairs	
6. *Patthama*	Activations	

Tables 3.1 and 3.2 are adapted from Richard H. Robinson, *The Buddhist Religion* (Belmont, CA: Dickenson Publishing Company, 1970), pp. 125–128. Copyright © 1970, Dickenson Publishing Company. Used by permission of Wadsworth, a division of Thomson Learning.

Abhidhamma [ahb-hee-DAHM-muh] Pitaka ("Special Teaching Basket"). We will consider each basket in turn, and then survey the structure of the Chinese and Tibetan forms of the canon.

The Vinaya Pitaka is so named because it contains the regulations for the communal life of the monks and nuns. All these rules are said to be the words of the Buddha. The Vinaya has three divisions: the *Sutta-vibhanga,* "Discourse on Rules"; the *Khandhakas,* "Sections"; and the *Parivaras,* "Accessory," a short summary of the rules and how to apply them. Each of the first two are divided into two other groups. The Vinaya Pitaka presents 227 different rules, most of them prohibitions of forbidden activities, which are grouped according to importance. They range from a few offenses that result in permanent expulsion from the order to minor offenses that need only be confessed to one's monastic leader. All the rules for monks apply in a general way to the nuns as well, but a special section of the *Suttavibhanga* gives specific regulations for them. The size of the Vinaya Pitaka is indicated by its most recent English translation, which runs to six substantial volumes. That the Vinaya is first among the *pitakas* attests to the leading role that monasticism has played in the history of Buddhism as a whole and its scriptures in particular.

The Sutta Pitaka contains teachings attributed to Gotama Buddha. Buddhists divide this largest of the baskets into five collections called *nikayas:* Long Discourses, Medium-Length Discourses, Kindred Discourses, Item-More (or Gradual) Discourses, and Short Texts. Each discourse has many subdivisions, and most follow a common structure. First comes "Thus I have heard [from the Buddha]," second comes a statement of the place and occasion of the hearing, third is the body of the teaching, and last the listener's confession of the truth of the teaching and acknowledgment that he is Buddha's disciple. The Discourse Basket is probably the best-known basket of the *Tipitaka*. For students of Buddhism it provides the best access to the essence of this tradition, with its rationale for the first basket, collections of wise sayings, stories of former lives of the Buddha and other Buddhist worthies, and its general *suttas* on doctrines and ethics.

The Abhidhamma Pitaka contains seven scholastic treatises based on the teachings of Buddha. They deal with advanced, difficult topics that are often highly philosophical. Although the Sanskrit and Pali versions of the first two baskets are similar in content, they vary quite a bit in the third basket. The Pali version, used by South Asian Theravada Buddhism, tries to adhere conservatively to the exact words of Buddha. Its seven treatises are: "The Summary of **Dhamma** [DAH-muh; this is the same term as the Sanskrit *dharma*]," "Divisions," "Discussion of Elements," "The Designation of Person," "Subjects of Discussion," "The Pairs," and "Activations." The Sanskrit Abhidharma is important for the growth of Buddhist philosophy because these Sanskrit books deal with the *ideas* of Buddha more than with his words. Like the Pali version, the Sanskrit has seven books, but they are different in names and content, and they vary between the Chinese and Tibetan translations. The seven most commonly recognized are "The Method of Knowledge," "The Treatise," "The Overview of Consciousness," "Collection on the Law [Dharma]," "Treatise on Communication," "Overview of the Elements," and "Discourse on Sacred Beliefs."

The Mahayana canon did not adopt the threefold basket-division of the Pali canon; it has no main divisions (see Table 3.2). But many of the more important books of the Pali canon were incorporated in the Mahayana canon. The Pali and Mahayana canons

Table 3.2

The Mahayana or Chinese Canon: The San-Ts'ang

Name of Section	Translation	Size
Agama	Limbs	2 vols., 151 texts
Jatakas	Lives	2 vols., 68 texts
Prajna-Paramita	Perfect Wisdom	4 vols., 42 texts
Saddharma-pundarika	—	1 vol., 16 texts
Avatamsaka	—	2 vols., 31 texts
Ratnakuta	—	
Mahaparinirvana	Great Decease	1 vol., 23 texts
—	Great Assembly	1 vol., 28 texts
Sutra-Pitaka	Sutra Collection	4 vols., 423 texts
Tantra	Tantra	4 vols., 572 texts
Vinaya	Discipline	3 vols., 86 texts
—	Commentary on Sutras	3 vols., 31 texts
Adhidharma	Special Teaching	4 vols., 28 texts
Madhyamika		1 vol., 15 texts
Yogacara	Yoga Practice	2 vols., 49 texts
—	Treatises	1 vols., 65 texts
—	Commentaries on Sutras	7 vols.
—	Commentaries on *Vinaya*	1 vol.
—	Commentaries on Shastras	5 vols.
—	Chinese Sectarian Writings	5 vols.
—	History and Biography	4 vols., 95 texts
—	Encyclopedias and Dictionaries	2 vols., 16 texts
—	Non-Buddhist Writings	1 vol., 8 texts
—	Catalogues	1 vol., 40 texts

share such important works as the **Jatakas** [JAH-tah-kuhs], the *Death of the Buddha* (*Mahaparinibbana*, Sanskrit *Mahaparinirvana*), Vinaya texts on monastic discipline, various Abhidhamma texts, and the like. Some books from the Mahayana canon have even penetrated Theravada Buddhism, recognized and used as scripture while not being formally admitted to the historic Pali canon. In Sri Lanka, for example, the *Buddhacarita* and the *Visuddhimagga* are widely received and used as scripture.

The Mahayana canon also added many other new books, all of them claiming to be the true word of the Gotama Buddha. One of the most important is the **sutra** [writing, scripture; Pali, sutta] group of *Prajna-Paramita*, or "Perfection of Knowledge." These books discuss philosophically the denial of the reality of existence and nonexistence. They feature an almost constant repetitiveness that has contributed to their great length. Another work is the *Sukhavativyuha*, "Description of the Happy Land" where the gracious Buddha Amitabha rules and invites his followers to share eternal life with him. This text has become important in the Japanese Pure Land Buddhist sect. A third work is the *Saddharmapundarika*, "Lotus of the Good Law." This work has become the leading text of Nichiren Buddhism. In sum, with its adoption of many older books along with an astonishing variety of new books, the literature of Mahayana Buddhism is vast and complex.

The third main Buddhist canon is the Tibetan (see Table 3.3). In the seventh century c.e., Buddhism came to Tibet, where it is known as Lamaism (from the Tibetan

Table 3.3

The Tibetan Canon

Name	Translation	Size
I. *Kanjur:*	Translation of the Ordinances	108 vols.
'Dul-ba	Discipline [for monastics]	13 vols.
Shes-rab-kyi-pha-rol-tu-phyin-pa	Supreme Otherworldly Knowledge	21 vols.
Phal-chen	Buddhist Cosmology	6 vols.
dKon-brtsegs	Heap of Jewels	6 vols.
mDo	Teaching Lectures	30 vols.
Mya-ngan-'das	Nirvana	2 vols.
rGyud	Texture [Tantra]	22 vols.
II. *Tanjur:*	Translation of the Doctrine	225 vols.
mDo	Teaching	136 vols.
rGyud	Texture [Tantra]	87 vols.
	A book of Hymns	1 vol.
	An index	1 vol.

bla-ma, the "superior" religion). The Tibetan king sent a delegation to India, where an alphabet was devised for the Tibetan language and the entire Buddhist literature translated into it. To this Indian literature, the Tibetans added many books of their own, secular as well as religious. The final and official assembling of these books came in the fourteenth century, when they were fixed into two collections, the *Kanjur* ("Translation of the Ordinances") and the *Tanjur* ("Translation of the Doctrine").

The *Kanjur* (or *bKa'-'gyur*) contains 689 books of various lengths in 100 or 108 volumes. It contains only those texts that the Buddha himself is said to have taught. The first main division is the "Discipline," for monks; the second is the "Supreme Otherworldly Knowledge"; the third deals with the Buddha community (Sangha); the fourth is the "Heap of Jewels"; the fifth is the "Teaching Lectures"; the sixth is "Nirvana"; the last is the *Tantra.* The *Tanjur* (or *bsTan-'gur*) is not, as is often stated, a commentary on the *Kanjur.* It contains 225 volumes in two main sections, Sutra and Tantra. The Sutra section includes many translations of Indian commentaries on older scriptures. The *Tanjur* deals in an even wider variety of topics than the *Kanjur:* traditional religious teachings, magical texts drawn mainly from native Tibetan religion, and texts on alchemy and astrology. Today the preservation and further dissemination of Tibetan scriptures is a primary task of Tibetan Buddhist exiles.

Origin and Development

The development of Buddhist scripture begins with Gotama Buddha himself. Buddhists believe that Prince Gotama established among his monk-disciples an oral transmission of his teachings on which later written scriptures are based. They trace all the varied scripture collections and their contents back to Buddha; all are his word.

When Gotama died, he had not appointed a human successor. Indeed, he taught instead that the leader of the Buddhists was to be his Teaching (Dhamma) and the monastic order (Sangha) he founded. Soon after his death, his disciples gathered at the first general council of Buddhists, held at Rajagaha in 483 B.C.E., to formalize his teachings. After seven months of work collecting and examining the purported sayings of Buddha for authenticity, they drafted an official version and committed it to memory. His chief disciple Ananda is said to have recited them all. The sayings were then written down on palm leaves (more durable than paper or parchment in the hot, humid Indian climate) and then separated into baskets. Mahayana Buddhists believe that all three were developed at this time. Theravada Buddhists believe that the last basket, Special Teaching, was formed at the third general council of Buddhists in 253 B.C.E. Most modern scholars would agree that the nature of this basket seems to suggest a later origin.

Even after this initial conversion to writing, oral transmission continued and was seen as the primary mode of scripture preservation by all early Buddhists. An early Special Teaching Basket text, the *Samuccaya,* indicates the reasons for this preference. Among them are: memorizing is easy, accumulates merit, aids understanding, brings mental satisfaction, and promotes one's good standing among others. In addition, early Buddhists saw transmission by an exacting oral tradition as more reliable in preserving the exact words of the Buddha than writing.

When **Mahayana** ("Large Vehicle," more liberal and mostly north-Asian) Buddhism arose in the first century C.E., it had a new concern for liberation through the **bodhisattva** [bohd-hee-SAHT-vuh], one who postpones his own full enlightenment in order to help others. The older idea of self-redemption characteristic of **Theravada** ("Tradition of the Elders"; more conservative and south-Asian) Buddhism gave way to redemption through the grace of this Buddha, who postponed enlightenment to aid others. The new movement required a new body of scripture, and so began the Mahayana canon. This collection is typically called the "Chinese canon," but it is important to note that this canon is also used in Japan, usually in its Chinese-language form.

Use

Buddhist usage of scripture centers around monastic activity. Since early times, when the teaching of Buddha was passed along orally and then written down, the role of monks (not nuns) in scriptural activity has been primary. The scriptures themselves bear the marks of this orientation. For example, the first and the third baskets are explicitly for monastics. Other reasons also figure in. The expense in owning such a large canon makes it accessible mainly to monastic orders. Its size demands a lifetime of study to master it; its content is challenging and specialized, calling for special teachers who can only be found among the monks. Buddhism in general demands withdrawal from the distractions of daily life in order to give the scriptures the kind of in-depth study they deserve.

What does this monastic usage entail? First, Buddhism has traditionally distinguished between "study monks" and "insight monks." The very term "study monk" indicates the first usage of scripture, the study of the content of its teachings. The new monk studies scripture to learn the first and most important of the monastic rules that govern his life. He also studies the most easily understood texts in the Sutta Pitaka, such as the *Dhammapada* and the *Jataka* verses. As time progresses and he masters this material, he proceeds to learn the other rules in the Vinaya Pitaka and the other texts of the Sutta Pitaka. If, at the height of his monastic career, he displays an excellence in study and teaching, he may go on to master the intricacies of the Abhidhamma Pitaka.

Because study of the scriptures is in most forms of Buddhism a prerequisite for becoming a meditation monk, all monks pass through this first phase. Moreover, throughout the history of Buddhism and even today, monks designated as "study monks" greatly outnumber those labeled "meditation monks." This is especially the case in modern times, when the general conviction has grown in many Buddhist circles that one cannot reach enlightenment in this life.

In all this study and teaching, the goal is to realize in one's own life the teachings of the Buddha that lead toward enlightenment. The scripture itself, as a book, is worth little or nothing. The *meaning* of the words, not the words themselves, has value in the search for purification.

Monks also pursue scriptural activity for the laity. At funerals they recite texts for the merit of the deceased. Monks often officiate at wedding ceremonies. They lecture on the scriptures to the laity, both individuals and groups. Some monks will preach the scriptures to the laity, often using such popular material as the *Jatakas,* or birth tales. Wealthy layfolk will often sponsor long recitations of scripture in the monasteries and will pay for the publication of scriptures, all for the sake of making merit for loved ones. But all these activities with the laity are mostly incidental to a monk's main activity—studying and meditating on scripture in order to travel the road to personal enlightenment.

Of all forms of Buddhism, the Tibetan holds its scriptures in a great ritual esteem characteristic of bibliolatry. The books are venerated in worship, with incense and prayer offered to them. They are produced in the traditional way, either printed by hand or with woodblocks, and are preserved in the monasteries with great care. Although these books are produced and preserved in Tibet, no scholarly critical edition of them has been compiled, modern language translations are very incomplete, and only a few European libraries possess a complete copy of the *Kanjur* and *Tanjur.*

HISTORY

The Past Lives of Gotama Buddha*

After his enlightenment, the Buddha knew all his past lives. In the Jatakas *("Birth Stories"), he recounts in detail 550 episodes from as many past lives, each revealing his gradual progress to perfection in his last incarnation as Gotama. These Jatakas each teach one point, always to edify the reader. Only the verses at the end are considered inspired, and the stories are built from them. They come from a Mahayana setting that features the bestowal of merit from one person to another, but they* *are widely known in Theravada lands as well. In this story the layman transfers merit to the barber.[2]*

The Master told this story about a believing layman while staying in Jetavana. This was a faithful, pious soul, and a chosen disciple. One evening, on his way to Jetavana, he came to the bank of the river Aciravati, when the ferrymen had pulled up their boat on the shore in order to attend

---

* *Jataka* 190, the Birth-Story of the Blessing of the Commandments

[2] Taken, with editing, from E. B. Cowell, ed., *The Jataka,* vol. 2 (Cambridge: Cambridge University Press, 1895), pp. 77–78.

service. As no boat could be seen at the landing, and our friend's mind was full of delightful thoughts of the Buddha, he walked into the river. His feet did not sink below the water. He got as far as mid-river walking as though he were on dry land, but then he noticed the waves. Then his ecstasy subsided, and his feet began to sink. Again he strung himself up to high tension [by meditation], and walked on over the water. So he arrived at Jetavana, greeted the Master, and took a seat on one side. The Master entered into conversation with him pleasantly. "I hope, good layman, you had no mishap on your way." "O Sir," he replied, "on my way I was so absorbed in thoughts of the Buddha that I set foot upon the river; but I walked over it as though it had been dry ground!" "Ah, friend layman," said the Master, "you are not the only one who has been kept safe by remembering the virtues of the Buddha. In older days pious laymen have been shipwrecked in mid-ocean, and saved themselves by remembering the Buddha's virtues." Then, at the man's request, he told the following story from the past.

Once upon a time, in the days when Kassapa was Supreme Buddha, a disciple who had entered on the Paths took passage on board ship in company with a barber of some considerable property. The barber's wife had given him charge of our friend, to look after him in better and in worse.

A week later, the ship was wrecked in mid-ocean. These two persons clinging to one plank were cast up on an island. There the barber killed some birds, and cooked them, offering a share of his meal to the lay brother. "No, thank you," said he, "I have had enough." He was thinking to himself, "In this place there is no help for us except the Three Jewels,"[3] and so he pondered upon the blessings of the Three Jewels. As he pondered and pondered, a Serpent-king who had been born in that isle changed his own body to the shape of a great ship. The ship was filled with

the seven kinds of precious things. An ocean god was the helmsman. The three masts were made of sapphire, the anchor of gold, the ropes of silver, and the planks were golden.

The Sea-spirit stood on board, crying, "Any passengers for India?" The lay brother said, "Yes, that's where we are headed." "In with you then, on board with you!" He went aboard, and wanted to call his friend the barber. "You may come," said the helmsman to the lay brother, "but not he." "Why not?" "He is not a man of holy life, that's why; I brought this ship for you, not for him." The lay brother replied, "Very well; the gifts I have given, the virtues I have practiced, the powers I have developed—I give him the fruit of all of them!" "I thank you, master!" said the barber. "Now," said the Sea-spirit, "I can take the barber aboard." So he conveyed them both over sea, and sailed upstream to Benares. There, by his power, he created a store of wealth for both of them, and spoke this to them:

"Keep company with the wise and good. If this barber had not been in company with this pious layman, he would have perished in the midst of the deep." Then he uttered these verses in praise of good company:

"Behold the fruit of sacrifice, virtue, and piety:
A serpent in ship-shape conveys the good man
    o'er the sea.

Make friendship only with the good, and keep
    good company;
Friends with the good, this Barber could his
    home in safety see."

Thus the Spirit of the Sea spoke, poised in mid-air. Finally he went to his own abode, taking the Serpent-king along with him.

The Master, after finishing this discourse, declared the Truths and identified the [connection to his] Birth. At the conclusion of the Truths the pious layman entered on the Fruit of the Second Path.[4] "On that occasion the converted lay brother attained Nirvana; Sariputta was the Serpent-king, and I myself was the ocean god."

---

[3] *Three Jewels:* the Buddha, the Dhamma ("Teaching"), and the Sanga ("Monastic Society"); also called the "three refuges."

[4] *the Fruit of the Second Path:* the path of those who are reborn again only once.

The Life of Gotama Buddha*

The Acts of the Buddha *by Ashvaghosha (first century B.C.E.) is often placed between Theravada and Mahayana Buddhism and is a favorite book in the latter. It deals in poetic form with the life and teachings of the Buddha. This selection recounts the birth of Gotama, the "Four Sights," his "Great Retirement," and his enlightenment. It portrays the life of the Buddha as an example for all Buddhists: all his followers should reach Nirvana in this manner. It opens, as do many Buddhist scriptures, with an invocation to Gotama Buddha.*[5]

That Arhat is here saluted, who has no counterpart. Bestowing the supreme happiness, he surpasses Brahman the Creator. Driving away darkness, he vanquishes the sun. Dispelling all burning heat, he surpasses the beautiful moon.

There was a city, the dwelling-place of the great saint Kapila, that had its sides surrounded by the beauty of a lofty broad plain like a line of clouds. With its high-soaring palaces, it was immersed in the sky. . . . [9] A king by the name of Suddhodana ruled over the city. He was a relative of the sun, anointed to stand at the head of earth's monarchs. He adorned it as a bee adorns a full-blown lotus. [10] He was the very best of kings, intent on liberality yet empty of pride. . . .

[15] He had a queen named Maya, who was free from all deceit [*maya*]. She was a brilliance proceeding from his brilliance, like the splendor of the sun when it is free from all the influence of darkness. . . . Truly the life of women is always darkness; yet when it encountered her, it shone brilliantly. . . .

[19] Falling from the host of beings in the Tushita heaven, and illumining the three worlds, the most excellent of Bodhisattvas[6] suddenly entered at a thought into her womb. [20] He assumed the form of a huge elephant as white as Himalaya, armed with six tusks, with his face perfumed with flowing ichor. Then he entered the womb of the queen of king Suddhodana to destroy the evils of the world. The guardians of the world hastened from heaven to watch over the world's one true ruler. . . . [23] Then one day by the king's permission the queen, having a great longing in her mind, went with the residents of the women's apartments into the garden Lumbini. As the queen supported herself by a bough that hung with a weight of flowers, the Bodhisattva suddenly came forth, splitting open her womb. [25] Then the constellation Pushya was auspicious. From the side of the queen, who was purified by her vow, her son was born for the welfare of the world. He was born without pain and without illness [for his mother]. . . .

[30] Having thus in due time come from the womb, he shone as if he had come down from heaven. He had not been born in the natural way. He was born full of wisdom, not foolish, as if his mind had been purified by countless aeons of contemplation. With glory, endurance and beauty he shone like the young sun descended upon the earth. He attracted all eyes like the moon, although he had a surpassing brightness. . . . [34] [He said:] "I am born for supreme knowledge, for the welfare of the world. Therefore, this is my last birth. . . ."

[54] The great seer Asita learned by signs and through the power of his penances this birth of him who was to destroy all birth. In his thirst for the excellent Law, he came to the palace of the Sakya king. . . . [59] The sage, being invited by the king, filled with properly intense feeling, uttered his deep and solemn words [to the king] as his large eyes opened wide with wonder: ". . . . 62] Hear now the motive for my coming and

---

* *Buddhacarita* 1.1–2, 9–10, 15–17, 19–21, 23–25, 30–34, 54, 59, 62, 64–68, 72–74, 83; 2.24–26, 28–32; 3.1–10, 26–33, 40–44, 53–61; 5.7–20; 12.88–105; 14.1–9, 35–37, 64–68, 79–81.

[5] Taken, with editing, from E. B. Cowell, trans., *Buddhist Mahayana Texts, Sacred Books of the East*, vol. 49 (Oxford: Oxford University Press, 1894), pp. 1–157.

[6] *Boddhisattva:* one who has reached enlightenment but postpones entering nirvana in order to help others reach it.

rejoice in it. I have heard a heavenly voice in the heavenly path, [saying] that your son has been born for the sake of supreme knowledge. . . ."

[64] When he heard this address, the king had his steps bewildered with joy. He took the prince, who lay on his nurse's side, and showed him to the holy ascetic. [65] Thus the great seer saw the king's son with wonder. His foot was marked with a wheel, his fingers and toes webbed, with a circle of hair between his eyebrows, and signs of vigor like an elephant.[7] Asita stood with tears hanging on the ends of his eyelashes, and he looked up toward heaven sighing. Seeing Asita with his eyes filled with tears, the king was agitated by his love for his son. . . .

[72] Knowing the king to be disturbed through his fear of some impending evil, the sage addressed him: "Let not your mind, O monarch, be disturbed. All that I have said is certainly true. I have no feeling of fear about his being subject to change, but I am distressed for my own disappointment. It is my time to depart, and this child is now born. He knows the mystery hard to attain, the means of destroying rebirth. Having forsaken his kingdom, becoming indifferent to all worldly things, and having attained the highest truth by his strenuous efforts, he will shine forth as a sun of knowledge to destroy the darkness of illusion in the world. . . ."

[83] When he heard these words, the king, his queen and his friends abandoned sorrow and rejoiced. Thinking, "Such is this son of mine," he considered that his son's excellence was his own. But he let his heart be influenced by the thought, "He will travel by the noble path." He was not opposed to religion, yet he still was alarmed at the prospect of losing his child. . . .

[2.24] When the young prince had passed the period of childhood and reached his middle youth, he learned in a few days the various sciences suitable to his race, which generally took

many years to master. [25] But remembering what the great seer Asita said about his destined future that was to embrace transcendental happiness, the anxious care of the king . . . turned the prince to sensual pleasures. He sought for him from a family of unblemished moral excellence a bride possessed of beauty, modesty, gentle bearing, and widespread glory. Yasodhara was her name, a name well worthy of her, a very goddess of good fortune. . . .

[28] "He might see some inauspicious sight that could disturb his mind." Reflecting this way, the king had a dwelling prepared for his son in the private recesses of the palace. Then the son spent his time in those royal apartments. They were furnished with the delights proper for every season, gaily decorated like heavenly chariots upon the earth, and bright like the clouds of autumn. He spent time among the splendid musical concerts of singing women. [30] With the softly-sounding tambourines beaten by the tips of the women's hands, and ornamented with golden rims, and with the dances that were like the dances of the heavenly nymphs, that palace shone like Mount Kailasa. The women delighted him with their soft voices, their beautiful pearl-garlands, their playful intoxication, their sweet laughter, and their stolen glances concealed by their brows. Carried away in the arms of these women well-skilled in the ways of love, and reckless in the pursuit of pleasure, he fell from the roof of a pavilion and yet did not reach the ground, like a holy sage stepping from a heavenly chariot. . . .

[3.1] On a certain day he heard about the forests carpeted with tender grass. They had been all bound up in the cold season, but now their trees resounded with the kokilas birds and they were adorned with lotus-ponds. When he heard of the delightful appearance of these parks beloved by the women, he resolved to go outdoors. He was like an elephant long shut up in a house.

When the king learned the wish expressed by his son, he ordered a pleasure-party to be prepared, one worthy of his own affection and his son's beauty and youth. But he prohibited any

---

[7] This sentence describes some of the birthmarks of Gotama, some of which can be seen on statues of the Buddha and which are important in Tibetan Buddhism for identifying new lamas.

encounter with any afflicted common person in the highroad. He said, "Heaven forbid that the prince with his tender nature should even imagine himself to be distressed." [5] Then he removed from the road with the greatest gentleness all those who had mutilated limbs or maimed senses, the decrepit and the sick and all squalid beggars. They made the highway assume its perfect beauty. Along this road made beautiful, the fortunate prince with his well-trained attendants came down one day at a proper time from the roof of the palace and went to visit the king to gain his permission to leave. Then the king, with tears rising in his eyes, smelled his son's head and gazed for a long time upon him. He gave him his permission, saying, "Go." But in his heart he did not want him to depart.

He [Gotama] then mounted a golden chariot. It was adorned with reins bright like flashing lightning, and yoked with four gentle horses, all wearing golden trappings. With a worthy entourage he entered the road that was strewn with heaps of gleaming flowers, with garlands suspended and banners waving, like the moon with its stars entering the sky. [10] He passed very slowly along the highway, watched on every side by the citizens, and showered with curiosity by their eyes opened wide like blue lotuses. . . .

[26] But then the gods, dwelling in their pure abodes, saw the city rejoicing like heaven itself. They created an old man to walk along and to stir the heart of the king's son. The prince saw him overcome with decrepitude and different in form from other men. With his gaze intently fixed on him, he addressed his driver with simple confidence. "Who is this man that has come here, with white hair and his hand resting on a staff, his eyes hidden beneath his brows, his limbs bent down and hanging loose? Is this a change produced in him, or his natural state, or an accident?"

The charioteer revealed to the king's son the secret that should have been kept so carefully. He thought no harm in his simplicity, for those same gods had bewildered his mind, and he said, [30] "Old age has broken him down. It is the ravisher of beauty, the ruin of vigor, the cause of

sorrow, the destruction of delights, the affliction of memories, the enemy of the senses. He too once drank milk in his childhood, and in time he learned to crawl on the ground. Having step by step become a vigorous youth, he has step by step in the same way reached old age."

The startled prince spoke these words to the charioteer: "What! Will this evil come to me also?" To him the charioteer spoke again, "It will certainly come in time even to my long-lived lord. All the world knows that old age will destroy their beauty, and they are content to have it so. . . ."

[40] Then the same deities created another man with his body all afflicted by disease. On seeing him the son of Suddhodana addressed the charioteer, having his gaze fixed on the man. "That man with a swollen belly, his whole frame shaking as he pants, his arms and shoulders hanging loose, his body all pale and thin, uttering plaintively the word 'mother' when he embraces a stranger—who is this?"

Then his charioteer answered, "Gentle Sir, it is a very great affliction called sickness that has grown up, caused by the inflammation of the three humors. It has made even this strong man no longer master of himself."

Then the prince again addressed him, looking upon the man compassionately, "Is this evil peculiar to him, or are all people threatened by sickness?" The charioteer answered, "O prince, this evil is common to all. Pressed by diseases, people run to pleasure, though racked with pain. . . ."

[53] When the royal road was especially adorned and guarded, the king let the prince go out once more. He ordered the charioteer and chariot to proceed in a direction different from the previous one. But as the king's son was going on his way, the very same deities created a dead man. Only the charioteer and the prince, and no one else, saw him as he was carried dead along the road. [55] Then the prince spoke to the charioteer, "Who is this carried by four men, followed by mournful companions, who is adorned but no longer breathing?"

Then the driver, whose mind was overpowered by the gods who possess pure minds and pure dwellings, and who knew the truth, uttered to his lord this truth which he had been forbidden to tell. "This is some poor man who, bereft of his intellect, senses, vitality and qualities, lying asleep and unconscious, like mere wood or straw, is abandoned by both friends and enemies after they have carefully swathed and guarded him."

Hearing these words of the charioteer he was startled. He said to him, "Is this an accident peculiar to him alone, or is such the end of all living creatures?" Then the charioteer replied to him, "This is the final end of all living creatures. Be one a poor man, a man of middle state, or a noble, destruction will come to all in this world."

[60] Then the king's son, calm though he was, when he heard of death, immediately sank down overwhelmed. . . . He spoke with a loud voice, "This is the end appointed to all creatures, and yet the world throws off all fear and is infatuated! The hearts of men must be hard, for they can be self-composed in such a situation. . . ."

[5.7] Then he wanted to become perfectly alone in his thoughts, and stopped those friends who were following him. He went to the root of a rose-apple in a solitary spot, with its beautiful leaves all quivering [in the wind]. There he sat on the ground covered with leaves, and with its young grass bright like lapis lazuli. Meditating on the origin and destruction of the world, he laid hold of the path that leads to firmness of mind. [10] Having attained firmness of mind, and being immediately set free from all sorrows such as the desire of worldly objects, he attained the first stage of contemplation.

Having obtained the highest happiness sprung from deliberation, he next pondered this meditation. He thoroughly understood in his mind the course of the world. "It is a miserable thing that humankind, though powerless and subject to sickness, old age, and death, is blinded by passion and ignorance. People look with disgust on another who is afflicted by old age or diseased or dead. If I, being such myself, should feel disgust for another who has such a nature, it would not be worthy or right, for I know the highest duty."

As he considered thoroughly these faults of sickness, old age, and death that belong to all living beings, all the joy that he had felt in the activity of his vigor, in his youth, and in his life vanished in a moment. [15] He did not rejoice, he did not feel remorse. He suffered no hesitation, indolence, nor sleep. He felt no attraction to the qualities of desire. He neither hated nor scorned another person. This pure, passionless meditation grew within the great-souled one. Then unobserved by the other men with him, a man in a beggar's clothing crept up.

The king's son asked him a question. He said, "Tell me, who are you?" He replied, "O bull of men, I who am terrified at birth and death have become an ascetic for the sake of liberation. Desiring liberation in a world subject to destruction, I seek that happy indestructible abode. I am isolated from mankind. My thoughts are unlike those of others, and my sinful passions are turned away from all objects of sense. Dwelling anywhere, at the root of a tree, or in an uninhabited house, a mountain or a forest, I wander without a family and without home. I am a beggar ready for any food, and I seek only the highest good."

[20] When he had spoken, while the prince was looking on, he suddenly flew up to the sky. This ascetic was a heavenly inhabitant who, knowing that the prince's thoughts were other than what his outward form promised, had come to him to rouse his recollection. When the other man had gone like a bird to heaven, the foremost of men rejoiced and was astonished. Having comprehended the meaning of the term dhamma, he set his mind on how to accomplish his deliverance. . . .

[12.88] Then the saint whose every effort was pure [Gotama] fixed his dwelling on the pure bank of the Nairangana. He wanted a lonely habitation. Five beggars who desired liberation came up to him when they saw him there. . . . [90] He was honored by these disciples who were dwelling in that family. . . . Thinking, "This may be the means of abolishing birth and death," he at once began a series of difficult austerities by fasting. For six years, vainly trying to attain merit, he practiced self-mortification. He performed many rules of abstinence which are hard for a man to carry out. At the hours of eating, longing to cross the world whose farther shore is so difficult to reach, he broke his vow with single jujube fruits, sesame seeds, and rice. But the emaciation that was produced in his body by that asceticism became positive fatness because of his splendor. [95] With his glory and his beauty unimpaired although he was thin, he caused gladness to other eyes, as the autumnal moon in the beginning of her bright fortnight gladdens the lotuses. He had only skin and bone remaining. His fat, flesh and blood had faded completely. Yet, though diminished, he still shone with undiminished grandeur like the ocean.

Then the seer, having his body emaciated to no purpose in a cruel self-mortification, and dreading continued existence, reflected in his longing to become a Buddha. "This is not the way to passionlessness, nor to perfect knowledge, nor to liberation. That was certainly the true way that I found at the root of the Gambu tree. But that cannot be attained by one who has lost his strength." So resuming his care for his body, he next pondered how best to increase his bodily vigor. [100] "Wearied with hunger, thirst, and fatigue, with his mind no longer self-possessed through fatigue, how can one who is not absolutely calm reach the purpose that is to be attained by his mind? True calm is properly obtained by the constant satisfaction of the senses. The mind's self-possession is only obtained when the senses are perfectly satisfied. True meditation is produced in one whose mind is self-possessed and at rest. In one whose thoughts are engaged in meditation the exercise of perfect contemplation begins at once. By contemplation are obtained those conditions through which supreme calm is eventually gained. This is the undecaying, immortal state, which is so hard to be reached." Having thus resolved, "This means is based upon eating food," the wise seer of unbounded wisdom decided to accept the continuance of life.

[105] Having bathed, thin as he was, he slowly came up the bank of the Nairangana River. He was supported like a hand by the trees on the shore, which bent down the ends of their branches in adoration. . . .

[14.1] When he attained the highest mastery in all kinds of meditation, he remembered in the first watch the continuous series of all his former births. "In such a place I was so and so by name, and from there I passed and came here." Thus he remembered his thousands of births, experiencing each as it were over again. Having remembered each birth and each death in all those various transmigrations, the compassionate one then felt compassion for all living beings. [5] This world of living beings rolls on helplessly like a wheel, having wilfully rejected the good guides in this life and done all kinds of actions in various [previous] lives. As he remembered, in his strong self-control this conviction came to him, "All existence is unsubstantial, like the fruit of a banana plant."

When the second watch came, he was possessed of unequalled energy. He who was the highest of all seeing beings received a preeminent divine sight. By that divine, perfectly pure sight he saw the whole world as in a spotless mirror. He saw the various transmigrations and rebirths of the various beings with their several lower or higher merits from their actions, and compassion grew up more within him. . . .

[35] Having pondered all this, in the last watch he reflected, "Alas for this whole world of living beings who are doomed to misery, all wandering astray! They do not know that all this universe, destitute of any real refuge, is born and decays through that existence which is the site of the skandhas[8] and pain. It dies and passes into a new state and then is born anew. . . ."

[64] The all-knowing Bodhisattva, the illuminated one, after pondering and meditating again came to his conclusion. [65] "This is pain; this

---

[8] *skandhas:* the five components that constitute the human person.

also is the origin of pain in the world of living beings; this also is the stopping of pain; this is that course which leads to its stopping."[9] Having determined this, he knew everything as it really was. He, the holy one, sitting there on his seat of grass at the root of the tree, pondered by his own efforts and attained perfect knowledge. Then he bursted the shell of ignorance, and gained all the various kinds of perfect intuition. He attained all the partial knowledge of alternatives that is included in perfect knowledge. He became the perfectly wise, the Bhagavat,[10] the **Arhat** ["Worthy One," who has achieved enlightenment], the king of the Law, the **Tathagata** [tah-THAH-gah-tuh, "one who has come/gone thus," and reached enlightenment], the one who has attained the knowledge of all forms, the Lord of all knowledge. . . .

[79] The gods rejoiced, and paid him worship and adoration with divine flowers. All the world, when the great saint had become all-wise, was full of brightness. Then the holy one descended and stood on his throne under the tree.[11] There he passed seven days filled with the thought, "I have here attained perfect wisdom." [80] When the Bodhisattva had attained perfect knowledge, all beings became full of great happiness. All the different universes were illumined by a great light. The happy earth shook in six different ways like an overjoyed woman. The Bodhisattvas, each dwelling in his own special abode, assembled and praised him.

---

[9] *This is pain . . . its stopping:* the Buddhist reader would easily recognize here the Four Noble Truths.
[10] *Bhagavat:* the Blessed One.

[11] *the tree:* the *bo* tree, so called because there Gotama achieved enlightenment (*Bodhi*).

The Death of Gotama Buddha*

In "The Book of the Great Decease," Buddha makes provision for life in the monastic community after his death. (Buddhists typically do not say that Gotama died, rather that he entered **parinibbana,** *or the state of nirvana achieved after death.) The unity and knowledge of the community is stressed —the Buddha leaves it in an ideal state.[12]*

The Blessed One addressed the venerable Ananda, and said, "It may be, Ananda, that in some of you the thought may arise, 'The word of the Master is ended, we have a teacher no more!' Do not think this way. The truths and the rules of the order that I have set forth and laid down for you all, let them be your Teacher when I am gone.

"Ananda! When I am gone, do not address one another in the way in which the brothers have until now addressed each other, with the title of Avuso' [Friend]. A younger brother may be addressed by an elder with his name, or his family name, or the title 'Friend.' But an elder should be addressed by a younger brother as 'Lord' or as 'Venerable Sir.'

"When I am gone, Ananda, let the order, if it should so wish, abolish all the lesser and minor precepts. . . ."[13]

The venerable Ananda said to the Blessed One, "How wonderful a thing is it, Lord, and how marvelous! I truly believe that in this whole assembly of the brothers there is not one brother who has any doubt or misgiving as to the Buddha, or the truth, or the path, or the way!"

"It is out of the fullness of faith that you have spoken, Ananda! The Tathagata knows that in this whole assembly of the brothers there is not one brother who has any doubt or misgiving as

---

* *Mahaparinibbana Sutta* 6.1–14, 31–35, 45–48
[12] Taken, with editing, from T. W. Rhys Davids, trans., *Buddhist Suttas, Sacred Books of the East,* vol. 11 (Oxford: Oxford University Press, 1881), pp. 112–30.

[13] This was not done because the monastic order could not decide between major and minor rules.

to the Buddha, or the truth, or the path, or the way! For even the most backward, Ananda, of all these five hundred brothers has become converted. They are no longer liable to be born in a state of suffering, and they assured of final salvation."

[10] Then the Blessed One addressed the brothers, and said, "Behold now, brothers, I exhort you, saying, 'Decay is inherent in all component things! Work out your salvation with diligence'!" This was the last word of the Tathagata! . . .

Then the Blessed One, passing out of the state in which both sensations and ideas have ceased to be, entered the state between consciousness and unconsciousness. Passing out of the state between consciousness and unconsciousness, he entered the state of mind to which nothing at all is specially present. Passing out of the consciousness of no special object, he entered the state of mind to which the infinity of thought is the only thing present. Passing out of the mere consciousness of the infinity of thought, he entered the state of mind to which the infinity of space is alone present. Passing out of the mere consciousness of the infinity of space, he entered the fourth stage of deep meditation. Passing out of the fourth stage, he entered the third. Passing out of the third stage, he entered the second. Passing out of the second, he entered the first. Passing out of the first stage of deep meditation, he entered the second. Passing out of the second stage, he entered the third. Passing out of the third stage, he entered the fourth stage of deep meditation. Then he passed out of the last stage of deep meditation, and immediately he died.

When the Blessed One died, at the moment of his passing out of existence, a mighty earthquake arose, terrible and awe-inspiring. The thunders of heaven burst forth. . . .

When the Blessed One died, of those of the brothers who were not yet free from the passions, some stretched out their arms and wept. Others fell head first on the ground, rolling around in anguish at the thought, "Too soon has the Blessed One died! Too soon has the Happy One passed away from existence! Too soon has the Light gone out in the world!"

But those brothers who were free from the passions [the Arhats] bore their grief collected and composed at the thought. "All component things are impermanent! How is it possible that [they should not be dissolved]?" . . .

[33] Then the Mallas of Kusinara said to the venerable Ananda, "What should be done, Lord, with the remains of the Tathagata?"

"As men treat the remains of a king of kings, so should they treat the remains of a Tathagata."

"And how, Lord, do they treat the remains of a king of kings?"

"They wrap the body of a king of kings in a new cloth. When that is done, they wrap it in cotton wool. When that is done, they wrap it in a new cloth, and so on till they have wrapped the body in five hundred successive layers of both kinds. Then they place the body in an oil vessel of iron, and cover that up with another oil vessel of iron. They then build a funeral pyre of all kinds of perfumes, and burn the body of the king of kings. Then at the four crossroads they build a dagaba [14] to the king of kings. This is the way in which they treat the remains of a king of kings. As they treat the remains of a king of kings, so should they treat the remains of the Tathagata. At the four crossroads a dagaba should be built to the Tathagata. Whoever shall place garlands or perfumes or paint there, or make salutation there, or become in its presence calm in heart, shall have a profit and a joy for a long time."

Then the Mallas gave orders to their attendants, saying, "Gather all the carded cotton wool of the Mallas!" [35] Then the Mallas of Kusinara wrapped the body of the Blessed One in a new cloth. And when that was done, they wrapped it in cotton wool. And when that was done, they wrapped it in a new cloth, and so on till they had wrapped the body of the Blessed One in five hundred layers of both kinds. Then they placed the body in an oil vessel of iron, and covered that up with another oil vessel of iron. Then they built

---

[14] *dagaba:* a burial mound.

a funeral pile of all kinds of perfumes, and they placed the body of the Blessed One on it. . . .

[45] Then the venerable Maha Kassapa went . . . to the funeral pile of the Blessed One. When he had come up to it, he arranged his robe on one shoulder. Bowing down with clasped hands, he walked three times reverently around the pile. Then, uncovering his feet, he bowed down in reverence at the feet of the Blessed One. Those five hundred brethren arranged their robes on one shoulder. Bowing down with clasped hands, they walked reverently around the pile three times, and then bowed down in reverence at the feet of the Blessed One. When the homage of the venerable Maha Kassapa and of those five hundred brothers was ended, the funeral pile of the Blessed One caught fire by itself. Now as the body of the Blessed One burned itself away, neither soot nor ash was seen from the skin and the covering, and from the flesh and the nerves and the fluid of the joints. Only the bones remained behind. . . . Of those five hundred pieces of clothing the very innermost and outermost were consumed.

The Life of Milarepa*

Milarepa was a leader in bringing Buddhism to Tibet in the twelfth century C.E. This near-autobiographical account has achieved scriptural status, and is one of the most beloved stories among Tibetan Buddhists. In this reading, he renounces ordinary life and withdraws to meditate in the mountains.[15]

They [his friends] left, and I ate the good food they had brought. The sensation of pleasure and pain and the feelings of hunger increased so much that I could no longer meditate. I thought that there was no greater obstacle for me than this inability to meditate. Breaking the seal of the scroll that the lama had given me, I looked at it. It contained the essential instructions to overcome obstacles and improve practice, instructions for transforming vice into virtue, and more especially the advice to take good food at this time.

I understood that, through the force of my former perseverance in meditation, my nerves had absorbed creative energy. Due to my inferior food the energy remained inactive. The beer had stimulated my nerves to some extent and [my sister's] beer and food had completed the process. Following the directions on the scroll, I worked hard on the vital exercises recommended for body, breathing, and meditation. As a result, the obstructions in the smaller nerves as well as those in the median nerves were cleared away. I attained an experience of joy, lucidity, and pure awareness similar to what I had known about in theory. In fact it was an extraordinary experience of illumination which was very powerful and stable. Having overcome the obstacles, I realized imperfections as perfections; even through discriminating thought, I perceived the inherent simplicity of the Dharmakaya.

I understood that in general all things related to samsara and nirvana are interdependent. Furthermore I perceived that the source-consciousness is neutral. Samsara is the result of a wrong point of view. Nirvana is realized through perfect awareness. I perceived that the essence of both lay in an empty and luminous awareness. More particularly, this special experience of my illumination was the fruit of my previous meditations and the immediate effects of the food and the profound instructions of the lama. I also had a very special understanding that the methods of the Esoteric Path (Vajrayana) are for the transformation of all sensory experience into spiritual attainment. . . .

---

* gTsan-smyon He-ru-ka, *The Life of Milarepa* 2.7
[15] Taken, with editing, from W. Y. Evans-Wentz, *The Life of Milarepa* (Oxford: Oxford University Press, 1925).

I thought that I should now work for the good of sentient beings. As I was reflecting on this a prophecy came to me: "Devote yourself wholly to meditation in this life, in accordance with the lama's instructions. There is nothing greater than serving the teachings of the Buddha and thereby saving sentient beings through meditation." Again I thought, "If I meditate as long as I live, I will be setting the best example for future disciples to renounce the world and meditate." And I was certain that both the tradition of the Dharma and sentient beings would derive much benefit from that.

Then I thought, "I have stayed in this place too long and have talked too much about my knowledge of the Dharma to those who visited me. People saw me flying after my experience of illumination. If I stay here any longer I will fall under the influence of the world. There exists a risk of encountering Mara's obstacles, and the Eight Worldly Reactions will disturb my meditation. I must go and meditate at Chuwar according to the prophecy of the lama." . . .

When I arrived at Dingri, by the Chuwar road going through Peykhu, I sat down by the side of the road and watched what was going on. Some pretty young girls wearing jewels passed me on their way to Nokme. Seeing my emaciated body, one of them said, "Look! What misery! May I never be reborn as such a creature." Another one said, "How pitiful! A sight like that depresses me." I thought to myself, "I have compassion for these ignorant beings." And, feeling pity, I stood up and said to them, "Daughters, do not speak in this way. There is no reason for you to be so distressed. You could not be born like me, even if you wished. It is astonishing that you feel compassion, but your compassion comes from pride and a wrong understanding. . . ."

Then Bodhi Raja of Ngandzong asked: "Lama Rimpoche, it seems to me that you are either the incarnation of Vajradhara Buddha and that you engage in all these actions for the benefit of sentient beings, or you are a great Bodhisattva who has attained the state of 'Non-returning' and who has accumulated immense merit for many aeons. In you, I see all the characteristics of a true yogin who sacrifices his life for the Dharma practice. We human individuals cannot even conceive the extent of your asceticism and your devotion to your lama, let alone practice it ourselves. If we dared to practice in this way, our bodies could not bear such an ordeal. That is why it is certain that you were a Buddha or Bodhisattva from the very beginning. And so, although I am incapable of religion, I believe that we sentient beings will be led toward liberation from samsara through seeing your face and hearing your words. Revered Master, I beg you to tell us if you are the incarnation of a Buddha or a Bodhisattva."

The master replied: "I never heard whose incarnation I am. Maybe I am the incarnation of a being from the three lower realms, but if you see me as Buddha you will receive his blessing by virtue of your faith. Although this belief that I am an incarnation springs from your devotion to me, actually there is no greater impediment to your practice. It is a distortion of the true Dharma. The fault lies in not recognizing the true nature of the achievement of great sinner like myself has reached a stage not far from Enlightenment due to my belief in karma, my subsequent renunciation of the aims of worldly life, and due especially to my single-minded devotion to meditation.

"More particularly, if you receive initiation and the secret instruction which brings spontaneous awakening unclouded by conceptualizations, and if you then mediate under the guidance of an enlightened lama, you will undoubtedly attain Enlightenment.

"If you commit the ten harmful deeds and the five deadly sins, without doubt you will be reborn into the torments of the lowest realms. This is because there is no belief in karma and but little devotion to the Dharma.

"Whoever wholeheartedly believes in karma and dreads the suffering of the lower realms, a great longing for illumination will arise in him. This will lead him to devote himself to a lama, to meditation, and to maintaining a deeper insight.

It is possible for every ordinary man to persevere as I have done. To consider a man of such perseverance as the reincarnation of a Buddha or as a Bodhiasattva is a sign of not believing in the short path. Put your faith in the great law of cause and effect. Contemplate the lives of enlightened teachers; reflect upon karma, the misery of the cycle of existence, the true value of human life, and not knowing the hour of death. Devote yourselves to the practice of the Vajrayana!"

TEACHING

The Sermon on the Four Noble Truths*

This excerpt from The Turning the Wheel of the Law Sutra *is known as the Benares Sermon. It is an excellent statement of the essentials of Buddhist teaching: the middle way, the Four Noble Truths and the Eightfold Path.*[16]

Reverence to the Blessed One, the Holy One, the Fully Enlightened One!

Thus have I heard. The Blessed One was once staying at Benares, at the hermitage called Migadaya. The Blessed One addressed the company of the five monks, and said, "There are two extremes, O monks, which the man who has given up the world ought not to follow. The first is the habitual practice of those things whose attraction depends upon the passions. This is especially true of sensuality. It is a low and pagan way, unworthy, unprofitable, and fit only for the worldly minded. Second is the habitual practice of asceticism, which is painful, unworthy, and unprofitable.

"There is a middle path, O monks, avoiding these two extremes, discovered by the Tathagata. This path opens the eyes, bestows understanding, leads to peace of mind, to the higher wisdom, to full enlightenment, and to Nirvana! What is that middle path, O monks, avoiding these two extremes, discovered by the Tathagata, the path that opens the eyes, and bestows understanding, which leads to peace of mind, to the higher wisdom, to full enlightenment, to Nirvana? Truly, it is this Noble Eightfold Path, that is to say: Right views; Right aspirations; Right speech; Right conduct; Right livelihood; Right effort; Right mindfulness; and Right contemplation. . . .

[5] "Now this, O monks, is the noble truth concerning suffering. Birth brings pain, decay is painful, disease is painful, death is painful. Union with the unpleasant is painful, painful is separation from the pleasant. Any craving that is unsatisfied, that too is painful. In brief, the five aggregates that spring from attachment, the conditions of individuality and their cause, are painful. This, O monks, is the noble truth concerning suffering.

"Now this, O monks, is the noble truth concerning the origin of suffering. Truly, it is the thirst or craving, causing the renewal of existence, accompanied by sensual delight, seeking satisfaction now here, now there. That is to say, it is the craving for the gratification of the passions, or the craving for a future life, or the craving for success in this present life. This, O monks, is the noble truth concerning the origin of suffering.

"Now this, O monks, is the noble truth concerning the destruction of suffering. Truly, it is the destruction, in which no passion remains, of this very thirst. It is the laying aside of, the get-

* *Dhammacakkappavattana Sutta* 1–8
[16] Taken, with editing, from Rhys Davids, *Buddhist Suttas,* pp. 146–155.

ting rid of, the being free from, the harboring no longer of this thirst. This, O monks, is the noble truth concerning the destruction of suffering.

"Now this, O monks, is the noble truth concerning the way which leads to the destruction of sorrow. Truly, it is this Noble Eightfold Path. . . .

[21] "As long, O monks, as my knowledge and insight were not quite clear regarding each of these Four Noble Truths in this triple order, in this twelvefold manner, I was uncertain whether I had attained to the full insight of that wisdom that is unsurpassed in the heavens or on earth, among the whole race of Samanas and Brahmins, or of gods or men. But as soon as my knowledge and insight were quite clear regarding each of these four noble truths, in this triple order, in this twelvefold manner, then I became certain that I had attained to the full insight of that wisdom that is unsurpassed in the heavens or on earth, among the whole race of Samanas and Brahmins, or of gods or men. Now this knowledge and this insight has arisen within me. The emancipation of my heart is immovable. This is my last existence. Now there will be no rebirth for me!"

Thus spoke the Blessed One. The five monks praised the words of the Blessed One and were glad. When the discourse had been uttered, there arose within the venerable Kondanna the eye of truth, spotless, and without a stain. He saw that whatever has an origin also inherently must end.

[25] And when the royal chariot wheel of the truth had been set rolling by the Blessed One, the gods of the earth . . . the attendant gods of the four great kings . . . and the gods in the highest heaven gave forth a shout. They said, "In Benares, at the hermitage of the Migadaya, the supreme wheel of the empire of Truth has been set rolling by the Blessed One. That wheel can never be turned back by any Samana or Brahmin, nor by any god, nor by any Brahma or Mara, not by anyone in the universe!" In an instant, a second, a moment, this sound went up to the world of Brahma. This great ten-thousand-world-system quaked and trembled and was shaken violently. An immeasurably bright light appeared in the universe, beyond even the power of the gods!

The *Skandhas* and the Chain of Causation*

The skandhas *are the elements that together make up the human personality. They relate to the no-soul doctrine of Theravada Buddhism. This passage outlines these* skandhas *and then traces the chain of causation that leads to suffering.*[17]

The omniscient lion of the Sakyas [i.e., Buddha] then caused all the assembly, headed by those who belonged to the company of Maitriya, to turn the wheel of the Law.[18] . . .

[28] The body is composed of the five skandhas, and produced from the five elements. It is all empty and without soul, and arises from the action of the chain of causation. This chain of causation is the cause of coming into existence, and the cessation of this chain is the cause of the state of cessation.

[30] He who knows this wants to promote the good of the world. Let him hold fast the chain of causation, with his mind fixed on wisdom. Let him embrace the vow of self-denial for the sake of wisdom, and practice the four perfections, and go through existence always doing good to all beings. Then having become an Arhat and conquered all the wicked, even the hosts of Mara, and attained the threefold wisdom, he

---

* *Buddhacarita* 16.1, 28–50

[17] Taken, with editing, from Cowell, *Buddhist Mahayana Texts,* pp. 174–80.

[18] *turn the wheel of the Law:* give and spread the true teaching.

shall enter Nirvana. Whoever has his mind indifferent and is empty of all desire for any further form of existence, let him abolish one by one the several steps of the chain of causation. When these effects of the chain of causation are ended one by one, he at last, being free from all stain and substratum, will pass into a blissful Nirvana.

[35] "Listen, all of you, for your own happiness, with your minds free from stain. I will declare to you step by step this chain of causation. The idea of ignorance is what gives the root to the huge poison-tree of mundane existence with its trunk of pain. The impressions are caused by this, which produce [the acts of] the body, voice, and mind. Consciousness arises from these impressions, which produces the five senses and the mind. The organism that is sometimes called samgna or samdarsana, springs from this; and from this arises the six organs of the senses, including the mind.

"The association of the six organs with their objects is called 'contact.' The consciousness of these different contacts is called 'sensation.' [40] Craving is produced by this, which is the desire of being troubled by worldly objects. 'Attachment to continued existence,' arising from this, sets itself in action towards pleasure and the rest. From attachment springs continued existence, which is sensual, possessing form, or formless. From existence arises birth through a returning to various wombs. On birth is dependent the se-

ries of old age, death, sorrow and the like. By putting a stop to ignorance and what follows from it, all these cease successively. This is the chain of causation, which has many turns, whose sphere of action is created by ignorance. This is to be meditated upon by you who enjoy dwelling tranquilly in lonely woods. He who knows it thoroughly reaches at last to absolute thinness. Then he becomes blissfully extinct.

"When you have learned this, to be freed from the bond of existence you must cut down ignorance with all your efforts, for it is the root of pain. [45] Then, set free from the bonds of the prison-house of existence, you will possess as Arhats natures perfectly pure. You shall attain Nirvana."

Having heard this lesson preached by the chief of saints, all the mendicants understood the course and the cessation of embodied existence. As these five ascetics listened to his words, their intellectual eye was purified for the attainment of perfect wisdom. The eye of dharma was purified in six hundred millions of gods, and the eye of wisdom in eight hundred millions of Brahmans. The eye of dharma was purified in eighty thousand men, and even in all beings an ardor for the Law was made visible. [50] Everywhere all kinds of evil became tranquilized, and everywhere an ardor for all that helps the good Law manifested itself.

The Essence of Buddhism*

With its full title The Heart of Transcendent Wisdom, *this scripture is one of the best known in Buddhism. The* Heart Sutra *personifies wisdom as a woman, especially at its beginning and end. In a religion often given to verbose writings, this one is remarkable for its brevity.*[19]

* Heart Sutra
[19] From Douglas A. Fox, trans., *The Heart of Buddhist Wisdom* (Lewiston, NY: Mellen, 1986). Copyright 1985 by Douglas A. Fox. Used by permission.

Honor to the Omniscient. [or, Honor to the Lady, Noble Transcendent Wisdom.]

The noble bodhisattva Avalokitesvara was brooding in the flowing depths of the course of Transcendent Wisdom. Looking about, he sees the five skandhas to be empty of essence.

Here, Sariputra, form is emptiness, emptiness is form. Form is not other than emptiness, and emptiness is not other than form. That which is form equals emptiness, and that which is emptiness is also form. Precisely the same may be said of form and the other skandhas: feeling, perception, impulse, and consciousness.

Here, Sariputra, all dharmas bear the marks of emptiness, which are: not to have arisen nor to have been suppressed, neither to be corrupt nor pure, and to be neither unfinished nor complete.

Therefore, Sariputra, emptiness is not form, nor feeling, perception, impulse, nor consciousness. It is not the eye, ear, nose, tongue, body, or mind. It is not shape, sound, odor, flavor, nor object of touch or thought. It is not the experience of vision (and so on until we reach) it is not elements of mental discrimination. It is not learning or ignorance, and it is not the elimination of learning or ignorance (and so on until we reach) it is not senility and death, and it is not the elimination of senility and death. It is not suffering, beginning, ceasing, or a path. It is not knowledge, not attainment or realization, and therefore neither is it nonattainment.

[5] The bodhisattva, bound to Transcendent Wisdom, lives with nothing clouding his mind. Lacking confusion, he is intrepid, and having passed beyond error, reaches nirvana.

All Buddhas, of the past, present, or future, bound to irrefutable Transcendent Wisdom, reach completely full understanding and the highest awakening.

Therefore Transcendent Wisdom should be known as the great mantra, the great knowledge mantra, the invincible mantra, the unsurpassable mantra, causing all suffering to cease. It is trustworthy because it is not false. It is the mantra proclaimed in the *Prajnaparamita,* and it is this: Oh, you [Lady] who are gone, gone, gone beyond, gone utterly beyond: Hail Wisdom!

With these words *The Heart of Transcendent Wisdom* is complete.

A Tibetan Commentary on the *Heart Sutra**

Although this commentary is not part of Buddhist scripture, it illustrates how scripture is interpreted and used in Tibet. The author bsTandar-lha-ram-pa, (ca. 1758–1839) belonged to the dGe-lugs-pa school.[20]

Regarding how [the Perfection of Wisdom Sutras] were propagated in the snowy land of Tibet, during the time of Khri-srong-sde-btsan (740–ca. 798), Nyang-kham-pa, also known as rLangs-kham-pa Go-cha-bya-pa, acquired the ability to memorize without forgetting and was sent to [India] to bring back the Perfection of Wisdom. He memorized the *Vast Mother,* covered his back with a cover of gold, covered his front with a cover of turquoise, tied it with a string of pearls, and returned [to Tibet]. What he had in his mind was dictated in four volumes.

It did not say *uatasahasrika* in Sanskrit and is called "the red draft," "the translation of the mind of rLangs," and "[the text] kept in a deer leather bag." Also, Manjusri of sBas and Indravaro of Nyang translated the Indian text in four volumes. It . . . was called the "hundred thousand taxes" and the blue draft. These versions were greatly condensed books, almost like notes. The red [draft] was written with vermillion mixed with blood from the nose of the Dharma king [Khri-srong-sde-btsan] himself. The blue [draft] received its name from being written with indigo mixed with singed hair from [his] head. The [text] kept in a leather bag was named for the vessel in which it was kept. The container in which it was placed was a deer skin bag. The "hundred thousand taxes" was so-called because it was translated after taxes had been gathered from the subjects. . . .

With regard to the second, the meaning of the parts [of the *Heart Sutra*], there are two sections, the preliminary [stanzas] and the actual [sutra]. Regarding the first, in great monasteries

* *Jewel Light Illuminating the Meaning*
[20] From Donald S. Lopez, Jr., *The Heart Sutra Explained: Indian and Tibetan Commentaries* (Albany: State University of New York Press, 1988). Used by permission.

such as Se-ra and 'Bras spung (Drepung), before reciting the sutra, it is customary [to recite] these verses of praise and obeisance:

I bow down to the mother of the Conquerors
    of the three times,
The perfection of wisdom, inexpressible by
    words or thoughts,
Which is unproduced and unceased [like] the
    entity of the sky,
The object of the wisdom of unique knowledge.

It is said that these verses are words recited by the [Buddha's] son, Rahula, to his mother. The meaning is that the wisdom that goes and is gone beyond samsara does so by means of the wisdom that directly realizes emptiness; [that wisdom] is not an object that can be expressed by speaking words or thinking thoughts. Because that wisdom is not created by way of its own entity, it is not destroyed, but, like the expanse of the sky, is the negation of being established by way of its own entity. That very thing which serves as the sphere of the unique knowledge of meditative equipoise is the mother that gives birth to all the Conquerors of the three times. It is obeisance to the wisdom that know emptiness directly.

With respect to the second, the actual explanation, there are also two parts, the meaning of the title and the meaning of the text. That which in the language of India is Bhagavatiprajnaparamitahrdaya, when translated into Tibetan is "The Heart of the Transcendent and Victorious Perfection of Wisdom," and that is the title of the sutra. Regarding the purpose for stating the title,

if a name were not given, there would be no way of finding out which sutra it was. Hence, the name is stated at the beginning. Regarding the word "heart," for example, [the place] where all the consciousnesses that pervade the entire body gather is called the heart. In the same way, all the meanings of the vast, intermediate, and condensed Mother sutras are gathered here. Therefore, it is called the sutra of sutras or the heart of sutras. All of the intentions of the Transcendent Victor are gathered in this sutra. As Tsong-kha-pa says in his *Legs bshad snying po chung ba*:

Whatever you have spoken
Begins from dependent arising
And is for the purpose of passing beyond
    sorrow.
You have no activities that do not bring peace.

The Transcendent Victor thinks only of methods by which sentient beings may pass beyond sorrow, and the method by which they pass beyond sorrow is the wisdom realizing emptiness. Therefore, it is called the essence of wisdom. That which passes beyond sorrow is the reality of sentient beings' minds. Therefore, it is called the essence of Tathagatas. When it is understood that everything in the sutras and tantras only sets forth methods for purifying the taints of sentient beings' minds, it is realized that all the teachings are without contradiction. Therefore, because all the Buddhas of the three times are born from the wisdom realizing emptiness, that wisdom is referred to with the term "mother." This is the idea behind *bhagavati*.

A Description of Nirvana*

The Milindapanha, *or "Questions of King Milinda," is a famous text illustrating the kind of doctrinal conversations that took place as Buddhism spread through Asia. Although it is not canonical, it has the use and wide influence of scripture.*

King Milinda (Menander) was a king of Greek descent who ruled in the far northwest of India in the second century B.C.E. *This passage explains basic Buddhist teaching on Nirvana.*[21]

* Milinda-panha 4.8.65–66

[21] Taken, with editing, from T. W. Rhys Davids, *The Questions of King Milinda* (Oxford: Oxford University Press, 1894), pp. 188–89.

King Milinda said: "I will grant you, Nagasena, that nothing is like nirvana. It is pure bliss. One cannot point to its form or shape, its duration or size, either by simile or explanation, by reason or by argument. But is there perhaps some quality of nirvana which it shares with other things, and which lends itself to a metaphorical explanation?"

"Its form, O king, cannot be elucidated by similes, but its qualities can."

"How good to hear that, Nagasena! Speak then, quickly, so that I may have an explanation of even one of the aspects of nirvana! Appease the fever of my heart! Allay it with the cool sweet breezes of your words!"

"Nirvana shares one quality with the lotus, two with water, three with medicine, ten with space, three with the wishing jewel, and five with a mountain peak. As the lotus is unstained by water, so is nirvana unstained by all the defilements. As cool water allays feverish heat, so also nirvana is cool and allays the fever of all the passions. Moreover, as water removes the thirst of men and beast who are exhausted, parched, thirsty, and overpowered by heat, so also nirvana re-moves the craving for sensuous enjoyments, the craving for further becoming, the craving for the cessation of becoming. As medicine protects from the torments of poison, so nirvana from the torments of the poisonous passions. Moreover, as medicine puts an end to sickness so nirvana to all sufferings. Finally, nirvana and medicine both give security. And these are the ten qualities which nirvana shares with space. Neither is born, grows, old, dies, passes away, or is reborn; both are unconquerable, cannot be stolen, are unsupported, are roads . . . to all one can desire, bring joy, and shed light. As a mountain peak is lofty and exalted, so is nirvana. As a mountain peak is unshakeable, so is nirvana. As a mountain peak is inaccessible, so is nirvana inaccessible to all the passions. As no seeds can grow on a mountain peak, so the seeds of all the passions cannot grow in nirvana. And finally, as a mountain peak is free from all desire to please or displease, so is nirvana."

"Well said, Nagasena! So it is, and as such I accept it."

A Mahayana View of the Buddha*

In Mahayana, the Buddha is a gracious savior who enables both monks and laity to reach nirvana. This first selection from the Lotus Sutra of the True Law *argues that the Mahayana ("Large Vehicle") is in fact the only vehicle in Buddhism. In the second, the* Lotus Sutra *itself is the gift of the Buddha that enables those who read and venerate it to come to nirvana. This veneration is today especially prominent in Nichiren Buddhism.*[22]

Only now and then, Sariputra, does the Tathagata preach such a discourse on the law as this. Just as only now and then is seen the blossom of the fig tree, Sariputra, so does the Tathagata only now and then preach such a discourse on the law. Believe me, Sariputra. I speak what is real, I speak what is truthful, I speak what is right. It is difficult to understand the exposition of the mystery of the Tathagata, Sariputra. For in explaining the law, Sariputra, I use hundreds of thousands of various skilful means, such as different interpretations, indications, explanations, illustrations. It is not by reasoning, Sariputra, that the law is to be found: it is beyond the pale of reasoning, and must be learned from the Tathagata. For, Sariputra, it is for a sole object, a sole aim, truly a lofty object, a lofty aim that the Buddha, the Tathagata, appears in the world. And what is that sole object, that sole aim, that lofty object, that lofty aim of the Buddha, the Tathagata, appearing in the world? To show all creatures

---

* *Saddharma-pundarika Sutra* 2.36; 10.1
[22] Taken, with editing, from H. Kern, trans., *The Saddharma-Pundarika, Sacred Books of the East,* vol. 21 (Oxford: Oxford University Press, 1884), pp. 39–49, 213–214.

the sight of Tathagata-knowledge, the Buddha, the Tathagata, appears in the world. To open the eyes of creatures for the sight of Tathagata-knowledge, the Buddha, the Tathagata, appears in the world. . . .

For, Sariputra, I show all creatures the sight of Tathagata-knowledge. I open the eyes of creatures for the sight of Tathagata-knowledge. I firmly establish the teaching of Tathagata-knowledge, Sariputra. I lead the teaching of Tathagata-knowledge on the right path, Sariputra. By means of one sole vehicle, namely, the Buddha-vehicle, Sariputra, I teach creatures the law. There is no second vehicle, nor a third. This is the nature of the law, Sariputra, universally in the world, in all directions. For all the Tathagatas, who in times past existed in countless, innumerable spheres in all directions for the welfare of many, the happiness of many, out of pity to the world, for the benefit, welfare, and happiness of the great body of creatures, preached the law to gods and men with able means. These means include several directions and indications, various arguments, reasons, illustrations, fundamental ideas, interpretations. They pay regard to the dispositions of creatures whose inclinations and temperaments are so varied. All those Buddhas and Lords have preached the law to creatures by means of only one vehicle, the Buddha-vehicle, which finally leads to omniscience. It is identical with showing all creatures the sight of Tathagata-knowledge; with opening the eyes of creatures for the sight of Tathagata-knowledge; with the awakening (or admonishing) by the display (or sight) of Tathagata-knowledge; with leading the teaching of Tathagata-knowledge on the right path. Such is the law they have preached to creatures. And those creatures who have heard the law from the past Tathagatas have all reached supreme, perfect enlightenment.

The Tathagatas who shall exist in future, Sariputra, in countless, innumerable spheres in all directions for the weal of many, the happiness of many, out of pity to the world, for the benefit, weal, and happiness of the great body of creatures, shall preach the law to gods and men. . . .

Such is the law they shall preach to creatures. Those creatures, Sariputra, who shall hear the law from the future Tathagatas shall all reach supreme, perfect enlightenment.

The Tathagatas who now are staying, living, existing, Sariputra, in countless, innumerable spheres in all directions preach the law to gods and men. . . . Such is the law they are preaching to creatures. Those creatures, Sariputra, who are hearing the law from the present Tathagatas shall all reach supreme, perfect enlightenment.

I myself also, Sariputra, am at the present period a Tathagata, for the weal of many. . . . I myself, also, Sariputra, am preaching the law to creatures. . . . Such is the law I preach to creatures. Those creatures, Sariputra, who now are hearing the law from me shall all reach supreme, perfect enlightenment. In this sense, Sariputra, it must be understood that nowhere in the world a second vehicle is taught, far less a third.

[10.1] The Lord then addressed the eighty thousand Bodhisattvas Mahasattvas by turning to Bhaishajyaraga as their representative. "Do you see, Bhaishajyaraga, in this assembly the many gods, Nagas, goblins, Gandharvas, demons, Garudas, Kinnaras, great serpents, men, and beings not human, monks, nuns, male and female lay devotees, votaries of the vehicle of disciples, votaries of the vehicle of Pratyekabuddhas, and those of the vehicle of Bodhisattvas, who have heard this teaching from the mouth of the Tathagata?"

"I do, Lord; I do, Sugata."

The Lord proceeded: "All those Bodhisattvas Mahasattvas who in this assembly have heard well only a single stanza, a single verse [or word], or who even by a single rising thought have joyfully accepted this Sutra, to all of them, Bhaishajyaraga, among the four classes of my audience I predict their destiny to supreme and perfect enlightenment. Whoever after the complete extinction of the Tathagata shall hear this Dharmaparyaya and after hearing, if only a single stanza, joyfully accept it, even with a single rising thought, to those also, Bhaishajyaraga, be they young men or young women of good family,[23] I predict their destiny to supreme and perfect enlightenment. Those young men or women of good family, Bhaishajyaraga, shall be worshippers of many hundred thousand myriads . . . of Buddhas. Those young men or women of good family, Bhaishajyaraga, shall have made a vow under hundreds of thousands of myriads of Buddhas. They must be considered as reborn among the people of Jambudvipa, out of compassion to all creatures. They shall be reborn who shall take, read, make known, recite, copy, and after copy-

ing always keep in memory and from time to time regard were it but a single stanza of this teaching; who by that book shall feel veneration for the Tathagatas, treat them with the respect due to Masters, honor, revere, worship them; who shall worship that book with flowers, incense, perfumed garlands, ointment, powder, clothes, umbrellas, flags, banners, music, etc., and with acts of reverence such as bowing and joining hands. In short, Bhaishajyaraga, any young men or young women of good family who shall keep or joyfully accept only a single stanza of this teaching, to all of them, Bhaishajyaraga, I predict their destiny of supreme and perfect enlightenment."

---

[23] *Young men or women of good family:* layfolk can also reach nirvana.

Poems of Early Nuns*

Buddhist scripture records many poems from the first generations of nuns. The first one given here is by Pajapati, Gautama's "nanny"; here she tells of her previous lives and liberation from the Buddha. In the second poem, Buddha and Pajapati's daughter Nanda converse prior to her entering the sangha. The final poem is by Vaddhesi, Pajapati's friend, and relates her enlightenment.[24]

A POEM BY PAJAPATI

Homage to you Buddha,
best of all creatures,
who set me and many others
free from pain.

All pain is understood,
the cause, the craving is dried up,
the Noble Eightfold Way unfolds,
I have reached the state where everything stops.

I have been
mother,
son,

father,
brother,
grandmother;
knowing nothing of the truth
I journeyed on.

But I have seen the Blessed One;
this is my last body,
and I will not go
from birth to birth
again.

Look at the disciples all together,
their energy,
their sincere effort.
This is homage to the buddhas.

Maya gave birth to Gautama
for the sake of us all.
She has driven back the pain
of the sick and the dying.

A POEM BY NANDA

[Buddha:] Nanda,
look at the body,
diseased, impure, rotten.
Focus the mind
on all this foulness.

---

* *Therigatha*
[24] From Susan Murcott, *The First Buddhist Women: Translations and Commentaries from the Therigatha* (Berkeley, CA: Parallax Press, 1991). Used by permission.

(Then the Buddha made an image of a lovely
   woman and it aged before Nanda's eyes. He
   went on:)

Your body is like this,
and this is like your body.
It stinks of decay,
only a fool would love it.

[Nanda:] So day and night
without letting up,
I looked at it this way,
and by my own wisdom,
I perceived it fully,
I saw.

Watching carefully,
I plumbed to the very origin,
and saw this body as it really is,
inside and out.

Deep inside myself,
I have lost interest in passion.
I am careful, quenched,
calm, and free.

[A POEM BY VADDHESI]

It was twenty-five years
since I left home,
and I hadn't had a moment's peace.

Uneasy at heart,
steeped in longing for pleasure,
I held out my arms and cried out
as I entered the monastery.

I went up to a nun
I thought I could trust.
She taught me the Dharma,
the elements of body and mind,
the nature of perception,
and earth, water, fire, and wind.

I heard her words
and sat down beside her.
Now I have entered the six realms of sacred
   knowledge:
I know I have lived before,
the eye of heaven is pure,
and I know the minds of others.

I have great magic powers
and have annihilated
all the obsessions of the mind.
The Buddha's teaching has been done.

ETHICS

Conduct of the Monk*

The Dhammapada *("Path of Teaching") is one of
the fifteen books in the* Khuddaka-nikaya *of the*
Sutta Pitaka. *A first-century* B.C.E. *collection of
wise sayings, it summarizes Buddhist moral wisdom. Monks and nuns often memorize it at the beginning of their training, and it is studied as well
by the laity.*[25]

Restraint in the eye is good, restraint in the ear is
good, restraint in the nose is good, restraint in
the tongue is good. In the body restraint is good,
in speech restraint is good, in thought restraint is
good. Restraint is good in all things. A monk restrained in all things is freed from all pain.

People call a monk one who controls his
hand, who controls his feet, who controls his
speech, who is well controlled, who delights inwardly, who is collected, who is solitary and content. The monk who controls his mouth, who
speaks wisely and calmly, who teaches the meaning and the law, his word is sweet.

---

* *Dhammapada* 25:360–382
[25] Taken, with editing, from Max Müller, *The Dhammapada,
Sacred Books of the East,* vol. 10 (Oxford: Oxford University
Press, 1881), pp. 85–88.

He who dwells in the law, delights in the law, meditates on the law, follows the law, that monk will never fall away from the true law.

[365] Let him not despise what he has received, nor ever envy others; a mendicant who envies others does not obtain peace of mind.

Even the gods will praise a monk who, though he receives little, does not despise what he has received, if his life is pure and if he is not lazy.

He who never identifies himself with his name and form, and does not grieve over what he has left behind, he indeed is called a monk.

The monk who acts with kindness, who is calm in the doctrine of Buddha, will reach the quiet place [Nirvana], cessation of natural desires, and happiness. O monk, empty this boat! If emptied, it will go quickly. When you have cut off passion and hatred, you will go to Nirvana.

[370] Cut off the five senses, leave the five, rise above the five. A monk who has escaped from the five fetters is called Oghatinna, "saved from the flood."

Meditate, O monk, and do be not careless! Do not direct your thought to what gives pleasure. Then you may not have to swallow the iron ball (in hell), and that you may not cry out when burning, "This is pain."

Without knowledge there is no meditation, without meditation there is no knowledge. He who has knowledge and meditation is near to Nirvana.

A monk who has entered his empty house, whose mind is tranquil, feels a super-human delight when he sees the law clearly. When he has considered the origin and destruction of the elements (skandhas) of the body, he finds happiness and joy that belong to those who know the immortal (Nirvana).

[375] This is the beginning here for a wise monk: watchfulness over the senses, contentedness, restraint under the law; keeping noble friends whose life is pure and who are not lazy.

Let him live in charity, let him be perfect in his duties. Then in the fullness of delight he will put an end to his suffering.

As the Vassika plant sheds its withered flowers, men should shed passion and hatred, O monks!

The monk whose body and tongue and mind are quieted, who is collected, and has rejected the baits of the world, he is called quiet.

Rouse yourself by yourself, examine yourself by yourself, thus self-protected and attentive you will live happily, O monk!

[380] The self is the lord of self, self is the refuge of self. Therefore curb yourself as the merchant curbs a good horse.

The monk full of delight, who is calm in the doctrine of Buddha, will reach the quiet place (Nirvana), cessation of natural desires, and happiness.

Even a young monk who applies himself to the doctrine of Buddha will brighten up this world like the moon when free from clouds.

Admonition to Laity*

At the end of a discussion of monastic morality, the Buddha lays down instructions for householders (laity). Note how the rules given are modeled on those given to monks.

I will also tell you about the householder's work. . . .

Let him not kill, nor cause to be killed any living being, nor let him approve of others killing. Let him refrain from hurting all creatures, both those that are strong and those that tremble.

[20] Then let [him] abstain from taking anything in any place that has not been given to

---

* *Cullavagga, Dhammikasutta* 18–29

him, knowing it to belong to another. Let him not cause anyone to take, nor approve of those that take. Let him avoid all theft.

Let the wise man avoid an unchaste life as a burning heap of coals. If he is not able to live a life of chastity, let him not transgress with another man's wife.

Let no one speak falsely to another in the hall of justice or in the hall of the assembly. Let him not cause anyone to speak falsely, nor approve of those that speak falsely. Let him avoid all sort of untruth.

Let the householder who approves of the Dhamma not give himself to intoxicating drinks. Let him not cause others to drink, nor approve of those who drink, knowing it to end in madness. For through intoxication stupid people commit sins and make other people intoxicated. Let him avoid this seat of sin, this madness, this folly, which is delightful to the stupid.

[25] Let him not kill any living being, let him not take what has not been given [to him], let him not speak falsely, and let him not drink intoxicating drinks, let him refrain from unchaste

sexual intercourse, and let him not eat untimely food at night. Let him not wear wreaths nor use perfumes, let him lie on a couch spread on the earth. They call this the eightfold abstinence (*uposatha*), proclaimed by Buddha, who has overcome pain.

Having with a believing mind kept abstinence (*uposatha*) on the fourteenth, fifteenth, and the eighth days of the half-month, and having kept the complete *Patiharakapakkha*[26] consisting of eight parts, then in the morning, after having kept abstinence, let a wise man with a believing mind make distributions according to his ability. Thus he will gladden the assembly of monks with food and drink.

Let him dutifully maintain his parents, and practice an honorable trade. The householder who observes this strenuously goes to the gods called Sayampabhas.

---

[26] *Patiharakapakkha:* further rules for continual abstinence and self-control.

Wisdom of the Buddha*

This passage, often called "Twin Verses," is a general treatment of Buddhist morality. Each paragraph has two verses, usually opposites. A second section, from the chapter "On the Self," urges the virtue of self-reliance and self-dedication in the path to enlightenment.[27]

All that we are is the result of what we have thought: it is founded on our thoughts, it is made up of our thoughts. If a man speaks or acts with an evil thought, pain follows him, as the wheel follows the foot of the ox that draws the carriage. All that we are is the result of what we have

thought. It is founded on our thoughts, it is made up of our thoughts. If a man speaks or acts with a pure thought, happiness follows him like a shadow that never leaves him.

"He abused me, he beat me, he defeated me, he robbed me"—in those who harbor such thoughts hatred will never cease. "He abused me, he beat me, he defeated me, he robbed me"—in those who do not harbor such thoughts hatred will cease.

[5] For hatred does not cease by hatred at any time. Hatred ceases by love; this is an old rule. The world does not know that we must all come to an end here. But for those who know it, their quarrels cease at once.

He who lives looking for pleasures only, his senses uncontrolled, immoderate in his food,

---

* *Dhammapada* 1–20, 157–166
[27] Taken, with editing, from Müller, *The Dhammapada,* pp. 1–8, 45–46.

idle, and weak, Mara [the tempter] will certainly overthrow him, as the wind throws down a weak tree. He who lives without looking for pleasures, his senses well controlled, moderate in his food, faithful and strong, him Mara will certainly not overthrow, any more than the wind throws down a rocky mountain.

He who wishes to put on the yellow clothing²⁸ without having cleansed himself from sin, who disregards also temperance and truth, is unworthy of the yellow clothing. [10] But he who has cleansed himself from sin is well grounded in all virtues, and also keeps temperance and truth, he is worthy of the yellow clothing.

They who imagine truth in untruth, and see untruth in truth, never arrive at truth, but follow empty desires. They who know truth in truth, and untruth in untruth, arrive at truth, and follow true desires.

As rain breaks through a poorly thatched house, passion will break through an unreflecting mind. As rain does not break through a well-thatched house, passion will not break through a well-reflecting mind.

[15] The evildoer mourns in this world, and he mourns in the next; he mourns in both. He mourns and suffers when he sees the evil of his own work. The virtuous man delights in this world, and he delights in the next; he delights in both. He delights and rejoices when he sees the purity of his own work.

The evildoer suffers in this world, and he suffers in the next; he suffers in both. He suffers when he thinks of the evil he has done. He suffers more when going on the evil path. The virtuous man is happy in this world, and he is happy in the next; he is happy in both. He is happy when he thinks of the good he has done. He is still more happy when going on the good path.

The thoughtless man, even if he can recite a large portion [of the law], but is not a doer of it, has no share in the priesthood. He is like a cowherd counting the cows of others. [20] The follower of the law, even if he can recite only a small portion [of the law], but, having forsaken passion and hatred and foolishness, possesses true knowledge and serenity of mind, he, caring for nothing in this world or that to come, has a share in the order of monks.

[157, On the Self] If a man hold himself dear, let him watch himself carefully. During at least one out of the three watches [of the night] a wise man should be watchful.

Let each man direct himself first to what is proper, then let him teach others. Thus a wise man will not suffer.

If a man make himself as he teaches others to be, being himself well subdued, he may subdue [others]. One's own self is indeed difficult to subdue.

[160] The self is the lord of self; who else could be the lord? With self well subdued, a man finds a lord such as few can find.

The evil done by oneself, self-begotten, self-bred, crushes the foolish, as a diamond breaks a precious stone.

He whose wickedness is very great brings himself down to that state where his enemy wishes him to be, as a creeping vine does with the tree that it surrounds.

Bad deeds and deeds hurtful to ourselves are easy to do. What is beneficial and good is very difficult to do.

The foolish man who scorns the rule of the venerable [Arhat], of the elect [Ariya], of the virtuous, and follows false doctrine, bears fruit to his own destruction, like the fruits of the Katthaka reed.

[165] By oneself evil is done, by oneself one suffers. By oneself evil is left undone, by oneself one is purified. Purity and impurity belong to oneself; no one can purify another.

Let no one forget his own duty for the sake of another's, however great. Let a man, after he has discerned his own duty, always be attentive to his duty.

---

²⁸ *the yellow clothing:* the saffron gown of the monk.

The Bodhisattva Ideal*

This simple and eloquent passage describes all the moral qualities of the bodhisattva. It comes from a text that is a transition from Theravada to Mahayana.

They are Bodhisattvas who live on from life to life in the possession of manifold good qualities. They are Bodhisattvas who have won the mastery over karma, and made their deeds renowned through their accumulation of merit. They are resolute and valiant, intent on endurance, trustworthy, upright and sincere. They are generous, firm, gentle, tender, patient, whole and tranquil of heart, difficult to overcome and defeat, intent on what is real, charitable, and faithful to their promises. They are intelligent, brilliantly intelligent, gifted with insight, and not given to gratification of sensual desires. They are devoted to the highest good. They win converts by the means of sympathetic appeal. They are pure in conduct and clean of heart, full of exceeding great veneration, full of civility to elder and noble. They are resourceful, in all matters using conciliatory and agreeable methods, and in affairs of government they are adept in persuasive speech. They are men whose voice is not checked in the assembly, men who pour forth their eloquence in a mighty stream. With knowledge as their banner they are skilled in drawing the multitude to them. They are endowed with equanimity, and their means of living is beyond reproach. They are men of successful achievements, and are ready to come to the assistance of others and help those in distress. They do not become enervated by prosperity, and do not lose composure in adversity. They are skilled in uprooting the vices of mean men. They are unswerving in clothing the nakedness of others. They are anxious not to blight the maturing of their karma, and they acquire the roots of virtue by keeping themselves aloof from passion, hatred and folly. They are skilled in bringing solace to those in trouble and misfortune. They do no hesitate to render all kinds of service.

In all matters they are untiring in their purpose. They are endowed here in this world with the profound attributes of a Buddha. In their progress towards their goal they are undefiled in acts of body, speech and thought. Through the uprightness of their lives in former existences they are untarnished and pure in conduct. Possessing perfect knowledge they are men of undimmed understanding. They are eager to win the sphere of power of a Buddha—so far are they from refusing it. With knowledge as their banner they are untiring in speech and skilled in teaching. Being of irreproachable character they are immune from disaster. They are free from sin. They shun the threefold distractions. Leaving vain babblers alone, they love their enemies. They do not indulge in sexual pleasures. They know how to win the affection of all creatures. When they enter the world they have become endowed with powers that are in accordance with the vow they have made. In all matters they are skilled in the knowledge of correct and faulty conclusions. They are rich in goodness and blessed with good qualities. Eminent, wise in their illimitable virtue, they are serene among their fellows. On this matter it is said: As it is not possible for any bird to reach the confines of the sky, so it is not possible for any man to comprehend the good qualities of the self-becoming Buddhas.

---

* *Mahavastu*

ORGANIZATION

Founding of the Order*

After his enlightenment, the Buddha converts the five Hindu ascetics who earlier had left him when he had given up their practice of extreme asceticism. This Vinaya Pitaka selection offers a succinct view of general Buddhist teaching. Just as important, it offers a good view of the founding of the Buddhist order of monks, and therefore of the Buddhist tradition itself.[29]

The Blessed One, wandering from place to place, came to Benares, to the deer park Isipatana, to the place where the five monks were. The five monks saw the Blessed One coming from a distance. When they saw him, they agreed with each other, saying, "Friends, there comes the samana Gotama. He lives in abundance, has given up his exertions, and has turned to an abundant life. Let us not salute him, nor rise from our seats when he approaches, nor take his bowl and his robe from his hands. But let us put there a seat; if he likes, let him sit down. . . ."

When they spoke to him, the Blessed One said to the five monks, "Monks, do not address the Tathagata by his name or with the appellation 'Friend.' The Tathagata is the holy, absolute Sambuddha.[30] Give ear, O monks! Immortality has been won by me. I will teach you; I will preach the doctrine to you. If you walk in the way I show you, you will, before long, have penetrated to the truth. You yourselves will know it and see it face to face. You will live with the highest goal of the holy life, for which noble youths

give up the world completely and go forth into the houseless state."

When he had spoken, the five monks said to the Blessed One, "Friend Gotama, by those observances, by those practices, and by those austerities you have not been able to obtain power surpassing that of other men. You have not obtained the superiority of full and holy knowledge and insight. Now that you are living in abundance, have given up your exertions, and have turned to an abundant life, how will you be able to obtain power surpassing that of men? How will you obtain the superiority of full and holy knowledge and insight? . . . "

[15] The five monks spoke to the Blessed One a second time as before. And the Blessed One replied to the five monks a second time as before. And the five monks spoke to the Blessed One a third time as before. When they had spoken thus, the Blessed One said to the five monks, "Do you admit, O monks, that I have never spoken to you in this way before this day?"

"You have never spoken so, Lord."

"The Tathagata, O monks, is the holy, absolute Sambuddha. Give ear, O monks. . . ."

The Blessed One was able to convince the five monks. The five monks listened willingly to the Blessed One. They gave ear, and fixed their mind on the knowledge which Buddha imparted to them. . . . [There follows a statement of the Four Noble Truths and the Eightfold Path.]

[27] "O monks, as long as I did not possess with perfect purity this true knowledge and insight into these four Noble Truths . . . I knew that I had not yet obtained the highest, absolute Sambodhi in the world of men and gods, in Mara's and Brahma's world, among all beings, Samanas and Brahmanas, gods and men. But when I possessed with perfect purity this true knowledge and insight into these four Noble Truths . . . then I knew that I had obtained the

---

* *Mahavagga* 1.6.10, 11–16, 27–30, 32, 34, 37
[29] Taken, with editing, from T. W. Rhys Davids and Hermann Oldenberg, trans., *Vinaya Texts*, part 1, *Sacred Books of the East*, vol. 13 (Oxford: Oxford University Press, 1881), pp. 91–102.
[30] *Sambuddha:* one who has reached the insight essential to the higher stages of arhatship.

highest, universal Sambodhi in the world of men and gods. . . . This knowledge and insight arose in my mind: This emancipation of my mind cannot be lost. This is my last birth; I shall not be born again!"

Thus the Blessed One spoke. The five monks were delighted, and they rejoiced at the words of the Blessed One. When this exposition was given, the venerable Kondanna obtained the pure and spotless Eye of this truth: "Whatever is subject to the condition of origination, is subject also to the condition of cessation."

[30] And when the Blessed One had founded the Kingdom of Truth by propounding the Four Noble Truths, the earth-inhabiting gods shouted, "Truly the Blessed One has founded at Benares, in the deer park Isipatana, the highest kingdom of Truth, which may be opposed neither by a Samana nor by a Brahmana, neither by a deva, nor by Mara, nor by Brahma, nor by any being in the world." . . .

[32] The venerable Kondanna . . . overcame uncertainty, dispelled all doubts, and gained full knowledge. He was dependent on nobody else for knowledge of the doctrine of the teacher. He said to the Blessed One, "Lord, let me receive the pabbajja and upasampada ordinations from the Blessed One."

"Come, monk," said the Blessed One, "for the doctrine is well taught. Lead a holy life for the sake of the complete extinction of suffering." Then this venerable person received the ordination. . . .

[34] Then [the other monks] spoke to the Blessed One: "Lord, let us receive the pabbajja and upasampada ordinations from the Blessed One."

"Come, monks," said the Blessed One, "for the doctrine is well taught. Lead a holy life for the sake of the complete extinction of suffering." Thus these venerable persons received ordination. . . .

[47] Thus the Blessed One spoke. The five monks were delighted, and rejoiced at the words of the Blessed One. When this exposition had been given, the minds of the five monks became free from attachment to the world, and were released from the Asavas.[31] Then there were six arhants in the world.

---

[31] *Asavas:* mental defilement; the four asavas are sensuality, lust for life, false views, and ignorance.

The Rules of Defeat*

In this scripture from the Vinaya Pitaka, the "rules of defeat" are given and explained. "Defeat" means expulsion with no possibility of return. These rules govern the life of nuns as well as monks. Note at the end of the passage the ritual for confession of these faults in the monastery, the basic method of which is similar for confession of all other faults. The four prohibitions here—against sexual intercourse, theft, killing, and lying—form the basis of Buddhist morality for the laity. The only qualification is that the prohibition of sexual intercourse is modified to a prohibition of intercourse outside marriage.[32]

The four Rules concerning those acts that cause Defeat now come into recitation.

If any monk who has taken upon himself the monks' system of self-training and rule of life and has not after that withdrawn from the training, or declared his weakness, shall have sexual intercourse with anyone, down even to an ani-

---

* *Patimokkha, Parajika Dhamma* 1–4

[32] Taken, with editing, from Davids and Oldenberg, *Vinaya Texts,* part 1, pp. 3–6.

mal, he has fallen into defeat; he is no longer in communion.

If any monk shall take, from village or from forest, anything not given—what men call "theft"—he, too, has fallen into defeat; he is no longer in communion.

If any monk shall knowingly deprive a human being of life, or shall seek out an assassin against a human being, or shall utter the praises of death, or incite another to self-destruction, saying, "Ho, my friend! What good do you get from this sinful, wretched life? Death is better to you than life!"—he, too, is fallen into defeat; he is no longer in communion.

A monk, without being clearly conscious of possessing extraordinary qualities, may perhaps pretend that he has gained insight into the knowledge of the noble ones, saying, "Thus I know, thus I perceive." At some subsequent time

whether on being pressed, or without being pressed he feel guilty and may want to be cleansed from his fault. He shall say, "Brothers, when I did not know, I said that I knew; when I did not see, I said that I saw—telling a fruitless falsehood." Then, unless he spoke through undue confidence he has fallen into defeat; he is no longer in communion.

Venerable Sirs, the four Conditions of Defeat have been recited. When a monk has fallen into one or other, he is no longer allowed to reside with the monks. As before, so afterwards, he is defeated; he is not in communion.

Concerning them I ask the venerable ones, "Are you pure in this matter?" A second time I ask, "Are you pure in this matter?" A third time I ask, "Are you pure in this matter?" The venerable ones are pure. Therefore they keep silence. Thus I understand.

Rules Requiring Formal Meetings*

The next set of monastic rules covers thirteen matters for which a formal meeting of the order (samghadisesa) *is required. The precise punishment, to be decided at a meeting of the whole monastic assembly, amounts to something less than permanent expulsion, often suspension for one month. All the rules are given here.*[33]

The thirteen things which in their earlier and in their later stages require formal meetings of the Order now come into recitation.

1. If a monk intentionally emits his semen, except while sleeping.

2. If a monk, being degraded with perverted mind, comes into bodily contact with a woman by taking hold of her hand or her hair, or by touching any part of her body.

3. If a monk, being degraded with perverted mind, addresses a woman with wicked words, exciting her to passion as young men do to young women.

4. If a monk, being degraded with perverted mind, magnifies service to himself in the hearing of a woman, saying, "This, Sister, would be the noblest of services, that to so righteous and exalted a religious person as myself you should serve by that act," meaning sexual intercourse.

5. If a monk acts as a go-between for a woman to a man, or for a man to a woman, or for a wife, or for a mistress, or even for a prostitute.

6. If a monk, at his own request, has a hut put up on a dangerous site, without the open space around it, or does not bring the monks to approve the site, or exceeds the due measure.

7. If a monk has a large house made on a dangerous site, without the open space around it, or does not bring the monks to the place to approve the site.

---

* *Patimokkha, Samghadisesa Dhamma 1–13*
[33] Taken, with editing, from Davids and Oldenberg, *Vinaya Texts,* part 1, pp. 7–14.

8. If a monk, in harshness, malice, or anger, harasses another monk by a groundless charge of having committed a Parajika offence, thinking to himself, "Perhaps I may get him to fall from this religious life"—and then later, either when he is pressed, or without his being pressed, the case turns out to be groundless, and the monk confesses his malice.

9. If a monk, in harshness, malice, or anger, harasses another monk by a groundless charge of having committed a Parajika offence, supporting himself by some point or other of no importance in a case that really rests on something of a different kind; thinking to himself, "Perhaps I may get him to fall from this religious life"—and then later, either when he is pressed, or without his being pressed, the case turns out to rest on something of a different kind, and that monk confesses his malice.

10. If a monk causes division in a community that is at union, or persists in calling attention to some matter calculated to cause division, that monk should be addressed by the monks, "Sir, do not go around causing division in a community that is at union"; if that monk, when he has thus been spoken to by the monks, should persist as before, then let that monk be [formally] admonished about it by the monks as a body, even to the third time, to the intent that he abandon that course. If, while being so admonished up to the third time, he abandons that course, it is well; if he does not abandon it, it is a Samghadisesa.

11. Now other monks, one, two, or three, may become adherents of that monk, and may raise their voices on his side. If they should say this, "Do not say, Sirs, anything against that monk! That monk speaks according to the Dhamma, and he speaks according to the *Vinaya;*"—then let those monks be addressed by the other monks in this way, "Do not say this, Sirs! That monk does not speak according to the Dhamma, neither does he speak according to the *Vinaya.* Let not the causing of division in the community be pleasing to you!" If those monks, when they have thus been spoken to by the monks, should persist as before, those monks should be formally judged by the monks, as a body, even to the third time, so that they abandon that course. If, while being judged up to three times they abandon that course, it is well. If they do not abandon it, it is a Samghadisesa.

12. A monk may refuse to listen to what is said to him. When spoken to by the monks, according to the Dhamma, about the precepts handed down in the body of recited law, he will allow nothing to be said to him, objecting, "Say nothing to me, Sirs, either good or bad; and I will say nothing, either good or bad, to you. Be good enough, Sirs, to refrain from speaking to me!" Then let that monk be addressed by the monks, "Do not, Sir, make yourself a person who cannot be spoken to. Make yourself a person to whom we can speak. Speak to the monks, Sir, according to the Dhamma; and the monks, Sir, will speak to you according to the Dhamma. For the society of the Blessed One grown large by mutual discussion and by mutual help." If that monk, when he has thus been spoken to by the monks, should persist as before, then let that monk be formally judged by the monks as a body as many as three times, so that he may abandon that course. If, while being judged up to the third time, he abandons that course, it is well. If he does not abandon it, it is a Samghadisesa.

13. If a monk dwells near a certain village or town, leading a life hurtful to the laity and devoted to evil, so that his evil deeds are seen and heard, and the families led astray by him are seen and heard, let that monk be spoken to by the monks. The monks must say, "Your life, Sir, is hurtful to the laity, and evil. Your evil deeds, Sir, are seen and heard; and families are seen and heard to be led astray by you. Be so good, Sir, as to depart from this residence; you have lived here long enough." If that monk, when thus spoken to by the monks, should persist as before, that monk should be formally judged by the monks as a body as many as three times, so that he abandon that course. If, while being so judged up to three times, he abandons that course, it is well. If he does not abandon it, it is a Samghadisesa.

The Order of Nuns*

This selection narrates the story about how women were admitted into the monastic order as nuns. The Buddha was at first very reluctant to admit them, but he relented, giving special rules for an order of nuns. These nuns have historically played a much smaller role in Buddhism than the order of monks, a situation that continues today.[34]

Now at that time the Blessed Buddha was staying among the Sakyas in Kapilavatthu, in the Nigrodharama. And Maha-pajapati the Gotami[35] went to the place where the Blessed One was. When she arrived there, she bowed down before the Blessed One, and remained standing to one side. She said to the Blessed One, "It would be well, Lord, if women should be allowed to renounce their homes and enter the homeless state under the doctrine and discipline proclaimed by the Tathagata."

The Buddha replied, "Enough, O Gotami! Let it not please you that women should be allowed to do so." A second and a third time Maha-pajapati made the same request in the same words, and received the same reply. Then Maha-pajapati, sad and sorrowful that the Blessed One would not allow women to enter the homeless state, bowed down before the Blessed One. Keeping him on her right hand as she passed him, she departed weeping and in tears.

Now when the Blessed One had remained at Kapilavatthu as long as he thought fit, he set out on his journey towards Vesali. Travelling straight on, in due course he arrived there. The Blessed One stayed there in the Mahavana, in the Kutagara Hall.

Maha-pajapati cut off her hair, and put on orange-colored robes. She set out, with several women of the Sakya clan, towards Vesali. In due course she arrived at Vesali, at the Mahavana, at the Kutagara Hall. And Maha-pajapati, with swollen feet and covered with dust, sad and sorrowful, weeping and in tears, took her stand outside under the entrance porch.

The venerable Ananda saw her standing there, and on seeing her so, he said to Maha-pajapati, "Why do you stand there, outside the porch, with swollen feet and covered with dust, sad and sorrowful, weeping and in tears?"

"Because, Ananda, the Lord and Blessed One does not allow women to renounce their homes and enter the homeless state under the doctrine and discipline proclaimed by the Tathagata."

Then the venerable Ananda went up to the place where the Blessed One was. Bowing down before the Blessed One, he took his seat on one side. And, so sitting, the venerable Ananda said to the Blessed One:

"Behold, Lord, Maha-pajapati is standing outside under the entrance porch. She has swollen feet and is covered with dust. She is sad and sorrowful, weeping and in tears, because the Blessed One does not allow women to renounce their homes and enter the homeless state under the doctrine and discipline proclaimed by the Blessed One. It would be well, Lord, if women were to have permission granted to them to do as she desires."

The Buddha replied, "Enough, Ananda! Let it not please you that women should be allowed to do so." A second and a third time Ananda made the same request, in the same words, and received the same reply.

Then the venerable Ananda thought, "The Blessed One does not give his permission. I will now ask the Blessed One on another ground." And the venerable Ananda said to the Blessed One, "Lord, can women—when they have gone forth from the household life and entered the homeless state, under the doctrine and discipline

---

* *Cullavagga* 10.1.1–6
[34] Taken, with editing, from T. W. Rhys Davids and Hermann Oldenberg, trans., *Vinaya Texts,* part 3, *Sacred Books of the East,* vol. 20 (Oxford: Oxford University Press, 1885), pp. 320–26.
[35] *the Gotami:* a relative of Gotama, and his nurse when he was an infant.

proclaimed by the Blessed One—can they gain the fruit of conversion, or of the second Path, or of the third Path, or of Arhatship?"

"They are capable, Ananda."

"Lord, Maha-pajapati has proved herself of great service to the Blessed One, when as aunt and nurse she nourished him and gave him milk, and on the death of his mother she nursed the Blessed One at her own breast. It would be well, Lord, that women should have permission to go forth from the household life and enter the homeless state, under the doctrine and discipline proclaimed by the Tathagata."

"Ananda, if Maha-pajapati takes upon herself the Eight Chief Rules, let that be reckoned as her initiation. (1) Even if a woman has been a nun for a hundred years, she shall make salutation to, shall rise in the presence of, shall bow down before, and shall perform all proper duties towards a monk, even if he is only just initiated. (2) A nun is not to spend the rainy season in a district in which there is no monk. (3) Every half month a nun is to await from the monks two things, the request about the date of the Uposatha ceremony, and the time when the monk will come to give the Exhortation. (4) After keeping the rainy season, the nun is to enquire whether any fault can be laid to her charge before both Samghas—of monks and of nuns—with respect to three matters: what has been seen, what has been heard, and what has been suspected. (5) A nun who has been guilty of a serious offence is to undergo the Manatta discipline towards both the Samghas. (6) When a nun, as novice, has been trained for two years in the Six Rules, she is to ask permission for the upasampada initiation from both Samghas. (7) A nun is never to revile or abuse a monk. (8) From this time on, nuns are forbidden to admonish monks, but the official admonition of nuns by monks is not forbidden.

"Ananda, if Maha-pajapati takes upon herself these Eight Chief Rules, let that be reckoned to her as her initiation."

[5] Then the venerable Ananda, when he had learned from the Blessed One these Eight Chief Rules, went to Maha-pajapati and told her all that the Blessed One had said. She replied, "A man or a woman, when young and of tender years, accustomed to adorn himself, would bathe his head and receive with both hands a garland of lotus or jasmine or atimuttaka flowers, and place it on the top of his head. In the same way, I take upon myself these Eight Chief Rules, never to be transgressed my life long."

Then the venerable Ananda returned to the Blessed One, and bowed down before him, and took his seat on one side. So sitting, the venerable Ananda said to the Blessed One, "Lord, Maha-pajapati has taken upon herself the Eight Chief Rules; the aunt of the Blessed One has received the upasampada initiation."

Then the Buddha said, "Ananda, if women had not received permission to go out from the household life and enter the homeless state under the doctrine and discipline proclaimed by the Tathagata, then the pure religion would have lasted long; the good law would have stood fast for a thousand years. But since women have now received that permission, the pure religion will not now last so long, and the good law will now stand fast for only five hundred years. Houses in which there are many women but only a few men are easily violated by robber burglars. In the same way, Ananda, under whatever doctrine and discipline women are allowed to go out from the household life into the homeless state, that religion will not last long. So, Ananda, in anticipation I have laid down these Eight Chief Rules for the nuns, never to be transgressed for their whole life."

RITUAL AND MEDITATION

The Relics of the Buddha*

One of the most important features of Buddhist worship has been veneration of the relics (physical remains, mostly bones) of the Buddha. To a Buddhist, these are the holiest physical objects in the world. This selection from The Book of the Great Decease *tells the story of how the followers of the Buddha settled many arguments about how the relics of the cremated body of the Buddha should be distributed.*[36]

When they heard these things, the Mallas of Kusinara spoke to the assembled brothers. "The Blessed One died in our village domain. We will not give away any part of the remains of the Blessed One!"

When they had thus spoken, Dona the Brahmin addressed the assembled brothers. He said,

"Hear, reverend sirs, one word from me. Our Buddha accustomed to teach moderation. It is unseemly that strife should arise, and wounds, and war, over the distribution of the remains of him who was the best of beings! Let us all, sirs, unite in friendly harmony to make eight portions. Let thupas[37] arise widespread in every land, that humanity may trust in the Enlightened One! Brahmin, divide the remains of the Blessed One equally into eight parts, with fair division."

"Let it be so, sir!" Dona said in assent to the assembled brothers. He divided the remains of the Blessed One equally into eight parts, with fair division. He said to them, "Give me, sirs, this vessel, and I will set up over it a sacred memorial mound, and in its honor I will establish a feast." And they gave the vessel to Dona the Brahmin.

---

* *Mahaparinibbana Sutta 6.58–60*

[36] Taken, with editing, from Davids, *Buddhist Suttas,* pp. 133–34.

[37] *thupas* (or *stupas*): a house of worship enshrining relics of the Buddha.

Mindfulness in Meditation**

Buddhist monks must have a powerful concentration to fix their minds on the abstract processes and products of meditation. This passage from an influential Theravada meditation scripture discusses the way to full mindfulness.[38]

Monks, there is one road, one path for beings to purify themselves, to transcend sorrow and grief, to overcome suffering and melancholy, to attain the right way, to realize nirvana: that is the fourfold establishment of mindfulness. What are the four mindfulnesses? They are . . . the mind-

ful contemplation of the body . . . the mindful contemplation of the feelings . . . the mindful contemplation of thoughts . . . and the mindful contemplation of the elements of reality.

How does a monk practice the mindful contemplation of the body? In this way: He goes to the forest, or to the foot of a tree, or to an empty room, and he sits down, cross-legged, keeps his back straight, and directs his mindfulness in front of him. Mindfully, he breathes in, mindfully, he breathes out; breathing in a long breath, he knows "I am breathing in a long breath"; breathing out a long breath, he knows "I am breathing out a long breath"; breathing in a short breath, he knows "I am breathing in a short breath"; breathing out a short breath, he knows "I am breathing out a short breath." . . . He should be

---

** *Majjhima-Nikaya, Satipatthanasutta 10.1–9*

[38] Taken, with editing, from V. Trenckner, *The Majjhima-Nikaya,* vol. 1 (London: Pali Text Society, 1888) pp. 55–63.

like a lathe operator who knows that "I am making a long turn" when he is making a long turn
and that "I am making a short turn" when he is
making a short turn. . . . Thus a monk practices
mindfully contemplating his body.

Furthermore, when a monk is walking, he
knows "I am walking," and when he is standing, knows "I am standing," and when he is sitting, knows "I am sitting," and when he is lying
down, knows "I am lying down." Whatever posture his body may take, he knows that he is taking it. . . . Thus a monk practices mindfully contemplating his body.

And also, a monk is fully mindful of what he is
doing, both going and coming, looking straight
ahead and looking away, holding out his bowl or
retracting it, putting on his robes, carrying his
bowl, eating, drinking, chewing, tasting, defecat-
ing, urinating, moving, standing, sitting, sleeping, waking, talking, being quiet. . . . Thus a monk
practices mindfully contemplating his body.

And also, a monk considers his body itself,
from the soles of his feet upward and from the
top of his head downward, wrapped as it is in
skin and filled with all sorts of impurities. He
reflects, "In this body, there is hair, body-hair,
nails, teeth, skin, flesh, sinews, bones, marrow,
kidneys, heart, liver, pleura, spleen, lungs, colon,
intestines, stomach, feces, bile, phlegm, pus,
blood, sweat, fat, tears, lymph, saliva, snot, sy-
novia, and urine." . . . Thus a monk practices
mindfully contemplating his body.

And also, a monk considers his body . . . with
regard to the elements that compose it. He reflects, "In this body, there is earth, water, fire, and
air. . . ." He should think of these elements that
make up the body as though they were pieces of
the carcass of a cow that a butcher had slaughtered and displayed in a market. . . . Thus a monk
practices mindfully contemplating his body.

And also, if a monk should see a corpse abandoned in a cemetery, dead one day or two or
three, swollen, turning blue, and beginning to
fester, he should concentrate on his own body
and think, "This body of mine is just like that
one; it has the same nature, and it will not escape

this fate." . . . And should he see a corpse abandoned in a cemetery, being eaten by crows,
hawks, vultures, dogs, jackals, or various kinds of
vermin, he should concentrate on his own body
and think, "This body of mine is just like that
one; it has the same nature, and it will not escape
this fate." . . . And should he see a corpse abandoned in a cemetery, a skeleton still covered with
some flesh and blood and held together by ten-
dons, or without flesh but smeared with blood
and still held together, or without flesh or blood
but still held together, or just bones no longer
held together but scattered in different directions—here the bones of a hand, there the bones
of a foot, here a tibia, there a femur, here a hip-
bone, there a backbone, over there a skull—he
should concentrate on his own body and think,
"This body of mine is just like that; it has the
same nature, and it will not escape this fate. . . ."
And should he see a corpse abandoned in a cemetery, bones bleached white as shells, old bones in
a heap, bones that have completely decayed and
become dust—he should concentrate on his
own body and think, "This body of mine is just
like that; it has the same nature, and it will not
escape this fate." . . . Thus a monk keeps mindfully contemplating his body.

And how, monks, does a monk practice the
mindful contemplation of feelings? In this way:
Experiencing a pleasant feeling, he knows "I am
experiencing a pleasant feeling"; experiencing an
unpleasant feeling, he knows "I am experiencing
an unpleasant feeling." Experiencing a feeling
that is neither pleasant nor unpleasant, he knows
"I am experiencing a feeling that is neither pleasant nor unpleasant." Experiencing a pleasant
physical feeling, he knows "I am experiencing a
pleasant physical feeling"; experiencing a pleasant spiritual feeling, he knows "I am experiencing a pleasant spiritual feeling"; experiencing
an unpleasant physical feeling . . . an unpleasant
spiritual feeling . . . a physical feeling that is neither pleasant nor unpleasant . . . a spiritual feeling
that is neither pleasant nor unpleasant, he knows
he is experiencing those feelings. . . . Thus a monk
practices mindfully contemplating feelings.

And how, monks, does a monk practice the mindful contemplation of thoughts? In this way: He knows a passionate thought to be a passionate thought; he knows a passionless thought to be a passionless thought; he knows a hate-filled thought to be a hate-filled thought; he knows a hate-free thought to be a hate-free thought; he knows a deluded thought . . . an undeluded thought . . . an attentive thought . . . a distracted thought . . . a lofty thought . . . a lowly thought . . . a mediocre thought . . . a supreme thought . . . a concentrated thought . . . a diffused thought, . . . a thought that is free . . . a thought that is still bound . . . to be such thoughts as they are. Thus a monk practices mindfully contemplating his thoughts.

And how, monks, does a monk practice the mindful contemplation of the elements of reality? In this way: He practices the mindful contemplation of the elements of reality with regard to the five hindrances. And how does he do that? In this way: When there is within him sensual excitement, he knows that "sensual excitement is occurring within me"; when there is within him no sensual excitement, he knows that "sensual excitement is not occurring within me." . . . When there is within him some ill will, he knows that "ill will is occurring within me"; when there is within him no ill will, he knows "ill will is not occurring within me." . . . And similarly he knows the presence and the absence within himself of laziness and lethargy, agitation and worry, and doubt. . . . Thus he practices mindfully contemplating elements of reality within himself, he practices mindfully contemplating elements of reality outside of himself, . . . and he practices mindfully contemplating elements of reality as they arise . . . and as they pass away. . . . And thinking that "this is an element of reality," he is concerned with it only insofar as he needs to be for the sake of knowledge and recognition; so he abides free from attachment and does not cling to anything in this world.

A monk also practices the mindful contemplation of the elements of reality with regard to the five aggregates of attachment. And how does he

do that? In this way: He reflects "Such is physical form, such is the origin of physical form, such is the passing away of physical form." "Such is feeling, such is the origin of feeling, such is the passing away of feeling." "Such is perception, such is the origin of perception, such is the passing away of perception." "Such are karmic constituents, such is the origin of karmic constituents, such is the passing away of karmic constituents." "Such is consciousness, such is the origin of consciousness, such is the passing away of consciousness. . . ."

A monk also practices the mindful contemplation of the elements of reality with regard to the six senses and sense-objects. How does he do this? In this way: He knows his eyes, he knows visible forms, and he knows the attachments that develop in connection with the two of them. . . . Similarly he knows his ears, and he knows sounds. . . . He knows his nose and he knows smells. . . . He knows his tongue and he knows tastes. . . . He knows his body and he knows tactile things. . . . He knows his mind and he knows thoughts. And he knows the attachments that develop in connection with any of them. . . .

A monk also practices the mindful contemplation of the elements of reality with regard to the seven factors of enlightenment. How does he do that? In this way: When the first factor of enlightenment, which is mindfulness, is within him, he knows it to be present; when it is not within him, he knows it to be absent. . . . And similarly, he knows the presence and absence within himself of the other factors of enlightenment: the investigation of Dharma . . . energetic effort . . . enthusiasm . . . serenity . . . meditative concentration . . . and equanimity. . . .

A monk also practices the mindful contemplation of the elements of reality with regard to the Four Noble Truths. How does he do that? In this way: He knows "suffering" the way it really is, and he knows "the origination of suffering" the way it really is, and he knows "the cessation of suffering" the way it really is, and he knows "the way leading to the cessation of suffering" the way it really is.

The Merit of Making Images*

Another prominent (and much more widespread than relic veneration) feature of Buddhist worship is using statues of the Buddha to focus one's thoughts toward enlightenment. In this passage from the Mahayana Buddhist canon, the Buddha is said to lavish great merit on those who make his images. The belief that the Buddha gives his gracious blessing to those who seek it is a prominent theme in Mahayana Buddhism.[39]

And the Blessed One sat upon his lotus throne, upon the terrace of enlightenment; and each person in the four assemblies thought to himself: Truly we wish to hear the Blessed One teach us the meritorious virtue of making images of the Buddha. For what blessings could we gain if we made an image in the form of the Buddha, yet with our meager talent failed to capture his likeness?

And the bodhisattva Maitreya knew their thoughts: he arose from his seat, placed his robe over his right shoulder, and knelt upon the ground. He joined his palms together, and said to the Blessed One: "King Udayana has made an image of the Buddha. Whether the Buddha is in the world or has passed away into nirvana, how much merit does one gain who follows the dictates of a faithful heart and builds an image such as his? My one wish is that the Blessed One explain this thing to me."

And the Buddha said to the bodhisattva Maitreya: "Listen attentively! Listen attentively, and ever bear in mind what I shall explain to you.

"Let a son of good family or a daughter of good family but be pure and faithful, and fix his mind solely upon the virtues of the Buddha, and meditate unceasingly upon his awe-inspiring virtue and majesty.

"Let him think upon the ten powers of the Buddha, and upon his fourfold fearlessness; upon his eighteen special qualities, and upon his great love and compassion; upon his omniscience, and upon all his signs of greatness.

"Let him see how every single pore of the Buddha's body glows with measureless multicolored brilliant light, with immensities of surpassing blessings and adornments and accomplishments, with measureless insight and perfect enlightenment, with measureless meditation and forbearance, with measureless magic and spiritual power.

"Let him meditate upon the infinitude of all the virtues of the Buddha, upon his far removal from all the hosts of error, and upon his splendor unequaled in all the world.

"And let him fix his mind in this manner, and awaken deep faith and joy, and make an image of the Buddha with all its signs. Then he gains merit which is vast, and great, and measureless, and limitless, and which can be neither weighed nor counted.

"Maitreya, should a man draw and adorn an image with a host of varied colors; or cast an image of silver, or bronze, or iron, or lead, or tin; or carve an image of fragrant sandalwood; or cover an image with pearls, or shell, or well-woven and embroidered silk; or cover a wooden image with red earth and white lime plaster; or build an image to the best of his ability, even if it be so small as the size of a finger, as long as those who see it can see that it is in the form of the Blessed One—I shall now tell you what his blessed reward will be, and how he will fare in his next life.

"For a man who does these things may be born again into this world, but he will not be born into a poor family, nor will he be born in a barbarian border kingdom, nor into a lowly clan, nor as an orphan; he will not be born stupid or fierce, nor as a merchant or peddler or butcher; truly he will not be born into any low mean craft

---

* *Taisho Shinshu Daizokyo,* 16, no. 694

[39] From Stephan Beyer, *The Buddhist Experience: Sources and Interpretations* (Belmont, CA: Dickenson, 1974), pp. 47–50, 54–55. Copyright 1974, Dickenson Publishing Company. Used by permission of Wadsworth, a division of Thomson Learning.

or impure caste, into any heretical practices or heretical views.

"For by the power of his intention he has cast aside the cause for such rebirth, and he will not be born into such states; but rather he will always be born into the household of a universal emperor, having powerful clansmen, or perhaps into the household of a Brahmin of pure practices, rich and honorable, lordly and without error.

"And the place where he is born will always be where Buddhas are served and worshipped; and perhaps there he shall be a king, able to maintain and establish the Law, teaching the Law which converts those of evil practices; and perhaps he shall be a universal emperor, having the seven jewels, bringing forth a thousand sons, and mounting into the sky to convert the four corners of the world.

"And when his length of days has been exhausted, the lord will be abundantly joyful, perhaps to rule as the king of the gods, or as lord of the Heaven of Delights, or of the Heaven of Power; for there will be no joy either of gods or of men which he will not taste. And thus his blessed reward will continue in heaven and will not be cut off when he dies.

"And he will always be born as a man: he will not take on the body of a woman, or of a eunuch, or of a hermaphrodite. The body which he takes will be without defect or deformity: neither one-eyed nor blind; his ears not deaf; his nose not bent or twisted; his mouth not large or crooked; his lips not hanging down or wrinkled or rough; his teeth not broken or missing, not black or yellow; his tongue not slow; the back of his neck without tumor or boil; his form not hunched; his color not splotched; his arms not weak; his feet not large; and he will be neither too thin nor too tall, neither too fat nor too short. . . .

"Maitreya, if there is a man who, in the midst of this world, can awaken his faith and build an image of the Buddha, then between his having done so and his not having done so the difference is . . . great: for anywhere this man is born, he is purified and free of all his past sins, and

by all his skill may gain liberation even without a teacher. . . ."

And then the bodhisattva Maitreya said to the Buddha: "Blessed One, you have always said that good or evil deeds are never lost. Any being who has done such grievous sins should be born in a mean, low class and household, be poor and sick and die a speedy death. But if he can awaken his faith and build an image of the Buddha, then will he still experience the retribution for his host of sins?"

And the Buddha said to the bodhisattva Maitreya: "Maitreya, listen attentively, and I shall explain it to you. Should this being, who has done all those sins, put forth his heart to build a Buddha image, seek to wail and repent, take himself strongly in hand and vow to transgress no more, then everything that he has done before is all annulled. Let me illustrate this case for you.

"Maitreya, there was once a man who had been very stingy in a past life, and thus he now experienced poverty and suffered from his lack of wealth, for all his former possessions and pleasures were now exhausted. But one day it happened that a monk, who had entered into meditation, arose from his trance; and this man honored the monk and gave him alms of food and drink. And no sooner had he given alms than he was freed from poverty forever, and all that he wanted was just as he wished. Maitreya, that poor man had accumulated evil karma in a former life: but now what had happened to the retribution for what he had done?"

And the bodhisattva Maitreya said: "Blessed One, it was because he gave food to the monk that the evil karma of his past life was annulled and exhausted, and thereby he could be free of poverty forever, and endowed with a sufficiency of great wealth."

And the Buddha said to Maitreya: "It is just as you have said. And you should know that a man who builds a Buddha image is the same: because he builds an image his evil karma is exhausted forever, without any reminder; and he experiences none of the retribution which he should experience. . . .

"But if he repents his former deeds and vows to sin no more, awakens his faith, and builds a Buddha image, then the sins which he has done are all exhausted and annulled, and he will become loved and honored by all men.

"And why is that? It is because all Buddhas have the measureless limitless blessed virtues of their Buddhahood: measureless limitless great insight, measureless limitless meditation and freedom, and all manner of superlative qualities of meritorious virtue. . . . The virtue of the Blessed Buddha is without limit or measure, and it cannot even be thought or talked of. And that is why, if a man awakens his faith and builds a Buddha image, every single one of his evil deeds will be exhausted and annulled; and from the store of the Buddhas he gains meritorious virtue without limit or measure, until he himself gains Buddhahood, and himself saves beings from all their suffering and woe forever."

Scripture to Guide the Soul after Death*

Probably the most famous Tibetan scripture is the Bardo Thodol (*or* Bar-do thos-grol), *popularly known as the "Tibetan Book of Dead" but more accurately translated "Listen and Be Liberated from the Intermediate State." This book provides readings done at and after death to guide the soul of the deceased through the intermediate ("Bardo") state to a happy reincarnation. This key reading at the point of death first speaks of the "clear light" of pure Nirvana; the person cannot reach it, and guidance is given to lead the soul through demonic nightmares to shelter in the womb of a being who will later give birth to the dead person's reincarnation.*[40]

"Noble person, (his/her name), now the time has come for you to seek a path [through the Bardo]. After your breath has almost ceased that which is called the Clear Light of the first phase of the Intermediary State will dawn upon you. Its meaning was explained to you by your lama. It is existence as such, empty and bare like the sky; it will appear to you as the stainless and bare mind, clear and empty, without limitations or a center. At this moment you should recognize this and remain therein. I shall guide you to this insight." Before the physical breath has totally ceased one should repeat this close to the dying person's ear many times so that it is imprinted on the mind. . . .

"Noble son, (name), listen! The intrinsic light of true being will now become apparent to you. This you must recognize! Noble son, the innate being of your present cognition is this very naked voidness, which does not exist as a thing, phenomenon, or color; it is mere voidness. This is the absolute reality of the female Buddha Samantabhadra.[41] As your cognition consists in voidness, don't let this opportunity become meaningless. . . . The nature of your own mind is void of an inherent being and of any substance, but your intelligence is crystal clear. This nature of your mind is inseparable from your intelligence; together they are the true being, the Buddha. The nature of your mind, equally clear and void, consists in a mass of light, and because of being free of becoming and decaying it is the Buddha of boundless light. This you must recognize!. . .

"Noble son, for three and a half days you will be unconscious. When you awake from the coma

---

*Bardo Thodol 1.1- 2

[40] From H. Coward, E. Dargyay, and R. Neufeldt, *Readings in Eastern Religion* (Waterloo, Ontario: Wilfred Laurier University Press, 1988). Copyright 1988 by Wilfred Laurier University Press. Used by permission.

---

[41] *Samantabhadra:* As in Buddhist tantric texts, the feminine here represents perfect wisdom.

you will think: 'What happened to me?' For this reason you have to recognize that you are now in the intermediate state. At this time, when you depart from the world, all things will appear to you as light, and as celestial beings. The entire sky will shine with bright blue. . . .

"You should yearn for the light blue light, which is so brilliant and clear; and full of devotion you should address Vairocana with this prayer which you should repeat after me: 'Alas! At this time I am wandering through the world because of my great ignorance. I beg you, Vairocana, to guide me on the bright path of the primordial wisdom of the sphere being-as-such, the right path. May the divine mother, Akashesvari (Protector of the heavens) protect me from behind. I beg you, rescue me from the abyss of the intermediate state and guide me to perfect buddhahood.'

"Noble son, (name), hear me! You have not understood me even though I have directed you toward the right insight according to the instructions of this text. Now when you can't close the womb, then the time has truly come when you have to acquire a new body. There is more than only one profound and authentic instruction for closing the door of the womb. Remember them, be not distracted, imprint them on your mind.

"Noble son, although you are reluctant to go, torturers—which are evil deeds—chase you.

Powerless, you have to go where you don't want to. Torturers and executioners pull you and you feel as if you are running away from darkness, tornadoes, cries of war, snow, rain, hail, and blizzards. In your anxiety you are looking for a refuge, and you escape and hide—as I have said before—in mansions, rock crevasses, caves, thick undergrowth, or in lotus flowers which close over you. You ask yourself whether they will get you there. 'If they detect me here, then everything is lost,' and while questioning whether you have escaped you cling to this spot. If they take you from there you are afraid of being overcome by the anxieties and terrors of the intermediate state. Thus you feel fear and anxiety and you hide in the middle of these burrows. Therein you seize a bad body which did not exist before, and you will suffer from various ills. This is a sign that the devils and demons have prevented your escape.

"Listen and memorize this instruction suitable for such an occasion! When the torturers chase you into a state of helplessness, or when fear and anxiety threaten you then you should visualize a wrathful deity who destroys all these forms of threat. Quickly perfect your vision of the deity with all his limbs. . . . Through their blessing and compassion you will rid yourself from the torturers and will have the strength to close the door of the womb. This profound and accurate instruction you should keep in mind!"

GLOSSARY

Abhidhamma (ahb-hee-DAHM-muh) "Special Teaching," the third basket of the Buddhist canon [Sanskrit: *Abhidharma*].

Arhat (AHR-haht) "Worthy One," a title of those who achieve enlightenment [Sanskrit: *Arhant*].

bodhisattva (bohd-hee-SAHT-vuh) one who comes very close to Buddha nature (enlightenment) but postpones it for the sake of helping others to reach it.

Buddha (BUHD-ha) one who has reached enlightenment; although Gotama is the Buddha *par excellence,* this term applies to all others who attain this state.

dhamma (DAH-muh) teaching, path, way [Sanskrit: *dharma*]

Jataka (JAH-tah-kuh) the book of tales of Gotama Buddha's previous lives.

Mahayana (mah-hah-YAH-nuh) "the Great Vehicle," the more recent form of Buddhism found mostly in north and east Asia.

parinibbana (pah-ree-nihb-BAH-nuh) the ultimate peace that comes after death.

Sutta (SUH-tuh) a writing, a scripture; the second basket of the canon, featuring the basic teachings of Buddhism [Sanskrit: *sutra*].

Tathagata (tah-THAH-gah-tuh) "One who has come/gone thus," one who has reached enlightenment.

Theravada (ther-ah-VAH-duh) "tradition of the elders," the more conservative form of Buddhism found mostly in south Asia.

Tipitaka (tih-pee-TAH-kuh) "Three Baskets," the main internal divisions of the canon [Sanskrit: *Tripitaka*].

Vinaya (vih-NIGH-yuh) "Discipline," the first basket of the canon, which deals with the rules of monastic life.

QUESTIONS FOR STUDY AND DISCUSSION

1. What are the main features of the Buddhist scripture canon?

2. How is the life of Gotama Buddha an example for all Buddhists? Is it true to say that most of Buddhism is founded on the life of Gotama?

3. In what sense are the Four Noble Truths the essence of Buddhism?

4. What are the characteristics of monasticism as described in scripture?

5. To what degree is Buddhism a religion made for monastics?

6. How is the role of women in Buddhism described in its scripture? Consider especially the role of nuns.

7. In what ways do the scriptures reflect the basic differences (and the similarities) between southern (Theravada) and northern (Mahayana) Buddhism? Consider both canon and content.

8. Based on your understanding of Buddhist scripture, how would you describe nirvana?

9. What are some basic similarities and differences between Hinduism and Buddhism?

10. What to you is the most striking feature of Buddhism?

SUGGESTIONS FOR FURTHER READING

Primary Readings

The *Sacred Books of the East* series is still the fullest and most accessible collection of Buddhist scripture in English translation. Its volume 10 contains the *Dhammapada* translated by Max Müller and the *Sutta-Nipata* by V. Fausböll; vol. 11, various suttas by T. W. Rhys Davids; vols. 13, 17 and 20, the most important Vinaya texts by Rhys Davids and H. Oldenberg; vol. 19, a translation of the Chinese version of the *Acts of the Buddha;* vol. 21, the *Lotus Sutra* by H. Kern; vols. 35 and 36, the *Questions of King Milinda;* and vol. 49, various Mahayana texts, prominently the *Acts of the Buddha,* by E. B. Cowell, Müller, and J. Takakusu.

E. Conze, *Buddhist Scriptures.* London: Penguin, 1959. An excellent anthology by a leading expert on Buddhism.

W. T. de Bary, *The Buddhist Tradition in India, China and Japan.* New York: Vantage Books, 1972. Of all the anthologies of the three major traditions of Buddhism, this one is the finest.

J. Strong, *The Experience of Buddhism: Sources and Interpretations.* The Religious Life in History Series. Belmont, CA: Wadsworth, 1995. Perhaps the most comprehensive anthology of Buddhist scripture and other religious literature.

Secondary Readings

N. S. Barnes, "[Women in] Buddhism," in A. Sharma, ed., *Women in World Religions.* Albany: State University of New York Press, 1987. Gives good attention to the historical witness of Buddhist scriptures to this topic.

M. Levering, "Scripture and Its Reception: A Buddhist Case," in *Rethinking Scripture.* Albany: State University of New York Press, 1989, pp. 58–101. A fascinating glimpse of the use of scripture in a Buddhist nunnery.

Donald S. Lopez, Jr., *Elaborations on Emptiness: Uses of the* Heart Sutra. Princeton: Princeton University Press, 1996. Explores the philosophical and ritual uses of this most important text.

W. Rahula, *What the Buddha Taught,* rev. ed. New York: Grove Press, 1974. An excellent overview of basic Buddhist teachings and writings by a leading Buddhist monk and scholar.

R. A. Ray, "Buddhism: Sacred Text Written and Realized," in F. M. Denny and R. L. Taylor, *The Holy Book in Comparative Perspective.* Gives very good attention to orality.

K. A. Tsai, *Lives of the Nuns: Biographies of Chinese Buddhist Nuns from the Fourth to Sixth Centuries.* Honolulu: Hawaiian University Press, 1995. A translation and commentary of a Chinese book written to demonstrate the power of Buddhist scripture in the lives of female monastics.

Illustrated Folio from a Jain Kalpasutra *Palm-Leaf Manuscript*
This thirteenth-century manuscript shows a Shvetambara monk preaching to a prince, who raises his hands in reverence; the scriptures are open before them on a reading stand. Note the hole for threading the binding string at the center of the folio. Credit: Edwin Binney 3rd Collection, San Diego Museum of Art

CHAPTER FOUR

Jainism

❖ A Jaina man makes his way into a temple in Calcutta. He stands reverently before a life-sized statue of a naked man who in ancient times attained nirvana. As other worshippers walk respectfully around the statue several times, he stands still at its base and reads from the Jaina scriptures.

❖ A group of Jaina nuns walks slowly and carefully down a dirt road in northern India. Dressed in white, they have muslin cloths over their mouths to keep out flying insects. They use small brooms to sweep gently the ground in front of them as they walk, looking for even the smallest visible creatures. They are practicing the first and most important of their vows, noninjury to any living thing.

❖ In the streets of Bombay, two men come along carrying between them a light cot alive with bedbugs. They stop before the door of a Jaina household and cry, "Who will feed the bugs?" Someone tosses a coin from a window, and one of the men places himself carefully on the bed, offering himself as a living grazing ground to his fellow beings. The donor of the coin gains credit, and the man on the cot gains the coin.[1]

INTRODUCTION

Jainism was founded by Mahavira ("Great Hero") in the sixth century B.C.E. Mahavira taught a stricter version of the Hindu Upanishadic way, giving special emphasis to **ahimsa** [ah-HIM-suh], "noninjury" to all living beings. Rejecting belief in a supreme god, Jains seek release from endless reincarnation through a life of strict self-denial. Two million Jains in India have had an influence out of all proportion to their comparatively small numbers. Gandhi, for example, drew inspiration from their teaching of nonviolence. The Jaina scriptures, despite their fragmentary state, afford an excellent glimpse into this tenacious religion, especially its main teachings and monastic life.

Overview of Structure

Jaina scripture is known in religious scholarship as the **Agama** [ah-GAH-muh], "tradition." Most Jains call it the **Siddhanta** [sid-DAHN-tuh], "doctrine." The two main branches of Jainism, the Shvetambaras and the Digambaras, share a few books, but for the most part they have different canons. Shvetambara ("white-clad" monastics) is the larger group. It teaches that women can achieve nirvana without having to be reborn

---

[1] Heinrich Zimmer, *Philosophies of India* (New York: Meridian, 1957), p. 279; quoted from John A. Hutchison, *Paths of Faith,* 4th ed. (New York: McGraw-Hill, 1991), p. 98.

as a man and therefore has an order of nuns. Digambara (with "sky-clad" or naked monks) teaches that women cannot achieve nirvana.

The Shvetambara canon is commonly said by Western scholars to have forty-five books in six sections: *Angas* [AHN-guhs] ("limbs"), *Upangas* ("sub-*Angas*"), *Prakirnakas* (mixed texts), *Chedasutras* (on authority and discipline), *Culikasutras* ("appendixes"), and *Mulasutras* ("basic texts"). The **Angas** are the oldest part of the canon. The first *Anga* is the *Acarangasutra,* containing the most reliable Jain story of Mahavira and laws for monks and nuns. The second *Anga* is the *Sutrakritanaga,* which contains the main Jain teachings. The best-known *mulasutra* is the *Uttaradhyayana Sutra,* teachings believed by Jains to be the last words of Mahavira. Besides these books, Jains also say that their original and pure teachings were contained in fourteen *Purvas* ("Foundations"), now all lost. The difficulties among the two sects and within each sect's canon are traced to the loss of these books. (The least of the Jaina sects, the Sthanakavasis, deny the existence of any scripture.)

The Digambaras accept as canonical the ancient *Purvas* that survive. They also accept the **Prakaranas,** the main section of their canon: the *Mulacara* (on conduct), the *Samayasara* (on doctrine), the *Pravancanasara* (teaching), and the *Aradhana* ("Accomplishment"). They also treat as scripture many scholastic commentaries on the scriptures (*anuyoga*), which range from the first to the ninth centuries C.E. Both Jain groups accept the important *Tattvarthadhigama Sutra* ("Book for Attaining the Meaning of Principles") by Umasvamin, the first work on Jaina philosophy to be written in Sanskrit. The fixing of the number of Shvetamabara texts at forty-five, and their subdivision into six groups, was largely the work of the nineteenth-century German scholar Georg Bühler. Recently this partition has been called into question as too simplistic and not reflecting actual Jain usage. Kendall Folkert, for example, has stated, "When one asks contemporary Jains what their scriptures are, one receives widely varying answers, responses that vary not because of ignorance, but because there does not appear to be a wholly accepted body of scripture that is of equal value to the entire community." Folkert also states that Digambaras sometimes accept Shvetambara texts.[2]

The *Agama* discusses a vast number of subjects, with books written by many Jain leaders over a long period. Some of it is in prose, some in verse, and some mixed prose and verse. Its content, though frequently repetitious and diffuse, at times can be succinct and systematic.

Origin, Development, and Use

Jains believe that, when he achieved nirvana, Mahavira emitted a "sacred sound" that his followers translated into words. Thus the authority for the most ancient scriptures of both Jain sects is Mahavira himself, but (in typical Indian fashion) he is not thought to have written them. Some of them claim to be speeches given by Mahavira to Gautama Indrabhuti, whose disciple Sudharman gave them in turn to his pupil Jambusvamin. The types of literature mentioned earlier developed over time, all of it handed

---

[2] K. Folkert, "The 'Canons' of 'Scripture,'" in M. Levering, *Rethinking Scripture* (Albany: State University of New York Press, 1979), p. 175.

on orally in the monastic community until about 500 C.E., when it was edited and written down.

Like Theravada Buddhism, which it resembles, Jainism has put monks in control of the development and usage of its scriptures. Mahavira gave the holy teaching as an ascetic. He gave it to his monk followers, who passed it down through the ages for a thousand years until other monks wrote it down. Thus it is not surprising that the content of Jain scripture is dominated by monastic teachings, ideals, and rules. The *Agama* was never intended for a popular audience but for monks (and, to a much lesser degree, nuns), who have much time to study it, learn it, and teach it to one another. Typically, the monk studies the four *mulasutras* at the beginning of his career. If he masters them, he goes on to other more difficult texts and can perhaps become one of the highly respected monks who is a teacher of scripture in the monastery. Study of scripture is commanded in the rules for monks, and knowledge derived from the sacred books is typically the first step to release. This monastic orientation of scripture explains to a large degree their repetition, many lists of various items, and other features that make them more difficult for the layperson to comprehend.

Nevertheless, the Jain laity also uses its scriptures extensively. Literacy rates are high among Jains, who tend to be more well educated than the average Indian, and this has made its scriptures more accessible. Believers read and reflect upon them in houses of worship. Usage at festivals is also striking. For example, the *Kalpa Sutra* is formally read aloud at Paryusana, the end-of-the-year festival of confession and rededication.

HISTORY

The Life of Mahavira*

*This passage tells the story of Mahavira as an example for believers, and especially for monks and nuns, of one who has achieved nirvana. Mahavira renounced the world, gave away his property, pulled out his hair, and finally starved himself to death. The gods who see and admire these feats are not supreme gods, and Mahavira shows himself superior to them as a **Jina** [GEE-nuh] (one who has achieved nirvana). The* Kalpa Sutra *contains a story of Mahavira more legendary than this.*[3]

* *Acaranga Sutra* 2.15.6–9, 14, 16–20, 22–25, 27
[3] All scripture selections in this chapter are taken, with editing, from Hermann Jacobi, *Jaina Sutras, Sacred Books of the East,* vols. 22, 45 (Oxford: Oxford University Press, 1884, 1895).

In that period, in that age, once upon a time, after the lapse of nine complete months and seven and a half days, in the first month of summer . . . on its thirteenth day . . . the Kshatriya woman Trisala, perfectly healthy herself, gave birth to a perfectly healthy boy, the Venerable Ascetic Mahavira.

In that night in which the Kshatriya woman Trisala, perfectly healthy herself, gave birth to a perfectly healthy boy, the Venerable Ascetic Mahavira, there was a great divine, godly luster originated by descending and ascending gods and goddesses. They were of the four orders of Bhavanapatis, Vyantaras, Gyotishkas, and Vimanavasins. In the meeting of the gods their bustle amounted to confusion.

In that night . . . the gods and goddesses rained down a great shower of nectar, sandal powder, flowers, gold, and pearls. In that night the gods and goddesses performed the customary ceremonies of auspiciousness and honor, and anointed Mahavira as a **Tirthankara** [tihr-TAHN-kah-ruh][4]. . . .

[14] Then the Venerable Ascetic Mahavira, after his intellect had developed and his childhood had passed away, lived in the enjoyment of the allowed, noble, fivefold joys and pleasures: sound, touch, taste, color, and smell.

The Venerable Ascetic Mahavira belonged to the Kasyapa clan. His three names have thus been recorded by tradition. His parents called him Vardhamana,[5] because he is devoid of love and hate. He is called Sramana ("Ascetic") because he sustains dreadful dangers and fears, the noble nakedness, and the miseries of the world. The name Venerable Ascetic Mahavira has been given to him by the gods. . . .

[16] The Venerable Ascetic Mahavira's parents were worshippers of Parsva and followers of the Sramanas.[6] For many years they were followers of the Sramanas, and for the sake of protecting the six classes of lives they observed, blamed, repented, confessed, and did penance for their sins. On a bed of Kusa-grass they rejected all food, and their bodies dried up by the last mortification of the flesh, which is to end in death. Thus they died in the proper month, and, leaving their bodies, were born as gods in Adbhuta Kalpa. Descending after the end of their allotted length of life, with their departing breath they will reach absolute perfection in Mahavideha. They will reach wisdom, liberation, final Nirvana, and the end of all misery.[7]

In that period, in that age the Venerable Ascetic Mahavira . . . lived thirty years among the householders under the name of Videha.

After his parents had gone to the worlds of the gods . . . he gave up his gold and silver, his troops and chariots. He distributed, portioned out, and gave away his valuable treasures consisting of riches, plants, gold, pearls, etc., and distributed among those who wanted to make presents to others. Thus he gave away his possessions for a whole year. In the first month of winter, in the first fortnight, in the dark fortnight of Margasiras, on its tenth day, while the moon was in conjunction with Uttaraphalguni, he decided to retire from the world. . . .

Then the four orders of gods awakened the best of Jinas, the Venerable Mahavira, saying, "**Arhat** [AHR-haht, "worthy one" who has reached nirvana]! Propagate the religion which is a blessing to all creatures in the world!"

When the gods and goddesses . . . had become aware of the Venerable Ascetic Mahavira's intention to retire from the world, they assumed their proper form, dress, and ensigns. They ascended their own vehicles and chariots with their proper pomp and splendor, together with their whole retinue. Rejecting all large matter, they retained only tiny matter.[8] Then they rose up, and with that excellent, quick, swift, rapid, divine motion of the gods they came down again. They crossed numberless continents and oceans till they arrived in Gambudvipa at the northern Kshatriya part of the place called Kundapura. In the northeastern quarter of it they suddenly halted.

Sakra, the leader and king of the gods, quietly and slowly stopped his vehicle and chariot, quietly and slowly descended from it and went off alone. There he underwent a great transformation, and produced by magic a great, beautiful, lovely, fine-shaped divine pavilion. It was ornamented with many designs in precious stones,

---

[4]*Tirthankara:* a "ford-finder" who goes across the river of the world's misery to nirvana. Jains believe that Mahavira was the last of twenty-four Tirthankaras.

[5]*Vardhamana:* "the Increasing One," so called because his birth brought great wealth to his parents.

[6]*Sramanas:* monks.

[7]*Descending . . . misery:* they will in their next incarnation achieve nirvana and be reborn no more.

---

[8]*large matter . . . tiny matter:* the gods change their physical form to a more spiritual and less physical state.

gold, and pearls. In the middle of that divine pavilion he produced a great throne of the same description, with a footstool.

[20] Then he went to the Venerable Ascetic Mahavira, and three times circumambulating him from left to right,[9] he praised and worshipped him. Leading him to the divine pavilion, he softly placed him facing east, he anointed him with hundredfold and thousandfold refined oil and with perfumes and ointments, he bathed him with pure water, and he rubbed him with cool sandalwood oil. . . . He clad him in a pair of robes so light that the smallest breath would carry them away. They were manufactured in a famous city, praised by clever artists, soft as the fume of horses, interwoven with gold by skillful masters, and ornamented with designs of flamingos. Then the god adorned him with necklaces of many and few strings, with one hanging down over his chest and one consisting of one row of pearls. He put on him a garland, a golden string, a turban, a diadem, wreaths of precious stones, and decorated him with garlands, ribbons, scarves, and sashes. . . .

At that period, in that age, in the first month of winter . . . on its tenth day . . . fasting three days without taking water, having put on one garment, the Venerable Ascetic Mahavira with a train of gods, men, and Asuras[10] left the northern Kshatriya part of the place Kundapura by the high way for the park Gnatri Shanda. There, just at the beginning of night, he caused his palankin to stop quietly on a slightly raised untouched ground. He quietly descended from it, sat quietly on a throne with the face toward the east, and took off all his ornaments and finery.[11]

The god Vaisramana, prostrating himself, caught up the finery and ornaments of the Venerable Ascetic Mahavira in a cloth of flamingo pattern. Mahavira then plucked out his hair with his right and left hands on the right and left sides of his head, in five handfuls. But Sakra, the leader and king of the gods, falling down before the feet of the Venerable Ascetic Mahavira, caught up his hair in a diamond cup. Requesting his permission, he brought them to the Milk Ocean. After the Venerable Ascetic Mahavira had plucked out his hair in five handfuls, he paid obeisance to all liberated spirits. Vowing to do no sinful act, he adopted the holy conduct. Then the whole assembly of men and gods stood motionless, like the figures on a picture.

At the command of Sakra, the clamor of men and gods and the sound of musical instruments suddenly ceased when Mahavira chose the holy conduct. Day and night as he followed that conduct which is a blessing to all animated and living beings,[12] the zealous gods listened to him with joyful gooseflesh.

When the Venerable Ascetic Mahavira had adopted the holy conduct which produced that state of soul in which the reward of former actions is temporarily counteracted, he reached the knowledge called Manahparyaya, by which he knew the thoughts of all sentient beings. . . . Then he formed the following resolution: "I shall for twelve years neglect my body and abandon the care of it. I shall with a right disposition bear, undergo, and suffer all calamities arising from divine powers, men or animals."

The Venerable Ascetic Mahavira formed this resolution. Neglecting his body, he arrived in the village Kummara when only one division of the day remained. Neglecting his body, the Venerable Ascetic Mahavira meditated on his Self in blameless lodgings, in blameless wandering, in restraint, in kindness, in avoidance of sinful influence, in a chaste life, in patience, in freedom from passion, in contentment, in control, and in circumspectness, all while practicing religious postures and acts. He walked the path of Nirvana

---

[9]*circumambulating* [walking around] *from left to right:* as is done today in Jain temples with statues of the Jinas.
[10]*Asuras:* spirits.
[11] *took off . . . finery:* yet he is not naked, as he wears a cloth underneath. This reflects the Shvetambara orientation of this book.

---

[12] *conduct a blessing to all . . . beings:* ahimsa, also called here the "holy conduct."

and liberation, which is the fruit of good conduct. With right disposition he bore, endured, sustained, and suffered all calamities arising from divine powers, men, and animals. With undisturbed and unaffected mind, he was careful in body, speech, and mind.

The Venerable Ascetic Mahavira passed twelve years in this way of life. During the thirteenth year in the second month of summer . . . on its tenth day, on the northern bank of the river Rigupalika, in the field of the householder Samaga, in a north-eastern direction from an old temple, not far from a Sal tree, in a squatting position with joined heels exposing himself to the heat of the sun, with the knees high and the head low, in deep meditation, in the midst of abstract meditation, he reached Nirvana. He reached the complete and full, unobstructed, unimpeded, infinite and supreme, best knowledge and intui-

tion, called Kevala.[13] [25] When the Venerable One had become an Arhat and Jina, he was a Kevalin, omniscient and comprehending all objects. He knew all conditions of the world, of gods, men, and demons. He knew from where they come, where they go, whether they are born as men or animals, or become gods or hellbeings. He knew their food, drink, doings, desires, open and secret deeds, their conversation and gossip, and the thoughts of their minds. He saw and knew all conditions in the whole world of all living beings. . . . [27] On the day when the Venerable Ascetic Mahavira had reached the highest knowledge and intuition, he reflected on himself and the world. First he taught the law to the gods, and then to men.

---

[13] *Kevala:* knowledge that frees one from the cycle of rebirth.

TEACHING

The World Is Uncreated*

This passage considers some of the Hindu arguments for the existence of personal creators of the universe, and rejects them in favor of classic Jain atheism. Therefore, all persons are "on their own" in their search for liberation.

Foolish people say that a Creator made the world. The teaching that the world was created is wrong, and should be rejected.

If God created the world, where was he before creation?

If you say he was transcendent then, and needed no support, where is he now?

No single being had the skill to make this world. Besides, how can a spiritual god create

that which is material? How could God have made the world without any raw material? . . . If you say that this raw material arose naturally you fall into another error, for the whole universe might thus have been its own creator and have arisen naturally in the same way. If God created the world by an act of his own will, without any raw material, then the world is just his will and nothing else—and who will believe this nonsense? If he is ever perfect and complete, how could the will to create have arisen in him?

If, on the other hand, he is not perfect, he could no more create the universe than a potter could. If he is formless, actionless, and all-embracing, how could he have created the world? Such a soul, devoid of all modality, would have no desire to create anything.

---

* *Mahapurana* 4.16–31, 38–40

If he is perfect, he does not strive for the three goals of humanity,[14] so what advantage would be gained by creating the universe? If you say that he created for no purpose, because it was his nature to do so, then God is pointless. If he created in some kind of sport, it was the sport of a foolish child, leading to trouble. . . .

If God made the world out of love for living things and need of them, why did he not make creation wholly blissful, free from misfortune?

If he were transcendent he would not create, for he would be free. Nor would he create if in-volved in transmigration, for then he would not be almighty.

So the doctrine that the world was created by God makes no sense at all. God commits great sin in killing the children that he himself created. If you say that he kills only to destroy evil beings, why did he create such beings in the first place? . . .

Good men should combat the believer in divine creation, maddened by an evil doctrine. Know that the world is uncreated, as time itself is, without beginning and end. . . . it is uncreated and indestructible, it endures through the compulsion of its own nature.

---

[14] *three goals of humanity:* the Hindu goals of pleasure (*kama*), wealth (*artha*), and liberation (*mosksha*).

The Causes of Sin*

This reading teaches the understanding of all that hurts other beings and renunciation of it. The first section deals with reincarnation, the second with ahimsa *as the path out of it.*

O long-lived Gambusvamin! I Sudharman[15] have heard the following discourse from the venerable Mahavira:

Many do not remember whether they have descended in an eastern direction when they were born in this world, or in a southern, or in a western, or in a northern direction. . . . Similarly, some do not know whether their soul is born repeatedly or not. They do not know what they were before, nor what they will become after they die and leave this world. Now this is what one should know, either by one's own knowledge or through the instruction of the highest [i.e., a Tirthankara], or having heard it from others: that he descended in an eastern direction, or in any other direction. Similarly, some know that their soul is born repeatedly, that it arrives in this or that direction, whatever direction that may be. [5] He believes in soul, believes in the world, believes in reward, believes in action (acknowledged to be our own doing in such judgments as these): "I did it"; "I shall cause another to do it"; "I shall allow another to do it." In the world, these are all the causes of sin, which must be comprehended and renounced. A man that does not comprehend and renounce the causes of sin . . . is born repeatedly in manifold births, experiencing all painful feelings. The Revered One [Mahavira] has taught the truth of comprehension and renunciation. For the sake of the splendor, honor, and glory of this life, for the sake of birth, death, and final liberation, for the removal of pain, all these causes of sin are at work. They are to be comprehended and renounced in this world. He who . . . comprehends and renounces these causes of sin is called a karma-knowing sage. Thus I say.

[2:1] The living world is afflicted, miserable, difficult to instruct, and without discrimination.

---

* *Acaranga Sutra* 1.1–2
[15] *Gambusvamin* was the pupil of Sudharman.

In this world full of pain, with beings suffering by their different acts, benighted ones cause great pain. See! there are beings individually embodied.[16] See! there are men who control themselves, while others only pretend to be houseless.[17] One destroys this earth-body[18] by bad and injurious acts. He hurts many other beings besides, by means of earth, through his doing acts relating to earth. About this the Revered One has taught the truth. For the sake of the splendor, honor, and glory of this life, for the sake of birth, death, and final liberation, for the removal of pain, man acts sinfully toward earth, or causes others to act so, or allows others to act so. This deprives him of happiness and perfect wisdom. He is informed about this when he has understood or heard, either from the Revered One or

from the monks, the faith to be coveted. Some truly know this injuring to be bondage, delusion, death and hell. A man is longing for this when he destroys this earth-body by bad, injurious acts. He destroys many other beings as well, which he hurts by means of earth, through his deeds relating to earth. Thus I say.

[5] Somebody may cut or strike a blind man who cannot see the wound. Somebody may cut or strike his foot, ankle, knee, thigh, hip, navel, belly, side, back, chest, heart, neck, arm, finger, nail, eye, forehead, or head. Some kill openly, and some kill secretly. In the same way, the earth-bodies are cut, struck, and killed although their feeling is not apparent.

He who injures these earth-bodies does not comprehend and renounce the sinful acts. He who does not injure these comprehends and renounces the sinful acts. Knowing them, a wise man should not act sinfully toward the earth, nor cause others to act so, nor allow others to act so. He who knows these causes of sin relating to earth is called a karma-knowing sage. Thus I say.

---

[16] *beings individually embodied:* individual souls exist as absolute realities, not as a part of one world soul.

[17] *pretend to be houseless:* unfaithful monks.

[18] *earth-body:* all lives composed of the elements of the earth.

Can Women Achieve Liberation*

The two main groups of Jains disagree on whether women are able to achieve liberation from continued reincarnation. The first section outlines the Shvetambara affirmation of this possibility; the second states the fuller Digambara denial. Note how the argument turns on the issue of monastic clothing that separates the two groups.

[*Strinirvana-pariccheda* 2, 4] Women can be liberated, because women possess all the causes necessary for it. The cause of liberation is fulfillment of the three jewels [correct view, correct knowledge and correct conduct], and this is not incompatible with being a woman. So, nuns are able to understand the Jina's words, have faith in them, and practice them faultlessly. Therefore,

they can attain liberations as women. Someone might say that women cannot attain release because they wear clothes. . . . The Lord Arhats, our guides for the path to nirvana, taught that women must wear clothes and prohibited them from renouncing clothes. Therefore it follows that clothes are necessary for release, like a wisk broom [is necessary to protect small creatures from violence.

[*Sutraprabrita* 1.22–26] The [Shvetambara] nun eats food only once a day, but wears a piece of clothing; the novice nun wears two pieces of clothing. In the teaching of the Jina, no person who wears clothing attains liberation, even if that person is a Tirthankara. The path to liberation is that of nakedness, and all other paths are wrong. The sutras teach that the genital organs of women, the area between their breasts, their

---

* *Strinirvana-pariccheda* 2, 4; *Sutraprabrita* 1.22 26

navels and armpits have very small living beings, so how can women be ordained [since the care of their bodies would harm these beings]? If a woman is pure because of [the first jewel of] correct views, they become associated with the path. But even if she practices [the jewel of] cor-rect, ascetic conduct, nowhere in the teaching is it said that women can be ordained. Women do not have purity of mind, and their minds are slack. Since they get their period each month, they have no meditation free from anxiety.

The World Is Full Of Suffering*

This eloquent passage is spoken by Prince Mriga-putra to his parents. Seeking by a series of striking metaphors to persuade them to become monks, he impresses them with the horrors of constant suffer-ing born of constant reincarnation.

From clubs and knives, stakes and maces, breaking my limbs, an infinite number of times I
   have suffered without hope.
By sharp-edged razors, by knives and shears,
   many times I have been drawn and quar-
   tered, torn apart and skinned.
Helpless in snares and traps, like a deer, I have
   been caught and bound and fastened, and
   often I have been killed.

A helpless fish, I have been caught with hooks
   and nets; An infinite number of times I have
   been killed and scraped, split and gutted.
A bird, I have been caught by hawks or trapped
   in nets,
Or trapped by birdlime, and I have been killed
   an infinite number of times.
A tree, with axes and saws by the carpenters an
   infinite number of times I have been felled,
   stripped of my bark, cut up, and sawn into
   planks.
As iron, with hammer and tongs by black-
   smiths, an infinite number of times I have
   been struck and beaten, split and filed. . . .
Ever afraid, trembling, in pain and suffering,
   I have felt the greatest sorrow and agony.
In every kind of existence I have suffered pains
   that have known no reprieve for a moment.

---

* Utaradhyayana Sutra 19.61–67, 71, 74

The Road to Final Deliverance**

This passage presents a summary of the way to sal-vation. The four main steps are by knowledge, faith, conduct, and ascetic practice ("austerities"). Note the typically Indian penchant to number things up, useful in monastic teaching. Most original-language terms that follow all the numbers have been omitted.

Learn the true road leading to final deliverance, which the Jinas have taught. It depends on four causes and is characterized by right knowledge and faith. Right knowledge, Faith, Conduct, and Austerities; this is the road taught by the Jinas who possess the best knowledge. Right knowl-edge, faith, conduct, and austerities—beings who follow this road will obtain beatitude.

Knowledge is fivefold: (1) Sruta, knowledge derived from the sacred books; (2) perception; (3) supernatural knowledge; (4) knowledge of the thoughts of other people; (5) Kevala, the highest, unlimited knowledge. [5] This is the fivefold knowledge. The wise ones have taught the knowledge of substances, qualities, and all developments.

** Uttaradhyayana Sutra 28

Substance is the substrate of qualities; the qualities are inherent in one substance; but the characteristic of developments is that they inhere in either substances or qualities. Dharma, Adharma,[19] space, time, matter, and souls are the six kinds of substances. They make up this world, as has been taught by the Jinas who possess the best knowledge. Dharma, Adharma, and space are each one substance only; but time, matter, and souls are an infinite number of substances. The characteristic of Dharma is motion, that of Adharma immobility, and that of space, which contains all other substances, is to make room (for everything).

[10] The characteristic of time is duration, that of soul the realization of knowledge, faith, happiness, and misery. The characteristic of Soul is knowledge, faith, conduct, austerities, energy, and realization of its developments. The characteristic of matter is sound, darkness, luster, light, shade, sunshine, color, taste, smell, and touch. The characteristic of development is singleness, separateness, number, form, conjunction, and disjunction.

The nine truths are: (1) Soul; (2) the inanimate things; (3) the binding of the soul by Karma;[20] (4) merit; (5) demerit; (6) that which causes the soul to be affected by sins; (7) the prevention of asrava by watchfulness; (8) the annihilation of Karma; (9) final deliverance. He who truly believes the true teaching of the fundamental truths possesses righteousness.

Faith is produced by (1) nature; (2) instruction; (3) command; (4) study of the Sutras; (5) suggestion; (6) comprehension of the meaning of the sacred lore; (7) complete course of study; (8) religious exercise; (9) brief exposition; (10) the Law.

He who believes by nature truly comprehends, by a spontaneous effort of his mind, the nature of soul, inanimate things, merit, and demerit. He

puts an end to sinful influences. He who spontaneously believes the four truths (explicitly mentioned in the last verse), which the Jinas have taught, thinking they are of this and not of a different nature, believes by nature. But he who believes these truths, having learned them from somebody else, either a Khadmastha[21] or a Jina, believes by instruction. [20] He who has gotten rid of love, hate, delusion, and ignorance, and believes because he is told to do so, believes by command.

He who obtains righteousness by the study of the Sutras, either Angas or other works, believes by the study of Sutras. He who by correctly comprehending one truth arrives at the comprehension of more—just as a drop of oil expands on the surface of water—believes by suggestion. He who truly knows the sacred lore, namely the eleven Angas, the Prakirnas, and the Drishtivada, believes by the comprehension of the sacred lore. He who understands the true nature of all substances by means of all proofs and nayas,[22] believes by a complete course of study.

[25] He who sincerely performs all duties implied by right knowledge, faith, and conduct, by asceticism and discipline, and by all Samitis and Guptis,[23] believes by religious exercise.

He who holds no wrong doctrines though he is not versed in the sacred doctrines nor acquainted with other systems, believes by brief exposition. He who believes in the truth of the realities, the Sutras, and conduct, as it has been explained by the Jinas, believes by the Law.

Right belief depends on the acquaintance with truth, on the devotion to those who know the truth, and on the avoiding of schismatical and

---

[19] *Dharma, Adharma:* good and evil, respectively.

[20] *karma:* fruit of evil deeds, viewed by Jains as a physical accretion on the soul.

[21] *Khadmastha:* one who is advanced in knowledge, but not to the full knowledge of nirvana.

[22] *nayas:* literally, "leadings," probably referring to logical arguments.

[23] The five *Samitis,* rules for monks, are: how to walk in a noninjurious manner; how to speak; how to beg for food; how to relieve oneself in a noninjurious manner; how to use the few possessions allowed a monk. The three *Guptis* regulate thought, speech, and the body.

heretical tenets. There is no right conduct without right belief, and it must be cultivated for obtaining right faith. Righteousness and conduct originate together, or righteousness precedes conduct. [30] Without faith there is no knowledge, without knowledge there is no virtuous conduct, without virtues there is no deliverance, and without deliverance there is no perfection.

The excellence of faith depends on the following eight points: (1) that one has no doubts (about the truth of the tenets); (2) that one has no preference (for heretical tenets); (3) that one does not doubt its saving qualities; (4) that one is not shaken in the right belief (because heretical sects are more prosperous); (5) that one praises the pious; (6) that one encourages weak brethren; (7) that one supports or loves the confessors of the Law; (8) that one tries to exalt it.

Conduct, which produces the destruction of all Karma, is (1) the avoidance of everything sinful; (2) the initiation of a novice; (3) purity produced by peculiar austerities; (4) reduction of desire; (5) annihilation of sinfulness according to the precepts of the Arhats, as well in the case of a Khadmastha[24] as of a Jina.

Austerities are twofold, external and internal. Both external and internal austerities are sixfold. By knowledge one knows things, by faith one believes in them, by conduct one gets freedom from Karma, and by austerities one reaches purity. Having by control and austerities destroyed their Karma, great sages go to perfection and get rid of all misery.

Thus I say.

---

[24] *Khadmastha:* one who does not have full knowledge.

ORGANIZATION

The Five Great Vows*

These solemn, final vows are taken by a monk or nun entering the life of renunciation. Note that the vow of ahimsa comes first. The ideals of these vows are also influential among the laity, and they take "Lesser Vows" modeled on the full monastic vows, but not as strict. Because of faithfulness to their vows, Jains have a strong reputation in India for truthfulness (vow 2 below) and honesty (vow 3). The vows themselves are given, but their "clauses" (explanations) are omitted.

The Venerable Ascetic Mahavira, endowed with the highest knowledge and intuition, taught the five great vows, with their clauses . . . to the Sramanas and Nirgranthas,[25] to Gautama, etc.

The first great vow, Sir, is this. I renounce all killing of living beings, whether tiny or large, whether movable or immovable. I myself shall not kill living beings nor cause others to do it, nor consent to it. As long as I live, I confess and blame, repent and exempt myself of these sins, in the threefold way, in mind, speech and body. . . .

The second great vow is this. I renounce all vices of lying speech arising from anger or greed or fear or mirth. I shall neither myself speak lies, nor cause others to speak lies, nor consent to the speaking of lies by others. I confess and blame, repent and exempt myself of these sins in the threefold way, in mind, speech, and body. . . .

The third great vow is this. I renounce all taking of anything not given, either in a village or a town or a wood, either of little or of much, of small or great, of living or lifeless things. I shall neither

---

* *Acaranga Sutra* 2.15.i–v
[25] *Sramanas and Nirgranthas:* Jaina monks.

take myself what is not given, nor cause others to take it, nor consent to their taking it. As long as I live, I confess and blame, repent and exempt myself of these sins in the threefold way, in mind, speech and body. . . .

The fourth great vow is this. I renounce all sexual pleasures, either with gods or men or animals. I shall not give way to sensuality, nor cause others to give way to it, nor consent to their giving way. As long as I live, I confess and blame, repent and exempt myself [of these]. . . .

The fifth great vow is this, I renounce all attachments, whether little or much, small or great, living or lifeless. I myself shall not form such attachments, nor cause others to do so, nor consent to their doing so. As long as I live, I confess and blame, repent and exempt myself [of these].

ETHICS

Ahimsa*

This selection details the duty of noninjury or ahimsa, the first vow of monastics. This is one of the leading duties of the laity as well. For example, observant Jains do not eat after sunset because they are not able to see any insects in the dark.

These classes of living beings have been declared by the Jinas: earth, water, fire, wind; grass, trees, and plants; and the moving beings, both the egg-bearing and those that bear live offspring, those generated from dirt and those generated in fluids. Know and understand that they all desire happiness. By hurting these beings, people do harm to their own souls, and will repeatedly be born as one of them.

Every being born high or low in the scale of the living creation, among movable and immovable beings, will meet with its death. Whatever sins the evildoer commits in every birth, for them he must die.

In this world or in the next the sinners suffer themselves what they have inflicted on other beings, a hundred times, or suffer other punishment. Living in the Samsara[26] they always acquire new Karma, and suffer for their misdeeds.

[5] Some leave their mother and father to live as Sramanas, but they use fire. The prophet [Mahavira] says, "People are wicked who kill beings for the sake of their own pleasure." He who lights a fire kills living beings; he who extinguishes it kills the fire. Therefore a wise man who well considers the Law should light no fire. Earth contains life, and water contains life; jumping or flying insects fall in the fire; dirt-born vermin and beings live in wood. All these beings are burned by lighting a fire.

Plants are beings possessed of natural development. Their bodies require nourishment, and they all have their individual life. Reckless men who cut them down for their own pleasure destroy many living beings. By destroying plants, when young or grown up, a careless man does harm to his own soul. The prophet says, "People are wicked who destroy plants for their own pleasure."

---

* *Sutrakritanga* 1.7.1–9

[26] *Samsara:* the wheel of rebirth.

Rules for Monastic Life*

Rules for both conduct and thought govern the life of a monk or a nun. While the passage speaks of "compassion for living things" as a motivation for noninjury, the main motivation is less altruistic — to avoid as much as possible one's collection of karma.

Learn from me, with attentive minds, the road shown by the wise ones. This road leads a monk who follows it to the end of all misery.

Giving up the life in a house, and taking Pravragya,²⁷ a sage should know and renounce those attachments that take hold of men. A restrained monk should abstain from killing, lying, stealing, sexual intercourse, from desire, love, and greed.

Even in his thoughts a monk should not long for a pleasant painted house filled with the fragrance of garlands and frankincense, secured by doors, and decorated with a white ceiling-cloth. [5] For in such a dwelling a monk will find it difficult to prevent his senses from increased desire and passion. He should be content to live on a burial-place, in a deserted house, below a tree, in solitude, or in a place that had been prepared for the sake of somebody else. A well-controlled monk should live in a pure place that is not too crowded, and where no women live. He should not build a house, nor cause others to erect one. Many living beings both movable and immovable, both tiny and large, are killed when a house is being built; therefore a monk should abstain from building a house.

[10] The same holds good with the cooking of food and drink, or with one's causing them to be cooked. Out of compassion for living beings one should not cook nor cause another to cook. Beings which live in water, plants, or in earth and wood are destroyed in food and drink; therefore a monk should cause nobody to cook. Nothing is so dangerous as fire, for it spreads in all directions and is able to destroy many beings. One should not light a fire.

Even in his thoughts a monk should not long for gold and silver. Indifferent alike to dirt and gold, he abstains from buying and selling. If he buys, he becomes a buyer; if he sells, he becomes a merchant. A monk is not to engage in buying and selling. [15] A monk who is to live on alms should beg and not buy. Buying and selling is a great sin; but to live on alms is benefitting. He should collect his alms in small parts according to the Sutras and to avoid faults. A monk should contentedly go on his begging-tour, whether he gets alms or not.

A great sage should not eat for the sake of the pleasant taste [of the food] but for the sustenance of life. He should not be dainty nor eager for good fare, he should restrain his tongue, and be without desire. Even in his thoughts he should not desire to be presented with flowers,²⁸ to be offered a seat, to be eloquently greeted, to be offered presents, or to get a magnificent welcome and treatment. He should meditate on true things only, committing no sins and having no property.

He should walk about careless of his body until his end draws near. [20] Rejecting food when the time of his death is near, and leaving the human body, he becomes his own master, and is liberated from misery. Without property, without egoism, free from passions. . . . he obtains absolute knowledge, and reaches eternal blessedness.

Thus I say.

---

* *Uttaradhyayana Sutra* 35
²⁷ *Pravragya:* the vow of the monk's wandering way of life.

²⁸ *presented with flowers:* these and the following special treatments would come when a monk visits layfolk in public or their homes.

The True Monk*

This passage repeats many of the preceding rules, but in a more positive and winsome way. It receives its title from the repeated refrain, "he is a true monk."

He who adopts the Law in the intention to live as a monk should live in company with other monks, upright, and free from desire. He should abandon his former connections, and not longing for pleasures, he should wander about as an unknown beggar. Then he is a true monk.

He should live free from love, a model of righteousness, abstaining from sins, versed in the sacred lore, protecting his soul, wise, hardy, and observing everything. He who is attached to nothing is a true monk.

Ignorant of abuse and injury, a steadfast monk should be a model of righteousness, always protecting his soul, neither rash nor passionate. When he endures everything, then he is a true monk. He who is content with lowly beds and lodgings, bears heat and cold, flies and gnats, is neither rash nor passionate, and endures everything, he is a true monk.

[5] He does not expect respectful treatment, nor hospitality, nor reverence, nor praises. He controls himself, keeps the vows, practices austerities, lives together with other monks, and meditates on his soul; this is a true monk. If he does not care for his life, or abandons every delusion, if he avoids men and women, always practices austerities, and does not betray any curiosity, then he is a true monk.

He who does not profess and live on divination from cuts and shreds, from sounds on the earth or in the air, from dreams, from diagrams, sticks, and properties of buildings, from changes in the body, from the meaning of the cries of animals, he is a true monk. He who does not praise or pay attention to the warriors, Ugras, princes, Brahmins, Bhogas,[29] and artists of all sorts, who abstains from this, he is a true monk.

[10] He who does not, for earthly gain, improve his acquaintance with householders, with whom he fell in as a monk, or was in friendly relation before that time, he is a true monk. A Nirgrantha is forbidden to take a bed, lodging, drink, food, or any dainties and spices from householders, if they do not give it themselves. He who is not angry at such occasions is a true monk.

If a monk gets any food and drink, or dainties and spices, and does not feel compassion on a sick fellow-monk in thoughts, words, and deeds, then he is not a true monk. But if he has his thoughts, words, and acts under strict discipline, then he is a true monk. Dishwater, barley mush, cold sour gruel, water in which barley has been washed— such loathsome food and drink he should not despise, but call at the lowliest houses for alms; then he is a true monk. . . .

[15] He who understands all religious disputations, who lives with fellow-monks, who practices self-discipline, who meditates on his soul, who is wise, hardy, and observes everything, who is calm, and does not hurt anybody, he is a true monk.

He who, not living by any craft, without house, without friends, subduing his senses, free from all ties, sinless, and eating only a little, leaves the house and lives single, he is a true monk.

Thus I say.

---

*Uttaradhyayana Sutra 15.1–16

[29] *Ugras, Bhogas:* honored families from the warrior caste.

Stories from Jaina Scriptures and Commentary*

The Shvetamara Jain stories illustrate in a more popular way the basic teachings of the faith. The first passage illustrates the importance of respect, the second deals with deceit. The third story comes from around the eleventh century C.E. and illustrates overcoming difficulties and attachments to become a monk.[30]

[The story of the Brahmin and his wife] After hearing the Law from an authentic elder, a Brahmin and his wives gave up worldly life. They led a very rigorous religious life, but their love for each other did not leave them. One of the ladies still had some pride: she was a Brahmin indeed! After death they went to the world of the gods and enjoyed life for the life-time they had.

There was, on the other hand, the city of Ilavardhana which had Laa as its tutelary deity. The wife of a caravan-leader who had no child worshiped her. The former Brahmin fell from the world of the gods and was born as this lady's son. He was therefore given the name of Ilaputra. He studied the arts. As for the Brahmin's former wife, she was born in an acrobat's family.

Both the boy and the girl had now reached marriageable age. One day the boy fell in love with the girl's beauty. Though he asked for her, he did not get her. Her parents said, "We shall give you the equivalent of her weight in gold. She is our imperishable treasure. But if you set off on tour with us and learn our art, we shall give her to you."

So Ilaputra set off on tour with them and learned their art. Then he was asked to give a show in front of the king on the occasion of a wedding-ceremony. The company went to Bernatada. The king attended the show together with his harem. Ilaputra was on the stage, but the

king had eyes only for the girl. The king did not give any money. There was loud applause: 'Acrobat,' people said to Ilaputra, "Do a falling stunt."

On top of a bamboo there is a piece of wood. Two nails are fixed on it. The acrobat wears shoes which are pierced at the bottom. Then, holding a sword and a shield in his hands, he jumps into the sky. The nails should be fitted into the holes of the shoes by seven jumps forwards and backwards. If the acrobat fails, he falls down and is broken into pieces.

That was the feat Ilaputra did. The king went on gazing at the young girl. People created an uproar. Nobody gave any money since the king did not give anything. The king thought, 'If this acrobat dies, the girl will be mine.' So he said to Ilaputra, "I did not see. Do it again." The boy did it again, but again the king did not see. He did it a third time, a fourth time he was asked to do it again. The audience was disgusted. Standing on the top of the bamboo, Ilaputra thought, "Enough of worldly pleasures! This king is not even satisfied with so many wives. He wants to attach himself to this actress, and in order to fulfill his desire he wants to kill me." He was ready to give up worldly life.

One day in a merchant's house he saw some monks who were receiving alms from fully adorned ladies. He noticed that the monks looked very peaceful, and said "Happy are those who have no more desire for sexual enjoyments. I was a merchant's son. See what condition I have reached after having left my family!"

In that very place, having achieved indifference for worldly objects, he got Omniscience. The indifference of the girl too should be fully described, and also that of the chief queen. The king, too, felt remorse. All four became Omniscient and Emancipated.

[Two non-Jain ascetics] There was A Minister's Deceit; in Bhrgukaccha the king Nahapana whose power lay in his treasury. On the other hand, there was in Pratishana Satavahana who

---

* *Avasyakasutra* 1.484.11–485.13; 2.200.11–201.12; *Mulasuddhiprakarana*, 179–180

[30] From Phyllis Granoff, ed., *The Clever Adulteress and Other Stories* (Ontario: Mosaic Press, 1990). Translated by Nalini Balbir and Phyllis Granoff. Used by permission.

could give a hundred, thousands, a hundred thousands, or millions to those who would bring back a hand or a head. So every day Nahapana's men used to kill enemies. Satavahana's men also used to kill and bring back some, but their king did not give them anything. As Satavahana had no more soldiers, he retreated. The following year he came again, but then also he was defeated and went away. So time passed.

One day, his minister said to him, 'Accuse me of some crime, banish me, and imprison some men.' The king did exactly so. As for the minister, he left the place and went to Bhrgukaccha, taking a load of sweet-smelling balls. He stayed in a secluded temple. The news spread in the neighboring kingdoms that Satavahana had thrown out his minister. In Bhrgukaccha nobody knew him. If somebody asked him, 'Who are you?', the minister said, 'I have been given the name of Lord Guggula.' If anybody recognized him, he gave the reason why he had been thrown out. They considered it was rather trivial.

Then Nahapana came to know about all that. He sent some men to Guggula, but Guggula did not even want to hear about becoming Nahapana's minister. The king himself came. He took Guggula back with him and appointed him. The minister, knowing that he was trusted said, "Through good deeds one can get a kingdom. Let the path to another birth be prepared." Nahapana spent money on temples, stupas, ponds, and tanks, and thus all the money ran out. His former minister summoned Satavahana to come. Nahapana again spent everything. He said to his minister. "You are a resourceful man."

"I shall manage," Guggula said. "Bring the ladies' ornaments."

Again Satavahana went back to Pratishana, summoned to come by his former minister. Nahapana had nothing left which he could give. He ran away. The city was captured by Satavahana.

In Bhrgukaccha there were the teacher Jinadeva and two non-Jain disputants, the brothers Bhadantamitra and Kunala. They took the drum out in order to invite people to challenge them.

While going to visit a Jain temple, Jinadeva came to know about it. He took up the challenge. The dispute took place in the royal court. The red-robed ascetics were defeated. Later on those two realized that without knowing the Scriptures of these Jains they would never be able to answer questions. So they deceitfully left worldly life at Jinadeva's feet. (See the account of Govinda for the full description.) Then they studied and understood the Scriptures. They really believed in them and became Jain monks.

[The Story of the Merchant Abhinava] There is in our own continent of Jambudvipa, in the very center of the area known as Southern Bharata, an ancient city named Vesali, which was exceedingly famous. There once reigned King Cedaa, who like some mythical beast that slays the proud lion of the jungle, had slain his proud and mighty enemies. He was lord over eighteen vassal kings. And there dwelt in that city two merchants. One was named Junnasetthi, "The Old Merchant," and the other was called Ahinavasetthi, "The Young Merchant." The first was as poor as poor can be, while the other was as rich as rich can be.

Now one day the lord of the triple world, the lord of heaven, earth and the nether world, the Jina Mahavira came into that city in the course of his monastic wanderings. This was in the time before he had reached his state of perfect enlightenment. And one night the rains began. Mahavira took refuge in some shelter there and assumed a posture of meditation that he would keep for the four months of the rainy season.

The old merchant saw him there and his heart was filled with feelings of awe and reverence. Waves of joy flowed over his whole body and he proclaimed, "Today truly my whole life's purpose is fulfilled. Today my life indeed seems worth living. For today I can bow down to the feet of the Blessed One, which are like pure water to cleanse the dirt of sin." And with feelings like this every day he went to bow down to the feet of the Blessed One. He would stay a few moments each day, with his hands joined together and held over his head in a gesture of reverence, and worship the Blessed One. And he thought, "Now I come here every day and it seems that the Blessed One never moves from this place. He is every day engaged in meditating, his body unmoving, as he observes the fast for four months of the rainy season. If only the Blessed One would break his fast at my house when the time comes, then truly I would consider myself to be the most fortunate man in the world."

And while he occupied himself with pious thoughts like these, in no time at all the four months of the rainy season passed and there came the day for the Blessed One to break his fast. Bowing down to the Blessed One the old merchant said, "Friend to all the world! Lord of Ascetics! Blessed One, bless me today by breaking your fast at my house." And with these words he returned home. There he made everything ready and he waited expectantly looking at the door. He kept thinking to himself all the while, "The Blessed One is coming, the Blessed One is coming, and I shall fulfill my every desire by giving him food to break his fast. If the Lord of the Inas comes to my house, then I shall have crossed this ocean of rebirths, whose waves are our sufferings, and in whose depths lurk countless misfortunes like so many sharks."

And as his desire for the highest bliss grew and grew and waves of joy coursed through his body while he waited there, the Jina passed him by and went into the house of the young merchant. And the young merchant, recalling the teaching that a gift given to the proper recipient leads to fruits right in that very same lifetime, fed the Blessed One. And at the very moment that he did so the five marvelous signs appeared on account of the power of that gift that was given to such a worthy person as Mahavira. A rain of jewels fell from the sky, while the Gods waved the ends of their robes in congratulations. The Gods beat their heavenly drums and a fragrant perfumed rain fell from the sky. Heavenly voices could be heard, praising the gift.

Now when the old merchant heard the sound of the heavenly drums beating he wondered what

had happened. Someone then told him, "The Blessed One has been given food to break his fast." His earlier religious resolve was thus broken. In the meantime the Blessed One continued on his wanderings, leaving that city.

Now it chanced that the Jina Parsvanatha came there. All of the townspeople reverently rushed out to greet the Jina. And that Blessed One discoursed on the Jain religion, which is like a boat for fortunate souls, ferrying them across the ocean of rebirths.

"Listen, all of you fortunate souls who are destined to achieve final release! The Jain faith alone is your refuge in this cycle of rebirths. All of the rest is mere delusion.

"All material prosperity, every worldly joy comes from this religion if it is well practiced. Indeed it leads even to heaven and final release.

"And its duties are said by the Jinas to be fourfold, giving to others, observing a moral life, practicing austerities, and engaging in right meditation. And so you should practice these things, particularly giving, so that you may obtain the bliss of true peace."

Now at that time, all the townspeople, who had been amazed by the great merit that the young merchant obviously had, seeing their chance, humbly asked the Blessed One: "Blessed One! Right now, here in this city, who is the person who has the most merit?" And at that the Blessed One pronounced the old merchant to have the greatest merit.

The people all quickly replied, "Blessed One! But he was not the one to give the Jina food to break his fast. The other one did, and the five divine signs appeared in his house."

But the Blessed One told them, "If the old merchant had not heard that the Jina had already been given food to break his fast, for sure he would have obtained omniscience just one second later. Now it is true that the young merchant experienced the divine signs in his house, and it is true that he achieved merit that will give rise to its fruit right here in this very lifetime, but he did not acquire any merit that will carry over into a future rebirth, for he lacked the proper mental attitude for that when he gave his gift."

And when they heard that answer all the townspeople felt great respect for the old merchant. Having bowed down to the Blessed One they all went back to their own homes.

GLOSSARY

Agama (AH-gah-muh) "tradition," the Western name for the Jain canon.

ahimsa (ah-HIM-suh) "noninjury" to any living being.

Angas (AHN-guhs) "limbs," the first and main section of the Shvetambara canon.

Arhat (AHR-haht) one who has reached nirvana.

Jina (GEE-nuh) a "conqueror," one who has reached nirvana.

Prakaranas (prah-KAR-ah-nuhs) the main section of the Digambara canon.

Siddhanta (sid-DAHN-tuh) "doctrine, teaching," the name that Jains use for their scripture.

Tirthankara (tihr-TAHN-kah-ruh) "ford-finder," one who has traveled from the misery of this world across the river of existence to liberation, and who enables others to do so by teaching and example.

QUESTIONS FOR STUDY AND DISCUSSION

1.   Compare the life of Mahavira and Siddharta Gotama (the Buddha). How are they remarkably alike, and what might their dissimilarities be?

2.   One scholar has called Jainism the "unhappy face of Buddhism." Judging from their scriptures, would you agree or disagree? Why?

3.   Discuss the division between the Shvetambara and Digambara sects on the issue of the place of women as monastics. To what degree may this issue be reflected in arguments over the role of women in the monastics or clergy of other faiths?

4.   Discuss the basic idea of *ahimsa* in Jainism. Why has it been influential in the wider Indian tradition? How might it be applicable to the peoples of other, non-Indian faiths?

SUGGESTIONS FOR FURTHER READING

Primary Readings

A. L. Basham, "Jainism and Buddhism," in W. T. deBary, ed., *Sources of Indian Tradition.* New York: Columbia University Press, 1958, pp. 39–92. Excellent translations with introductions of about twenty short but important passages in Jain religion and philosophy.

Hermann Jacobi, trans., *Gaina Sutras,* in M. Muller, ed., *Sacred Books of the East,* vols. 22 and 45. Oxford: Oxford University Press, 1884, 1895. Reprinted, Delhi: Motilal Banarsidass, 1964. Contains selections of two *angas,* a *mulasutta* and a *cheyasutta;* still the fullest English translation.

Secondary Readings

Paul Dundas, *The Jains.* London: Routledge, 1993. The best and most recent introduction to Jainism, with an excellent examination of Jain attitudes to scripture.

Kendall W. Folkert, "The 'Canons' of 'Scripture,'" in M. Levering, ed., *Rethinking Scripture.* Albany: State University of New York Press, 1989, pp. 170–179. A thought-provoking analysis of the present reception of Jaina scriptures in light of the comparative study of world scriptures.

Kendall W. Folkert, *Scripture and Community: Collected Essays on the Jains,* ed. J. E. Cort. Studies in World Religions Series. Cambridge: Harvard University Center for the Study of World Religions, 1995. Treats the various aspects of Jain tradition, with special attention to scriptures and monastic practice.

P. Jaini, *The Jain Path of Purification.* Berkeley: University of California Press, 1979. A good all-around recent introduction to Jainism, with good treatment of scripture.

Recitation of the Guru Granth Sahib
An official reader recites the holy book in the Golden Temple of Amristar, India, while an attendant behind him waves a horse-hair fan to venerate the book. Credit: Gunter Reitz / Barnaby's Picture Library

CHAPTER FIVE

Sikhism

❖ A turbaned man walks down a bridge to the gate of the Golden Temple of Amritsar, India. Once inside, he approaches the central and only object of veneration, the large scripture book called the *Adi Granth*. Placed on cushions on a raised platform under a richly ornamented canopy, the *Granth* is read by an official reader as an attendant waves a ceremonial whisk over it. The worshipper bows reverently before the book with folded hands, listening to the melodious reading.

❖ Residents of a northern Indian city pause as a religious procession comes down their street. Music from instruments and singers reaches their ears before they see the procession itself. As the procession comes into view, they do not see a statue of a Hindu divinity but rather the *Adi Granth,* mounted on a truck and driven in solemn veneration.

❖ Worshippers at a Sikh temple see, in quick succession, three life-cycle ceremonies. First, a baby is brought in for naming; as the *Adi Granth* is opened at random, the first letter on the left-hand page becomes the first letter in the child's first name. Second, a young couple comes to be married; during the ceremony, the couple circle the *Granth* several times to the accompaniment of verses from its marriage hymns. Third, the relatives of a recently deceased Sikh come for the conclusion of funeral rites; a prominent part of it is the continuous reading of the entire *Granth,* and they are present for the solemn conclusion of the reading.

INTRODUCTION

The Sikh religion was founded about 1500 c.e. by Guru Nanak. It has made its home in the Punjab region of northern India, where today it numbers more than 9 million believers. Designed to appeal to Hindus and Muslims, it contains elements of both faiths. With Hinduism it shares mysticism and devotion; with Islam, a rigid monotheism. Yet it rejects elements of both these traditions, especially their leaders and rituals. Sikhism grew through a line of ten gurus until it reached its present form as expressed in its scripture, considered the successor of this line. In its veneration of scripture, Sikhism is unsurpassed among world religions.

Overview of Structure

The scripture book **Adi Granth** [AH-dee GRAHNTH] has three main parts, arranged in order of their importance. First is the **Japji** [JAHP-jee], written by Guru Nanak, which the faithful consider a summary and capstone of Sikhism. Teaching in the form of a poem, it differs from the rest of the *Adi Granth* by having no hymn tune. Appended to the *Japji* are fourteen hymns, all of which are found later in the

Adi Granth. The second part, by far the longest, is the collection of **Rags** [rahgs] ("tunes"), thirty-nine in all. Each rag is divided by different poetic meters and lengths. These divisions are further divided by guru-author, proceeding chronologically through the line of gurus. Each guru calls himself "Nanak," usually at conclusion of the hymn, but the different guru-authors are noted by the numbered use of the term **Mahala** [ma-HAH-luh]. Mahala 1 denotes the compositions of Guru Nanak; Mahala 2, of Guru Angad, etc.; up to Mahala 5 for Guru Arjan. The third part is a mixed collection of twenty-six small books, most elaborating on the rags. It also features hymns of many *bhakti* (Hindu) saints and Sufi (Muslim) mystics, which early Sikhs found congenial, and which Sikhs have always seen as proof of the universality of their tradition. As it now stands, the *Adi Granth*'s material ranges in time from the twelfth-century hymns of Jaidev to the hymns of the ninth guru, Tegh Bahadur, who died in 1675.

The ***Dasam Granth,*** or "Tenth Book," is mostly composed of legendary narratives, which are not to be found in the *Adi Granth*. Modern scholarship has traced many of them to Hindu Puranic sources. But certain parts of the *Dasam Granth* are well known and much used among Sikhs, especially the teachings of the tenth guru, Gobind Singh. Often quoted is his famous statement, "The temple and the mosque are one; so too are *puja* [Hindu worship] and [Muslim] prostration. All men are one though they seem to be many." Coupled with these more ecumenical sayings are statements of the rising militancy of the Sikhs.

The content of the *Adi Granth* states in hymnic form the main beliefs of the Sikhs. The *Adi Granth* rejects what it perceives as the ritualism and formalism of Islam and especially of Hinduism, arguing for moral purity as the chief basis of religion. Hindu caste structure is repeatedly rejected; all men are to live as equals. Karma and reincarnation are accepted, but the practice of the Sikh religion will release one from rebirth and lead to blessedness in heaven. Above all, the *Adi Granth* promotes the strict doctrine of one God and mystical devotion to his name. This loving God offers salvation by his grace to those who meditate on him and live in his truth. The reader looks in vain for stories about the life of the founder or other gurus. These have been collected instead into the ***janam-sakhis*** [JAH-num SAH-kees], traditional narratives that are highly legendary. The *janam-sakhis* have a semicanonical status among devout Sikhs.

The main language of the *Adi Granth* is Punjabi, written in the Gurmukhi ("mouth of the Guru") script. It also shows strong traces of influence from the Hindi language and from several other north Indian languages. The *Adi Granth* employs the Sadhukari (or Sant-Basha) dialect, which was used by religious poets in North India in the fifteenth and sixteenth centuries. Its language is complicated enough to necessitate special training for the **granthis** [GRAHN-thees], official readers, but most observant Sikhs can understand the scripture well enough to read it on their own.

Origin and Development

The overall structure of the *Adi Granth* suggests its origins and growth. Guru Nanak (1469–1539), in a typical Hindu attitude, rejected the authority of the written word, stressing instead the interior meditation on the "holy [oral] word." The *Japji* and the various hymns he composed were passed along orally. Guru Angad, whom Nanak made his successor, devised a Punjabi alphabet for the Gurmukhi language, and the *Adi Granth* was later written in this script. Guru Amar Das, third in the line, compiled a hymnal of his own poems, the poems of his two predecessors, and poems from pre-Sikh mystics. The fifth guru, Arjan, revised this hymnal and compiled the oral and written work of all his predecessors into the *Adi Granth* in 1603–1604. Tradition says that Arjan's opponents were writing and circulating books falsely attributed to Nanak in an effort to corrupt Sikhism and turn it away from Arjan's leadership. In response, Arjan compiled the *Adi Granth.*

The sixth guru, Arjan's son Har Gobind, altered the Sikh movement's original pacifism to a newfound militancy. The final guru, Gobind Singh, is considered by Sikhs to be, after Nanak, their most important leader. Before his death in 1708, he declared that the line of gurus was complete. From this time on, the only guru of the community was to be the *Adi Granth* itself, which Gobind edited in its final, present form. (He himself wrote portions of the *Dasam Granth,* as mentioned earlier.) Therefore, the *Adi Granth* has served as the teacher and authority for Sikhs, quite literally as the book containing the soul of the gurus. Nothing expresses this conviction as well as the Sikh daily prayer, the *Ardas:* "From the Timeless One [God] there came the bidding, in accordance with which was established the Panth [Sikh community]. To all Sikhs there comes this command: acknowledge as the Guru the *Granth.* Acknowledge the *Granth* as Guru, for it is the manifest body of the Masters. You whose hearts are pure, seek Him in the Word!" [1]

Use

All Sikh usage of the *Adi Granth* is steeped in an attitude of profound respect. Devout Sikhs generally refer to the *Adi Granth* by a more venerable name, the *Sri Guru Granth Sahib* (*Guru Granth* for short), or "Revered Teacher Granth." This name is based on the origin of the Sikh scripture. Sikhs believe that each of their ten gurus had the same soul, the soul of Nanak. The last guru bestowed this soul and its guru status on the *Granth.* It became the book-embodiment of the soul of the gurus, the statement of the essence of Sikhism and the final authority for its continuing life.

Sikhs also call the *Adi Granth* the "living embodiment of the Guru." One of their leading theologians has claimed, "This is the only scripture of the world which was compiled by one of the founders of a religion himself and whose authenticity has never been questioned." [2] Moreover, the *Adi Granth* has served for almost three hundred years as a force for unity in Sikhism. Doctrinal disputes are traditionally ended by consulting it, at random if need be. Sikhs have a strong mystical feeling for the *Granth* and treat it as an icon. No doubt the musical nature of its recitation contributes to its emotive power. Nevertheless, Sikhism also stresses the importance of meditating on and comprehending the meaning of its scripture.

---

[1] W. H. McLeod, *The Evolution of the Sikh Community* (Oxford: Clarendon Press, 1976), p. 66.
[2] Gopal Singh, ed., *Sri Guru Granth Sahib* (Calcutta: M. P. Birla, 1989), p. 1.

The Sikh temple is in essence a shrine for the *Adi Granth*. Temple officials ceremoniously close it and "put it to bed" at night. Before dawn they bring it out again, install it in its place, and open it. All this is done to the accompaniment of hymns from the *Adi Granth*'s pages. Despite its large-format size, Sikhs carry their guru above their heads, and those who carry it must wear gloves. When open, the *Granth* is draped in fine silk and placed on a special cot under a rich canopy at the focal point of the temple. Worshippers come to walk around it, bow to it, listen to its reading, and sometimes even pray to it. They must never turn their back on it. The official readers or granthis (often mistaken for "priests" by outsiders) often wear white scarves on their mouths as they read so that their breath will not touch the holy book. Sikh men take turns standing near it with a horsehair whisk (the **chaur** [chowr], one of the symbols of Sikhism), fanning it and keeping away flies with back-and-forth motions. This scripture-centered activity goes on every day at the temple; there is no weekly service. At special festivals, a nonstop oral reading by a team of granthis is held that lasts two days and nights. Every major life-cycle celebration centers in some way around the *Adi Granth*. In sum, it is no exaggeration to say that all the worship of the Sikhs centers on and originates in the *Adi Granth*.

This usage also carries over into the Sikh home. A prosperous Sikh household has a special room solely for the prominent placement of the *Granth*. Almost every other Sikh household has a **gutka** [GUHT-kuh], an anthology of the *Adi Granth* with a few passages from the *Dasam Granth*. Daily readings are held in the home. Early-morning recitation by memory of the *Japji* and other long sections is common, often lasting for more than an hour. Devout Sikhs have committed large portions of the *Adi Granth* to memory, and it is constantly on their lips during the day and night, especially in the five required daily prayers.

A memorable feature of Sikh scripture usage is **vak lao** [vahk low], "taking (God's) word." In the home or in the temple, the scripture is always opened at random, and the reading begins from the top of the lefthand page. This reading is thought to hold special significance for the occasion; it is God's word for the moment, which must be "taken" into the believer's life.

TEACHING

Selections from the *Japji**

This entire poem is repeated from memory by practicing Sikhs every morning during prayers—no small feat, as it is almost twice as long as the excerpts given here. They consider it the essence and epitome of their faith. The Japji *moves back and forth between several topics: (1) God's name, greatness, and power; (2) God's creation of the world; (3) the way of salvation by meditating on God's name; (4) good and evil; (5) relations with Hinduism and Islam. The rich sonority of the* Japji*'s poetry comes through in this translation. It begins with the* **Mul** *("root")* **Mantra** *[mool*

*1–3, 5–6, 9–10, 12–13, 15, 17–18, 20–22, 25, 28–29, 33, 37-Epilogue

MAHN-truh], a confession of faith considered the capstone of the whole composition.[3]

There is only one God whose name is true, the Creator, devoid of fear and enmity, immortal, unborn, self-existent; by the favor of the Guru.[4] Repeat His Name!

The True One was in the beginning; the True One was in the primal age.
The True One is now also, O Nanak; the True One also (forever) shall be.

[1] By thinking I cannot obtain a conception of Him, even though I think hundreds of thousands of times.
Though I be silent and keep my attention firmly fixed on Him, I cannot preserve silence.
The hunger of the hungry for God does not subside, though they obtain the load of the worlds.

If man should have thousands and hundreds of thousands of devices, even one would not assist him in obtaining God.
How shall man become true before God? How shall the veil of falsehood be torn?
By walking, O Nanak, according to the will of the Commander as preordained.

By His order bodies are produced; His order cannot be described.
By His order souls are infused into them; by His order greatness is obtained.
By His order men are high or low; by His order they obtained preordained pain or pleasure.
By His order some obtained their reward; by His order others must ever wander in transmigration.
All are subject to His order; none is exempt from it.

He who understands God's order, O Nanak, is never guilty of egoism.

Who can sing His power? Who has power to sing it?
Who can sing His gifts or know His signs?
Who can sing His attributes, greatness, and deeds?
Who can sing His knowledge, whose study is arduous?
Who can sing Him, who fashions the body and destroys it?
Who can sing Him, who takes away life and restores it?
Who can sing Him, who appears to be far, but is known to be near?
Who can sing Him, who is all-seeing and omnipresent?
In describing Him there would never be an end.

Millions of men give millions upon millions of descriptions of Him, but they fail to describe Him.
The Giver gives; the receiver grows weary of receiving.
In every age man subsists by His bounty.
The Commander by His order has laid out the way of the world.
Nanak, God the unconcerned[5] is happy. . . .

[5] He is not established, nor is He created.
The Pure One exists by Himself.
They who worshipped Him have obtained honor.
Nanak, sing His praises who is the Treasury of excellences.
Sing and hear and put His love into your hearts.
Thus shall your sorrows be removed, and you shall be absorbed in Him who is the abode of happiness.
Under the Guru's instruction God's word is heard; under the Guru's instruction its

---

[3] All selections from the Sikh scriptures are taken from Max A. Macauliffe, *The Sikh Religion: Its Gurus, Sacred Writings and Authors* (Oxford: Oxford University Press, 1909).
[4] *by the favor of the Guru:* known through the Guru.

---

[5] *unconcerned:* free of care.

knowledge is acquired; under the Guru's instruction man learns that God is everywhere contained.

The Guru is Shiva; the Guru is Vishnu and Brahma; the Guru is Paarbati, Lakhshmi, and Saraswati.[6]

If I knew Him, should I not describe Him? He cannot be described by words.

My Guru has explained one thing to me—
That there is but one Bestower on all living beings; may I not forget Him!

If I please Him, that is my place of pilgrimage to bathe in; if I please Him not, what ablutions shall I make?

What can all the created beings I behold obtain without previous good acts?

Precious stones, jewels, and gems shall be treasured up in your heart if you hearken to even one word of the Guru.

The Guru has explained one thing to me—
That there is but one Bestower on all living beings; may I not forget Him! . . .

[9] By hearing the Name man becomes as Shiva, Brahma, and Indra.

By hearing the Name even the low become highly lauded.

By hearing the Name the way of Yoga and the secrets of the body are obtained.

By hearing the Name man understands the real nature of the Shastras, the Smritis, and the Vedas.

Nanak, the saints are ever happy.

By hearing the Name sorrow and sin are no more.

[10] By hearing the Name truth, contentment, and divine knowledge are obtained.

Hearing the Name is equal to bathing at the sixty-eight places of pilgrimage.

By hearing the Name and reading it man obtains honor.

By hearing the Name the mind is composed and fixed on God.

Nanak, the saints are always happy.

By hearing the Name sorrow and sin are no more. . . .

[12] The condition of him who obeys God cannot be described.

Whoever tries to describe it shall afterward repent.

There is no paper, or pen, or writer
To describe the condition of him who obeys God.

So pure is His name—
Whoever obeys God knows the pleasure of it in his own heart.

By obeying Him wisdom and understanding enter the mind;

By obeying Him man knows all worlds;

By obeying Him man suffers no punishment;

By obeying Him man shall not depart with Jam[7]—

So pure is God's name—
Whoever obeys God knows the pleasure of it in his own heart. . . .

[15] By obeying Him man attains the gate of salvation;

By obeying Him man is saved with his family;

By obeying Him the Guru is saved, and saves his disciples;

By obeying Him, O Nanak, man wanders not in quest of alms—

So pure is God's name—
Whoever obeys God knows the pleasure of it in his own heart. . . .

[17] Numberless Your worshippers, and numberless Your lovers;

Numberless adorers, and numberless they who perform austerities for You;

Numberless the reciters of sacred books and Vedas;

---

[6]*Shiva . . . Saraswati:* all are Hindu divinities.

[7]*Jam:* the god of death. By obeying God, a person will not be reborn to die again.

Numberless Your Yogins whose hearts are indifferent to the world;

Numberless the saints who ponder on attributes and divine knowledge;

Numberless Your true men; numberless almsgivers;

Numberless Your heroes who face the steel of their enemies;

Numberless Your silent worshippers who lovingly fix their thoughts upon You.

What power have I to describe You?

So lowly am I, I cannot even once be a sacrifice to You.

Whatever pleases You is good.

O formless One, You are always secure.

Numberless are the fools appallingly blind;

Numberless are the thieves and devourers of others' property;

Numberless those who establish their sovereignty by force;

Numberless the cut-throats and murderers;

Numberless the sinners who pride themselves on committing sin;

Numberless the liars who roam about lying;

Numberless the filthy who enjoy filthy gain;

Numberless the slanderers who carry loads of calumny on their heads;

Nanak thus describes the degraded.

So lowly am I, I cannot even once be a sacrifice to You.

Whatever pleases You is good.

O Formless One, You are always secure. . . .

[20] When the hands, feet, and other members of the body are covered with filth,

It is removed by washing with water.

When your clothes are polluted,

Apply soap, and the impurity shall be washed away.

So when the mind is defiled by sin,

It is cleansed by the love of the Name.

Men do not become saints or sinners by merely calling themselves so.

The recording angels take with them a record of man's acts.

It is he himself sows, and he himself eats.

Nanak, man suffers transmigration by God's order.

Pilgrimage, austerities, mercy, and almsgiving on general and special occasions

Whoever performs, may obtain some little honor;

But he who hears and obeys and loves God in his heart

Shall wash off his impurity in the place of pilgrimage within him.

All virtues are Yours, O Lord; none are mine.

There is no devotion without virtue.

From the Self-existent proceeded Maya,[8]

whence issued a word which produced Brahma and the rest—

"You are true, You are beautiful, pleasure is ever in Your heart!"

What the time, what the epoch, what the lunar day, and what the week-day,

What the season, and what the month when the world was created,

The Pandits[9] did not discover; had they done so, they would have recorded it in the Puranas.

Nor did the Qazis[10] discover it; had they done so, they would have recorded it in the Quran:

Neither the Yogi nor any other mortal knows the lunar day, or the week-day, or the season, or the month.

Only the Creator who fashioned the world knows when He did so.

How shall I address You, O God? How shall I praise You? How shall I describe You? And how shall I know You?

Says Nanak, everybody speaks of You, one wiser than another.

Great is the Lord, great is His name; what He does comes to pass.

---

[8]*Maya:* "deceit, illusion," God's mystical power by which he created matter.

[9]*Pandits:* highly learned Brahmins.

[10]*Qazis:* Islamic judges.

Nanak, he who is proud shall not be honored
on his arrival in the next world.

There are hundreds of thousands of nether and
upper regions.
Men have grown weary at last of searching for
God's limits; they say one thing, that God
has no limit.

The thousands of Puranas and Muslim books
tell that in reality there is but one principle.
If God can be described by writing, then
describe Him; but such description is
impossible.
O Nanak, call Him great; only He Himself
knows how great He is. . . .

[25] His many bounties cannot be recorded,
He is a great giver and has not a particle of
covetousness.
How many, yes countless heroes beg of Him!
How many others whose number cannot be
conceived!
How many persons receive yet deny God's
gifts!
How many fools there are who merely eat!
How many are ever dying in distress and
hunger!
O Giver, these are also Your gifts.
Rebirth and deliverance depend on Your will:
Nobody can interfere with it.
If any fool tries to interfere with it,
He himself shall know the punishment he shall
suffer.
God himself knows to whom He may give, and
He Himself gives:
Very few acknowledge this.
He to whom God has given the boon of prais-
ing and lauding Him,
O Nanak, is the King of kings. . . .

[28] Make contentment and modesty your ear-
rings, self-respect your wallet, meditation the
ashes to smear on your body;
Make your body, which is only a morsel for
death, your beggar's coat, and faith your rule
of life and your staff.

Make association with men your Ai Panth,[11]
and the conquest of your heart the conquest
of the world.
The primal, the pure, without beginning, the
indestructible, the same in every age!

Make divine knowledge your food, compassion
your storekeeper, and the voice which is in
every heart the pipe to call to feast.
Make Him who has strung the whole world on
His string your spiritual Lord; let wealth and
supernatural power be relishes for others.

Union and separation is the law which regulates
the world. By destiny we receive our portion.
Hail! Hail to Him, the primal, the pure, without beginning, the indestructible, the same
in every age! . . .

[33] I have no strength to speak and no
strength to be silent.
I have no strength to ask and no strength
to give;
I have no strength to live, and no strength
to die,
I have no strength to acquire empire or wealth
which produce a commotion in the heart.
I have no strength to meditate on You or ponder on divine knowledge;
I have no strength to find the way to escape
from the world.
He in whose arm there is strength, may see
what he can do.
Nanak, no one is of superior or inferior
strength before God. . . .

[37] Make continence your furnace, resignation
your goldsmith,
Understanding your anvil, divine knowledge
your tools,
The fear of God your bellows, austerities
your fire,
Divine love your crucible, and melt God's name
in it.

---

[11] *Ai Panth:* a sect of (Hindu) yogins.

In such a true mint the Word shall be coined.
This is the practice of those on whom God
looks with an eye of favor.
Nanak, the Kind One by a glance makes them
happy.

[Epilogue] The air is the guru, water our father,
and the great earth our mother;
Day and night are our two nurses, male and
female, who set the whole world playing.

Merits and demerits shall be read out in the
presence of the Judge.
According to men's acts, some shall be near,
and others distant from God.
They who have pondered on the Name and
departed after the completion of their toil,
Shall have their countenances made bright, O
Nanak; how many shall be emancipated in
company with them!

Remembering God*

*In Sikhism, the way of salvation is by profound re-
flection on, and commitment to, God's name. "Remembering" is not the opposite of "forgetting," but
a way to deep reflection. These are the words of
Guru Arjan, often repeated after the* Japji *in the
morning prayer service.*

I bow to the primal Guru;
I bow to the Guru of the primal age;
I bow to the true Guru;
I bow to the holy divine Guru.

Remember, remember God;
By remembering Him you shall obtain
happiness,
And erase from your hearts trouble and
affliction.
Remember the praises of the one all-
supporting God.
Numberless persons utter God's various names.
Investigating the Vedas, the Puranas, and the
Smritis,
Men have made out the one word which is
God's name.
His praises cannot be recounted,
Who treasures God's name in his heart even
for a moment.

Says Nanak, save me, O Lord, with those who
are desirous of one glance of You.
In this Sukhmani is the name of God which like
ambrosia bestows happiness,
And gives peace to the hearts of the saints.

By remembering God man does not again enter
the womb;
By remembering God the tortures of Death
disappear;
By remembering God death is removed;
By remembering God enemies retreat;
By remembering God no obstacles are met;
By remembering God we are watchful night
and day;
By remembering God fear is not felt;
By remembering God sorrow troubles not:
Men remember God in the company of the
saints.
Nanak, by the love of God all wealth is
obtained.

By remembering God we obtain wealth, supernatural power, and the nine treasures;
By remembering God we obtain divine knowledge, meditation, and the essence of
wisdom;
Remembrance of God is the real devotion,
penance, and worship;
By remembering God the conception of duality
is dispelled;

*Gauri Sukhmani, Mahala 5

By remembering God we obtain the advantages of bathing at places of pilgrimage;

By remembering God we are honored at His court;

By remembering God we become reconciled to His will;

By remembering God men's lives are very profitable;

They whom He has caused to do so remember Him.

Nanak, touch the feet of such persons.[12]

---

[12]*touch the feet of such persons:* Nanak approves of them.

Creation of the World*

The world was directly and purposefully created by God; it still reflects God's goodness. This composition by Guru Nanak extolling God's creation is sung in every Sikh temple in the morning.

Wonderful Your word, wonderful Your knowledge;

Wonderful Your creatures, wonderful their species;

Wonderful their forms, wonderful their colors;

Wonderful the animals which wander naked;

Wonderful Your wind; wonderful Your water;

Wonderful Your fire which sports wondrously;

Wonderful the earth, wonderful the sources of production;

Wonderful the pleasures to which mortals are attached;

Wonderful is meeting, wonderful parting from You;

Wonderful is hunger, wonderful repletion;

Wonderful Your praises, wonderful Your eulogies;

Wonderful the desert, wonderful the road;

Wonderful Your nearness, wonderful Your remoteness;

Wonderful to behold You present.

Beholding these wonderful things I remain wondering.

Nanak, they who understand them are supremely fortunate.

By Your power we see, by Your power we hear, by Your power we fear, or enjoy the highest happiness;

By Your power were made the nether regions and the heavens; by Your power all creation;

By Your power were produced the Vedas, the Puranas, the Muslim books, and by Your power all compositions;

By Your power we eat, drink, and clothe ourselves; by Your power springs all affection;

By Your power are the species, classes, and colors of creatures; by Your power are the animals of the world.

By Your power are virtues; by Your power are vices: by Your power, honor and dishonor;

By Your power are wind, water, and fire; by Your power is the earth.

Everything exists by Your power; You are the omnipotent Creator; Your name is the holiest of the holy.

Says Nanak, You behold and pervade all things subject to Your command: You are altogether unrivalled.

---

*Asa Ki Var, Mahala 1

Dancing for Krishna*

Sikhism developed out of devotional Hinduism. Here Guru Amar Das rejects the Krishnavites' idea that merit is earned by participation in the dancing for Krishna that occurs at his festivals. In typical Guru-Granth *style, it adapts the practices of other religions to Sikhism by reinterpreting them for the new faith.*

I dance, but it is my heart I cause to dance;
By the favor of the Guru I have effaced myself.
He who keeps his mind firmly fixed on God
    shall obtain deliverance and the object of his
    desires.
Dance, O man, before your Guru;
He who dances as it pleases the Guru shall ob-
    tain happiness, and at the last moment the
    fear of Death shall forsake him.

He whom God causes to dance and whom He
    loves is a saint.
He himself sings, he himself instructs, and puts
    ignorant man on the right way.
He who banishes worldly love shall dance day
    and night in God's house and never sleep.

---

*Rag Gurji, Mahala 3

Every one who dances, leaps, and sings of other
    gods is lulled to sleep in the house of riches;
    such are the perverse who have no devotion.
Demigods and men who abandon the world
    dance in religious works; Munis and men
    dance in the contemplation of divine
    knowledge.
The Sidhs, Strivers, and holy men who have ac-
    quired wisdom to meditate on God dance in
    God's love.
The regions, worlds, beings endowed with the
    three qualities, and they who love You, O
    God, dance.
Men and the lower animals all dance, the four
    sources of life dance.
They who please You dance, the pious who love
    the Word. . . .
He to whom You are gracious shall obtain You
    by the favor of the Guru.
If I forget the True One even for a moment,
    that moment passes in vain.
Remember Him at every breath and He will
    pardon you from His own grace.
It is they who please You, O God, and who
    meditate on the Word, who really dance.
Says Nanak, they to whom You are merciful
    shall easily obtain bliss.

The Hindu Thread**

This passage from Guru Nanak features a strong rejection of Hindu ritual practices, especially those of the Brahmin (priestly) caste. As in the previous selection, Hindu practice is reinterpreted for Sikhs: "Make a sacred thread for the soul."

Make mercy your cotton, contentment your
    thread, continence its knot, truth its twist.

**Asa Ki Var, Mahala 1

That would make a sacred thread for the soul;
    if you have it, O Brahmin, then put it on me.
It will not break, or become soiled, or be
    burned, or lost.
Blest is the man, O Nanak, who has such a
    thread on his neck.
You purchase a sacred thread for four damris,
    and seated in a square [13] put it on;

---

[13]*seated in a square:* a square drawn on the ground in which the thread ceremony occurs.

You whisper instruction that the Brahmin is
the guru—
Man dies, the sacred thread falls, and the soul
departs without it.

Though men commit countless thefts, countless adulteries, utter countless falsehoods and
countless words of abuse;
Though they commit countless robberies and
villainies night and day against their fellow
creatures;
Yet the cotton thread is spun, and the Brahmin
comes to twist it.
For the ceremony they kill a goat and cook and
eat it, and everybody then says, "Put on the
sacred thread."
When it becomes old, it is thrown away and another is put on.
Nanak, the string does not break if it is strong.
By adoring and praising the Name honor and a
true thread are obtained.
In this way a sacred thread shall be put on
which will not break, and which will be fit
for entrance into God's court.

There is no string for the sexual organs (to
wear), no string for women;
There is no string for the impure acts which
cause your beards to be daily spat upon.
There is no string for the feet, no string for the
hands,
No string for the tongue, no string for the eyes.
Without such strings the Brahmin wanders
astray,
Twists strings for the neck, and puts them on
others.
He takes a fee for marrying;
He pulls out a paper, and shows the fate of the
wedded pair.[14]
Hear and see, you people; it is strange
That, while mentally blind, a man is
named wise.

---

[14]*He pulls . . . pair:* shows them an astrological prediction,
still an important part of Hindu marriage.

ETHICS

Truth Is the Basis of Conduct*

*This passage expresses the simplicity of Sikh ethics.
All good conduct comes from a love of the truth,
which in turn comes from being filled with God.*

He alone is truly truthful
In whose heart is the True One living,
Whose soul within is rinsed of falsehood
And his body without is cleansed by
washing.
He alone is truly truthful
Who loves truth with passion,
Whose heart rejoices in the Name
And finds the door to salvation.
He alone is truly truthful

Who knows the art of living,
Who prepares his body like a bed
And plants the seed of the Lord therein.
He alone is truly truthful
Who accepts the true message,
Toward the living shows mercy
Gives something as alms and in charity.
He alone is truly truthful
Whose soul in pilgrimage resides,
Who consults the true Guru
And by his counsel ever abides.
Truth is the nostrum for all ills.
It exorcizes sin,
washes the body clean.
Those that have truth in their aprons
Before them doth Nanak himself demean.

---

* *Hymns of Guru Nanak*

Prayer for Forgiveness*

This lyrical prayer by Guru Arjan expresses the moral structure of Sikhism. God is holy and forgives those who confess their sin. The prayer ends with the worshipper assured of forgiveness.

Hear my supplication, O my Lord God,
Though I am full of millions of sins, nevertheless I am Your slave.
O You Dispeller of grief, merciful, fascinating,
Destroyer of trouble and anxiety,
I seek Your protection; protect my honor.
You are in all things, O spotless One;
You hear and behold us; You are with us all, O God;
You are the nearest of all to us.
O Lord, hear Nanak's prayer; save the slave of Your household.

You are ever omnipotent; we are poor and beggars.
O God, save us who are involved in the love of money.
Bound by covetousness and worldly love, we have committed various sins.
The Creator is distinct and free from entanglements; man obtains the fruit of his acts.
Show us kindness, You purifier of sinners; we are weary of wandering through many a womb.

Nanak represents—I am the slave of God who is the
Support of the soul and life.
You are great and omnipotent; my understanding is feeble.
You cherish even the ungrateful; You look equally on all.
Unfathomable is Your knowledge, O infinite Creator;
I am lowly and know nothing.

Having rejected the gem of Your name, I have amassed kauris;[15]
I am a degraded and silly being.
By the commission of sin I have amassed what is very unstable and forsakes man.
Nanak has sought Your protection, O omnipotent Lord; preserve his honor.
When I sang God's praises in the association of the saints,
He united me, who had been separated from Him, with Himself.
By ever thoroughly singing God's praises, He who is happiness itself becomes manifest.
My couch, when God accepts me as His own, is adorned by Him.
Having dismissed anxiety I am no longer anxious, and suffer no further pain.
Nanak lives beholding God and singing the praises of the Ocean of excellences.

---

*Rag Bihagra, Mahala 5

---

[15]*kauris:* human money, worthless with God.

Against the Use of Wine**

Although the Sikh scriptures contain no formal listing of ethical commands, one of the firmest and most explicit moral commands of Sikhism is the prohibition of alcoholic beverages. Note once again

the reinterpretation of an evil practice: "Make . . . God's name your wine."

The barmaid is misery, wine is lust; man is the drinker.
The cup filled with worldly love is wrath, and it is served by pride.

**Rag Bihagra, Mahala 1

The company is false and covetous, and is ruined by excess of drink.

Instead of such wine make good conduct your yeast, truth your molasses, God's name your wine;

Make merits your cakes, good conduct your clarified butter, and modesty your meat to eat.

Such things, O Nanak, are obtained by the Guru's favor; by partaking of them sins depart.

RITUAL

Hymn for the Installation of the *Guru Granth**

Although the content of this hymn seems to be unrelated to the Guru Granth, *it is sung by Sikhs in the temple as the holy book is brought out in the morning and put to rest at night.*

O God, this is the desire of my heart:

That You, the Treasure of mercy, the Compassionate, should make me the slave of Your saints;

That I should devote my body and soul to their service and sing God's praises with my tongue;

That I should ever abide with the saints and remember You at every breath I draw.

The Name is my sole support and wealth; from it Nanak obtains delight.

*Rag Devgandhari, Mahala 5

A Marriage Hymn**

Here is a hymn typically sung at Sikh weddings. Devotion to God and to one's spouse are masterfully blended. The believer is represented as the bride, God as the groom.

The stars glitter on a clear night.

Holy men, the beloved of my Lord, are awake;

The beloved of my Lord are ever awake, and remember His name night and day.

They meditate in their hearts on His lotus feet, and forget Him not for a moment.

They renounce the mental sins of pride and worldly love, and efface the pain of wrong-doing.

Nanak represents, the servants of God, the dear saints are ever awake.

My couch has splendid trappings.

In my heart joy has sprung up since I heard that my Lord was approaching.

On meeting my Lord I have entered on happiness and am filled with the essence of joy and delight.

He embraced me; my sorrows fled; my soul, mind, and body all bloomed afresh.

I have obtained my heart's desires by meditating on God; the time of my union with Him I account auspicious.

Nanak testifies, when he met the Bearer of prosperity, the essence of all pleasure was prepared for him.

**Rag Asa, Mahala 5

My companions meeting me asked me to describe my Spouse.

I was so filled with the sweets of love that I could not speak.

The attributes of the Creator are deep, mysterious, and boundless; the Vedas have not found His limit.

She who meditates on the Lord with devotion and love, who ever sings His praises,

And is pleasing to her God, is full of all virtues and divine knowledge.

Nanak testifies, she who is dyed with the color of God's love shall be easily absorbed in Him.

When I began to sing songs of joy to God,

My friends became glad, my troubles and my enemies fled away,

My happiness and comfort increased, I rejoiced in God's name, and He Himself bestowed mercy on me.

I clung to His feet, and being ever wakeful I met Him.

Happy days came, I obtained peace with all treasures and was blended with God.

Nanak testifies, the saints of God are ever steadfast in seeking His protection.

ORGANIZATION

The Guru*

This hymn by Guru Amar Das expresses the characteristic attitude of later Sikhs toward the line of the gurus. Though the Sri Guru Granth Sahib *is not explicitly mentioned, Sikhs hearing this hymn would think that everything said about the guru applies to their* Guru Granth, *in which the soul of the guru is incarnated.*

Through the Guru a few obtain divine knowledge;

He who knows God through the Guru shall be acceptable.

Through the Guru there results divine knowledge and meditation on the True One;

Through the Guru the gate of deliverance is attained.

It is only by perfect good fortune the Guru comes in one's way.

The true become easily absorbed in the True One.

On meeting the Guru the fire of avarice is quenched.

Through the Guru peace dwells in the heart.

Through the Guru man becomes pure, spotless, and immaculate.

Through the Guru the Word which unites man with God is obtained.

Without the Guru every one wanders in doubt.

Without the Name great misery is suffered.

He who is pious meditates on the Name.

On beholding the True One, true honor is obtained.

Whom shall we call the giver? The One God.

If He be gracious, the Word by which we meet Him is obtained.

May Nanak meet the beloved Guru, sing the True One's praises,

And becoming true be absorbed in the True One!

---

*Rag Gauri, Mahala 3

God's Power in the Sikh Community*

The final shape of the Sikh community (panth) *was established by the tenth guru, Gobind Singh. This hymn by Guru Arjan contains a line, "Victory be ever to the society of the saints," very reminiscent of the shout used to close almost every Sikh service, "The Khalsa shall rule!"*

There is none beside Him,
In whose power are lords and emperors;
In whose power is the whole world;
Who has created everything.
Address your supplication to the true Guru,
That he may arrange all your affairs.

_____

*Rag Gauri, Mahala 5

His court is the most exalted of all;
His name is the prop of all the saints.
The Lord whose glory shines in every heart
Is contained in everything, and fills creation.
By remembering Him the abode of sorrow is
    demolished;
By remembering Him death molests us not;
By remembering Him what is withered be-
    comes green;
By remembering Him the sinking stone floats.
Victory be ever to the society of the saints!
God's name is the support of the lives of His
    servants.
Says Nanak, hear, O God, my supplication—
By the favor of the saints, grant me to dwell in
    Your name.

APPENDIX: SELECTIONS FROM THE *DASAM GRANTH*

A. Guru Gobind Singh's Story**

Guru Gobind tells not just his own story, but the story of the one soul of the line of Gurus.[16]

I shall now tell my own history,
How God brought me into the world as I was
    performing penance
On the mountain of Hem Kunt,
Where the seven peaks are conspicuous—
The place is called the Sapt Shring—
Where King Pandu practiced Yoga.
There I performed very great austerities
And worshipped Great-death.
I performed such penance
That I became blended with God.
My father and mother had also worshipped the
    Unseen One,

_____

**Vichitar Natak, 6
[16] From Max Macauliffe, *The Sikh Religion*, vol. 5 (Oxford: Oxford University Press, 1909), pp. 296–300.

And strove in many ways to unite themselves
    with Him.
The Supreme Guru was pleased
With their devotion to Him.
When God gave me the order
I assumed birth in this age.
I did not desire to come,
As my attention was fixed on God's feet.
God remonstrated earnestly with me,
And sent me into this world with the following
    orders:
"When I created this world
I first made the demons, who became enemies
    and oppressors.
They became intoxicated with the strength of
    their arms,
And ceased to worship Me, the Supreme Being.
I became angry and at once destroyed them.
In their places I established the gods.
They also busied themselves receiving sacrifices
    and worship,

And called themselves supreme beings.
Mahadev called himself the imperishable God.
Vishnu too declared himself to be God;
Brahma called himself the supreme Brahma,
And nobody thought Me to be God. . . .
They altogether forgot My orders.
Each became absorbed in his own praise,
When they did not recognize Me. Then I created men.
They too fell under the influence of pride,
And made gods out of stones. Then I created the Sidhs and the Sadhs,
But they too found not the Supreme Being.
Whoever was clever in the world
Established his own sect,
And no one found the Creator.
Enmity, contention, and pride increased. . . .
Brahma made the four Vedas
And caused all to act according to them;
But they whose love was attached to My feet
Renounced the Vedas.
They who abandoned the tenets of the Vedas and other books
Became devoted to Me, the supreme God.
They who follow true religion
Shall have their sins of various kinds blotted out.
They who endure bodily suffering
And cease not to love Me,
Shall all go to paradise,
And there shall be no difference between Me and them.
They who shrink from suffering,
And, forsaking Me, adopt the way of the Vedas and Smritis shall fall into the pit of hell,
And continually suffer transmigration. . . .
They who were created by Me

Struck out their several paths.
I then created Muhammad,
And made him king of Arabia.
He too established a religion of his own,
Cut off the foreskins of all his followers,
And made every one repeat his name;[17]
But no one fixed the true Name in man's heart.
All these were wrapped up in themselves;
None of them recognized Me, the Supreme Being.
I have cherished you as My son,
And created you to extend My religion.
Go and spread My religion there,
And restrain the world from senseless acts."

I stood up, clasped my hands, bowed my head, and replied:
"Your religion shall prevail in the world when You assure me your assistance."
On this account God sent me.
I took birth and came into the world.
As He spoke to me so I speak unto men.
I bear no enmity to any one.
All who call me the Supreme Being
Shall fall into the pit of hell.
Recognize me as God's servant only:
Have no doubt whatever of this.
I am the slave of the Supreme Being,
Come to behold the wonders of the world.
I tell the world what God told me,
And will not remain silent through fear of mortals.

---

[17]*repeat his name:* in the confession of Islam, "There is no God but God, and Muhammad is his prophet."

B. God as the Holy Sword*

One of the most important developments in the early history of Sikhism was the shift from pacifism to militancy. This famous hymn expresses this militancy with its personification of the sword as God.

Today the Sikh child is baptized with water that has been stirred by a two-edged sword, and the dagger between two swords is a prominent symbol of modern Sikhism.[18]

Vichitar Natak, 1

[18] From Macauliffe, *Sikh Religion*, vol. 5, pp. 286–87.

I bow with love and devotion to the Holy
Sword.
Assist me that I may complete this book.

You are the Subduer of countries, the Destroyer
of the armies of the wicked, in the battlefield
You greatly adorn the brave.
Your arm is unbreakable, Your brightness resplendent, Your radiance and splendor dazzle
like the sun.
You bestow happiness on the good, You terrify
the evil, You scatter sinners, I seek Your
protection.
Hail! hail to the Creator of the world, the Savior of creation, my Cherisher, hail to You,
O Sword!

I bow to Him who holds the arrow in His
hand; I bow to the Fearless One;
I bow to the God of gods who is in the present
and the future.
I bow to the Scimitar, the two-edged Sword,
the broad-bladed sword, and the Dagger.
You, O God, always have one form; You are
always unchangeable.

I bow to the Holder of the mace,
Who diffused light through the fourteen
worlds.
I bow to the Arrow and the Musket,
I bow to the Sword, spotless, fearless, and
unbreakable;
I bow to the powerful Mace and Lance
To which nothing is equal.
I bow to Him who holds the discus,[19]
Who is not made of the elements and is
terrible.
I bow to Him with the strong teeth;
I bow to Him who is supremely powerful,
I bow to the Arrow and the Cannon
Which destroy the enemy.
I bow to the Sword and the Rapier
Which destroy the evil.
I bow to all weapons called Shastar, which may
be held.
I bow to all weapons called Astar, which may
be hurled or discharged.

---

[19]*discus:* a circular, hurled weapon.

GLOSSARY

Adi Granth (AH-dee GRAHNTH) "the first/original book," the primary scripture of Sikhism,
consisting primarily of the words of the first five gurus; also known as the *Sri Guru Granth
Sahib* or *Guru Granth.*

chaur (chowr) a horsehair whisk used to venerate the *Adi Granth* by waving it over the scripture to cool the book and repel flies.

Dasam Granth (DAH-sum GRAHNTH) the "tenth book," the secondary scripture consisting
mostly of the words of the tenth guru, Gobind Singh.

granthi (GRAHN-thee) an official reader of the *Guru Granth.*

gutka (GUHT-kuh) an anthology for private use of the most important passages from the *Adi
Granth* and a few from the *Dasam Granth.*

janam-sakhis (JAH-num SAH-kees) literally, "birth stories" or traditional narratives about the
lives of the gurus, especially Nanak.

Japji (JAHP-jee) the first main section of the *Adi Granth,* a poem by Nanak considered to express the essence of Sikhism.

Mahala (ma-HAH-luh) a term used by the *Adi Granth* to differentiate the contributions of the
five gurus.

Mul Mantra (mool MAHN-truh) "root formula," the opening of the *Japji.*

Rags (rahgs) the thirty-one rudimentary "tunes" on which melodies used for singing the *Adi
Granth* are based.

vak lao (vahk low) "taking (God's) word" by opening the *Granth* at random and beginning the reading from the top of the left-hand page.

QUESTIONS FOR STUDY AND DISCUSSION

1. Describe the main teachings of the *Adi Granth*. Which do you see as most important, and why?

2. "Of all the religions of the world, Sikhism has the best claim to be 'a religion of the book.'" Do you agree or disagree? Why or why not?

3. Which attitudes, teachings, and practices of Sikhism seem to you to resemble Hinduism? Which seem to resemble Islam? Which seem to be distinct?

4. How does Sikh tradition, as expressed in its scriptures, vary between inclusiveness to other faiths and exclusiveness toward them?

5. Describe the shift from pacifism to militarism in Sikh tradition. Can you think of similar shifts in other religions?

SUGGESTIONS FOR FURTHER READING

Primary Readings

Max A. Macauliffe, *The Sikh Religion: Its Gurus, Sacred Writings and Authors.* 6 vols. Oxford: University Press, 1909. Reprinted New Delhi: S. Chand, 1963. Provides full selections from the Sikh scriptures, with good, literal translations.

W. H. McLeod, *Textual Sources for the Study of Sikhism.* Totowa, NJ: Barnes & Noble, 1984. An excellent anthology of Sikh scriptures and more recent writings.

Trilochan Singh et al., eds., *Selections from the Sacred Writings of the Sikhs.* London: Allen & Unwin, 1960. Generous selections from the *Adi Granth* and the *Dasam Granth*.

Secondary Readings

M. Juergensmeyer and N. G. Barrier, eds., *Sikh Studies.* Berkeley: Graduate Theological Union, 1979. This volume contains the papers from the Berkeley Conference on Sikh Studies; see especially the essays on scripture by W. McLeod, S. Singh, and F. Staal.

Surindar Singh Kohli, *A Critical Study of the* Adi Granth. New Delhi: Punjabi Writers' Co-operative Industrial Society, 1961. A scholarly study of the structure and theology of the *Adi Granth*.

H. McLeod, "The Sikh Scriptures," in his *Evolution of the Sikh Community.* Oxford: Clarendon Press, 1976, pp. 59–82. A succinct survey of the origin, development, and use of Sikh scriptures, with special emphasis on textual problems.

T. N. Madan, "The Double-Edged Sword: Fundamentalism and the Sikh Religious Tradition," in M. E. Marty and R. S. Appleby, eds., *Fundamentalisms Observed.* Chicago: University of Chicago Press, 1991, pp. 594–627. A study of the "fundamentalist" dimensions of the recent militarist movement led by J. S. Bhindranwale, with good attention to its approach to scripture.

Zoroastrian Ritual
A Zoroastrian priest in India offers a sacrifice with the _Avesta_ at his right hand for ready reference. Credit: Jehangir Gazdar/Woodfin Camp & Associates

CHAPTER SIX

Zoroastrianism

[handwritten margin note: Avesta most important book is Yasna - Zor. scripture]

❖ In a house in Bombay, India, a seven-year-old girl is being received into the Zoroastrian religion. A priest stands behind her, guiding her hands as she ties a sacred cord around her waist. She will wear this cord, which serves as a belt, for the rest of her life, except while bathing or sleeping. Five times a day she will ceremonially loosen it, say her prayers, and retie it. This cord has seventy-two threads representing the seventy-two chapters of the chief book of the Zoroastrian scripture, the *Yasna*.

❖ As he sits on the floor in a Zoroastrian temple, a priest offers sacrifice. Before him are spread a variety of consecrated objects, mostly fruits, vegetables and herbs, and a small flame. Usually he recites the scriptural words of sacrifice from memory, but today is one of the seven great yearly festivals of the faith, so a large-print *Avesta* book rests on a small stand to his right. He refers to the book from time to time to read some passages aloud and refresh his memory for other passages.

INTRODUCTION

[handwritten margin note: - prophet: Zarathushtra]

Begun perhaps as long as three thousand years ago in ancient Iran by its prophet Zarathushtra, Zoroastrianism was the state religion of the ancient Sasanid empire. Today its numbers are severely reduced, with no more than 250,000 adherents in the world. Some are clustered now in eastern Iran, most are in and near Bombay, India, and a few thousand adherents live in North America. The scriptures of Zoroastrianism combine its strong message of living a moral life with concerns for ritual purity in worship and in daily life. Because of their obscure ancient language, troubled history of transmission, and fragmentary character, these scriptures are often difficult to translate and understand. But the main beliefs of Zoroastrianism come through these writings as well today as perhaps as at any time in the three millennia of this religion, and Zoroastrians are as concerned as ever about how the message of their writings is embodied in daily life.

[handwritten margin note: - most in: E. Iran, Bombay, N. Am.]

Overview of Structure

The *Avesta* [ah-VES-tuh] has four major divisions, each with a ritual content and orientation. The first and most important is the *Yasna* [YAHZ-nuh], "Sacrifice," composed of hymns for worship in seventy-two chapters. The *Visparad* [VEE-spuh-rahd], "All the [divine] Lords," has hymns in twenty chapters. The *Yashts* [yahshts] are twenty-one "Hymns" to as many divinities. The *Vendidad* [VEN-dih-dahd] of twenty-two chapters is "The Law against Demons." Minor texts include the *Nyayishn*, "Litanies" or short prayers to the gods of nature and to angels; *Gahs*, hymns to the spirits of the five periods of the day; two *Sirozahs*, each with thirty paragraphs that

[handwritten margin note: Avesta consists of 4 ÷ - Yasna - Visparad - Yashts - Vendidad]

157

invoke the deities of each day of the month; and *Afrigans,* four "Blessings." We now will examine the four major divisions more closely.

The earliest and most important part of the *Yasna* is the collection of seventeen hymns called the **Gathas** [GAH-tahs]. They now stand in five sections in the *Yasna* as chapters 28–34, 43–51, and 53. Although orthodox Zoroastrians believe the whole of the *Avesta* to be the work of Zarathushtra, they hold these *Gathas* especially as his. Modern scholarship agrees, using the *Gathas* as the primary source for our knowledge of Zarathushtra. Written in an earlier type of Avestan language, the *Gathas* are distinguished from the other hymns of the *Yasna* by their emphasis on ethical dualism and lack of attention to ritual concerns. One main topic of the *Yasna* is the haoma ritual, by which the juices of the haoma plant are ground out and mixed with milk and herbs (chapters 9–11, 22–27). Other topics include prayer (19–21), a confession of faith (12), and sacrifices to water (45–48). All seventy-two chapters are recited daily by priests (from memory!) during Zoroastrianism's main sacrificial ceremony, the sacrifice of the haoma before the fire. This sacrifice is called the Yasna, from which this collection of scripture gets its name.

The *Visparad* is about one-sixth as long as the *Yasna*. It contains poetic invocations, praises, and sacrifices to all the divine lords of Zoroastrianism. Because its words are recited in different parts of the *Yasna* ceremony, when it is separated into its own collection it seems disjointed. Zoroastrians also recite the *Visparad* during their six holy days of obligation, especially New Year's Day.

The *Yashts* are hymns of praise to twenty-one divinities, angels, and human heroes of ancient Iran. Among the most important are hymns to Mithra, who was to become a god in his own religion of Mithraism (chapter 10), and a hymn to the guardian spirits (**Fravashis**) of the old saints (13). Much of the material in the *Yashts* is drawn from pre-Zoroastrian religion and provides an interesting glimpse on how later Zoroastrianism (after the prophet himself, who according to the *Gathas* made a clean break with older religion) adapted these older Indo-European religious ideas to its own usage.

The *Vendidad* begins with two myths about the creation and a primeval flood that tell how the divine law came to humans. The remaining sixteen chapters form a law code that prescribes purifications and penalties for priests. Chapters 3 and 5, for example, contain regulations for funerals; chapter 18 deals with the difference between the true and false priest. Like the *Yashts,* the *Vendidad* is inserted into the *Yasna* for ritual reasons.

Avesta is a word of uncertain meaning. Usually translated as "injunction" or "command," it has also been translated as "wisdom" or "knowledge," as "authoritative utterance," and as "scripture." It probably derives from the Middle Persian word *avastaq,* "law." The "injunction" is that of the god Ahura Mazda through the prophet Zarathushtra. This name is broad enough to encompass all the commands of Zoroastrianism: to serve good and turn from evil; to be both morally and ceremonially pure; to worship Ahura Mazda and the good spirits by sacrifice and praise.

Origin and Development

The *Avesta* begins with Zarathushtra himself. Though a date for the prophet in the sixth century B.C.E. is still held by most scholars, some (especially Boyce) would push Zarathushtra back to 1400–1000 B.C.E. The oral tradition that was later written down

(handwritten margin notes) god is Ahura Mazda / Zara Thushtra existed in 1400-1000 BCE

into our *Gathas* can be traced more or less to Zarathushtra for reasons both of style and content.

Next to arise over probably a millennium were the other poetic sections of the *Avesta*, which scholars today call the "Younger *Avesta*." The rest of the *Yasna* and the *Yashts* are in metrical poetry. Last to be written were the prose portions of the *Avesta*. The whole process was complete, and the canon of the *Avesta* fixed, at about 325 C.E.

In its original form, the *Avesta* was probably about four times larger than it is now. Besides the liturgical texts now in the *Avesta*, it probably treated cosmogony, eschatology, astronomy, natural history, the history of Zarathushtra, and several other topics. The *Zand* contains many references to a large loss of Zoroastrian scripture during the invasions of Alexander the Great (fourth century B.C.E.). What remained from these persecutions was material that was fixed in the memory of the priests, liturgical scripture. A collection was made under the Sasanian dynasty of Iran in the third and fourth centuries C.E. The *Avesta* as we know it comes from this period and was probably first written down at this time. Zoroastrianism was now the state religion of the Sasanid empire, and a written text may have been viewed as promoting uniformity in religious doctrine and practice.

Islam then pressed hard on the religion of Ahura Mazda. Although it officially tolerated Zoroastrianism as a monotheistic religion, Islam also sought to end the faith by suppressing its temples and burning its scripture books. Some Zoroastrians fled Muslim intolerance for a more congenial life around Bombay in India. During this period the *Avesta* was reduced to its present size, preserved by the small Zoroastrian community left to continue to this day. The oldest manuscript that has survived dates to 1323 C.E.; the entire Avestan collection was printed only in the nineteenth century.

Use

As one can infer from the names of the Avestan books, they are strongly oriented to worship and sacrifice. The scriptures are the hymn texts for sacrifice, and sacrifice is done to the constant accompaniment of scripture recitation, usually by memory. Scripture usage throughout Zoroastrian history has therefore been almost exclusively performative. Scripture is used for the enactment of ritual, not for study, meditation, or the formation and teaching of doctrine. The Avestan language used in formal worship and in the traditional main prayers of the faithful is largely unknown to priest and layperson alike. Thus, Zoroastrians typically have had little knowledge of what their scriptures actually "teach." For example, a nineteenth-century British missionary to Bombay, John Wilson, was able to confuse and embarrass a high-ranking Zoroastrian priest in a public debate when he made it apparent that the priest did not know the contents of the *Avesta* and was not able to defend them.

At the end of nineteenth century, a movement of reform sought to change this age-old usage of the *Avesta*. Under the influence of Western religion and European methods of religious scholarship, reformers claimed that the *Gathas* are the center and only authentic part of the *Avesta*. Everything else is to be judged by its leading ideas. Rituals were regarded as secondary to moral teachings and were interpreted symbolically, altered, or sometimes disregarded altogether. The rational, philosophical, and moral elements of the faith were given priority. This shift from a performative to a cognitive usage among a minority of Zoroastrians in India and North America is the source of one of the chief internal disagreements in Zoroastrianism.

HISTORY

The Call of Zarathushtra* — appning zar. as a prophet

This gatha is a conversation between four main characters: (1) the collective soul of the cattle, which represents the means of livelihood for the people of the Zoroastrian faith; (2) Asha, or "Righteousness," one of the immortals; (3) Ahura Mazda, the Lord and Creator; and (4) Zarathushtra. It closes with Zarathushtra's prayer for divine aid. This passage is used by worshippers as a prayer for divine help to destroy the powers of deceit and to promote peace and truth.[1]

The Soul of the Cattle and the people cried aloud to you, O Ahura and Asha, "For whom did you create me, and by whom did you fashion me? The assaults of wrath and violent power come upon me, with desolating blows, audacious insolence, and thieving might. I have no other pasture-giver than you. Teach me good cultivation of the fields, which is my only hope of blessing!"

Then the Creator of the Cattle asked Righteousness: "How did you appoint a guardian for the cattle when you made her? How did you secure for her both pasture and a Cattle-chief who was skilled and energetic? Did you select as her master one who might hurl back the fury of the wicked?"

The Divine Righteousness answered in his holiness, "We were very perplexed. We could not obtain a leader who was capable of striking back their fury, and who himself was without hate. We cannot know the influences which approach and move the heavenly fires, fires which reveal the favor and the will of God. God is the mightiest of beings. Those who have performed their actions approach him with invocations. He has no need to ask!"

Zarathushtra said, "The Great Creator is most mindful of the commands that have been fulfilled in the deeds of demon-gods and good or evil men. He knows the commands that they will fulfill. Ahura is the discerning judge. It shall be to us as he desires! [5] Therefore we both, my soul and the soul of the mother Cattle, are making our requests for the two worlds[2] to Ahura. With hands stretched out in entreaty, we pray to the Great Creator with questions in our doubt. He will answer. Destruction will not come to the one who lives righteously, or to the careful farmers of the earth!"

Then the Lord, the Great Creator who understands the mysterious grace by his insight, spoke. "A spiritual master is not found for us in this way. Nor can we find in this way a leader moved by Righteousness and appointed by its spirit. Therefore I have named you as the leader of the diligent tillers of the ground!"

The Amesha-Spentas[3] said, "Mazda has created the inspired Word of reason that is a Mathra[4] of fatness for the offering. The Divine Righteousness consented to Mazda's deed. He has prepared food for the cattle and food for the eaters. He is bountiful with his saving doctrine.

---

* *Yasna* 29

[1] Except where noted, all passages from Zoroastrian scripture are taken, with editing, from J. Darmesteter and L. H. Mills, trans., *The Zend-Avesta*, vols. 4, 23, 31, *Sacred Books of the East* (Oxford: Oxford University Press, 1880–1887).

[2] *the two worlds:* this present world and the world to come at the end of time.

[3] *Amesha-Spentas:* "immortal holy ones," seen sometimes as aspects of God's being, or other times as beings in their own right.

[4] *Mathra:* a special sacrificial formula; cf. Sanskrit *mantra*.

But who is endowed with the Good Mind, who can give those teachings by word of mouth to mortals?"

Ahura said, "I have found this man, Zarathushtra Spitama, who alone has listened to our words! He desires to announce our mighty and completed acts of grace, for me the Great Creator, and for Righteousness. Therefore I will give him the good dwelling and the authoritative position of one who speaks for us!"

Then the Soul of the Cattle lamented, "Woe is me, for I have obtained a lord who is powerless to carry out his wish! He is only the voice of a feeble and timid man. I desire one who is lord over his will, one who is able like a king to carry out what he desires." The Amesha-Spentas said, "Yes, when shall one who brings strong help to her[5] ever appear?"

---

[5] *her:* the (female) Soul of the Cattle.

[10] Zarathushtra said, "O Ahura, O Righteousness, grant gladness to these our disciples. Grant them the sovereign kingdom of the Deity, which is established in his Good Mind. This kingdom gives them the peaceful amenities of home and quiet happiness, instead of the terrible ravages that they suffer. O Great Creator, I have always thought You to be the first possessor of these blessings! O Great Creator and Living Lord, when shall the Divine Righteousness, the Good Mind of the Lord, and his Sovereign Power hurry to me? When will they give me strength for my task and my mission? Without this I cannot advance or even undertake my work. Give us your aid in abundance for our great cause. May we partake in the bountiful grace of your equals, your counselors and servants!"

A Hymn of Praise to Zarathushtra*

With this hymn Zoroastrians venerate the memory of Zarathushtra. Note the recurring use of "who/he first." The end of this selection recounts a legend of the cosmic praise offered to the baby Zarathushtra.

We worship the piety and the *Fravashi*[6] of the holy Zarathushtra. He was the first who thought what is good, the first who spoke what is good, the first who did what is good. He was the first Priest, the first Warrior, the first Plower of the ground. He first knew and first taught. He first possessed and first took possession of the Bull, of Holiness, of the Word, the obedience to the Word, the dominion, and all the good things made by Mazda, the good things that are the offspring of the good Principle.

He was the first Priest, the first Warrior, the first Plower of the ground. He first took the turning of the wheel[7] from the hands of the Daeva[8] and the cold-hearted man. He was first in the material world to pronounce the praise of Asha, thus bringing the Daevas to nothing. He confessed himself a worshipper of Mazda, a follower of Zarathushtra. He is one who hates the Daevas, and obeys the laws of Ahura.

[90] He was first in the material world to say the word that destroys the Daevas, the law of Ahura. He was first in the material world to proclaim the words that destroy the Daevas, the law of Ahura. He was the first in the material world to declare all the creation of the Daevas unworthy of sacrifice and prayer. He was strong, giving all the good things of life, and he was the first bearer of the law among the nations.

In him was heard the whole Mathra, the word of holiness. He was the lord and master of the world. He was the praiser of Asha who is the

---

* *Yasht* 24: 87b–94
[6] *Fravashi:* guardian spirit.

---

[7] *turning of the wheel:* the life of the created world.
[8] *Daeva:* evil spirit.

most great, most good and most fair. He had a revelation of the law, that most excellent of all beings.

For him the Amesha-Spentas longed, in one accord with the sun, in the fullness of the faith of a devoted heart. They longed for him as the lord and master of the world, as the praiser of the most great, most good and most fair Asha. He had a revelation of the Law, that most excellent of all beings.

In his birth and growth the waters and the plants rejoiced. In his birth and growth the waters and the plants grew. In his birth and growth all the creatures of the good creations cried out, "Hail! Hail to us! For he is born, the Athravan,[9] Spitama Zarathushtra. Zarathushtra will offer us sacrifices with drink offerings and bundles of baresma.[10] The good Law of the worshippers of Mazda will come, and it will spread through all the seven Karshvares[11] of the earth."

---

[9] *Athravan:* priest.
[10] *baresma:* sandalwood twigs, present at every sacrifice.
[11] *Karshvares:* divisions.

TEACHING

Hymn to Ahura and the Purifying Fire*

This hymn to Ahura Mazda and to the spirit of the fire is set in the fire temple. Note the emphasis on morality in thought, word, and deed. Today the fire is still a symbol of moral purity and the center of every Zoroastrian temple.

[1] We would approach you . . . in the house of this your holy Fire, O Ahura Mazda, most bounteous Spirit! If anyone brings pollutions to this flame, you will cover him with pollutions. O most friendly one, O Fire of the Lord, give us zeal! Come to us with the loving blessing of one who is most friendly, with the praise of the one most adored. Yes, come to us and aid us in this great task!

You truly are the Fire of Ahura Mazda. Yes, you are the most bounteous one of his Spirit. Therefore yours is the most potent of all names for grace, O Fire of the Lord! Therefore we come to you, O Ahura, with the help of your Good Mind that you implant in us. We come to you with your good Righteousness, and with actions and words implanted by your good wisdom!

[5] We bow before you, and we direct our prayers to you with confessions of our guilt, O Ahura Mazda! With all the good thoughts that you inspire, with all the words well said, and the deeds well done, with these we come to you. To your most beautiful body we make our deep acknowledgments, O Ahura Mazda. We acknowledge those stars that are your body, and we acknowledge that one star, the highest of the high, as the sun was called!

---

* *Yasna 36*

Hymn to Ahura Mazda the Creator*

This selection is a beautiful expression of faith and devotion to Ahura Mazda the Creator, and the spirits associated with him.

We worship Ahura Mazda, who made the Cattle, Righteousness, the waters, the wholesome plants, the stars, the earth, and all existing things that are good. Yes, we worship him for his Sovereign Power and his greatness. They are full of blessing, and have priority among the Yazads who abide beside the Cattle in protection and support.

We worship him under his name as Lord, Mazda dear, the most gracious of names. We worship him with our bones and with our flesh. We worship the **Fravashis** of the saints, of holy men and holy women. We worship Righteousness the Best, the most beautiful, the Bountiful Immortal, who is endowed with light in all things good.

[5] We worship the Good Mind of the Lord, and his Sovereign Power, and the Good Faith, the good law, and Piety the ready mind within your people!

---

* *Yasna* 37:1–5

The Doctrine of Dualism** *very important*

This gatha instructs the believer in the basic teachings of Zarathushtra on good and evil. It speaks of the ancient character of good and evil, their role in creation of the world, their present struggle for domination, and their destiny at the end of history. The believer must constantly choose the good and thereby build up its power in the universe. Note the nonritual character of righteousness.

[1] You who are drawing near and want to be taught, now I will proclaim to you my observations about him who knows all things. I will proclaim the praises of Ahura, the sacrifices that spring from the Good Mind, and the blessed meditations inspired by Righteousness. I pray that favorable results may be seen in the lights. Hear then with your ears; see the bright flames with the eyes of the Better Mind. It is a decision about religions, man and man, each individual himself. Before taking up this cause, awake to our teaching!

The primeval spirits as a pair combined their opposite strivings, and yet each is independent in his action. They have long been famous. One is better, the other worse, in thought, in word, and in deed. Let those who act wisely choose correctly between these two. Do not choose as evil-doers choose!

When the two spirits came together at first, they made life and life's absence. They decided how the world shall be ordered at its end. The wicked receive Hell, the worst life; the holy receive Heaven, the Best Mental State. [5] He who was the evil one chose the evil realm, working the worst possible results. But the more gracious spirit chose the Divine Righteousness. Yes, he who clothes himself with the firm stones of heaven as his robe made this choice. He also chose those who make Ahura happy by their actions, actions performed in accordance with the faith.

The Demon-gods and those who worship them can make no righteous choice between these two spirits, since they have been deceived.

** *Yasna* 30

As they were questioning and debating in their council, the Worst Mind approached them that he might be chosen. They made their fatal decision. Then they rushed to the Demon of Fury, that they might pollute the lives of mortals.

Then Aramaiti, the personified Piety of the saints, approached. The Sovereign Power, the Good Mind, and the Righteous Order came with her. Aramaiti gave a body to the spiritual creations of good and of evil; she is the abiding and ever-strenuous one. O Mazda, let that body for your people be at the end like it was when you first created it! At the end the great struggle shall be fought out which began when the Daevas first seized the Demon of Wrath as their ally, and then just vengeance shall come upon these wretches. Then, O Mazda, the Kingdom shall be gained for you by your Good Mind within your people. O living Lord, the Good Mind speaks his command to those who will deliver the Demon of the Lie into the two hands of the Righteous Order, like a captive is delivered to a destroyer.

May we be like those who bring on this great renovation. May we make this world progressive, until its perfection is reached. May we be like the Ahuras of Mazda. Yes, may we be like you, in helpful readiness to meet your people, presenting benefits in union with the Righteous Order. Our thoughts will be where true wisdom shall live in her home.

[10] When perfection will be attained, then the blow of destruction shall fall upon the Demon of Falsehood, and her adherents shall perish with her. But the righteous saints, who walk on earth in good reputation and in honor, will gather swiftly in the happy home of the Good Mind and of Ahura.

Therefore, O mortals, you are learning these religious commands that Ahura gave in our happiness and our sorrow. You are also learning the long punishment of the wicked, and the blessings that are in store for the righteous. When these begin their course, salvation will be yours!

ETHICS

Personal Virtues*

To encourage virtue and discourage vice, Zoroastrians have strong rules of moral duties to accompany their ritual observances. The instructions are typically in the form of a proverb or aphorism, as in this passage.

There are five best things in religion. These are truthfulness, generosity, being possessed of virtue, diligence and advocacy. This [kind of] truthfulness is the best; one who acts [so truthfully] to the creatures of Ahura Mazda that the recipient of his action has so much more benefit

when he acts like that to him. This generosity is best: One who makes a present to a person from whom he has no hope of receiving anything in reward in this world, and he has not even given the hope that the recipient of his gift should hold him in gratitude and praise. This possession of virtue is best: One who makes battle against the non-material demons, whatever they may be. In particular one does not let these five demons into one's body: Greed, Envy, Lust, Wrath and Shame. This diligence is best: One who does one's work in such a manner that at every moment he is certain that if he were to die at that hour it would not be necessary to do anything differently from how he is doing it. That advo-

---

* *Denkard* 6:23, 24

cacy is best: One who speaks for a person who is inarticulate, who cannot speak his own misery and complaint. That person speaks out the voice of his own soul and of that of the poor and good person to the people of this world and these six Amesha Spentas.

They held this too: Wisdom is manifest in work, character in rule, friend in hardship.

Six Ritual Obligations*

Ritual and ethical obligations are closely intertwined in Zoroastrianism. Six of the primary ritual obligations from the Sad Dar (Hundred Doors) are listed in the following. Strong punishment in the last judgment of the soul is promised for those who fail to keep these obligations.

The sixth subject is this, that of the many good works there are of those which, when they accomplish them, obtain great rewards; and if one does not perform them severe punishment seizes upon one at the head of the Chinvat bridge.[12]

One is the celebration of the season of festivals. The second is keeping the days of the guardian spirits.[13] The third is attending to the souls of fathers, mothers, and other relations. The fourth is reciting the Sun Litany three times every day. The fifth is reciting the Moon Litany three times every month, once when it becomes new, once when it becomes full, and once when it becomes slender. And the sixth is celebrating the Rapithwin ceremony once every year.

If not able to celebrate them oneself, it is requisite to order them [to be done], so that they may celebrate them every single time. These six good works are things indispensable for everyone.

[5] They call the transgression of each of these six a "bridge-sin." That is, every one who broke one of these they keep back, at the head of the Chinvat bridge, until punishment for it happens to him. No good work is possible in this place, which is a place of torment and punishment for him.

Therefore one must make an effort to perform each one at its own time, so that one may obtain a reward, and not a severe punishment.

---

* *Sad Dar 6 : 1–7*

[12] *Chinvat bridge:* where the last judgment of the soul takes place.

[13] *days of the guardian spirits* [fravashis]: the last ten days of the religious year.

RITUAL

The Place of the *Gathas***

This passage, which stands at the end of the Gathas, *serves to show their high place in the Zoroastrian faith.*

As our offering to the bountiful *Gathas* that rule as the leading chants within the appointed times and seasons of our ritual, we present all our riches of land, and our persons, together with our very bones and tissues. We present our forms and forces, our consciousness, our soul, and *Fravashi.*

The *Gathas* are our guardians and defenders, and our spiritual food. Yes, they are both food and clothing to our souls. These *Gathas* are guardians and defenders and spiritual food, both

---

** *Yasna 55 : 1–3*

food and clothing to our souls. May they be an offering for us. May they give abundant rewards . . . for the world beyond the present world, after the parting of our consciousness and body. May these Praises of the Offering come forth, and appear for us with power and victory, with health and healing, with progress, with growth, with preparation and protection, and with blessing and holiness. May they abound with gifts for those who can understand.

Let them appear with free generosity to the enlightened; let them appear as Mazda, the most beneficial, has produced them. He is the one who is victorious when he strikes. He helps our settlements advance, he protects and guards the religious order of the settlements which are even now being furthered. He guards those who will bring salvation to us, and protects the entire creation of holy and clean things.

The Zoroastrian Confession*

This stately creed of Zoroastrianism is called the Faravane. *Recited daily by every faithful worshipper of Mazda, it outlines an important Zoroastrian doctrine, the dualism of good and evil as cosmic forces. Believers pledge themselves to Mazda and the good, and reject the Daevas [evil spirits] in the universe and their lives.*

[1] I drive the Daevas away. I confess myself a Mazda-worshipper of the order of Zarathushtra. I renounce the Daevas and devote myself to the lore of the Lord. I am a praiser of the Bountiful Immortals. I attribute all things good to Ahura Mazda, the Holy and Resplendent One. To Him belong all things good: the Cattle, Asha, and the stars, in whose lights the glorious beings and objects are clothed. I choose Piety, the generous and the good. I loudly condemn all robbery and violence against the sacred Cattle, and all drought that wastes the Mazdayasnian villages. I put away the thought of wandering at will, of pitching my tent freely like a nomad. I wish to remove all wandering from the Cattle which abide steadfastly on this land. Bowing down in worship to Righteousness, I dedicate my offerings with praise. May I never be a source of decline, may I never be a source of withering to the Mazdayasnian villages, not for the love of body or life.

I renounce the shelter and headship of the Daevas, evil as they are. They are utterly empty of good and void of Virtue. They are deceitful in their wickedness. Of all beings they are most like the Demon of the Lie, the most loathsome of existing things. They are completely empty of good.

[5] I renounce and renounce again the Daevas and all possessed by them, the sorcerers and all who use their methods, and every being of the sort. I renounce their thoughts, their words and actions, and the seed that propagates their sin. I renounce their shelter and their headship. I renounce sinners of every kind who act as Rakhshas[14] act!

Thus indeed might Ahura Mazda have shown to Zarathushtra, answering every question which Zarathushtra asked, in all the consultations in which they conversed together. Thus might Zarathushtra have renounced the shelter and the headship of the Daevas in all the questions, and in all the consultations with which Zarathushtra and the Lord conversed together. And so I myself, in whatever circumstances I may be placed, as a worshipper of Mazda and of Zarathushtra's order, so renounce the Daevas and their shelter. The holy Zarathushtra renounced them the same way in old times.

I belong to that religious holiness to which the waters belong, to that holiness to which the plants, to that holiness to which the Cattle of blessed gift, to that religious holiness to which Ahura Mazda, who made both cattle and holy

---

* *Yasna* 12

[14] *Rakhshas:* demons.

men, belongs. To that holiness I belong. I am of the creed which Zarathushtra held, which Kavi Vistaspa, and those two, Frashaostra and Gamaspa, held.[15] Yes, I am of that faith as every **Saoshyant** [future savior] who shall come to us, the holy ones who do truly significant things. Of that creed, of that tradition, am I.

I am a Mazda-worshipper of Zarathushtra's order. So I confess, as a praiser and confessor. I praise aloud the thing well thought, the word well spoken, and the deed well done. Yes, I praise at once the Faith of Mazda, the Faith that has no saying that fails, the Faith that wields the deadly halberd,[16] the Faith of kindred marriage.[17] I praise the holy Creed, which is the most imposing, best, and most beautiful of all religions which exist, and of all that in the future shall come to knowledge. I praise Ahura's Faith, the Zarathushtrian creed. I ascribe all good to Ahura Mazda, and such shall be the worship of the Mazdayasnian belief!

---

[15] King *Kavi Vistaspa* was Zarathushtra's royal patron and protector. *Frashaostra* was an early follower of Zarathushtra, whose daughter Hvovi was Zarathushtra's third wife. *Gamaspa* was the chief counselor of King Vishtaspa and a friend of the new faith.

---

[16] *halberd:* battle-axe.

[17] *kindred marriage:* refers to the Zoroastrian practice of marrying distant relatives.

The Four Great Prayers*

These four prayers are the most important in Zoroastrian worship. They are named after their first words.[18]

A. *Ahuna vairyo*

As is the Master, so is the Judge to be chosen in accord with truth. Establish the power of acts arising from a life lived with good purpose, for Mazda and for the lord whom they made pastor for the poor.

---

* From the *Yasna*
[18] This prayer, and the *Ashem vohu,* are taken from M. Boyce, *A History of Zoroastrianism,* 2 vols. (Leiden: Brill, 1975, 1982).

B. *Airyema ishyo*

May longed-for Airyaman come to the support of the men and women of Zarathushtra, to the support of our good purpose. The Inner Self earns the reward to be chosen. I ask for it the longed-for recompense of truth, which the Lord Mazda has in mind.

C. *Ashem vohu*

Asha is good, it is best. According to wish it is, according to wish it shall be for us. Asha belongs to Asha Vahishta.

D. *Yenhe hatam*

Those Beings, male and female, whom Lord Mazda knows the best for true worship, we worship them all.

Disposal of the Dead**

This passage describes the Zoroastrian "towers of silence," in which the dead are exposed to birds of prey so that their ritually defiling bodies may not pollute the sacred earth. First, provision is made for the on-ground exposure of the dead in places where "towers of silence" cannot be built.

** *Vendidad, Fargard* 6, section 5, 44–51

"O Maker of the material world, you Holy One! Where shall we bring the bodies of the dead, where shall we lay their bodies, O Ahura Mazda?"

[45] Ahura Mazda answered, "On the highest summits, where you know there are always corpse-eating dogs and corpse-eating birds, O holy Zarathushtra! There the worshippers of

Mazda shall secure the corpse by the feet and by the hair. They shall secure it with brass, stones, or lead, lest the corpse-eating dogs and the corpse-eating birds go and carry the bones to the water and to the trees."

"If they shall not secure the corpse, so that the corpse-eating dogs and the corpse-eating birds carry the bones to the water and to the trees, what is the penalty that they shall pay?"

Ahura Mazda answered: "They shall be Peshotanus.[19] They shall receive two hundred stripes with the Aspahe-astra, two hundred stripes with the Sraoshokarana."[20]

"O Maker of the material world, you Holy One! Where shall we bring the bones of the dead, where shall we lay them, O Ahura Mazda?"

[50] Ahura Mazda answered: "The worshippers of Mazda shall build a building out of the reach of the dog, of the fox, and of the wolf, and in which rain water cannot stay. Such a building shall they build, if they can afford it, with stones, mortar, and earth. If they cannot afford it, they shall lay the dead man on the ground, on his carpet and his pillow, clothed with the light of heaven,[21] and beholding the sun."

---

[19] *peshotanus:* ones subject to punishment.
[20] The same type of whip is probably meant here, so that the total number of lashes would be two hundred.

[21] *clothed with the light of heaven:* naked. Exposed to the birds of prey, the body will undergo the same ritual disposal as corpses put in towers of silence.

GLOSSARY

Avesta [ah-VES-tuh] the name of the Zoroastrian scriptures.

Fravashis [frah-VAH-shees] guardian spirits.

Gathas [GAH-tuhs] the collection of seventeen hymns in the *Yasna*.

Saoshyant [sa-OSH-yant] a future savior who will help purify the world.

Vendidad [VEN-dih-dahd] The *Law against Demons,* a division of the *Avesta*.

Visparad [VEE-spuh-rahd] "All the [Divine] Lords," a twenty-chapter collection of hymns in the *Avesta*.

Yashts [yahshts] "Hymns," twenty-one in number, a division of the *Avesta*.

Yasna [YAHZ-nuh] "Sacrifice," or hymns for worship; the first and foremost division of the *Avesta*.

QUESTIONS FOR STUDY AND DISCUSSION

1. What, to judge from the *Gathas,* were the main religious ideas of the prophet Zarathushtra?

2. What sort of changes occurred in Zoroastrian religion after the passing of Zarathushtra? For your answer, compare the *Gathas* with the rest of the *Avesta*.

3. Explain how Zarathushtra is worshipped by way of these scriptures.

4. How do the striking funeral and cleanliness rituals described here testify to the strong connection made in Zoroastrianism between ritual and moral purity?

SUGGESTIONS FOR FURTHER READING

Primary Sources

M. Boyce, *Textual Sources for the Study of Zoroastrianism*. Chicago: University of Chicago Press, 1990. A full selection of texts, with introductions but few annotations.

J. Darmesteter and L. H. Mills, *The Zend-Avesta*. In Max Müller, ed., *Sacred Books of the East*, vols. 4, 23, and 31. Oxford: Oxford University Press, 1880–87. Its Victorian English often interferes, but this is the only relatively complete translation of the *Avesta* in English.

J. Insler, *The Gathas of Zarathushtra*. Leiden: Brill, 1975. Contains the Avestan text, English translation and notes, and excellent commentary.

Secondary Sources

J. Barr, "The Question of Religious Influence: The Case of Zoroastrianism, Judaism, and Christianity." *Journal of the American Academy of Religion*, 53 (1985): 201–235. A reexamination of the notion, commonly accepted in religious scholarship, that Zoroastrian teachings had a great influence on Judaism and through it on Christianity.

M. Boyce, *A History of Zoroastrianism*, 2 vols. Leiden: Brill, 1975, 1982. The standard history of Zoroastrianism, with comprehensive treatment of the *Avesta* as the main source of our knowledge of early Zoroastrianism.

M. Boyce, *A Persian Stronghold of Zoroastrianism*. Oxford: Oxford University Press, 1977. Though no explicit and extended treatment of scripture is included here, this firsthand report on the life of Iranian Zoroastrians will shed much light on present-day use of the *Avesta*.

J. W. Boyd, "Zoroastrianism: Avestan Scripture and Rite," in F. M. Denny and R. L. Taylor, eds., *The Holy Book in Comparative Perspective*. Charleston: University of South Carolina Press, 1985, pp. 109–125. An excellent discussion of orthodox versus reformist reception and use of the *Avesta*.

Confucius and His Books
Confucius appears in rich robes on the title page of this modern Taiwanese edition of the Four Books. Credit: David Alexander

CHAPTER SEVEN

Confucianism

- ❖ In a high school in Beijing, China, students read and consider the meaning of the main Confucian book, the *Analects*. They read aloud, listen to their teacher's lecture, and discuss its meaning for China today. This study of Confucian scripture is undertaken by many Chinese throughout the world, but its recent revival in Communist China heralds the return of classic Chinese values and the waning, some hope, of communist ideology.

- ❖ In Hong Kong, a solitary sage studies ancient Chinese poems. He pauses to reflect on their meaning, especially on how they relate to his Confucian beliefs. After reflecting, he writes out the passage calligraphically. He is practicing self-cultivation toward becoming a "superior man," the highest goal of the Confucian tradition, and his study of the ancient classics is a key ingredient in bringing about this perfection.

- ❖ In Los Angeles, a sociologist researches the extraordinary success of Chinese-American students in the University of California system. Her conclusion: The social and intellectual values of these students' Confucian tradition—family loyalty, love of learning, self-cultivation, all values of the Confucian scriptures—have produced a remarkable academic achievement.

INTRODUCTION

Confucianism is the system of religion and philosophy begun by the sage Kung Fu-tzu ("Master Kung," died 479 B.C.E.), known to the Western world as Confucius. Although his teachings had little impact during his lifetime, they were kept alive by the efforts of his disciples. In the second century B.C.E., Confucianism became the official religion of China. Since then it has been closely identified with the essence of traditional Chinese culture, forming the basis of Chinese education, ethics, and statecraft and influencing some of the lands surrounding China, especially Korea and Japan. In Taiwan, study of the Confucian books is required in schools. No longer the state religion of China since the communist takeover in 1949, Confucianism has experienced a rebirth of sorts in other parts of Asia. It teaches a personal and social morality stressing the practice of key virtues such as filiality, humaneness, propriety, and faithfulness. Its full and well-defined scriptural canon, reflecting the Chinese love of books and learning, provides excellent insight into Confucianism.

Overview of Structure

Confucianists call their earlier scriptures the "Classics" or **Ching** [jing]. In Chinese as in English, "classic" suggests a literary work that embodies principles accepted as authoritative over a long time up through the present. The Confucian canon is divided into two parts, the earlier Five Classics (*Wu Ching*) and the later Four Books (*Ssu Shu*).

The Five Classics form the foundation of the later works written by Confucius and his followers. These early books were known, respected, and authoritative hundreds of years before the birth of Confucius. According to some lists, they number as many as thirteen, but the best-known list has five books. Confucianists believe that Confucius edited all these classics and wrote commentaries for some. Though this is doubtful as fact, most scholars do hold that the early Confucian tradition played a strong role in shaping and transmitting these books when it took them into its canon. This claim does express the high value the Confucian tradition placed on the ancient classics. As Confucius himself once said, "It is by the *Poetry* that the mind is aroused; by the *Rites* that the character is established; by the *Music* [now lost, but perhaps incorporated in part into the *Rites*] that the finish is received" (*Analects* 8.8). We now will deal briefly with each.

First and the oldest is the **I Ching** [ee jing], the *Classic of Changes,* a diviner's manual that developed over several hundred years, beginning with the early part of the Chou dynasty (1120–221 B.C.E.). The book contains pairs of eight basic trigrams (combinations of three horizontal lines) used to provide information on the future and recommend a course of action to meet it. The *I Ching* is built on the yin-yang, the two great interactive cosmic forces of passive-active, dark-light, and similar polarities. This cosmology has given it great popularity among more educated Chinese. In Confucian history it was also sometimes used philosophically, especially because of the "wings" or commentary appended to the hexagrams. Of all Chinese literature, the *I Ching* has been the most often translated into English and other modern European languages, because of its cosmological appeal rather than as a book of divination; more than twenty translations are currently in print. In China, however, the religio-magical use has tended to predominate. (This book is important for Taoists as well and is a prominent part of their canon.)

Second is the *Shu Ching,* the *Classic of History/Documents*. It consists of royal chronicles, narratives, decrees, and the like from the early Chou dynastic period, a period Confucius looked on as ideal. Much of its contents are later, forged additions.

Third is the *Shih Ching* [shir jing], the *Classic of Poetry*. It consists of 305 relatively short poems from the tenth to the seventh centuries B.C.E., all set to music. These songs deal with love, rituals, family relations, and government. The religious songs were sung in worship services, especially in sacrifice to ancestors. The *Poetry* became, even by the time of Confucius, the leading model of Chinese literary expression. The writings of Confucius are filled with allusions to this classic.

Fourth is the *Ch'un ch'iu,* the *Spring and Autumn Annals*. "Spring and Autumn" is an expression that stands for the entire year, not just for those seasons. The *Annals* is a sober and rather reliable chronological account of events in the state of Lu, Confucius' home state, from 720 to 480 B.C.E. Its ideas of respect for law and custom in government are only implicitly Confucian.

Last is the *Li Chi* [lee kee], the *Classic of Rites*. This collection features rituals and ceremonies of ancient China, both public and private. The *Li Chi* was probably collected in the second century B.C.E. *Li* can be variously translated "ritual," "propriety," or "manners," and all these ideas are important in the *Li Chi*.

The Four Books are built on what Confucius and his followers saw as the main teachings of this earlier canon. First among them is the *Lun yu,* or *Analects* (collected sayings) of Confucius. The *Analects* is by far the most important text in the history of Confucianism and our most reliable source for a knowledge of Confucius himself. It contains sayings of the Master, and occasionally anecdotes about him, as remembered by his disciples and recorded after his death. The *Analects* contains 12,700 characters (ideograms) in twenty short books. Like most other collections of sayings, the *Analects* is loosely organized and repetitive at times. Yet it treats well all the important concepts of the Confucian tradition: the cardinal virtues of humanity, propriety, respect for parents; becoming a superior man; proper government.

The second of the Four Books is the *Meng-tzu* or *Mencius.* This book is named for its author, who after Confucius was the most significant figure in Confucian tradition. Mencius lived in the fourth century B.C.E., and his disciples compiled this book after his death. More than twice as long as the *Analects,* the *Mencius* has well-developed treatments of several important topics, especially proper government. Mencius saw filiality as the greatest of the virtues and held strongly to the teaching of innate human goodness.

Third is the *Ta hsueh,* the *Great Learning.* This short book is an excerpt on virtuous government from the *Li Chi,* where it is chapter 39 in Legge's translation. Its first, short chapter is held to be by Confucius. The next ten chapters are a commentary on the first by Tseng-tzu, one of Confucius' disciples. The *Great Learning* teaches that rulers govern by example. If the ruler is morally good, so will be his government and his subjects; if he is not good, his subjects will incline to evil and his rule, along with the Mandate of Heaven to govern, will collapse.

Fourth is the *Chung yung,* the *Doctrine of the Mean.* Like the *Great Learning,* it was originally a chapter (31) in the *Li Chi.* "Mean" is a broad concept embracing many aspects of virtue: moderation, right conduct, decorum, sincerity. The good Confucianist is expected to "keep to the middle" between emotional and intellectual extremes. It is in the middle that the superior man is formed and comes into harmony with the **Tao** [dow], the cosmic Way of life. This book was important in the Neoconfucian movement that arose in the twelfth century.

Origin and Development

We have already discussed briefly the older Classics. We will treat more fully here the two main Confucian works, the *Analects* and the *Mencius,* and the development of the Confucian canon as a whole.

The Confucian canon has not come down to us in an easy chain of tradition. The *Analects* and the *Mencius* were probably first written down in the century following the death of their authors. The *Great Learning* and *Doctrine of the Mean* were separated from the *Classic of Rites* and made independent books. But in 213 B.C.E., Emperor Shih Huang-ti, who as a radical innovator was opposed to ancient traditions, gave orders that all Confucian books be destroyed. This famous "Burning of the Books" resulted in the loss of several versions of the Confucian books, but most books survived in some form.

The Confucian canon was reedited and republished under the next dynasty, the Han (206 B.C.E. to 220 C.E.). During this dynasty Confucianism was made the official state religion, and the Confucian canon was officially adopted as the basis of thought and conduct—indeed, of all official Chinese culture. In the twelfth century, the Four Books were recognized as an independent collection, and they soon became more central to Confucian life than the older Classics, which came to be interpreted through the Four Books. The state sanction for the Confucian scriptures lasted until 1905, when China abolished the civil service system as based on the canon.

Use

The official use of the Confucian scriptures flows from its adoption as the state literature of China. For more than two thousand years, all education was based either directly or indirectly on them. The first books a child studied and memorized in elementary school were the Four Books, especially the *Analects* and *Great Learning*. The rigorous civil service exams to become a government official, whether on the county, provincial, or national level, were also based on the scriptures. Each county in China had a school where the scriptural lore was taught. Those who became unusually expert in the scriptures as applied to government were known as "mandarins"; the last known mandarin died in 1991. The imperial university in Peking had five professorial posts in scripture that were designed to promote the excellence of the whole system. The personal intention of Confucius was thus fulfilled, not during his lifetime but after it, when the government of China came to be based on his leading ideas.

But Confucius' ideal of providing education to all who desired and could master it fell by the wayside as this training for government became limited to the upper classes who could pay for it. Although only a small percentage of the population of China has been able to read, the influence of the Confucian scriptures through oral teaching and general cultural transmission has been so thorough that the social relationships and cultural attitudes of most Chinese have become essentially Confucian. It is often remarked that no matter the specific religion of the Chinese—Buddhist, Taoist, Christian, or whatever—they are also Confucian. Thus, largely through the influence of its scripture, Confucianism has taken its place as perhaps the leading historic religion of China. Now that communist values are waning in the People's Republic of China, educators are returning to Confucian scriptures to provide a core moral education, especially the values of civility and obedience to law.

The Confucian approach to its scripture is almost exclusively cognitive. Confucius and his followers rejected mysticism, and in subsequent centuries the sometimes bitter struggle with the more mystical Taoist tradition reinforced this cognitive orientation. Teacher and student discuss scriptural meaning in an orderly, rational way. The individual scholar often practices "quiet sitting," solitary study that involves recitation of the text, meditation on its meaning, and often calligraphic reproduction of the text itself.

The literary style of the Confucian canon influences this use. Confucian scriptures share a basic literary style known as **wen-yen** (roughly translated as "formal-classical"). This style is known for brief, even compressed composition. Each Chinese ideogram character must be considered carefully to bring out the meaning. This style is one reason why Confucianists have generated a massive commentarial literature that seeks to shed more light on the canon itself. In the Confucian tradition, these commentaries have become accepted works in understanding the canon. Moreover, this formal-classical style means that translations of Confucian scripture will often vary greatly among themselves. This compressed style invites the reader of both the Chinese original and the English translation to meditate carefully and deeply about its meaning.

HISTORY

The Character of Confucius*

The Analects *depicts Confucius as a model of the "superior man." By following his own teaching, he became an example to his followers. The first passage is Confucius' own summary of his progress in self-cultivation. The second describes key elements in his character. The third gives fascinating detail on some of his daily habits.*[1]

[2.4] The Master said, "At fifteen, I had my mind bent on learning. At thirty, I stood firm. At forty, I had no doubts. At fifty, I knew the decrees of Heaven.[2] At sixty, my ear was an obedient organ for the reception of truth. At seventy, I could follow what my heart desired, without transgressing what was right."

[7.1] The Master said, "I am a transmitter and not a maker, believing in and loving the ancients. I venture to compare myself with our old P'eng."[3]

The Master said, "The silent treasuring up of knowledge; learning without tiring; and in-

structing others without being wearied—which one of these things belongs to me?"

The Master said, "Leaving virtue without proper cultivation; not thoroughly discussing what is learned; not being able to move towards righteousness of which a knowledge is gained; and not being able to change what is not good —these are the things which cause me much concern."

When the Master was unoccupied with business, his manner was easy, and he looked pleased.

[5] The Master said, "My decline is extreme. For a long time, I have not dreamed, as I used to do, that I saw the duke of Chou."[4]

The Master said, "Let the will be set on the path of duty. Let every attainment in what is good be firmly grasped. Let perfect virtue be accorded with. Let relaxation and enjoyment be found in the arts."

The Master said, "From the man bringing his bundle of dried meat[5] for my teaching, or more than that, I have never refused instruction to any one."

The Master said, "I do not open up the truth to one who is not eager to get knowledge, nor

---

* *Analects* 2.4, 7.1–9, 19–24; 10.1–4, 8–12
[1] All selections from the *Analects* and the *Mencius* are taken from James Legge, trans., *The Chinese Classics* (Oxford: Oxford University Press, 1893).
[2] *decrees* (or "mandates") *of Heaven:* understood today by most Confucianists as the working of Nature in people and events, not primarily as the working of God.
[3] *old P'eng:* a sage from ancient times.

[4] *duke of Chou:* in the view of Confucius, one of the greatest of the early Chinese sage kings.
[5] *dried meat:* the smallest possible payment for instruction. Confucianism believes that learning and self-cultivation should be open to all who desire it.

help out any one who is not anxious to explain himself. When I have presented one corner of a subject to any one, and he cannot from it learn the other three, I do not repeat my lesson."

When the Master was eating by the side of a mourner, he never ate to the full. He did not sing on the same day in which he had been weeping. . . .

[19] The Master said, "I am not one who was born in the possession of knowledge; I am one who is fond of antiquity,[6] and earnest in seeking it there."

[20] The subjects on which the Master did not talk were extraordinary things,[7] feats of strength, disorder, and spiritual beings.

The Master said, "When I walk along with two others, they may serve me as my teachers. I will select their good qualities and follow them, their bad qualities and avoid them."

The Master said, "Heaven produced the virtue that is in me. What can Hwan T'ui[8] do to me?"

The Master said, "Do you think, my disciples, that I have any concealments? I conceal nothing from you. There is nothing which I do that is not shown to you, my disciples. That is my way."

There were four things which the Master taught—letters, ethics, devotion of soul, and truthfulness.

[10.1] Confucius, in his village, looked simple and sincere, and as if he were not able to speak. When he was in the prince's ancestral temple, or in the court, he spoke minutely on every point, but cautiously.

When he was on duty at court, in speaking with the great officers of the lower grade he spoke freely, but in a straightforward manner. In speaking with those of the higher grade, he did so mildly, but precisely. When the ruler was pre-

sent, his manner displayed respectful uneasiness; it was serious, but self-possessed.

When the prince called on him to receive a visitor, his countenance appeared to change, and his legs to move forward with difficulty. He inclined himself to the other officers among whom he stood, moving his left or right arm, as their position required, but keeping the skirts of his robe before and behind evenly adjusted. He hastened forward, with his arms like the wings of a bird. When the guest had left, he would report to the prince, "The visitor is not looking back any more."

When he entered the palace gate, he seemed to bend his body, as if it were not sufficient to admit him. When he was standing, he did not occupy the middle of the gateway; when he passed in or out, he did not tread upon the threshold. When he was passing the vacant place of the prince, his countenance appeared to change, and his legs to bend under him, and his words came as if he hardly had breath to speak them. He ascended the reception hall, holding up his robe with both his hands, and his body bent. He held in his breath also, as if he dared not breathe.

[8] He liked to have his rice finely cleaned, and to have his minced meat cut quite small. He did not eat rice which had been injured by heat or damp and turned sour, nor fish or meat which was gone. He did not eat what was discolored, or what was of a bad flavor, nor anything which was badly cooked, or was not in season. He did not eat meat which was not cut properly, nor what was served without its proper sauce. Though there might be a large quantity of meat, he would not allow what he took to exceed the due proportion for the rice. It was only in wine that he laid down no limit for himself, but he did not allow himself to be confused by it. He did not partake of wine and dried meat bought in the market. He was never without ginger when he ate. He did not eat much. When he had been assisting at the prince's sacrifice, he did not keep the meat which he received overnight. The meat of his family sacrifice he did not keep over three

---

[6] *antiquity:* Confucianists emphasize the Chinese custom of seeking direction from the ancient writings.

[7] *extraordinary things:* strange events in nature.

[8] *Hwan T'ui:* an army officer who had attempted to kill Confucius.

days. If kept over three days, people could not eat it. When eating, he did not converse. When in bed, he did not speak. Although his food might be coarse rice and vegetable soup, he would offer a little of it in sacrifice with a serious, respectful air.

If his mat was not straight, he did not sit on it.

[10] When the villagers were drinking together, after those who carried walking staffs left, he went out immediately. When the villagers were going through their ceremonies to drive away pestilential influences, he put on his court robes and stood on the eastern steps.

When he was sending complimentary inquiries to any one in another state, he bowed twice as he escorted the messenger away.

When Chi K'ang sent him a present of medicine, he bowed and received it, saying, "I do not know it. I dare not taste it."

The stable burned down when he was at court, and on his return he said, "Has any person been hurt?" He did not ask about the horses.

ETHICS

The Virtues of the Superior Man*

Confucius taught self-cultivation in knowledge and virtue. When one reaches moral and intellectual maturity, he is a "superior man." The Chinese phrase for "superior man," **chun-tzu** *[jun-tzoo], literally means "prince's son," but Confucius taught that by education even a common man could become superior. (The noninclusive language is intentional—women were not expected or encouraged to pursue this self-cultivation.) Neoconfucianism applies these passages to the closely related goal of becoming a sage.*

[1.1] The Master said, "Is it not pleasant to learn with a constant perseverance and application? Is it not delightful to have friends coming from distant quarters? Is he not a man of complete virtue, who feels no discomposure though men may take no note of him?"

The philosopher Yu said, "Few are those who, being filial and fraternal, are fond of offending their superiors. There have been none, who, not liking to offend their superiors, have been fond of stirring up confusion. The superior man bends his attention to the foundation. That being established, all practical courses naturally grow up. Filiality and fraternal submission—are they not the root of all benevolent actions?"

The Master said, "Fine words and an insinuating appearance are seldom associated with true virtue."

The philosopher Tsang said, "I daily examine myself on three points: whether, in transacting business for others, I have been faithful; whether, in dealings with friends, I have been sincere; whether I have mastered and practiced the instructions of my teacher." . . .

[6] The Master said, "A youth, when at home, should be filial, and away from home he should be respectful to his elders. He should be earnest and truthful. He should overflow in love to all, and cultivate the friendship of good people. When he has time and opportunity, after the performance of these things, he should employ them in the arts."

Tsze-hsia said, "If a man withdraws his mind from the love of beauty, and applies it as sincerely to the love of the virtuous; if, in serving his parents, he can exert his utmost strength; if, in serving his prince, he can devote his life; if, in his

---

* *Analects* 1.1–4, 6–9, 14; 15.17–23

dealings with his friends, his words are sincere—although men say that he has not learned, I will certainly say that he has."

The Master said, "If the scholar is not serious, he will not call forth any veneration, and his learning will not be solid. Hold faithfulness and sincerity as first principles. Have no friends not equal to yourself. When you have faults, do not fear to abandon them."

The philosopher Tsang said, "Let there be a careful attention to perform the funeral rites to parents, and let them be followed when long gone with the ceremonies of sacrifice. Then the virtue of the people will resume its proper excellence." . . .

[14] The Master said, "He who aims to be a man of complete virtue in his food does not seek to gratify his appetite, nor in his dwelling place does he seek the appliances of ease. He is earnest in what he does, and careful in his speech. He frequents the company of men of principle that he may be rectified. Such a person may be said indeed to love to learn."

[15.17] The Master said, "The superior man considers righteousness to be essential in everything. He performs it according to the rules of propriety. He brings it forth in humility. He completes it with sincerity. This is indeed a superior man."

The Master said, "The superior man is distressed by his lack of ability. He is not distressed by his lack of fame."

The Master said, "The superior man dislikes the thought of his name not being mentioned after his death."

[20] The Master said, "What the superior man seeks is in himself. What the inferior man seeks is in others."

The Master said, "The superior man is dignified, but does not wrangle. He is sociable, but not a partisan."

The Master said, "The superior man does not promote a man simply on account of his words, nor does he put aside good words because of the man."

Tsze-kung asked, saying, "Is there one word which may serve as a rule of practice for all one's life?" The Master said, "Is not Reciprocity[9] such a word? What you do not want done to yourself, do not do to others."

---

[9] *Reciprocity:* the virtue *shu.*

Benevolence*

*Benevolence (**jen** [ren]) is the chief of the Confucian virtues. It denotes humaneness, fellow feeling, even love; in this translation it is rendered by the word "virtue." Confucianists, especially those aspiring to sagehood, have trained themselves in benevolence by reflecting on their lives in the light of the scriptures.*

The Master said, "Virtuous manners constitute the excellence of a neighborhood. If a man in selecting a residence does not fix on one where such manners prevail, how can he be wise?"

The Master said, "Those who are without virtue cannot abide long either in a condition of poverty and hardship, or in a condition of enjoyment. The virtuous rest in virtue; the wise desire virtue."

The Master said, "It is only the [truly] virtuous man who can love, or who can hate, others."

The Master said, "If the will is set on virtue, there will be no practice of wickedness."

[5] The Master said, "Riches and honors are what men desire. If it cannot be obtained in the proper way, they should not be held. Poverty and a low condition are what men dislike. If it cannot be obtained in the proper way, they should not be avoided. If a superior man abandons virtue,

---

* *Analects* 4.1–6

how can he fulfill the requirements of that name? The superior man does not, even for the space of a single meal, act contrary to virtue. In moments of haste, he clings to it. In seasons of danger, he clings to it."

The Master said, "I have not seen a person who loved virtue, or one who hated what was not virtuous. He who loved virtue would esteem nothing above it. He who hated what is not virtuous would practice virtue in such a way that he would not allow anything that is not virtuous to approach his person. Is any one able for one day to apply his strength to virtue? I have not seen the case in which his strength would be sufficient. Should there possibly be any such case, I have not seen it."

The Actions of Filiality*

Filiality (**hsiao**), *called filial piety in the older literature, is reverence for one's living ancestors, and extends itself to worship of one's dead ancestors. This* Classic of Rites *passage goes into great detail in laying down rules for proper filial conduct. It stresses deference, obedience, and faithfulness to one's parents.*[10]

The sovereign king orders the chief minister to send down his lessons of virtue to the millions of the people. . . .

[4] [After getting properly] dressed [in the morning], [sons] should go to their parents and parents-in-law.[11] On getting to where they are, with bated breath and gentle voice they should ask if their clothes are too warm or too cold, whether they are ill or pained, or uncomfortable in any part. If they are, they should proceed reverently to stroke and scratch the place. They should in the same way, going before or following after, help and support their parents in leaving or entering the apartment. In bringing in the basin for them to wash, the younger will carry the stand and the elder the water. They will beg to be allowed to pour out the water, and when the washing is concluded, they will hand them the towel. They will ask whether they want anything, and then respectfully bring it. All this they will do with an appearance of pleasure to make their parents feel at ease. They should bring gruel, thick or thin, spirits or juice, soup with vegetables, beans, wheat, spinach, rice, millet, maize, and glutinous millet—whatever they wish, in fact. They should bring dates, chestnuts, sugar and honey to sweeten their dishes; the ordinary or the large-leaved violets, leaves of elm-trees, fresh or dry, and the most soothing rice-water to lubricate them; and fat and oil to enrich them. The parents will be sure to taste them, and when they have done so, the young people should withdraw. . . .

From the time that sons receive an official appointment,[12] they and their father occupy different parts of their residence. But at dawn, the son will pay his respects, and express his affection by the offer of pleasant delicacies. At sunrise he will leave, and he and his father will attend to their different duties. At sundown, the son will pay his evening visit in the same way. . . .

[10] While the parents are both alive, at their regular meals, morning and evening, the eldest son and his wife will encourage them to eat everything, and what is left after all, they themselves will eat. When the father is dead, and the mother still alive, the eldest son should wait upon her at her meals. The wives of the other

---

* *Classic of Rites* 10.1, 4, 7, 10–11,13–15
[10] Taken, with editing, from James Legge, trans., *The Sacred Books of China: The Texts of Confucianism*, part 3, *Sacred Books of the East*, vol. 27 (Oxford, Oxford University Press, 1885), pp. 449–57.
[11] The passage presupposes that one's parents have an apartment or room in one's house, typically the case in traditional China.

---

[12] *official appointment:* in a government position.

sons will do with what is left as in the former case. The children should have the sweet, soft and oily things that are left.

When sons and their wives are ordered to do anything by their parents, they should immediately respond and reverently proceed to do it. In going forward or backward, or turning round, they should be careful and serious. While going out or coming in, while bowing or walking, they should not presume to belch, sneeze, or cough, to yawn or stretch themselves, to stand on one foot, or to lean against anything, or to look askance. They should not dare to spit or snivel, nor if it is cold to put on more clothes, nor if they itch anywhere, to scratch themselves. Unless for reverent attention to something, they should not presume to bare their [parents'] shoulders or chest. Unless it be in wading, they should not hold up their clothes. Of their private dress and coverlet, they should not display the inside. They should not allow the spittle or snivel of their parents to be seen. They should ask leave to rinse away any dirt on their caps or girdles, and to wash their clothes that are dirty with lye that has been prepared for the purpose; and to stitch together, with needle and thread, any tear. . . .

Sons and sons' wives, who are filial and reverential, when they receive an order from their parents should not refuse or delay executing it. When their parents give them anything to eat or drink, which they do not like, they will never-theless taste it and wait for their further orders. When they give them clothes which are not to their liking, they will put them on, and wait in the same way. If their parents give them anything to do, and then employ another to take their place, although they do not like the arrangement, they will in the meantime give it into his hands and let him do it, doing it again, if it is not done well. . . .

When sons and their wives have not been filial and reverential, the parents should not be angry and resentful with them, but endeavor to instruct them. If they will not receive instruction, they should then be angry with them. If that anger does no good, they can then drive out the son, and send the wife away, yet not publicly showing why they have treated them so.

[15] If a parent has a fault, the son should with bated breath, and bland aspect, and gentle voice, admonish him. If the admonition does not take effect, he will be more reverential and more filial; and when the father seems pleased, he will repeat the admonition. If he should be displeased with this, rather than allow him to commit an offense against anyone in the neighborhood or countryside, the son should strongly protest. If the parent is angry and more displeased, and beat him till the blood flows, he should not presume to be angry and resentful, but be still more reverential and more filial.

The Attitude of Filiality*

Confucius stresses not only the actions of filiality as related in the previous reading, but much more the attitude with which these acts are carried out. This attitude must be one of the genuine reverence implied in hsiao *or "piety."*

[2.5] Mang asked what filiality was. The Master said, "It is not being disobedient." Soon after, as Fan Ch'ih was driving him, the Master told him,

saying, "Mang-sun asked me what filiality was, and I answered him—'not being disobedient.'" Fan Ch'ih said, "What did you mean?" The Master replied, "That parents, when alive, should be served according to propriety; that, when dead, they should be buried according to propriety; and that they should be sacrificed to according to propriety."

Mang Wu asked what filiality was. The Master said, "Do not make your parents anxious about anything else than your being sick."

---

* *Analects* 2.5–8; 4.18–21; 13.18

Tsze-yu asked what filiality was. The Master said, "Filial piety nowadays means the support of one's parents. But dogs and horses likewise are able to do something in the way of support. Without reverence, what is there to distinguish the one support given from the other?"

Tsze-hsia asked what filiality was. The Master said, "The difficulty is with the countenance. When their elders have any troublesome affairs and the young do their work, and when the young have plenty of wine and food to set before their elders, how can this be considered filiality?"

[4.18] The Master said, "In serving his parents, a son may protest to them, but gently; when he sees that they do not incline to follow his advice, he shows an increased degree of reverence, but does not abandon his purpose; and should they punish him, he does not allow himself to murmur."

The Master said, "While his parents are alive, the son may not leave his home area to a far distance. If he does go away, he must have a fixed place to which he goes."[13]

[20] The Master said, "If the son for three years[14] does not alter from the way of his father, he may be called filial."

The Master said, "The age of one's parents should always be kept in the memory, as a reason for joy and for fear."

[13.18] The duke of Sheh informed Confucius, saying, "Among us here are those who may be styled upright in their conduct. If their father stole a sheep, they will bear witness to the fact." Confucius said, "Among us, in our part of the country, those who are upright are different from this. The father conceals the misconduct of the son, and the son conceals the misconduct of the father. Uprightness is to be found in this."

---

[13] *a fixed place:* so his parents know where he is.
[14] *for three years:* after the death of the father.

Propriety*

Li, "propriety," can also be translated as "ritual correctness" or "good manners." The following selection highlights the traditional Confucian connection between propriety in the rites and in everyday life. In typically Confucian style, the Poetry *is quoted to illustrate the point. Confucian rituals carried out in the temples of Korea, Taiwan, and other lands still keep to the meticulous care prescribed here. Just as important, emphasis on li has given Chinese peoples their highly developed sense of politeness.*

The Master said, "If a man lacks the virtues proper to humanity, what has he to do with the rites of propriety? If a man is without the virtues proper to humanity, what has he to do with music?"

Lin Fang asked what was the first thing to be attended to in ceremonies. The Master said, "A great question indeed! In festive ceremonies, it is better to be sparing than extravagant. In the ceremonies of mourning, it is better that there be deep sorrow than a minute attention to observances." . . .

[8] Tsze-hsia asked, "What is the meaning of the passage, 'The pretty dimples of her artful smile! The well-defined black and white of her eye! The plain ground for the colors'?"[15] The Master said, "The business of laying on the colors follows [the preparation of] the plain ground." "Ceremonies then are a subsequent thing?" The Master said, "It is you, Shang, who can bring out my meaning. Now I can begin to talk about the *Poetry* with you."

---

* *Analects* 3.3–4, 8–9, 12–15, 17–19

[15] A poem from the *Poetry.*

The Master said, "I could describe the ceremonies of the Hsia dynasty, but Chi cannot sufficiently attest my words. I could describe the ceremonies of the Yin dynasty, but Sung cannot sufficiently attest my words. [They cannot do so] because of the insufficiency of their records and wise men. If those were sufficient, I could adduce them in support of my words." . . .

[12] He sacrificed to the dead as if they were present. He sacrificed to the spirits as if the spirits were present. The Master said, "I consider my not being present at the sacrifice as if I did not sacrifice."

Wang-sun Chia asked, "What is the meaning of the saying, 'It is better to pay court to the furnace than to the southwest corner'?"[16] The Master said, "Not so. He who offends against Heaven has none to whom he can pray."

The Master said, "Chou had the advantage of viewing the two past dynasties. How complete and elegant are its regulations! I follow Chou."

---

[16] A traditional saying, meaning that it is better to serve the gods of food than the ancestral spirits of the shrine (at the southwest corner of the Chinese house).

[15] The Master, when he entered the Grand Temple (of Lu), asked about everything. Someone said, "Who says that the son of the man of Tsau knows the rules of propriety! He has entered the grand temple and asks about everything." The Master heard the remark, and said, "This [behavior of mine] is indeed a rule of propriety." . . .

[17] Tzu-kung wished to do away with the offering of a sheep connected with the inauguration of the first day of each month. The Master said, "Tzu, you love the sheep; I love the ceremony."[17]

The Master said, "The full observance of the rules of propriety in serving one's prince is accounted by people to be flattery."

The duke Ting asked how a prince should employ his ministers, and how ministers should serve their prince. Confucius replied, "A prince should employ his minister according to the rules of propriety; ministers should serve their prince with faithfulness."

---

[17] Also translated: "Tzu, you love the sheep, but I love the sacrifice."

The Way*

The "Way" (Tao) is an ancient idea in Chinese tradition. In Confucianism, it is understood as the moral way of heaven, to which the ruler as a superior man should aspire. In this selection, the relationship of the Way and good government is brought out.

Confucius said, "When good government prevails in the empire, ceremonies, music, and punitive military expeditions proceed from the son of Heaven. When bad government prevails in the empire, ceremonies, music, and punitive mili-

---

* *Analects* 16.2

tary expeditions proceed from the princes. When these things proceed from the princes, as a rule, the cases will be few in which they do not lose their power in ten generations. When they proceed from the great officers of the princes, as a rule, the cases will be few in which they do not lose their power in five generations. When the subsidiary ministers of the great officers hold in their grasp the orders of the state, as a rule, the cases will be few in which they do not lose their power in three generations. When right principles prevail in the kingdom, government will not be in the hands of the great officers. When right principles prevail in the kingdom, there will be no discussions among the common people."

The Love of Learning*

The love of learning is a leading moral quality among anyone who aspires to moral and intellectual superiority. Here Confucius explains its relationship to other prominent virtues.

The Master said, "Yu, have you heard the six words to which are attached six faults?" Yu replied, "I have not." "Sit down, and I will tell them to you. There is the love of being benevolent without the love of learning; the fault here leads to a foolish simplicity. There is the love of knowing without the love of learning; the fault here leads to dissipation of mind. There is the love of being sincere without the love of learning; the fault here leads to an injurious disregard of consequences. There is the love of straightforwardness without the love of learning; the fault

---

* *Analects* 17.8–9, 12

here leads to rudeness. There is the love of boldness without the love of learning; the fault here leads to insubordination. There is the love of firmness without the love of learning; the fault here leads to extravagant conduct."

The Master said, "My children, why do you not study the *Book of Poetry*? The poems serve to stimulate the mind. They may be used for purposes of self-contemplation. They teach the art of sociability. They show how to regulate feelings of resentment. From them you learn the more immediate duty of serving one's father, and the remoter duty of serving one's prince. From them we become largely acquainted with the names of birds, beasts, and plants." . . .

[12] The Master said, "He who puts on an appearance of stern firmness, while inwardly he is weak, is like one of the small, common people. Yes, is he not like the thief who breaks through, or climbs over, a wall?"

Early Debate over the Goodness of Human Nature**

Although Confucius did not discuss the question of goodness and evil in the human personality, Mencius took up this topic. He argued the optimistic idea that all people are by nature good. Therefore, the ruler must only be good himself and bring out the innate goodness of his subjects in order to establish his rule. In this selection, the philosopher Kao Tzu serves as a foil for the thoughts of Mencius. In the second passage, Mencius argues that four virtues sum up the ethics of Confucian thought—humaneness, righteousness, propriety, and wisdom. He maintains that these virtues are rooted in basic human nature, so they are the proper expression of human nature.

The philosopher Kao said, "Man's nature is like the ke willow, and righteousness is like a cup or

---

** *Mencius* 6.1.1–4, 6

a bowl. The fashioning benevolence and righteousness out of man's nature is like the making cups and bowls from the ke willow." Mencius replied, "Can you, leaving untouched the nature of the willow make with it cups and bowls? You must do violence and injury to the willow before you can make cups and bowls with it. If you must do violence and injury to the willow in order to make cups and bowls with it, on your principles you must in the same way do violence and injury to humanity in order to fashion from it benevolence and righteousness! Your words, alas! would certainly lead all men on to reckon benevolence and righteousness to be calamities."

The philosopher Kao said, "Man's nature is like water whirling round in a corner. Open a passage for it to the east, and it will flow to the east; open a passage for it to the west, and it will flow to the west. Man's nature is indifferent to good and evil, just as the water is indifferent to the east and west." Mencius replied, "Water indeed will flow indifferently to the east or west, but will it flow indifferently up or down? The tendency of man's nature to good is like the tendency of water to flow downwards. There are none but have this tendency to good, just as all water flows downwards. Now by striking water and causing it to leap up, you may make it go over your forehead, and, by damming and leading it, you may force it up a hill—but are such movements according to the nature of water? It is the force applied which causes them. When men are made to do what is not good, their nature is dealt with in this way."

The philosopher Kao said, "Life is what is to be understood by nature." Mencius asked him, "Do you say that by nature you mean life, just as you say that white is white?" "Yes, I do," was the reply. Mencius added, "Is the whiteness of a white feather like that of white snow, and the whiteness of white snow like that of a white gem?" Kao again said "Yes." "Very well," pursued Mencius. "Is the nature of a dog like the nature of an ox, and the nature of an ox like the nature of a man?"

The philosopher Kao said, "To enjoy food and delight in colors is nature. Benevolence is internal and not external; righteousness is external and not internal." Mencius asked him, "What is the ground of your saying that benevolence is internal and righteousness external?" He replied, "There is a man older than I, and I give honor to his age. It is not that there is first in me a principle of such reverence to age. It is just as when there is a white [pale] man, and I consider him white—according as he is so externally to me. On this account, I pronounce of righteousness that it is external." Mencius said, "There is no difference between our pronouncing of a white horse to be white and our pronouncing a white man to be white. But is there no difference between the regard with which we acknowledge the age of an old horse and that with which we acknowledge the age of an old man? And what is it which is called righteousness?—the fact of a

man's being old? or the fact of our giving honor to his age?" Kao said, "There is my younger brother—I love him. But the younger brother of a man of Ts'in I do not love; that is, the feeling is determined by myself, and therefore I say that benevolence is internal. On the other hand, I give honor to an old man of Ts'oo, and I also give honor to an old man of my own people: that is, the feeling is determined by the age, and therefore I say that righteousness is external." Mencius answered him, "Our enjoyment of meat roasted by a man of Ts'in does not differ from our enjoyment of meat roasted by ourselves. Thus, what you insist on takes place also in the case of such things, and will you say likewise that our enjoyment of a roast is external?" . . .

The disciple Kung-too said, "The philosopher Kao says, 'Man's nature is neither good nor bad.' Some say, 'Man's nature may be made to practice good, and it may be made to practice evil,' and accordingly, under Wan and Woo, the people loved what was good, while under Yew and Le, they loved what was cruel. Some say, 'The nature of some is good, and the nature of others is bad.' Hence it was that under such a sovereign as Yaou there yet appeared Seang; that with such a father as Koo-sow there yet appeared Shun; and that with Chow for their sovereign, and the son of their elder brother besides, there were found K'e, the viscount of Wei, and the prince Pe-kan. And now you say, 'The nature is good.' Then are all those wrong?" Mencius said, "From the feelings proper to it, it is constituted for the practice of what is good. This is what I mean in saying that the nature is good. If men do what is not good, the blame cannot be imputed to their natural powers. The feeling of commiseration belongs to all men; so does that of shame and dislike; and that of reverence and respect; and that of approving and disapproving. The feeling of commiseration implies the principle of benevolence; that of shame and dislike, the principle of righteousness; that of reverence and respect, the principle of propriety; and that of approving and disapproving, the principle of knowledge. Benevolence, righteousness, propriety, and knowledge are not infused into us from without. We are certainly furnished with them. And a different view is simply from want of reflection. Hence it is said: 'Seek and you will find them. Neglect and you will lose them.' Men differ from one another in regard to them—some as much again as others, some five times as much, and some to an incalculable amount—it is because they cannot carry out fully their natural powers. It is said in the *Book of Poetry*:

'Heaven, in producing mankind,
Gave them their various faculties and relations
  with their specific laws,
These are the invariable rules of nature of all to
  hold,
And all love this admirable virtue.'

Confucius said, 'The maker of this ode knew indeed the principle of our nature!' We may thus see that every faculty and relation must have its law, and since there are invariable rules for all to hold, they consequently love this admirable virtue."

Meng said: "All men are such that they cannot bear seeing others suffer. The kings of old had this king of compassion and it governed their policy. One could easily rule the whole world with attitudes like that: it would be like turning it round in the palm of the hand.

"I say that men are like that because anyone seeing a child fall into a well would have a feeling of horror and distress. They don't feel this out of sympathy for the parents, or to gain a reputation among friends and neighbors, or for fear of being considered unfeeling. Not to feel the distress would be against human nature. Not to feel shame and disgrace and not to feel respect for others and not to have a sense of right and wrong are contrary to human nature. The feeling of distress is the beginning of humaneness; the feeling of shame is the beginning of righteousness; the feeling of respect is the beginning of wisdom. People have these four sentiments as they have four limbs. To have these four beginnings and to say they can't be developed is to injure oneself; to say that the ruler has them but cannot develop them is to injure him. Since all have them all should be able to develop them and fulfil them. They are like embers ready to burst into flame, or a spring ready to gush forth from the earth. If in fact they can be realized, they will protect the whole world. if they are not then they will not be enough even to protect one's parents."

The Basis of Good Government*

The text of Confucius is given in sections 1–7; what follows is from the ninth chapter of the commentary by the philosopher Tsang, which is appended to the Great Learning. *This passage, originally a chapter in the* Classic of Rites, *was made a classic by itself in one of the Four Books and has had a great influence on the idea and practice of government in China and other lands influenced by it.*[18]

---

* *The Great Learning* 1–7; 9.1, 3–9
[18] Taken, with editing, from James Legge, trans., *The Sacred Books of China: The Texts of Confucianism*, part 4, *Sacred Books of the East* vol. 28 (Oxford: Oxford University Press, 1885), pp. 411–13, 417–19.

What the Great Learning teaches is to illustrate illustrious virtue, to love people, and to rest in the highest excellence.

The point where to rest being known, the object of pursuit is then determined; and, that being determined, a calm unperturbedness may be attained to. To that calmness there will succeed a tranquil repose. In that repose there will be careful deliberation, and that deliberation will be followed by the attainment of the desired end. Things have their root and their branches; affairs have their end and their beginning. To know what is first and what is last will lead near to what is taught in the Great Learning.

The ancients who wished to illustrate illustrious virtue throughout the kingdom, first ordered well their states. Wishing to order well their states, they first regulated their families. Wishing to regulate their families, they first cultivated their persons. Wishing to cultivate their persons, they first rectified their hearts. Wishing to rectify their hearts, they first sought to be sincere in their thoughts. Wishing to be sincere in their thoughts, they first extended to the utmost their knowledge.

The extension of knowledge is by the investigation of things. [5] Things being investigated, knowledge became complete. Their knowledge being complete, their thoughts were sincere. Their thoughts being sincere, their hearts were then rectified. Their hearts being rectified, their persons were cultivated. Their persons being cultivated, their families were regulated. Their families being regulated, their states were rightly governed. Their states being rightly governed, the whole kingdom was made tranquil and happy.

From the son of Heaven down to the multitudes of the people, all considered the cultivation of the person to be the root of everything else. It cannot be, when the root is neglected, that what should spring from it will be well ordered. It never has been the case that what was of great importance has been slightly cared for, and at the same time what was of slight importance has been greatly cared for. . . .

[9.1, from the commentary] What is meant by "In order rightly to govern the state, it is necessary first to regulate the family,"[19] is this. It is not possible for one to teach others, while he cannot teach his own family. Therefore, the ruler, without going beyond his family, completes the lessons for the state. There is filiality, with which the sovereign should be served. There is fraternal submission, with which elders and superiors should be served. There is kindness, with which the multitude should be treated. . . .

[3] From the loving example of one family a whole state becomes loving, and from its courtesies the whole state becomes courteous, while, from the ambition and perverseness of the one man [the emperor], the whole state may be led to rebellious disorder—such is the nature of the influence. This verifies the saying, "Affairs may be ruined by a single sentence; a kingdom may be settled by its one man."

Yao and Shun led the kingdom with benevolence, and the people followed them. Chieh and Chau led the kingdom with violence, and the people followed them. The orders which these issued were contrary to the practices which they loved, and so the people did not follow them. On this account, the ruler must himself be possessed of good qualities, and then he may require them in the people. He must not have bad qualities in himself, and then he may require that they shall not be in the people. Never has there been a man, who, not having reference to his own character and wishes in dealing with others, was able effectually to instruct them.

[5] Thus we see how the government of the state depends on the regulation of the family.

In the *Book of Poetry* it is said, "That peach tree, so delicate and elegant! How luxuriant is its foliage! This girl is going to her husband's house. She will rightly order her household." Let the household be rightly ordered, and then the people of the state may be taught.

In the *Book of Poetry* it is said, "They can discharge their duties to their elder brothers. They can discharge their duties to their younger brothers." Let the ruler discharge his duties to his elder and younger brothers, and then he may teach the people of the state.

In the *Book of Poetry* it is said, "In his deportment there is nothing wrong; he rectifies all the people of the state." Yes; when the ruler, as a father, a son, and a brother, is a model, then the people imitate him.

This is what is meant by saying, "The government of his kingdom depends on his regulation of the family."

---

[19] Not a direct quote from the text of *The Great Learning* above, but a good statement of an idea that occurs there.

The Ruler as Example to the People*

The teaching of Confucius on government follows closely that of the Great Learning. *Here he stresses the personal quality of the ruler, the humane nature of his government, and the rectification of names.*

[2.18] Tsze-chang was learning with a view to official emolument. The Master said, "Hear much and put aside the points of which you stand in doubt, while you speak cautiously at the same time of the others—then you will afford few occasions for blame. See much and put aside the things which seem perilous, while you are cautious at the same time in carrying the others into practice—then you will have few occasions for repentance. When one gives few occasions for blame in his words, and few occasions for repentance in his conduct,[20] he is in the way to get emolument."

The duke Ai asked, saying, "What should be done in order to secure the submission of the people?" Confucius replied, "Advance the upright and set aside the crooked, then the people will submit. Advance the crooked and set aside the upright, then the people will not submit."

[20] Chi K'ang asked how to cause the people to reverence their ruler, to be faithful to him, and to go on to nerve themselves to virtue. The Master said, "Let him preside over them with gravity; then they will reverence him. Let him be filial and kind to all; then they will be faithful to him. Let him advance the good and teach the incompetent; then they will eagerly seek to be virtuous."

[12.11] The duke Ching, of Ch'i, asked Confucius about government. Confucius replied,

"There is government when the prince is a prince, and the minister is a minister, when the father is a father, and the son is a son."[21] "Good!" said the duke. "If, indeed, the prince is not a prince, the minister not a minister, the father not a father, and the son not a son, although I may prosper, can I enjoy it?" . . .

[17] Chi K'ang asked Confucius about government. Confucius replied, "To govern means to rectify. If you lead the people with correctness, who will dare not to be correct?" . . .

[19] Chi K'ang asked Confucius about government, saying, "What do you say to killing the unprincipled for the good of the principled?" Confucius replied, "Sir, in carrying on your government, why should you use killing at all? Let your obvious desires be for what is good, and the people will be good. The relation between superiors and inferiors[22] is like that between the wind and the grass. The grass must bend, when the wind blows across it."

[13.5] The Master said, "Though a man may be able to recite the three hundred odes, yet if, when entrusted with a governmental charge, he knows not how to act, or if, when sent to any quarter on a mission, he cannot give his replies unassisted, notwithstanding the extent of his learning, of what practical use is it?"

The Master said, "When a prince's personal conduct is correct, his government is effective without the issuing of orders. If his personal conduct is not correct, he may issue orders, but they will not be followed."

---

* *Analects* 2.18–20; 12.11, 17, 19; 13.4–6
[20] *words . . . conduct:* note the equal stress on correctness in words and deeds, characteristic of Confucianism.

[21] This is the teaching of the "rectification of names": harmony in every social relationship depends on each person carrying out the duties that her/his name implies.
[22] *superiors and inferiors:* in terms of social and political power, not morality.

Confidence and Prosperity in Government*

The Mencius *has much to say about good government. The first excerpt deals with the need of the rulers to keep the confidence of the people. The second deals with the need for some level of economic prosperity so that both ruler and people may flourish.*

Mencius said, "It was by benevolence that the three dynasties gained the empire, and by not being benevolent that they lost it. It is by the same means that the decaying and flourishing, the preservation and perishing, of states are determined. If the emperor is not benevolent, he cannot preserve the empire from passing from him. If the sovereign of a state is not benevolent, he cannot preserve his kingdom. If a high noble or great officer is not benevolent, he cannot preserve his ancestral temple. If a scholar or common man is not benevolent, he cannot preserve his four limbs. Hating death and ruin, and yet delighting in being unbenevolent is like hating to be drunk, and yet loving to drink wine." . . .

Mencius said, "Chieh and Chou's losing the empire arose from their losing the people, and to lose the people means to lose their hearts. There is a way to get the empire: get the people, and the empire is obtained. There is a way to get the people: get their hearts, and the people are obtained. There is a way to get their hearts: collect for them what they like, and do not lay on them what they dislike. The people turn to a benevolent rule as water runs downward, and as wild beasts run to the wilderness."

[1.6.20–24] Mencius said [to King Hsuan of Ch'i] . . . "Only men of education are able to maintain a fixed heart without a fixed means of livelihood. As to the people, if they do not have a certain livelihood, then they will not have a fixed heart. And if they do not have a fixed heart, there is nothing which they will not do. They will go the way of self-abandonment, of moral

deflection, of depravity, and of wild license. When they have been involved in these crimes, to follow them up and punish them is to entrap the people. How can such a thing as entrapping the people be done under the rule of a benevolent man?

"Therefore an intelligent ruler will regulate the livelihood of the people, so as to make sure that they shall have enough to serve their parents, and enough to support their wives and children. He insures that in good years they shall always be abundantly satisfied, and that in bad years they shall escape the danger of perishing. Then he may urge them to what is good, and they will do it, for in this case the people will follow after the good with ease. But now the livelihood of the people is so regulated that they do not have enough to serve their parents, and enough to support their wives and children. Even though they may have good years, their lives are continually embittered, and in bad years they do not escape perishing. In such circumstances they only try to save themselves from death, and they are afraid they will not succeed. What leisure do they have to cultivate propriety and righteousness?

"If Your Majesty wishes to govern humanely the livelihood of the people, why not turn to that which is the essential step to it? Let mulberry trees be planted about the homesteads with their five sections of land, and persons of fifty years may then be clothed with silk. In keeping fowls, pigs, and swine, let not their times of breeding be neglected, and persons of seventy years may eat meat. Let there not be taken away the time that is proper for the cultivation of the farm with its hundred sections of land, and the family of eight that is supported by it shall not suffer from hunger. Let careful attention be paid to education in schools, especially its education of the filial and fraternal duties, and gray-haired men will not be seen upon the roads carrying burdens on their backs or on their heads. It never has been that the ruler of a state where such results

---

* *Mencius* 4.3, 9; 1.6.20–24

were seen—the old wearing silk and eating meat, and the black-haired people suffering neither from hunger nor cold—did not attain to the office of emperor."

RITUAL

Divination*

*The Classic of Changes (**I Ching**) has been used for philosophical meditation, but its main use has been in divination. The traditional ceremony with milfoil (light wood) sticks is often used, but dice or any other method of selecting numbers can be employed. When the hexagram that matches the numbers thrown is located, it is read and applied to the inquirer's situation, giving the inquirer insight and foresight into the future.*[23]

THE CH'IEN HEXAGRAM:

Ch'ien [represents] what is great and originating, penetrating, advantageous, correct and firm.

In the first [or lowest] line, undivided, [we see] the dragon lying hidden [in the deep]. It is not the time for active doing.

In the second line, undivided, [we see] the dragon appearing in the field. It will be advantageous to meet with the morally great man.

In the third line, undivided, [we see] the superior man active and vigilant all day, and in the evening still careful and apprehensive. [There is] danger, but there will be no mistake.

In the fourth line, undivided, [we see the dragon looking] as if he were leaping up, but still in the deep. There will be no mistake.

In the fifth line, undivided, [we see] the dragon flying in the sky. It will be advantageous to meet with the great man.

In the sixth [or topmost] line, undivided, [we see] the dragon exceeding the proper limits. There will be occasion for repentance.

[The lines of this hexagram are all strong and undivided, as appears from] the use of the number nine. If the host of dragons [thus] appearing were to divest themselves of their heads, there would be good fortune.[24]

THE K'UN HEXAGRAM:

In [the condition denoted by] K'un there may [yet be] progress and success. For the firm and correct, the [really] great man, there will be good fortune. He will fall into no error. If he make speeches, his words cannot be made good.

The first line, divided, shows its subject with bare buttocks in difficulty under the stump of a tree. He enters a dark valley, and for three years has no prospect [of deliverance].

The second line, undivided, shows its subject in difficulty amid his wine and food. Then comes to him the red knee-covers [of the ruler]. It will be well for him [to maintain his sincerity] in sacrificing. Active operations [on his part] will lead to evil, but he will be free from blame.

The third line, divided, shows its subject in difficulty before a [frowning] rock. He lays hold

---

* *Classic of Changes* 1, 47, 54
[23] Taken, with editing, from James Legge, trans., *The Sacred Books of China: The Texts of Confucianism*, part 2, *The Yi King, Sacred Books of the East* vol. 16 (Oxford: Oxford University Press, 1882), pp. 57–58, 161–63, 180–82.

---

[24] The point of this hexagram is that mildness of action plus firmness of decision leads to good fortune.

of thorns. He enters his palace, and does not see his wife. There will be evil.

The fourth line, undivided, shows its subject proceeding very slowly [to help the subject of the first line], who is in difficulty by the carriage adorned with metal in front of him. There will be occasion for regret, but the end will be good.

The fifth line, undivided, shows its subject with his nose and feet cut off. He is in difficulty by [his ministers in their] scarlet aprons. He is leisurely in his movements, however, and is satisfied. It will be well for him to be [sincere] in sacrificing [to spiritual beings].

The sixth line, divided, shows its subject in difficulty, as if bound with creepers; or in a high and dangerous position, and saying [to himself], "If I move, I shall regret it." If he does repent of former errors, there will be good fortune in his going forward.[25]

THE KUEI MEI HEXAGRAM:

Kwei Mei indicates that [under the conditions which it denotes] action will be evil, and in no way advantageous.

The first line, undivided, shows the younger woman married off in a position secondary to the real wife.[26] [It suggests the idea of] a person lame on one leg who yet manages to tramp along. Going forward will be fortunate.

The second line, undivided, shows her blind in one eye, and yet able to see. There will be advantage in her maintaining the firm correctness of a solitary widow.

The third line, divided, shows the younger woman who was to be married off in an inferior position. She returns and accepts an ancillary position.

The fourth line, undivided, shows the younger woman who is to be married off protracting the time. She may be late in being married, but the time will come.

The fifth line, divided, reminds us of the marrying of a younger woman to [king] Ti-yi, when the sleeves of the princess were not equal to those of the [still] younger woman who accompanied her in an inferior capacity. [The case suggests the thought of] the moon almost full. There will be good fortune.

The sixth line, divided, shows the young lady bearing the basket [of harvest offerings], but without anything in it, and the gentleman slaughtering the sheep, but without blood flowing from it. There will be no advantage in any way.[27]

---

[25] The point of this hexagram is that the person beset by problems can move out of them with a grasp of the situation and a change of attitude.

[26] *younger woman . . . real wife:* the symbolism here draws on the ancient Chinese custom of a man taking a concubine.

[27] The point of this hexagram is that new undertakings are not advantageous, especially for those who, like the young woman, have difficulty accepting a low social role.

Songs for Sacrifice*

These selections from the Classic of Poetry *show the deep connection of ritual and virtue in Confucianism. The first song is that sung at a sacrifice to Thang, the father of an ancient royal dynasty. The second is also for a sacrifice to an ancestor, and the third is a complaint to Heaven about the rule of an unjust king. The last song provides fascinating details on the sacrificial service in the temple.[28]*

---

* *Classic of Poetry, Shang* 1; *Kau* 7; *Minor Odes* 10.1,3; 5

[28] Taken, with editing, from James Legge, trans., *The Sacred Books of China: The Texts of Confucianism*, part 1, vol. 3, *Sacred Books of the East* (Oxford: Oxford University Press, 1879), pp. 304–305, 325–26, 357–58, 365–68.

SACRIFICIAL ODES OF SHANG, ODE 1

How admirable! how complete!
Here are set our hand-drums and drums.
The drums resound harmoniously and loudly,
To delight our meritorious ancestor.

The descendant of Thang invites him with this
    music,
That he may soothe us with the realization of
    our thoughts.
Deep is the sound of our hand-drums and
    drums;
Shrilly sound the flutes;
All harmonious and blending together,
According to the notes of the sonorous gem.
Oh! majestic is the descendant of Thang;
Very admirable is his music.

The large bells and drums fill the ear;
The various dances are grandly performed.
We have the admirable visitors,[29]
Who are pleased and delighted.

From of old, before our time,
The former men set us the example—
How to be mild and humble from morning to
    night,
And to be reverent in discharging the service.

May he regard our sacrifices of winter and
    autumn,
[Thus] offered by the descendant of Thang!

---

[29] *admirable visitors:* ancestors present at the ceremony.

SACRIFICIAL ODES OF KAU, ODE 7

They come full of harmony;
They are here in all gravity—
The princes assisting,
While the Son of Heaven[30] looks profound.

[He says], "While I present [this] noble bull,
And they assist me in setting forth the sacrifice,
O great and august Father,
Comfort me, your filial son.

With penetrating wisdom you played the man,
A sovereign with the gifts both of peace
    and war,
Giving rest even to great Heaven,
And ensuring prosperity to your descendants.

You comfort me with the eyebrows of
    longevity;
You make me great with manifold blessings.
I offer this sacrifice to my meritorious father,
And to my accomplished mother.

---

[30] *Son of Heaven:* the king or emperor.

MINOR ODES OF THE KINGDOM, ODE 10.1, 3

Great and wide Heaven,
How is it you have contracted your kindness,
Sending down death and famine,
Destroying all through the kingdom?
Compassionate Heaven, arrayed in terrors,
How is it you exercise no forethought, no care?
Let the criminals alone;
They have suffered for their guilt.
But those who have no crime
Are indiscriminately involved in ruin.

How is it, O great Heaven,
That the king will not listen to the most just
    words?
He is like a man going [astray],
Who knows not where he will proceed to.
All you officers,
Let each of you attend to his duties.
How do you not stand in awe of one another?
You do not stand in awe of Heaven.

MINOR ODES OF THE KINGDOM, ODE 5

Thick grew the tribulus [on the ground],
But they cleared away its thorny bushes.
Why did they do this of old?
That we might plant our millet and sacrificial
    millet;
That our millet might be abundant,
And our sacrificial millet luxuriant.
When our barns are full,
And our stacks can be counted by tens of
    myriads,
We proceed to make drinks and prepared grain,
For offerings and sacrifice.
We seat the representatives of the dead, and
    urge them to eat,[31]
Thus seeking to increase our bright happiness.

With correct and reverent deportment,
The bulls and rams all pure,
We proceed to the winter and autumnal
    sacrifices.
Some arrange [the meat]; some adjust [the
    pieces of it].[32]
The officer of prayer[33] sacrifices inside the
    temple gate,
And all the sacrificial service is complete and
    brilliant.
Grandly come our ancestors;
Their spirits happily enjoy the offerings;
Their filial descendant receives blessing.
They will reward him with great happiness,
With myriads of years, life without end.

They attend to the ovens with reverence;
They prepare the trays, which are very large—
Some for the roast meat, some for the broiled.
Wives presiding are still and reverent,
Preparing the numerous [smaller] dishes.
The guests and visitors
Present the cup all around.
Every form is according to rule;
Every smile and word are as they should be.

The spirits quietly come,
And respond with great blessings—
Myriads of years as the [fitting] reward.

We are very much exhausted,
And have performed every ceremony without
    error.
The able officer of prayer announces [the will of
    the spirits],
And goes to the filial descendant to convey it—
"Fragrant has been your filial sacrifice,
And the spirits have enjoyed your drinks
    and food.
They confer on you a hundred blessings;
Each as it is desired,
Each as sure as law.
You have been exact and expeditious;
You have been correct and careful;
They will always confer on you the choicest
    favors,
In myriads and tens of myriads."

The ceremonies having thus been completed,
And the bells and drums having given their
    warning,
The filial descendant goes to his place,
And the able officer of prayer makes his
    announcement,
"The spirits have drunk to the full."
The great representatives of the dead then rise,
And the bells and drums escort their with-
    drawal,
[On which] the spirits tranquilly return.
All the servants, and the presiding wives,
Remove [the trays and dishes] without delay.
The [sacrificer's] uncles and cousins
All repair to the private feast.[34]
The musicians all go in to perform,
And give their soothing aid at the second
    blessing.
Your foods are set forth;
There is no dissatisfaction, but all feel happy.
They drink to the full, and eat to the full;

---

[31] *We seat . . . eat:* people who, in the ceremony, represent the deceased ancestors are seated and feted.

[32] In Confucian sacrifice, the animals are killed before the ceremony, not as a part of it.

[33] *officer of prayer:* the chief officiant.

[34] *private feast:* where the remainder of the sacrificial food and drink is consumed.

Great and small, they bow their heads, [saying],
"The spirits enjoyed your drinks and foods.
They will cause you to live long.
Your sacrifices, all in their seasons,

Are completely discharged by you.
May your sons and your grandsons
Never fail to perpetuate these services!"

Music and Morality*

*Music has played a large role in Chinese culture
and religion. One of the ancient Classics dealt exclusively with music. Although this text has unfor-
tunately been lost, some of it probably has survived
in the* Li Chi *or* Classic of Rites. *Note here how
music expresses the cosmic forces of the universe,
and how its extensive use in sacrifice furthers the
meaning of the ceremony.*[35]

Therefore the ancient kings in framing their music laid its foundation in the feelings and nature of men; they examined the notes by the
measures for the length and quality of each; and
adapted it to express the meaning of the ceremonies in which it was to be used. They brought
it into harmony with the energy that produces
life, and to give expression to the performance of
the five regular constituents of moral worth.
They made it indicate that energy in its Yang or
phase of vigor, without any dissipation of its
power, and also in its Yin or phase of remission,
without the vanishing of its power. The strong
phase showed no excess like that of anger, and
the weak no shrinking like that of pusillanimity.
These four characteristics blended harmoniously
in the minds of men, and were similarly manifested in their conduct. Each occupied quietly its
proper place, and one did not interfere injuri-
ously with another.

After this they established schools for teaching their music, and different grades for the
learners. They marked most fully the divisions of
the pieces, and condensed into small compass

the parts and variations giving beauty and ele-
gance, in order to regulate and increase the inward virtue of the learners. They gave laws for
the great and small notes according to their
names, and harmonized the order of the beginning and the end, to represent the doing of
things. Thus they made the underlying principles of the relations between the near and distant relatives, the noble and inferior, the old and
young, males and females, all to appear mani-
festly in the music. Hence it is said that "In music we must endeavor to see its depths."

[15] Hence the superior man returns to the
good affections in order to bring his will into
harmony with them, and compares the different
qualities of actions in order to perfect his conduct. Notes that are evil and depraved, and sights
leading to disorder and licentiousness are not allowed to affect his ears or eyes. Licentious music
and corrupted ceremonies are not admitted into
the mind to affect its powers. The spirit of idle-
ness, indifference, depravity, and perversity finds
no exhibition in his person. And thus he makes
his ears, eyes, nose, and mouth the apprehen-
sions of his mind, and the movements of all the
parts of his body, follow the course that is correct, and do that which is right.

After this there ensues the manifestation
of the inward thoughts by the modulations of
note and tone, the elegant accompaniments
of the lutes, small and large, the movements with
the shield and battle-axe, the ornaments of the
plumes and ox-tails,[36] and the concluding with
the pipes and flutes. All this has the effect of ex-

---

* *Classic of Rites* 17.2.10–11, 15–18, 20–21
[35] Taken, with editing, from James Legge, trans., *The Sacred
Books of China: The Texts of Confucianism*, part 4 , vol. 28,
Sacred Books of the East (Oxford: Oxford University Press,
1885), pp. 108–12.

[36] *movements . . . ox-tails:* pantomime dancing often accom-
panies the important rituals; both military dances (with *shield
and battle-axe*) and civilian dances (with *plumes and ox-tails*)
are performed by the dancers.

hibiting the brilliance of complete virtue, stirring up the harmonious action of the four seasonal energies, and displaying the true natures and qualities of all things.

Hence in the fine and distinct notes we have an image of heaven; in the ample and grand, an image of earth; in their beginning and ending, an image of the four seasons; in the wheeling and revolutions of the pantomimes, an image of the wind and rain. The five notes, like the five colors, form a complete and elegant whole, without any confusion. The eight instruments of different materials, like the eight winds, follow the musical accords, without any irregular deviation. The lengths of all the different notes have their definite measurements, without any uncertainty. The small and the great complete one another. The end leads on to the beginning, and the beginning to the end. The key notes and those harmonizing with them, the sharp and the base, succeed one another in their regular order.

Therefore, when the music has full course, the different relations are clearly defined by it; the

perceptions of the ears and eyes become sharp and distinct; the action of the blood and physical energies is harmonious and calm; bad influences are removed, and manners changed; and all under heaven there is complete repose. . . .

[20] It is for this purpose that the superior man returns to the good affections proper to his nature, in order to bring his will into harmony with them, and makes extensive use of music in order to perfect his instructions. When the music has free course, the people direct themselves to the quarter to which they should proceed, and we can see the power of his virtue.

Virtue is the strong stem of man's nature, and music is the blossoming of virtue. Metal, stone, silk, and bamboo are the materials of which the instruments of music are made. Poetry gives expression to the thoughts; singing prolongs the notes of the voice; pantomimic movements put the body into action. These three things originate in the mind, and the instruments of the music accompany them.

APPENDIX: LATER DEVELOPMENTS OF EARLIER THEMES

Later Debate over Human Nature*

The first reading by Hsun-tzu (a younger peer of Mencius), argues that human nature is innately evil and that strict guidelines must keep subjects in line. Although he believed in strong rule and punishment, he also advocated education as a way for people to be taught to be good. Through education people can be taught to hold back their urges and to recognize good. For Hsun-tzu, this education includes work in the classics and the performance of rites.[37] In the second reading, Yang Hsiung (53 B.C.E.–18 C.E.) maintains the middle position

of the good and evil within a person. He argues that people have become either good or evil through their own learning or experiences.[38]

Human nature is evil; any good in humans is acquired by conscious exertion. Now, the nature of man is such that he is born with a love of profit. Following this nature will cause its aggressiveness and greedy tendencies to grow and courtesy and deference to disappear. Humans are born with feelings of envy and hatred. . . .

---

* *Xunzi* 3.150–151; *Fuyan* 3.1a–b

[37] Taken from John Knoblock, *Xunzi: A Translation and Study of the Complete Works* (Stanford: Stanford University Press, 1994), pp. 150–51. Used by permission.

[38] From Wing-Tsit Chan, ed., *A Sourcebook of Chinese Philosophy* (Princeton: Princeton University Press, 1963), pp. 289–90. Used by permission of Princeton University Press.

This being the case, when each person follows his inborn nature and indulges his natural inclinations, aggressiveness and greed are certain to develop. . . . Thus it is necessary that man's nature undergo the transforming influence of a teacher and the model that he be guided by is ritual and moral principles. Only after this has been accomplished do courtesy and deference develop. Unite these qualities with precepts of good form and reason, and the result is an age of orderly government. If we consider the implications of these facts, it is plain that human nature is evil and that any good in humans is acquired by conscious exertion.

[*Fuyan*] Man's nature is a mixture of good and evil. He who cultivates the good in it will become a good man, and he who cultivates the evil in it will become an evil man. The ch'i [material force] is the driving force that leads one to good or evil. . . . Therefore the superior man studies hard and practices earnestly. He waits till his good becomes a rare treasure before he sells it. He cultivates his personal life before he makes friends. And he plans well before he acts. This is how to fulfill the Way.

Attack on Buddhism*

Han Yu (768–824 c.e.) led a Confucian attack against Buddhism and Taoism in which he asked the emperor to intercede and suppress these religions. This a passage from a letter written to the emperor asks him to rethink his decision to view a relic of the Buddha. Han Yu believes that this will show the people imperial support of the Buddhist practice of relic worship.

Buddhism is no more than a cult of the barbarian peoples which spread to China in the time of the Latter Han. It did not exist here in ancient times. . . . When Emperor Kao-tsu received the throne from the House of Sui, he deliberated upon the suppression of Buddhism. But at that time the various officials, being of small worth and knowledge, were unable fully to comprehend the ways of the ancient kings and so could not implement the wisdom of the emperor and rescue the age from corruption. . . .

Now Buddha was a man of the barbarians who did not speak the language of China and wore clothes of a different fashion. His sayings did not concern the ways of our ancient kings, nor did his manner of dress conform to their laws. He understood neither the duties that bind sovereign and subject, nor the affections of father and son. If he were still alive today and came to our court by order of his ruler, Your Majesty might condescend to receive him, but. . . . he would then be escorted to the borders of the nation, dismissed, and not allowed to delude the masses. How then, when he has long been dead, could his rotten bones, the foul and unlucky remains of his body, be rightly admitted to the palace? Confucius said, "Respect ghosts and spirits, but keep them at a distance." Now without reason Your Majesty has caused this loathsome thing to be brought in and would personally go to view it. . . . Your servant is deeply shamed and begs that this bone be given to the proper authorities to be cast into fire and water, that this evil may be rooted out, the world freed from its error, and later generations spared this delusion. . . . If the Buddha does indeed have supernatural power to send down curses and calamities, may they fall only upon the person of your servant, who calls upon High Heaven to witness that he does not regret his words.

* *Ch'ang-li hsien-sheng wen-chi*, 39.2b–42

[38] From W. T. deBary, *Sources of Chinese Tradition* (New York: Columbia University Press, 1964), pp. 371–372. Copyright 1964 by Columbia University Press. Used by permission.

Advice for Reading Texts*

After Confucius and Mencius, Chu Hsi (1130–1200) is the single most influential figure in Confucianism and the Chinese cultural tradition. The entire educational and civil service exam structure of China from the fourteenth century until the early twentieth was based on his theoretical and practical teachings. Chu's central concern was how a person could become a sage—that is, morally good. To promote this state of being, he developed for his disciples a systematic program of self-cultivation. Here is a part of his lengthy advice on reading and learning.[39]

In a response to a student, Wen-kung explained the way of learning, citing Hsun-tzu's four lines, "[The superior man] recites texts in order to penetrate the Way, ponders in order to understand it, associates with men who embody it in order to make it part of himself, and shuns those who impede it in order to sustain and nourish it." Hsun-tzu's explanation is pretty good. As for the term "recite a text," I believe that when the ancients recited a text they kept track of the number of times. . . . It also means, "to understand thoroughly." Only if we're read to the point of intimate familiarity are we able to understand thoroughly. And if we haven't read to the point of intimate familiarity, there is nothing we can possibly ponder.

In reading, to comprehend a passage, you should have a detailed understanding of it. If you don't understand it in detail, your reading of other passages will be muddled too. If you understand one passage in detail, others will be easy to understand. Shan-ku's note explains the method of reading extremely well.

Students who are overzealous don't understand in detail the meaning of what they read. In reading, you have to be very careful; it's essential

that you understand every sentence and every character with certainty. If your effort is lax and you're not given to reflection, you'll simply conclude that there's nothing in your understanding of it that need be doubted; it isn't really that there's nothing to be doubted, but since your understanding isn't complete you just don't realize it. In learning, there's generally a distinction between young and old. When we're young, we have excess energy; it's essential that we leave nothing unread and that we analyze fully the meaning of what we read. By contrast, as we approach old age, we must select out what's important and devote our efforts to it; in reading a particular book, we're aware that later on it will be difficult to summon up the effort to look at it again. We must ponder it deeply and analyze it to its limits, and we'll understand its meaning. It would seem that in the moral principle of the universe there's nothing but right and wrong. Right is right, wrong is wrong, and once we're certain about which is which, though we may not reread a text, the principle in it will naturally infuse us. We'll see it once and never forget it. This may all be compared to eating and drinking. If we chew slowly, the flavor lasts. If we take big bites and big gulps, in the end we don't know the flavor. . . .

[4.41] The value of a book is in the recitation of it. By reciting it often, we naturally come to understand it. Now, even if we ponder over what's written on the paper, it's useless, for in the end it isn't really ours. There's value only in recitation, though I don't know how the mind so naturally becomes harmonious with the psycho-physical stuff, feels uplifted and energized, and remembers securely what it reads. Even supposing we were to read through a text thoroughly, pondering it over and over in our minds, it wouldn't be as good as reciting it. If we recite it again and again, in no time the incomprehensible becomes comprehensible and the already comprehensible becomes even more meaningful. But if the recitation doesn't reach

---

* Conversations of Master Chu 4.37–39, 41
[39] From Daniel K. Gardner, *Learning to be a Sage: Selections from the Conversations of Master Chu* (Berkeley: University of California Press, 1990), pp. 136–39. Used by permission.

the point of intimate familiarity, it won't be so meaningful at all. At the moment I'm not even speaking about the recitation of commentaries; let's simply recite the classical texts to the point of intimate familiarity. Whether we are walking or at a standstill, sitting or lying down, if our minds are always on these texts, we'll naturally come to understand them. It has occurred to me that recitation is learning. The Master said: "Learning without thinking is a waste; thinking without learning is dangerous."[41] Learning is reciting. If we recite it then think it over, think it over then recite it, naturally it'll become meaningful to us. If we recite it but don't think it over, we still won't appreciate its meaning. If we think it over but don't recite it, even though we might understand it, our understanding will be precarious. It's just like hiring somebody else to guard our home: because he isn't one of the family, in the end he can't be used as we would use a family member.

———————————

[41]This quote is from the *Analects* 2.15.

Neoconfucian Ethics*

Chang Tsai (1020–1077) was a leading Neoconfucianist. In the more developed doctrines of being that are a hallmark of Neoconfucianism, Chang taught that the universe is one but its manifestations are many. When applied to ethics, this teaching became the notion of Heaven and Earth as universal parents and humaneness toward all people. This the leading idea of the Western Inscription (so-called because it was inscribed on the western wall of Chang's study), the most beloved text of Neoconfucian literature.[43]

Heaven is my father and Earth is my mother, and even such a small creature as I finds an intimate place in their midst.

———————————

* Chang Tsai, *The Western Inscription*
[43]From Wing-tsit Chan, *A Source book in Chinese Philosophy* (Princeton: Princeton University Press, 1963), pp. 497–98. Used by permission of Princeton University Press.

Should we recite it to the point of intimate familiarity, and moreover think about it in detail, naturally our mind and principle will become one and never shall we forget what we've read. I used to find it hard to remember texts. Then I simply recited them aloud. What I remember now is the result of recitation. Old Su[42] simply took the *Book of Mencius,* the *Analects,* the *Han Fei-tzu,* and the writings of the various sages and for seven or eight years sat quietly reciting them. Afterward he wrote a number of things that were very good. To be sure, his natural abilities couldn't be matched, but still it was essential that he recite as he did. And yet, reciting the texts, he merely wanted to pattern his writing on what was written there. Now if we were to turn our minds and his sort of natural ability to the investigation of moral principle, we'd find it right there in the text. Thus we know that the value of a text is in the intimate recitation of it. There is no other way.

———————————

[42]*Old Su* lived from 1009 to 1061.

Therefore that which fills the universe I regard as my body and that which directs the universe I consider as my nature.

All people are my brothers and sisters, and all things are my companions.

The great ruler (the emperor) is the eldest son of my parents (Heaven and Earth), and the great ministers are his stewards. Respect the aged—this is the way to treat them as elders should be treated. Show deep love toward the orphaned and the weak—this is the way to treat them as the young should be treated. The sage identifies his character with that of Heaven and Earth, and the worthy is the most outstanding man. Even those who are tired, infirm, crippled, or sick; those who have no brothers or children, wives or husbands, are all my brothers who are in distress and have no one to turn to.

When the time comes, to keep himself from harm—this is the care of a son. To rejoice in

Heaven and to have no anxiety—this is filial piety at its purest.

He who disobeys [the Principle of Nature] violates virtue. He who destroys humanity is a robber. He who promotes evil lacks [moral] capacity. But he who puts his moral nature into practice and brings his physical existence into complete fulfillment can match [Heaven and Earth].

One who knows the principles of transformation will skillfully carry forward the undertakings [of Heaven and Earth], and one who penetrates spirit to the highest degree will skillfully carry out their will.

Do nothing shameful in the recesses of your own house and thus bring no dishonor to them. Preserve your mind and nourish your nature and thus (serve them) with untiring effort.

The Great Yu[44] hated pleasant wine but at-

tended to the protection and support of his parents. Border Warden Ying brought up and educated the young and thus extended his love to his own kind.

Shun's[45] merit lay in delighting his parents with unceasing effort, and Shen-sheng's[46] reverence was demonstrated when he awaited punishment without making an attempt to escape. . . .

Wealth, honor, blessing, and benefits are meant for the enrichment of my life, while poverty, humble station, and sorrow are meant to help me to fulfillment.

In life I follow and serve [Heaven and Earth]. In death I will be at peace.

---

[44] *Yu:* founder of the Hsia dynasty, who ruled ca. 2180–2175 B.C.E. This story refers to *Mencius* 4B.20.

[45] *Shun:* legendary sage-emperor from the third millennium B.C.E. This story refers to *Mencius* 4A.28.

[46] *Shen-sheng:* seventh-century B.C.E. heir to the imperial throne who took his own life after he was falsely accused of poisoning his father. This story is referred to in the *Classic of Rites* (*Li Ki*), T'an-kung 1.

GLOSSARY

(Pinyin spelling, where it differs from Wade-Giles, is given in brackets before the pronunciation.)

Ching [jing] (jing) the Classics, the early Confucian canon.

chun-tzu [jun-zi] (jun-tzoo) literally, "prince's son"; in the teaching of Confucius, a "superior man" made so by the study and practice of virtue.

hsiao [xiao] (syow), the virtue of filiality; love for and service of one's parents and deceased ancestors.

I Ching [Yi Jing] (ee jing) the *Classic of Changes.*

jen [ren] (ren) the virtue of benevolence or humaneness.

li (lee) the virtue of propriety, decorum, both in the rites and in everyday life.

Tao [Dao] (dow) the cosmic Way, way of life; in Confucian scripture, often related to heaven (e.g., the "Way of Heaven").

wen-yen the formal-classical style in which the Confucian classics are written.

QUESTIONS FOR STUDY AND DISCUSSION

1.   Compare and contrast the earlier Confucian canon, the Five Classics, with the later canon, the Four Books. What are their commonalities and differences?

2.   How do the Confucian scriptures bear witness to the importance of three elements often held to be common to all traditional Chinese religion: heaven, earth, and ancestor worship?

3.   Reflect on the lively political issue of the personal character of candidates for public office in contemporary North America. To what degree does Confucius' counsel about a morally superior ruler apply in our society?

4. To what degree may filiality be a prescription for social pressures on the modern Western family?

5. What is the continuing significance of the Confucian scriptures in modern life outside China?

6. Do you think, with Mencius, that human nature is innately good? Why, or why not?

7. After having read these Confucian scriptures, what is your own conclusion on this often-discussed issue: Is Confucianism a religion or a philosophy?

SUGGESTIONS FOR FURTHER READING

Primary Readings

The fullest English translation of the Confucian canon continues to be by James Legge and others in Max Müller, ed., *Sacred Books of the East*. Vol. 3 is the *Shu Ching*, the religious portions of the *Shih Ching*, and the *Hsiao Ching*; vol. 16 is the *I Ching*; vols. 27 and 28 are the *Li Chi*.

R. M. Barnhart, *Li Kung-lin's Classic of Filial Piety*. New York: Metropolitan Museum of Art, 1993. Features the paintings of Li Kung-lin (1041–1106) illustrating the *filiality*; one of the most important works of art in Chinese cultural history.

Wing-tsit Chan, *A Source Book in Chinese Philosophy*. Princeton: Princeton University Press, 1963. Full selections from religious-philosophical Confucian books and older classics, from a leading interpreter of Chinese religious literature to the West.

D. C. Lau, trans., *The* Analects. London: Penguin, 1979. An excellent contemporary translation, with good notes.

D. C. Lau, trans., *The* Mencius. London: Penguin, 1983. The same standard and format as in his translation of the *Analects*.

J. Legge, trans., *The Chinese Classics*. Oxford: Oxford University Press, 1893. The standard translation of the Four Books: *Analects, Mencius, Doctrine of the Mean*, and *Great Learning*.

L. G. Thompson, *The Chinese Way in Religion*. Religious Life in History Series. Belmont, CA: Wadsworth, 1973. An excellent anthology of texts of the main Chinese religious traditions.

R. Wilhelm, trans., *The I Ching*. Bollingen Series no. 19. New York: Pantheon, 1961. Perhaps the best current translation of the *Book of Changes*.

Secondary Readings

J. B. Henderson, *Scripture, Canon, Commentary: A Comparison of Confucian and Western Exegesis*. Princeton: Princeton University Press, 1991. An excellent treatment of the important question of the relationship and explanation of scripture and commentary, with valuable comparative analysis of Chinese commentary and the Western (mainly Christian) commentarial tradition.

T. Kelleher, "[Women in] Confucianism," in A. Sharma, ed., *Women in World Religions*. Albany: State University of New York Press, 1989, pp. 135–159. An insightful essay on the influence of Confucian tradition on the roles of women in China, with good attention to scripture.

R. L. Taylor, "Confucianism: Scripture and Sage," in F. M. Denney and R. L. Taylor, *The Holy Book in Comparative Perspective*. Columbia, SC: University of South Carolina Press, 1985, pp. 181–203. An excellent recent study of the use of scripture to achieve sagehood.

R. L. Taylor, *The Way of Heaven: An Introduction to Confucian Religious Life*. Leiden: Brill, 1986. A fine introduction to Confucian scripture in the context of religious life; many photographic illustrations of Confucian iconography and rituals.

Scripture in a Chinese Funeral
A Taoist priest in the Sichwan province of China reads a funeral text, and the men sitting around respond, to enable the soul of the deceased to pass successive judgments on its way to final blessing. Credit: Stevan Harrell, from the Image Bank of the Center for the Study of World Religions, Harvard University. Used by permission of Stevan Harrell.

CHAPTER EIGHT

Taoism

❖ A young man visits a Taoist temple in Hong Kong. He is puzzled about the course of his life and consults with a priest. They talk about the great Way and how he relates to it. The priest reminds him of several passages in the Taoist scriptures and explains their meaning. After some minutes of conversation, the young man goes away smiling, now more certain about the future.

❖ In a temple in Kaoshiung, Taiwan, a medium known as a "spirit writer" falls under the possession of the temple's god. As he speaks the words of the god, a scribe standing near writes down the words. These words will be published in the temple's magazine and may perhaps form the basis of new Taoist scripture.

❖ At the Hsing T'ien Temple in Taipei, Taiwan, the temple courtyard is filled with blue-robed women carrying out the faith healing for which the temple has gained its reputation. They lay hands on the sick or on clothing brought by the families of those too sick to come in person.[1] In this way they carry out an ancient tradition of Taoism as discussed in many of its scriptures, that of healing and longevity.

INTRODUCTION

Taoism is, after Confucianism, the most influential religion among Chinese people. According to Taoists, their faith was founded by Lao Tzu in the six century B.C.E. Since ancient times, the Taoist tradition has had two interacting parts: philosophical Taoism, rich in cosmological meditation and speculation; and religious (sometimes called "esoteric") Taoism, with its emphasis on exorcism, astrology, and gaining long life or even immortality. Although Taoism has had an important influence through history, its future is cloudy. Some scholars hold it to be a dying tradition. This only time will tell, but the scriptures of Taoism, especially the *Tao Te Ching* [DOW deh jing] and the *Chuang-tzu* [jwahng tzoo], have earned a undying place in the history of the world's cultures, and are still influential today.

Overview of Structure

The name of the Taoist scripture as a whole is the **Tao Tsang** [dow tsahng], or "Taoist canon/collection." Its last main printing in 1926 had 1120 volumes. The Tao Tsang has traditionally been grouped into the "Three Caverns" (*San-Tung*). The Three Caverns reflect three distinct historic traditions within Taoism. The first section

---

[1] B. E. Reed, "[Women in] Taoism," in A. Sharma, ed., *Women in World Religions* (Albany: State University of New York Press, 1989), p. 180.

is associated with the Supreme Clarity school, the second with the Numinous Trea-sure school, and the third with the Three Sovereigns school. Each one of the Three Caverns is itself divided into twelve sections, the names of which give a good indi-cation of the overall contents of the Taoist scriptures. They are: "original revela-tions"; divine talismans; interpretations; diagrams; chronologies and genealogies; moral codes; ceremonial decorum; rituals; esoteric techniques (alchemy, astrology, ex-orcism, etc.); lives of past Taoist worthies; hymns; and messages to the dead. To this basic tripartite form was added a later addition, the "Four Supplements," itself as mixed in contents as the caverns.

Origin, Development, and Use

Critical study of the history of the Taoist canon is still in its beginning stages, and its massive nature makes the task even more challenging. Certain conclusions, however, have been reached by scholarship. We will relate here those main points most impor-tant for understanding the scripture selections in this chapter.

Taoists trace the origins of their religion and scriptures to the claimed founder of their tradition, Lao Tzu. They hold that his disciples wrote down the first and most important work of the canon, the *Tao Te Ching,* shortly after his death. (Taoists often refer to the *Tao Te Ching* as the "Lao-Tzu.") Recent critical scholarship, however, has concluded that even though it may have begun at this time, this book is a collection of material from different authors finally assembled in the third century B.C.E. De-spite this later date, the *Tao Te Ching* is in fact the fountainhead of most of the Taoist scripture that followed. Its reflections on the **Tao** [dow] ("Way") and its **te** [duh] ("power") in eighty-one brief sections are written in a highly compressed style. The Chinese original features much parallelism among the lines of poetry, and also a good deal of rhyme, lost in most translations. It points to a Tao that is cosmic, the origin of heaven and earth. This Tao is a part of each individual's existence, and it is a social ideal as well.

Probably because of the cryptic quality and mixed contents of the *Tao Te Ching,* it could be appealed to by all Taoists to come. Indeed, it is one of the few scripture books to be extensively used in both philosophical Taoism and religious Taoism. To judge from the frequency with which it has been translated into English (more than one hundred times) and other European languages, the *Tao Te Ching* has also had a significant appeal to peoples of other religions and cultures; the appeal of this book is echoed in the titles of more than fifty books in print in English in 1998. Titles that draw on Taoism and the *Tao Te Ching,* almost all with the same *The Tao of X* format, include *The Tao of: Parenting, Dialogue, Spycraft, Coaching, Sales, Golf,* and even *Jesus* and *Islam.*

The next main text of Taoism is the *Chuang-tzu,* named for its author. This book is far removed from the *Tao Te Ching.* Full of anecdote and allegory, it challenges the reader with its provocative style and contents. It stresses the illusory nature of knowl-edge and the difficulty, if not impossibility, of separating right and wrong. Neverthe-less, the *Chuang-tzu* does include specific moral guidelines that proceed from the "two great sanctions," the requirement planted in nature and the inner conviction of what is right and wrong. Both of these principles are grounded in the great Tao.

Other important Taoist texts can only be mentioned here in passing. The *T'ai-shang* tractate deals with retribution on sin and reward for evil. If persons live a good life in harmony with the Tao, their lifespan will be lengthened; if an evil life, they will die early or have their punishment passed on to descendants. The *Tao-fa hui-yuan,* "Group of Taoist Rites," is a book of ceremonies to control demonic forces, both in nature and in the individual, when they result in sickness. The *Shang-ching hou-shen tao-chun lieh-chi,* or "Annals of the Lord of the Tao, the Sage-to-Come of Shang-ching," contains information on how certain Taoist masters (often called "adepts") used respiration techniques, alchemy, and other esoteric techniques to feed on astral powers and become immortal or even divine. But many texts of religious/esoteric Taoism are written in a special script taught only to initiates into special sects, and Taoists have in general been very secretive about sharing this literature.

TEACHING

The Nature of the Tao*

The leading themes in the Tao Te Ching *are the nature of the Tao and how one follows it. These passages present the way as unnameable (chapter 1), female in quality (6), the "mother" of heaven and earth (25), and accomplishing great things by means of small things (34). In the* Chuang-tzu, *the sage discusses the Tao in a more philosophic way, yet also in the playful and challenging manner so typical of the* Chuang-tzu.[2]

[1] Tao called Tao is not Tao.
Names can name no lasting name.

Nameless: the origin of heaven and earth.
Naming: the mother of ten thousand things.

Empty of desire, perceive mystery.
Filled with desire, perceive manifestations.

These have the same source, but different
  names.
  Call them both deep—
    Deep and again deep:
The gateway to all mystery.

[6] The Valley Spirit never dies.
It is called the Mysterious Female.

The entrance to the Mysterious Female
Is called the root of Heaven and Earth,

Endless flow
Of inexhaustible energy.

[25] Something unformed and complete
Before heaven and earth were born,
Solitary and silent,
Stands alone and unchanging,
Pervading all things without limit.
It is like the mother of all under heaven,
But I don't know its name—
  Better call it Tao.
  Better call it great.

Great means passing on.
Passing on means going far.
Going far means returning.

---

* *Tao Te Ching,* 1, 6, 25, 34; *Chuang-tzu* 29
[2] All readings from the *Tao Te Ching* are taken from Stephen Addiss and Stanley Lombardo, *Lao-Tzu, Tao Te Ching* (Cambridge, MA: Hackett, 1993). Copyright, 1993, Hackett Publishing Co, Inc. Used by permission. Selections from the *Chuang Tzu* are from James Legge, *The Texts of Taoism, Sacred Books of the East,* vols. 39 and 40 (Oxford: Oxford University Press, 1891).

Therefore,
    Tao is great,
    And heaven,
    And earth,
    And humans.

Four great things in the world.
Aren't humans one of them?

Humans follow earth
Earth follows heaven
Heaven follows Tao.
Tao follows its own nature.

[34] Great Tao overflows
To the left   To the right.

All beings owe their life to it
And do not depart from it.
It acts without a name.
It clothes and nourishes all beings
But does not become their master.

Enduring without desire,
It may be called slight.
All beings return to it,
But it does not become their master.

It may be called immense.
By not making itself great,
It can do great things.

[*Chuang-tzu* 29] Tung-kwo tze asked Chuang Tzu, saying, "Where is what you call the Tao to be found?" Chuang Tzu replied, "Everywhere." The other said, "Specify an instance of it. That will be more satisfactory." "It is here in this ant." "Give a lower instance." "It is in this earthenware tile." "Surely that is the lowest instance?" "It is in that excrement." To this Tung-kwo tze gave no reply.

Chuang Tzu said, "Your questions, my master, do not touch the fundamental point of the Tao. They remind me of the questions addressed by the superintendents of the market to the inspector about examining the value of a pig by stepping on it, and testing its weight as the foot descends lower and lower on the body. You should not specify any particular thing. There is not a single thing without the Tao. So it is with the Perfect Tao. And if we call it the Great Tao, it is just the same. It has the three terms, "Complete," "All-embracing, "the Whole." These names are different, but the reality sought in them is the same, referring to the One thing.

"Suppose we were to try to roam about in the palace of Nowhere. When met there, we might discuss the subject without ever coming to an end. Or suppose we were to be together in the region of Non-action. Should we say that the Tao was Simplicity and Stillness? or Indifference and Purity? or Harmony and Ease? My will would be aimless. It went nowhere, I would not know where it had gone; it went and came again, I wouldn't know where it had stopped; if it went on going and coming, I would not know when the process would end. In vague uncertainty, I would be in the vastest waste. Though I entered it with the greatest knowledge, I would not know how inexhaustible it was. That which makes things what they are does not have the limit which belongs to things; and when we speak of things being limited, we mean that they are so in themselves. The Tao is the limit of the unlimited, and the boundlessness of the unbounded.

"We speak of fullness and emptiness; of withering and decay. It produces fullness and emptiness, but is neither fullness nor emptiness; it produces withering and decay, but is neither withering nor decay. It produces the root and branches, but is neither root nor branch; it produces accumulation and dispersion, but is itself neither accumulated nor dispersed."

The World*

The typical Chinese expression for the world is "Heaven and Earth." These passages present the world, composed of the "ten thousand things," as proceeding from the Tao and holding to the way of inactivity. Wise persons will pattern their lives on the Tao that has made Heaven and Earth.

[7] Heaven is long, Earth enduring.
Long and enduring
Because they do not exist for themselves.

Therefore the Sage
　　Steps back, but is always in front,
　　Stays outside, but is always within.

No self interest?
Self is fulfilled.

[42] Tao engenders One,
One engenders Two,
Two engenders Three,³
Three engenders the ten thousand things.

The ten thousand things carry shade
And embrace sunlight.
　　Shade and sunlight, yin and yang,⁴
Breath blending into harmony.⁵

---

* *Tao Te Ching* 7, 42, 52
³ *the One* is *ch'i,* the primordial, cosmic breath; *the Two* are yin and yang; *the Three* are the waters under the earth, the earth, and heaven.
⁴ *Yin* and *Yang* are the cosmic principles or dualities: passive and active, earth and heaven, dark and light, etc.
⁵ *breath: ch'i,* the cosmic breath/wind.

Humans hate
To be alone, poor, and hungry.
Yet kings and princes
Use these words as titles.
　　We gain by losing,
　　Lose by gaining.

What others teach, I also teach:
A violent man does not die a natural death.
This is the basis of my teaching.

[52] The world has a source: the world's
　　mother.
Once you have the mother,
　　You know the children.
Once you know the children,
　　Return to the mother.

Your body dies.
There is no danger.

Block the passage,
Bolt the gate:
　　No strain
Until your life ends.

Open the passage,
Take charge of things:
　　No relief
Until your life ends.

Seeing the small is called brightness.
Maintaining gentleness is called strength.
Use this brightness to return to brightness.

Don't cling to your body's woes.
Then you can learn endurance.

The Domain of Nothingness*

A central teaching in Taoism is emptiness. When one becomes harmonious with the Tao, the world is without particulars. This is reflected in the idea that a true sage will not have a name. This passage alludes to related Buddhist themes.

T'ien Ken was traveling to the south of Yin Mountain. He had reached the river Liao when he met a nameless sage, to whom he said, "I beg to ask about governing the world."

"Go away," said the nameless man, "you are a low fellow. How unpleasant is your question! I would be in companionship with the Maker of things. When wearied, I would mount on the bird of ease and emptiness, proceed beyond the world, wander in the land of nowhere, and live in that domain of nothingness. Why do you come to worry me with the problem of setting the world in order?"

T'ien Ken again asked his question and the nameless man replied: "Make excursion in purest simplicity. Identify yourself with nondistinction. Follow the nature of things and have no personal bias, and then the world will be in peace."

---

* *Chuang-tzu*, book 7

ETHICS

Nonaction**

*The leading ethical ideal of Taoism is **wu-wei** [woo-WAY], nonaction or "active nonstriving." By nonaction, the sage seeks to come into harmony with the great Tao, which itself accomplishes by nonaction.*

Nonaction makes its exemplifier the lord of all fame; nonaction serves him as the treasury of all plans; nonaction fits him for the burden of all offices; nonaction makes him the lord of all wisdom. The range of his action is inexhaustible, but there is nowhere any trace of his presence. He fulfills all that he has received from Heaven, but he does not see that he was the recipient of anything. A pure vacancy of all purpose is what characterizes him. When the perfect man employs his mind, it is a mirror. It conducts nothing and anticipates nothing; it responds to what is before it, but does not retain it. Thus he is able to deal successfully with all things, and injures none.

** *Chuang-tzu*, book 7

Individual Life in Harmony with the Tao***

These selections, which emphasize the necessity of bringing individual life into accord with the Tao, give advice on how to accomplish this through nonaction and indirection.

[16] Attain complete emptiness,
Hold fast to stillness.

The ten thousand things stir about;
I only watch for their going back.

Things grow and grow,
But each goes back to its root.

*** *Tao Te Ching* 16, 22, 33, 44

Going back to the root is stillness.
This means returning to what is.
Returning to what is
Means going back to the ordinary.

Understanding the ordinary:
    Enlightenment.
Not understanding the ordinary:
    Blindness creates evil.
Understanding the ordinary:
    Mind opens.

Mind opening leads to compassion,
Compassion to nobility,
Nobility to heavenliness,
Heavenliness to Tao.

    Tao endures.
    Your body dies.

There is no danger.

[22] Crippled becomes whole,
Crooked becomes straight,
Hollow becomes full,
Worn becomes new,
Little becomes more,
Much becomes delusion.

Therefore Sages cling to the One
    And take care of this world;
Do not display themselves
    And therefore shine;
Do not assert themselves
    And therefore stand out;
Do not praise themselves
    And therefore succeed;
Are not complacent
    And therefore endure;
Do not contend

And therefore no one under heaven
    Can contend with them.

The old saying
Crippled becomes whole
Is not empty words.

It becomes whole and returns.

[33] Knowing others is intelligent.
Knowing yourself is enlightened.

Conquering others takes force.
Conquering yourself is true strength.

Knowing what is enough is wealth.
Forging ahead shows inner resolve.

Hold your ground and you will last long.
Die without perishing and your life will endure.

[44] Name or body: which is closer?
Body or possessions: which means more?
Gain or loss: which one hurts?

Extreme love exacts a great price.
Many possessions entail heavy loss.

Know what is enough—
    Abuse nothing.
Know when to stop—
    Harm nothing.

This is how to last a long time.[6]

---

[6] *last a long time:* lines like these in the *Tao Te Ching* encouraged later Taoist esoteric practices about gaining long life and even immortality through religious practices.

The Superior Man*

Here is a characteristically Taoist presentation of the superior man, designed of course to provide an alternative to the Confucian idea of superiority. The Taoist superiority comes not through self-cultivation in the virtues, but by tapping through inactivity into the superiority of the Tao. The full descriptions of the Taoist superior man form a complete list of the type of person that Taoists, especially philosophically oriented ones, seek to become.

The Master said, "The Tao overspreads and sustains all things. How great it is in its overflowing influence! The superior man ought by all means to remove from his mind all that is contrary to it. Acting without action is what is called Heaven-like. Speech coming forth of itself is what is called a mark of the true Virtue. Loving men and benefiting things is what is called Benevolence. Seeing wherein things that are different yet agree is what is called being Great. Conduct free from the ambition of being distinguished above others is what is called being Generous. The possession in himself of a myriad points of difference is what is called being Rich. Therefore to hold fast the natural attributes is what is called the Guiding Line of government; the perfecting of those attributes is what is called its Establishment; accordance with the Tao is what is called being Complete; and not allowing anything external to affect the will is what is called being Perfect.

"When the Superior man understands these ten things, he keeps all matters as it were sheathed in himself, showing the greatness of his mind; and through the outflow of his doings all things move and come to him. Being such, he lets the gold lie hid in the hill, and the pearls in the deep; he considers not property or money to be any gain; he keeps aloof from riches and honors; he rejoices not in long life, and grieves not for early death; he does not account prosperity a glory, nor is ashamed of indigence; he would not grasp at the gain of the whole world to be held as his own private portion; he would not desire to rule over the whole world as his own private distinction. His distinction is in understanding that all things belong to the one treasury, and that death and life should be viewed in the same way."

The Master said, "How still and deep is the place where the Tao resides! How limpid is its purity! Metal and stone without It would give forth no sound. They have indeed the power of sound in them, but if they be not struck, they do not emit it. Who can determine the qualities that are in all things?

"The man of kingly qualities holds on his way unoccupied, and is ashamed to busy himself with the conduct of affairs. He establishes himself in what is the root and source of his capacity, and his wisdom grows to be spiritlike. In this way his attributes become more and more great, and when his mind goes forth, whatever things come in his way, it lays hold of them and deals with them. Thus, if there were not the Tao, the bodily form would not have life, and its life, without the attributes of the Tao, would not be manifested. Is not he who preserves the body and gives the fullest development to the life, who establishes the attributes of the Tao and clearly displays It, possessed of kingly qualities? How majestic is he in his sudden issuings forth, and in his unexpected movements, when all things follow him!—This we call the man whose qualities fit him to rule.

"He sees where there is the deepest obscurity; he hears where there is no sound. In the midst of the deepest obscurity, he alone sees and can distinguish various objects; in the midst of a soundless abyss, he alone can hear a harmony of notes. Therefore where one deep is succeeded by a greater, he can people all with things; where one mysterious range is followed by another that is more so, he can lay hold of the subtlest character of each. In this way in his dealings with all

---

* *Chuang-tzu*, book 12

things, while he is farthest from having anything, he can yet give to them what they seek; while he is always hurrying forth, he yet returns to his resting place; now large, now small; now long, now short; now distant, now near."

Government*

The social ethic of Taoism is largely concerned with government. Here it presents a quietistic approach opposite of the activistic approach of Confucianism. By inactivity in following the Tao one can bring about the best state. This social ethic has led to several political options for Taoists: withdrawal from public life, mild participation in it, and at times participation in anarchy.

[3] Don't glorify heroes,
And people will not contend.
Don't treasure rare objects,
And no one will steal.
Don't display what people desire,
And their hearts will not be disturbed.

Therefore,
The Sage rules
    By emptying hearts and filling bellies,
    By weakening ambitions and strengthening
    bones;
Leads people
    Away from knowing and wanting;
Deters those who know too much
    From going too far:
Practices non-action
    And the natural order is not disrupted.

[18] Great Tao rejected:
    Benevolence and righteousness appear.

Learning and knowledge professed:
    Great hypocrites spring up.

Family relations forgotten:
    Filial piety and affection arise.

The nation disordered:
    Patriots come forth.

[57] Use the expected to govern the country,
Use surprise to wage war,
Use non-action to win the world.
How do I know?

    Like this!

The more prohibitions and rules,
    The poorer people become.
The sharper people's weapons,
    The more they riot.
The more skilled their techniques,
    The more grotesque their works.
The more elaborate the laws,
    The more they commit crimes.

Therefore the Sage says:
    I do nothing
And people transform themselves.
    I enjoy serenity
And people govern themselves.
    I cultivate emptiness
And people become prosperous.
    I have no desires
And people simplify themselves.

[64] At rest is easy to hold.
Not yet impossible is easy to plan.
Brittle is easy to break.
Fine is easy to scatter.

Create before it exists.
Lead before it goes astray.

A tree too big to embrace
    Is born from a slender shoot.
A nine-storey tower
    Rises from a pile of earth.

---

* *Tao Te Ching* 3, 18, 57, 64

A thousand-mile journey
    Begins with a single step.

Act and you ruin it.
Grasp and you lose it.
Therefore the Sage
    Does not act
    And so does not ruin
    Does not grasp
    And so goes not lose.

People commonly ruin their work
    When they are near success.

Proceed at the end as at the beginning
    And your work won't be ruined.

Therefore the Sage
    Desires no desires
    Prizes no prizes
    Studies no studies
        And returns
    To what others pass by.

The Sage
    Helps all beings find their nature,
    But does not presume to act.

Great and Small Rulers*

In this passage, the Chuang-tzu *offers a critique of rulers. It argues, in its characteristic style, that true greatness is much more than just the ability to do one's job in government. As the quail rightly laughs at the mythical bird, the wise laugh at those with pretensions to greatness.*

In the barren north . . . there is a bird named the p'eng, with a back like Mount T'ai, and wings like clouds across the sky. Upon a whirlwind it soars up to a height of ninety thousand leagues. Beyond the clouds and atmosphere, with the blue sky above it, it then directs its flight to the south, and thus proceeds to the ocean there.

A quail laughs at it, saying: "Where is that bird going? I spring up with a bound, and when I have reached no more that a few yards I come down again. I just fly about among the brushwood and the bushes. This is also the perfection of flying. Where is that bird going?" This is the difference between the great and the small.

There are some men whose knowledge is sufficient for the duties of some office. There are some men whose conduct will secure unity in some district. There are some men whose virtue makes them fit to be a ruler. There are some men whose ability wins credit in the country. In their opinion of themselves, they are just like the above.

---

* *Chuang-tzu,* book 1

On Death**

This often-quoted story is an excellent example of the striking literary features of the Chuang-tzu.

When Chuang Tzu went to Khu, he saw an empty skull, bleached but still retaining its shape. Tapping it with his horse-switch, he asked

it, "Did you, Sir, in your greed of life, fail in the lessons of reason, and come to this? Or did you do so, in the service of a perishing state, by the punishment of the axe? Or was it through your evil conduct, reflecting disgrace on your parents and on your wife and children? Or was it through your hard endurance of cold and hunger? Or was it that you had completed your term of life?"

** *Chuang-tzu,* book 18

Having given expression to these questions, he took up the skull, and made a pillow of it when he went to sleep. At midnight the skull appeared to him in a dream and said, "What you said to me was after the fashion of an orator. All your words were about the entanglements of men in their lifetime. There are none of those things after death. Would you like to hear me, Sir, tell you about death?" "I should," said Chuang Tzu, and the skull resumed: "In death there are not the distinctions of ruler above and minister below. There are none of the phenomena of the four seasons. Tranquil and at ease, our years are those of heaven and earth. No king in his court has greater enjoyment that we have." Chuang Tzu did not believe it, and said, "If I could get the Ruler of our Destiny to restore your body to life with its bones and flesh and skin, and to give you back your father and mother, your wife and children, and all your village acquaintances, would you wish me to do so?" The skull stared intently at him, knitted its brows, and said, "How should I cast away the enjoyment of my royal court, and undertake again the toils of life among mankind?"

Reward and Retribution*

Although the Tao does not have a strongly moral character, the Taoist tradition nonetheless developed the doctrine of reward for virtue (in long life) and punishment for evil (shortened life or punishment of descendants). This passage gives a lyrical list of good deeds and excerpts the beginning of an even longer section on evil deeds.

There are no special doors for calamity and happiness; they come as men themselves summon them. Their recompenses follow good and evil as the shadow follows the substance.

Accordingly, in heaven and earth there are spirits that take account of men's transgressions, and, according to the lightness or gravity of their offenses, take away from their term of life. When that term is curtailed, men become poor and reduced, and meet with many sorrows and afflictions. All (other) men hate them; punishments and calamities attend them; good luck and occasions for felicitation shun them; evil stars send down misfortunes on them. When their term of life is exhausted they die.

There also are the Spirit-rulers in the three pairs of the T'ai stars of the Northern Bushel[7] over men's heads, which record their acts of guilt and wickedness, and take away (from their term of life) periods of twelve years or of a hundred days.

There also are the three Spirits of the recumbent body which reside within a man's person. As each appointed day of reporting comes, they ascend to the court of Heaven, and report men's deeds of guilt and transgression. On the last day of the moon, the spirit of the Hearth does the same.

In the case of every man's transgressions, when they are great, twelve years are taken from his term of life; when they are small, a hundred days.

Transgressions, great and small, are seen in several hundred things. He who wishes to seek for long life must first avoid these.

If his way is right, he should go forward in it; if it is wrong, he should withdraw from it.

He will not tread in devious byways; he will not impose on himself in any secret apartment. He will amass virtue and accumulate deeds of merit. He will feel kindly towards all creatures. He will be loyal, filial, loving to his younger brothers, and submissive to his elder. He will make himself correct and so transform others. He will pity orphans, and have compassion on widows; he will respect the old and cherish the

---

* *T'ai-Shang*, book 1
[7] *Northern Bushel*: a constellation.

young. Even the insects, grass, and trees he should not hurt.

He ought to pity the evil tendencies of others; to rejoice over their excellences; to help them in their difficulties; to rescue them from their perils; to regard their gains as if they were his own, and their losses in the same way; not to publish their shortcomings; not to flaunt his own superiorities; to put a stop to what is evil, and exalt and display what is good; to yield much, and take little for himself; to receive insult without resenting it, and honor with an appearance of apprehension; to bestow favors without seeking for a return, and give to others without any subsequent regret—this is what is called a good man. All other men respect him; Heaven in its course protects him; happiness and financial rewards follow him; all evil things keep far from him; the spiritual Intelligences defend him; what he does is sure to succeed; he may hope to become Immaterial and Immortal.

He who would seek to become an Immortal of Heaven ought to give the proof of 1,300 good deeds; and he who would seek to become an Immortal of Earth should give the proof of three hundred.

But if the movements of a man's heart are contrary to righteousness, and his conduct is in opposition to reason; if he regards his wickedness as a proof of his ability, and can bear to do what is cruel and injurious; if he secretly harms the honest and good; if he treats with clandestine slight his ruler or parents; if he is disrespectful to his elders and teachers; if he disregards the authority of those whom he should serve; if he deceives the simple; if he calumniates his fellow-learners; if he vents baseless slanders, practices deception and hypocrisy, and attacks and exposes his kindred by blood or marriage; if he is hard, violent, and without humanity—in the case of crimes such as these, (the Spirits) presiding over the Life, according to their lightness or gravity, take away the culprit's periods of twelve years or of one hundred days. When his term of life is exhausted, death ensues. If at death there remains any unpunished guilt, judgment extends to his posterity.

RITUAL

Methods of Prolonging Life*

This text, considered the most important in religious Taoism, stresses the esoteric methods of achieving immortality. The first selection discusses the general principles of achieving longevity or immortality; the second points out how scripture texts can aid in this process.[8]

If you are going to do everything possible to nurture your life, you will take the divine medi-

cines. In addition, you will never weary of circulating your breaths; morning and night you will do calisthenics to circulate your blood and breaths and see that they do not stagnate. In addition to these things, you will practice sexual intercourse in the right fashion; you will eat and drink moderately; you will avoid drafts and dampness; you will not trouble about things that are not within your competence. Do all these things, and you will not fall sick. On the other hand, you are sure to become ill if you are afraid of not always having your own way in society and of instability in your affairs; also, if laxity and lack of diligence trouble you. If all you have is a heart faithful to God and yet do nothing for your own

---

* *Pao-p'u tzu* 15.6b–7a; 19.6b–7a

[8] From James R. Ware, *Alchemy, Medicine, Religion in the China of A.D. 320: The Nei P'ien of Ko Hung* (Pao-p'u tzu). Cambridge, MA: Massachusetts Institute of Technology Press, 1966. Copyright, 1966 by The Massachusetts Institute of Technology. Used by permission.

benefit—your predestined life span being defective and your body threatened with harm the Three Corpses[9] will take advantage of your weak months and perilous days, the hours when your longevity could be interrupted or sickness incurred, to summon vicious breaths and bring in any demons they might be able to find to do you injury. The danger is certainly great for any person for whom these six obstacles are grouped and the Three Destructives (from the duodenary cycle) united in the same quarter. And when this situation intensifies, it produces the various illnesses. But all of this was set in motion by the anxiety that was present in the first place.

Accordingly, those who first did something about God in antiquity exercised all the medical arts at the same time to save themselves from misfortunes that are ever present, but this principle is unknown to ordinary processors who, not understanding what they have been taught, pay no attention to the prescriptions for treating illness. Further, being unable to break with worldly life and live as hermits, and using only personal remedies to drive away illness, they lack all means for combating it and curing themselves. They are by no means as well off as the people in general who use various infusions. They are people to whom we may apply this adage: One may go to Han-tan and fail to acquire the gait used there, and then forget what was known in one's native Shou-ling (*Chuang [-tzu]* 17.79). . . .

I heard Cheng Yin say that no Taoist book surpasses *San huang nei wen* and *Wu yueh chen hsing t'u*[10] in importance. They were the honored secrets of the genies (spirit immortals) and superior men of antiquity, and could be taught only by those bearing the title of genie. Those receiving them transmitted them once after forty years, and in doing so oaths were taken by smearing the lips with the blood of a victim,[11] and agreements were entered into by the giving

of a present. Writings of this type are to be found in all the famous mountains and the five revered mountains, but they are stored in hidden spots in caves. In response to those who have secured the divine process and entered a mountain to give sincere thought to it, the god of the mountain will automatically open the mountain and let such persons see the texts, just as Po Ho got his in a mountain, and immediately set up an altar, made a present of silk, drew one ordinary copy,[12] and then left with them. A purified place is always prepared for such texts, and whenever anything is done about them one must first announce it to them, as though one were serving a sovereign or a father.

The classic itself states that if *San huang nei wen* is in a household, it will banish evil and hateful ghosts, soften the effects of epidemics, block calamities, and rout misfortunes. If anyone is suffering from illness or on the point of death, let someone believing in the process with all his heart give this text to the patient to hold, and he will be sure not to die. If a wife is having trouble in childbirth to the point of possible death, let her hold this text, and her son will be born immediately. If pilgrims wishing to seek Fullness of Life will hold this text when entering the mountains, it will rout tigers and wolves, and none of the mountain powers, poisons, or evils will dare approach. When crossing rivers and seas, the processors will be able to dispel crocodiles and dragons, and halt the wind and waves with this book.

With the method taught in this text it is possible to initiate undertakings positively or negatively without inquiring about the correct site or choosing the right day, and one's household will be free from calamities. If you wish to build a new house or tomb, write several dozen copies of the Earth Augustus text and spread them on the site. Look at them on the following day, and if a yellow color is seen adhering to them, one may begin the work there and the household will be sure to become rich and prosperous. When

---

[9] *Three Corpses:* worms in the body causing illness and death.
[10] Both these books were written by Po Ho.
[11] *victim:* a sacrificed animal.

[12] *drew one ordinary copy:* i.e., wrote out a copy.

others are being interred, copy the Man Augustus text and include your own full name written on a folded sheet of paper. Insert this in that person's grave without letting others know what you are doing, and you will be free from sudden misfortune and robbers. Anyone plotting against you will be sure to have his harm turned against himself.

The Life and Ascension of Shen Xi*

The highest form of attaining immortality in Taoism is ascension to heaven, there to become an immortal. Here is an eyewitness account of the ascension of Shen Xi from a fourth-century scripture, the Biographies of Spirit Immortals.[13]

Shen Xi was a native of Wu district in Jiangsu. He studied the Tao in Sichuan, attaining the magical powers of dissipating calamity, curing disease, and bringing relief to the common people. However, he knew nothing of the drugs of immortality and their use. Still, his virtue found favor in the sight of heaven and was duly recorded in the registers above.

On one occasion, Xi and his wife, Lady Jia, were returning from a visit to the family of their daughter-in-law when they encountered three chariots. One was drawn by a white deer, another by a green dragon, and the third by a white tiger. There were thirty or forty mounted attendants in dark red livery, armed with lances and swords. They crowded the narrow road, filling it with pomp and glitter.

They inquired if he was Shen Xi. The latter, wondering what to make of this astounding apparition, replied, "Indeed, I am. But why do you ask?"

"Mr. Shen, sir," one of them explained, "you have deserved well of the people. The Tao is forever present in your heart, and from your earliest childhood, your conduct has been free from blame. However, your allotted lifespan is short and your years are approaching their close. So the Yellow Venerable Lord has sent down three immortal officials with their chariots to escort you to heaven.

"The gentleman in the chariot with the white deer is Bo Yanzhi, a palace official.

"The gentleman in the chariot with the green dragon is Sima Sheng, a lord of transcendence.

"The gentleman in the chariot with the white tiger is Xu Fu, a master of ceremony."

Presently the three immortals came forward in their feathery robes. They held their official tablets in their hands and bestowed on Shen a tablet of white jade, a green jade scepter, and a set of red jade characters, which he could not read. After this formal ceremony, they took him to heaven.

His ascension was witnessed by a number of field laborers in the vicinity. They did not know what to make of it. After a little while there came a thick mist, and when it cleared away, the whole company had disappeared. All that remained were the oxen which had drawn Shen's carriage. They were peacefully grazing in the fields.

Someone recognized the animals as belonging to the Shen household and informed his family that he and his wife had vanished. Fearing that they had been carried off to the deep mountains by evil spirits, family and servants searched in every direction for a hundred miles around. But they did not find them.

Over four hundred years later, Shen Xi unexpectedly revisited his native village. He sought out one of his descendents, a man called Shen Huaixi, who explained that he had heard his elders speak of a certain ancestor who had become immortal. But, he said, this ancestor had never come back.

Shen stayed with his descendant for about a month. During that time, he recounted his first experience of ascension.

---

* *Shenxian zhuan, Daozang jinghua* 5.11
[13] From Livia Kohn, ed., *The Taoist Experience: An Anthology* (Albany: State University of New York Press, 1993), pp. 326–28. Used by permission.

"Although I was not brought before the Emperor of Heaven himself," he said, "I did get to meet the Venerable Lord, who is his right-hand man. The attendants instructed me not to make any formal acknowledgments, but simply to take my seat in silence.

"The celestial palace seemed composed of an insubstantial, luminous haze, shot through with an enormous variety of colors too fantastic to describe. There were hundreds of attendants, mostly female. In the gardens grew trees bearing pearls and jade; all sorts of immortality herbs and magic mushrooms sprouted in great profusion.

"Dragons and tigers," he continued, "assembled in groups and frolicked in their midst. I could hear a tinkling sound, like that of copper and iron ornaments, but I've never discovered where it came from. The walls on all sides shone with a bright glow; they were covered with talismanic inscriptions.

"The Venerable Lord himself was about ten feet in height. His hair hung loose, and he wore an embroidered robe. His entire person radiated light. After a while, several jade maidens brought in a golden table with jade goblets and set it before me. They told me that this was the divine cinnabar elixir. Whoever drinks it is exempt from death. Both my wife and I were given a cup and promised a long life of ten thousand years.

"Next we were told to make a formal obeisance to the Venerable Lord but offer no thanks. When we had finished the divine medicine, they brought us two dates as large as hens' eggs, and several five-inch slices of something that looked like dried meat. 'Return to the world of mortals for a time,' they told us, 'and there cure the manifold diseases of humanity. Whenever you wish to ascend again, just write out this talisman and hang it on the end of a pole. Then someone will come and get you.'

"So they said, and handed me the talisman and an immortal recipe. Soon afterward I fell into a drowse. Suddenly I seemed to wake as if from a long sleep and found that I was back on earth. Many times I have tried it on sick people. The recipe really works!"

The Relationship of Taoism to Confucianism*

Taoism and Confucianism have long been the two major traditions of China. Here is a statement from the Taoist side on their relationship, with the better judgment going of course to Taoism. The text deals with the question, Of Confucianism and Taoism, which is the easier?[14]

Confucianism is difficulty in the midst of facility [ease]; Taoism is facility in the midst of difficulties. The difficulties of Taoism are these: abandonment of social intercourse and renouncing wife and family; rejection of fame and loss of income; removal of brilliances from one's sight and suppression of the tinkling marks of office from one's ears; the silence and retirement where one's sole profession is preservation of one's own integrity; not to be depressed by criticism nor elated by praise; to look upon honors without desiring them and to dwell humbly without shame. But Taoism also has its attractive side; no visits of congratulation or condolence, and no critical glances and looks at one's abode; no troubling of the internal gods with the Seven Classics and never a concern for the calendar; no bother about the advancings of asterisms and no enslavement to a craft or to letters; all annoyances lifted, and an inner harmony that grows of itself; perfect freedom of action and thought, no fear, no grief. Therefore, I describe Taoism as facility in the midst of difficulties.

Everything done in Confucianism is modeled upon precedents. Leaving and staying have their

* *Pao-p'u Tzu* 7.5a

[14] From James R. Ware, *Alchemy, Medicine, Religion in the China of A.D. 320: The* Nei P'ien *of Ko Hung* (Pao-p'u tzu). Cambridge, MA: Massachusetts Institute of Technology Press, 1966. Copyright 1966 by the Massachusetts Institute of Technology. Used by permission.

set rules; speech and silence depend upon the hour. If a teacher is desired, he can be found in practically any house; it is a matter of written material, there are plenty of commentaries to resolve the doubts. This is what is easy in Confucianism. Its difficulties are these: grasping the profound and rendering present the distant, and also confronting and reconciling the regulations coming from the rulers of old; . . . and acquiring a wide knowledge of all those many things said by the various schools of philosophy; constantly accumulating good works among the people, and giving the last drop of loyalty to one's lord; being able to interpret any signs conferred by heaven, and giving thought to the meanings of winds and clouds; to be considered unsuccessful for not knowing some solitary matter and to have to face criticism for one word of imprecision; to have one's every step taken as a model by the world, and to have one's every utterance repeated by all. This is what I mean by difficulties in the midst of facility. But to put it honestly, Confucianism is difficult because of its multiplicities, while Taoism is easy with its conciseness.

APPENDIX: A COMPLETE TAOIST SCRIPTURE*

"The Great Emperor who Protects Life" is a local Taoist God in southeast China. This scripture was written in the fifteenth century C.E. A good example of a short Taoist text celebrating a god by retelling his legend and giving moral commands to his people, it also shows a Buddhist influence on Taoism. It is notable for its request that people hire Buddhist or Taoist priests to chant it, or form scripture-recitation societies to chant it themselves.[15]

Raising our heads we invoke the August Heavenly Great Emperor Wu. He lived in the Quanzhou Commandery but was born near Zhangzhou. His brave and valiant awesome spiritual powers arose from his merciful heart. Because he used ritual powers he became a Medicine King. To the masses of the people he brought most abundant advantages. His fulfillment of his merit moved the Jade Sovereign. He was asked by Imperial decree what karmic path he had followed. [He replied that] upon obtaining correct knowledge and perception [he] expanded the Tao. [The Jade Emperor] commanded that the great lofty title of the numinous doctor be enhanced. Also, he sent [as subordinates] an Immortal Medical Official named Huang, the Awesome Martial Retainer Jiang Si shi, the Perfect Man of the Green Kerchief and two pages, the Six Ding Generals [who are] Strong Soldiers who Expel Evil, Maiden Qin, the Taiyi Female Physician, together with the Great Messenger who Flies to Heaven. [All of these] work together to support the weak and expel disease and misfortune.

I today with all my heart and with complete obedience, express my desire that you will be happy to let fall your mercy at my recitation [of your names].

Chant for the Opening of the Scripture:
Great Saint, Physician Spirit, Perfected
　　Lord Wu
Wrote Talismans, let fall seal-script [revelations], and proclaimed scriptures
Swearing a vow that his Sacred Spell would
　　have awesome power,
And bring auspiciousness, gather good fortune,
　　and avoid disaster.

Formerly, the Perfected Lord of Merciful Salvation, attended an audience in the Taiqing Palace

---

* *The True Scripture of The Great Emperor*
[15] From Dean, Kenneth, *Taoist Ritual and Popular Cults of South-East China*. Princeton: Princeton University Press, 1993. Copyright 1993 by Princeton University Press. Reprinted by permission of Princeton University Press.

within the Hall of the Three Origins. All the gods of the Stars were gathered round. The Heavenly Venerable said:

Now when I observe the 3,000 million worlds below, and the multitudes dwelling in Jambudvipa, [they are] all practising the 10 evils and the 5 disobediences, disloyal and unfilial, unmannered and unrighteous, not revering the Three Treasures, ignorant of charity, unwilling to provide assistance, frequently carrying out evil deeds, killing living beings, behaving licentiously, stealing, coveting and getting angry, entangling themselves in a web of culpability, and disrupting the nation. [There] both kings and men are unjust; those above do not measure by the Tao, and those below do not uphold the Laws. The innocent are slaughtered, their spirits do not scatter, but instead turn into demonic flying zombies. Therefore the foreign borderland peoples raised up weapons of war, and the people of South China, in cold and hot seasons, fell victim to malarial miasmas and yellow fever, became dumb and died horrible painful deaths. Then arose a mosquito borne plague of measles, with symptoms of red eyes and dysentery. Pigs, sheep, oxen, and horses became afflicted and died. Mountain demons and pythons, vipers, tigers, and elephants, birds, beasts, and sea monsters [arose]. Wild winds drove the boats; dragons and demonic waves destroyed city walls and fords, and there were many floods and fires. And then there was trouble with [Imperial] Laws, for every year brought hunger and starvation, the five grains did not raise up. As for those of you who performed charity, but for whom things did not work out as you wished, you should know that this is the [work of] demons. These demons are all martial fellows and stout soldiers, with brave and valiant divine energy. They [formerly] aided heavenly spirits to move clouds and spread vapors, so that winds and rain were seasonal, and the grains and rice grew ripe, and the Empire enjoyed Great Peace. Yet today they have all increased in number to a total of 84,000 and have suddenly raised up tornadoes and floods. The 404 diseases circulate through the seasons, bringing little good fortune to the world. The evil and rebellious masses encounter disasters and die. The Heavenly Venerable took pity on those people who had cultivated good fortune [by carrying out] the 10 good deeds. [He then] extended divine protection to them. Study the words of the prophecy:

A green dog barks
A wooden pig squeals,
A rooster [crows] at the rabbit [in the] moon
A round moon without lustre.
Three disasters strike
Nine rebellions arise.

In the jia and yi years there will be military ravages
In the bing and ding years fearful fires
In the wu and ji years locusts will spread plague
In the geng and ren years storms and flood,
Thus from jia year to the gui year,
The first five years will have barren harvests,
The last five years will have good harvests.
Alas we have come to the end of the world
All the Buddhas will attain Nirvana
Saints and Sages will hide away
Common men and ignorant women are unaware and do not understand
Therefore I have transmitted this scripture
So that it may broadly save the world.
And pronounce this gatha:
The dogs barks, the pig squeals
The bad will vanish, the good will survive
Take refuge in the Three Treasures
Uphold and recite this Scripture.
Revere it wherever you go
And it will always hold down demonic soldiers
Heavenly spirits will protect you
Family and nation will be at peace
Widely transmit the Way of the Scripture
Pass it all around

The Most High Lord Lao said:

Whenever any good man or faithful woman worships the Three Treasures, and delights in charitable deeds, then on the gengshen, and jiazi days, and on the days of the Three Origins, the Seven [Dipper Stars], the Day of Destiny, and the winter sacrifice, they should fast and purify their hearts, recite this scripture, and revere these True Writings. Then spontaneously, heavenly spirits will protect them and they will not encounter any hardship. I, [Lord Lao], will carry on this great work, and obtain for them good fortune and longevity. I [hereby] issue secret instructions and sacred talismans, altogether 120, and announce to the Perfected Lord of Merciful Salvation: Your Tao is complete and your Virtue prepared. Your good deeds are pure and resplendent. In heaven you [observe the] prohibitions, and have thereby established marvellous powers of wisdom. On earth you have mercy and compassion and the great mission of the salvation of [humankind]. Amongst men you have the honorable title of Perfected Lord of Trustworthy Benevolence. You can move between the Three Realms. You can subdue these demons and transmit the message of this Scripture. Save and deliver the masses, bring them all back together to the Great Tao.

When the Most High had finished speaking, the Heavenly Venerable rode away, the spirits of the stars all made their farewells and withdrew. Then the Perfected Lord of Merciful Salvation carried out the command from on high, swiftly ordering the miraculous realm. In the guiyou year, in the 4th month, on the 7th day,[16] he paced the Mainstays [of Heaven] and sprayed out vapor. An earthquake struck three times. Then he descended into a true medium, and pronounced this scripture and made this spell:

Transformation body of Guanyin
Gathered up the sprites on Bohai Island
My heart sinks in the six Harmonies
My chi revolves the five Elements
Compassionately I save the world
Saving from disease, I am a Physician Spirit
A glass of water with seven salts
My precious sword held straight out
I pace the Mainstays, breathing in and out
The masses of demons all collapse
A thousand disasters forever annihilated
A myriad blessing arrive
In the space opened up by the smoke of incense
The sacred form ascends
Recite my sacred spell
And I will descend in my true shape
Om, swiftly, swiftly, in accordance with the ordinances.

The True Medium spoke:

In my life I dwelt in Quanzhou commandery, and left traces [of my deeds] near Zhangzhou. From then until now through over 300 years I have piled up merit in laborious deeds. Fine honors were commended and bestowed [upon me]. Formerly I shipped grain to save [people] in a drought. Also I led spirit soldiers and drove away pirate robbers. Recently I let flow a sweet spring to put an end to the sufferings of sickness. Now I transmit the Methods and Scriptures of the Spiritual Treasure in order to save the people of the world. If any man or woman obtain my true scripture with its marvelous seal, faithfully keep and worship them. Either invite Buddhist or Taoist priests to recite the scripture, or organize an association to read and recite it. Widely order its dissemination. Then as for anything your heart desires there will be nothing that does not satisfy your wishes. Whensoever anyone begins to build a well or a stove, or constructs a house or a tomb, or an enclosure for pigs, sheep, oxen, horses, chickens or ducks, and at that time there be vapors bearing sickness, then they may arrange incense, flowers, lamps, and tea, and offer up outstanding fruit, recite

---

[16] *In the guiyou year, in the 4th month, on the 7th day:* this "could be any year, in cycles of sixty, beginning with 1273 [C.E.], close to the fall of China to the Mongols." (K. Dean, *Taoist Ritual and Popular Cults of South-East China,* pp. 78–79).

this scripture and repeat my spell seven times successively, and write with red vermillion the talismans and [recite] the incantations that I have revealed, placing them upon the door, then demons of disaster will spontaneously dissipate, and members of the family will be fine. That which I desire with all my heart is that you will all ascend to the banks of the Tao. After the True Medium had finished speaking, he exhaled the soul and came to.

Perfected Lord, Perfected Lord
Regulate evil and behead plague [demons].
Employ your talisman, spells and
   [purificatory] water
Broadly save the myriad peoples
Pace the Mainstays with correct chi
Forever cutting off the roots of misfortune
Awesome radiance shines brightly
Your illustrious sobriquet has been succes-
   sively enhanced
With incense and temple sacrifices
Morning and night we earnestly worship you
The myriad spirits all pray
That they might all bathe in your divine
   merit
Recite my sacred spell
Sweep away the masses of evil
Swiftly, swiftly, in accordance with the
   ordinances.
[Spell for Commanding Water:]
Perfected Lord of Trustworthy Benevolence
Transformation body of Guanyin
Compassionately you broadly save [people]
Your spirit descends once invoked
Moving clouds and spreading vapors
Curing illness and eliminating adversity
His fire vehicle removes poison
His water vehicle all strike home
His wind vehicle and chi vehicle

Penetrate to the mysterious obscurity
The green dragon guards wood
The white tiger protects metal
The red pheasant guards fire
The Dark Warrior is the spirit of Water
I am the Lord of Earth,
Chaotic Origin,
Ancestor of the Tao
Pacing the Mainstays with correct breaths
I protect the myriad beings
My merit is accomplished
Ascend with me
Swiftly, swiftly, in accordance with the
   ordinances
The Physician Spirit's honored name is pro-
   claimed far and wide
Brightly shone his Spiritual Skill at his birth
   near Zhangzhou
Formerly the responsive transformation body
   of Guanyin
Removed by Ritual means the mass of
   demons and sprites from Bohai Island
Three shocks from the earthquake and the
   medium was possessed
Proclaimed the scripture and saves all beings
People of the world, burn incense and
   earnestly recite the scripture
A thousand disasters will be forever ended
And good fortune and longevity will come
   to you.

It is said that this scripture specifically cures periodic outbreaks of pestilence. Reciting it can liberate the masses from hardship. At the end of the original copy there was appended the Marvelous Scripture of Immortal Maiden of Merciful Salvation Who Saves [Those in] Childbirth, which still awaits reprinting. ([This appendage is] Noted by Yang [Jun].)

GLOSSARY

(Pinyin spelling, where it differs from Wade-Giles, is given in brackets before the pronunciation.)

Chuang-tzu [Zhuangzi] (jwahng tzoo) the second most important book of the Taoist scriptures.

Tao [Dao] (dow) the Way of the cosmos, to be "tuned into" in human life.

Tao Te Ching [Dao De Jing] (dow duh jing) the "Classic of the Way and its Working," the leading book of the Taoist scriptures.

Tao Tsang [Dao Zang] (dow tsahng) the Taoist canon.

te [De] (duh) virtue, power, working.

wu-wei (woo WAY) nonaction, nonstriving; passivity; the use of the natural power of the Tao in oneself.

QUESTIONS FOR STUDY AND DISCUSSION

1. From your reading of these texts, how would you define or describe the Tao?

2. In what ways is the *Tao Te Ching* the foundation of subsequent Taoist traditions?

3. Compare and contrast the Taoist and Confucian ideas of the sage or superior man.

4. Discuss the remarkable feminine imagery used, especially in the *Tao Te Ching*, to describe the Tao. Has this carried over into later Taoism in the form of a greater role for women in the religion? If not, why?

5. Discuss the Taoist goal of longevity. How is the pursuit of this goal different in religious and philosophical Taoism?

6. How might the perplexing style of the *Chuang-tzu* be particularly well designed to promote its goals?

7. Compare and contrast the Taoist and Confucian ideas of government. How is it possible, as the *Tao Te Ching* claims, to govern by nonaction?

8. Contrast "philosophical Taoism" and "religious Taoism." How are their differences and similarities reflected in their scriptures?

SUGGESTIONS FOR FURTHER READING

Primary Readings

S. Addiss and S. Lombardo, *Lao-Tzu, Tao Te Ching*. Cambridge, MA: Hackett, 1993. An excellent translation, characterized by literary grace and terse poetic power.

Wing-tsit Chan, *A Source Book in Chinese Philosophy*. Princeton: Princeton University Press, 1963. Full selections from key Taoist books, from a leading interpreter of Chinese religious literature to the West.

R. G. Henricks, *Lao Tzu, Te-Tao Ching*. New York: Ballantine, 1989. A lively translation, with full introduction and commentary, of the recently discovered *Ma-wang-tui* texts. [The usual name of this book is reversed in these texts.]

L. Kohn, *Taoist Mystical Philosophy: The Scripture of Western Ascension*. Albany: State University of New York Press, 1991. A translation and commentary of an important early text from philosophical Taoism.

L. Kohn, *The Taoist Experience: An Anthology*. Albany: State University of New York Press, 1993. An excellent selection of scriptural and nonscriptural texts illustrating the range of Taoism.

J. Legge, ed., *The Texts of Taoism*. New York: Julian, 1959; first published 1891 by Oxford University Press. A standard rendering of the *Tao Te Ching, Chuang-tzu,* and the *Thai Shang*.

The Multimedia I Ching. Princeton: Princeton University Press, 1997. This CD-ROM presents the classic Wilhelm/Baynes translation along with natural landscape scenes, architectural scenes and music.

S. R. Nickerson, *Early Daoist Scriptures.* Berkeley: University of California Press, 1997. A translation and commentary on Taoist scriptures previously unpublished in the West.

J. R. Ware, *Alchemy, Medicine, Religion in the China of A.D. 320: the* Nei P'ien *of Ko Hung* (Pao-p'u tzu). Cambridge, MA: M.I.T. Press, 1966. A complete and accurate translation of the single most important text in the history of religious Taoism.

Secondary Readings

R. E. Allinson, *Chuang-Tzu for Spiritual Transformation: An Analysis of the Inner Chapters.* Albany: State University of New York Press, 1989. A challenging philosophical analysis of the heart of this classic.

Chih-chung Tsai, *Zhuangzi Speaks: The Music of Nature.* Princeton: Princeton University Press, 1992. A bestselling book in its Chinese original, this volume features line-drawing and cartoon interpretations of the *Chuang-Tzu* to express the ineffable Tao.

B. E. Reed, "[Women in] Taoism," in A. Sharma, ed., *Women in World Religions.* Albany: State University of New York Press, 1989, pp. 161–181. An insightful analysis of the role of the feminine in Taoist scripture, especially the *Tao Te Ching,* and their less than prominent role in lived Taoist religion.

M. Saso, *Blue Dragon White Tiger: Taoist Rites of Passage.* Washington, DC: The Taoist Center, 1990. A treatment of various life-cycle rituals.

M. Saso, *The Teachings of Taoist Master Chuang.* New Haven: Yale University Press, 1978. A fascinating study of a contemporary religious Taoist teacher in Taiwan.

Izanagi Creating the Japanese Islands
This hanging scroll painting by Kobayashi Eitaku (1843–1890) depicts a leading theme of the
Shinto sacred writings. Credit: William Bigelow Collection. Courtesy, Museum of Fine Arts,
Boston.

CHAPTER NINE

Shinto

INTRODUCTION

Shinto, the ancient Japanese national religion, is unique among the religious traditions of Asia and the world. Of all major faiths based in historically literate cultures, it has no scripture as modern scholars understand that term. Shinto recognizes no book as officially authoritative; it has no canon; and it has no formalized doctrines or ethical systems that could be shaped by a scripture.

Nevertheless, two books in particular have a special standing in Shinto because of their antiquity and unique contents. They are the ***Kojiki,*** "Record of Ancient Matters," and the ***Nihongi,*** "Chronicles of Japan." Both written by imperial decree in the eighth century C.E., these books have held a place of honor in Shinto. Since ancient times, the Japanese have looked on them as the story of the foundation of Japan. For a thousand years schoolchildren were taught their stories as an education in patriotism. These books "are regarded as authoritative and provide [Shinto's] historical as well as its spiritual basis."[1]

Although not classified as scripture, these books give good evidence of the leading ideas of the Shinto tradition. First in importance is the existence of the many ***kami,*** gods and spirits, whom most Japanese view polytheistically. Second, humanity is the offspring of the ***kami*** and are continually supported by their power. Third, the Japanese nation, especially the imperial family, is the center of humanity. Fourth, a deep reverence is owed the emperor as the one through whom blessings flow to the nation.

Since the disestablishment of Shinto as the official state religion in 1945, however, the *Kojiki* and *Nihongi* are no longer taught in schools. Moreover, as a part of this disestablishment, the Japanese emperor renounced his divinity, which these books are largely designed to buttress. But much of the old feeling still lingers. For example, both pride and protests erupted in 1991 when the new emperor Akihito spent a night in a specially constructed Shinto shrine, a ritual in older days thought to bring about the emperor's rebirth as a child of the sun god Amaterasu. So, even though the imperial claims these books were written to support have been officially renounced, these sacred texts still provide valuable insight into the historical essence of Shinto and its traditional relationship to the Japanese national character.

The *Kojiki*

The *Kojiki,* finished in 712 C.E., is the oldest surviving book in Japan. The only knowledge we have of its origin comes from the preface by its author Yasumaro (given in full in the first reading). This preface records that Emperor Temmu (reigned 672–687) decreed that the falsified genealogical records, much of them mythological, of the

---

[1] Sokyo Ono, *Shinto, The Kami Way* (Rutland, VT: Charles Tuttle, 1962), p. 10.

leading Japanese families should be corrected by a new book. In this way the genealogical myths of the competing clans were incorporated into and subsumed by the genealogical myth of Temmu's clan. To do this, the *Kojiki* draws on two main works of the time, the *Teiki*, or *Imperial Sun-Lineage*, and the *Honji*, or *Ancient Dicta of Former Ages*. The first was a source of genealogies, the second a collection of myths, legends, and songs; both were probably oral collections. These two sources, when combined and reworked into the *Kojiki*, shape its characteristic emphasis on a reliable genealogy that goes back to the gods. Besides these changes, scholars discern other revisions to more ancient traditions in the *Kojiki*. For example, it is likely that earlier indigenous Japanese traditions on the complementarity of men and women were adapted to more Confucian ideas of male superiority.

The *Kojiki* itself is divided into three books. The first is a statement of early Japanese mythology that proclaims that the emperor's family, as the "offspring of the heavenly deities," is destined to rule Japan. The second and third books contain stories of the ancient emperors and their exploits, most of them legendary, up to the time of writing. Only a few of these stories have any explicit religious significance.

The *Nihongi*

More fully known as the *Nihonshoki*, or *Chronicles of Japan*, the *Nihongi* was written shortly after the *Kojiki*, in 720 C.E. Shotoku Daishi, its traditional author, compiled the *Nihongi* in thirty books. It narrates a closely related version of the same stories of the *Kojiki*, draws on the same sources, and is written in the same Chinese style. Its special concern is to show that the Teika reforms of 645, in which Shinto was brought under stricter government regulation, resulted in greater obedience to the way of the Kami.

SELECTIONS FROM THE *KOJIKI* AND THE *NIHONGI*

Preface to the *Kojiki*

This preface is the author's dedicatory address to Gemmei, niece and daughter-in-law of Emperor Kamu-Yamato [Temmu], who commissioned the work but died before its completion. The preface is a summary of much of the contents of the entire Kojiki. *The narrator tells of the creation of the world, the birth of the early gods, and the creation of Japan. The middle sections deal with various emperors, from the first emperor, Jimmu, to Temmu, although the narrative seems to be speaking of Temmu continually through this section. His decision to sponsor the writing of the* Kojiki *is given special attention. The final sections tell the praises of the Empress and provide the only information* we have on the writing of this book. The significance of the Kojiki *is given in this section: it is "the basis of the country, the grand foundation of the monarchy."*[2]

I, Yasumaro, say:

When chaos had begun to condense, but force and form were not yet manifest, and noth-

---

[2] All selections from the Kojiki are taken, with editing, from Basil Hall Chamberlain, trans., *Ko-ji-ki, Transactions of the Asiatic Society of Japan,* supplement to vol. 10 (Tokyo: Asiatic Society of Japan, 1906).

ing was named, nothing done, who could know its shape? Nevertheless Heaven and Earth first parted, and the Three Deities[3] performed the commencement of creation. The Passive and Active Essences[4] then developed, and the Two Spirits[5] became the ancestors of all things. Therefore he entered obscurity and emerged into light, and the Sun and Moon were revealed by the washing of his eyes. He floated on and plunged into the sea-water, and Heavenly and Earthly Deities appeared through the washings of his person. So in the dimness of the great commencement, we, by relying on the original teaching, learn the time of the conception of the earth and of the birth of islands. In the remoteness of the original beginning, we, by trusting the former sages, perceive the era of the genesis of Deities and of the establishment of men. Truly, we know that a mirror was hung up,[6] that jewels were spat out, and that then a Hundred Kings succeeded each other. We know that a blade was bitten, and a serpent cut in pieces, so that a Myriad Deities flourished. By deliberations in the Tranquil River the Empire was pacified; by discussions on the Little Shore the land was purified.

Then His Augustness Ho-no-ni-ni-gi first descended to the Peak of Takachi, and the Heavenly Sovereign Kamu-Yamato traversed the Island of the Dragon-Fly. A weird bear put forth its claws, and a heavenly saber was obtained at Takakura. Men with tails obstructed the path, and a great crow guided him to Yeshinu. Dancing in rows, they destroyed the brigands, and listening to a song they vanquished their foes. Being instructed in a dream, he was reverent to the Heavenly and Earthly Deities, and was therefore styled the Wise Monarch. Having gazed on the

smoke, he was benevolent to the people, and is therefore remembered as the Emperor-Sage.

Determining the frontiers and civilizing the country, he issued laws from the Nearer Afumi; reforming the surnames and selecting the gentile names, he held sway at the Further Asuka. Though each differed in caution and in ardor, though all were unlike in accomplishments and in intrinsic worth, yet they all by contemplating antiquity corrected manners that had fallen to ruin; by illumining recent times, they repaired laws that were approaching dissolution.

In the august reign of the Heavenly Sovereign who governed the Eight Great Islands from the Great Palace of Kiyomihara at Asuka, the Hidden Dragon[7] put on perfection, the Reiterated Thunder came at the appointed moment. Having heard a song in a dream, he felt that he should continue the succession; having reached the water at night, he knew that he should receive the inheritance. Nevertheless Heaven's time was not yet, and he escaped like the cicada to the Southern Mountains.[8]

Then[9] both men and matters were favorable, and he marched like the tiger to the Eastern Land. Suddenly riding in the imperial chariot, he forced his way across mountains and rivers. The Six Divisions rolled like thunder, the Three Hosts sped like lightning. The erect spears lifted up their might, and the bold warriors arose like smoke. The crimson flags glistened among the weapons, and the ill-omened crew were shattered like tiles. Before a day had elapsed, the evil influences were purified. Then the cattle were let loose and the horses given repose, and with shouts of victory they returned to the Flowery Summer. The flags were rolled up and the javelins put away, and with dances and chants they came to rest in the capital city.

The year was that of the Rooster, and it was the Second Moon. At the Great Palace of

---

[3] *Deities:* the Japanese *kami* is translated "Deities" throughout.
[4] *Passive and Active Essences:* yin and yang, respectively.
[5] *The Two Spirits* from which all creation came are Izanagi (the Male-Who-Invites) and Izanami (the Female-Who-Invites).
[6] *mirror:* in many Shinto shrines, a mirror is often the only visible symbol of the *kami*'s presence.

[7] *the Hidden Dragon:* the emperor as the crown prince.
[8] The emperor renounced ordinary life for a time.
[9] This paragraph tells how the emperor crushed an attempt by a rival to gain the emperor's throne by force.

Kiyomihara, he ascended to the Heavenly seat. In morality he outstripped the Yellow Emperor, in virtue he surpassed the king of Chou.[10] Having grasped the celestial seals, he was paramount over the Six Cardinal Points; having obtained the Heavenly supremacy, he annexed the Eight Wildernesses. He held the mean between the Two Essences,[11] and regulated the order of the Five Elements. He established divine reason to advance good customs; he disseminated brilliant usages to make the land great. Moreover, the ocean of his wisdom, in its vastness, profoundly investigated the highest antiquity. The mirror of his heart, in its fervor, clearly observed former ages.

Then the Heavenly Sovereign commanded, saying: "I hear that the chronicles of the emperors and likewise the original words in the possession of the various families deviate from exact truth, and are mostly amplified by empty falsehoods. If at the present time these imperfections be not amended, before many years shall have elapsed, the purport of this, the great basis of the country, the grand foundation of the monarchy, will be destroyed. So now I desire to have the chronicles of the emperors selected and recorded, and the old words examined and ascertained, falsehoods erased and truth determined, in order to transmit [the latter] to later ages."

At that time there was a retainer whose surname was Hiyeda and his personal name Are. He was twenty-eight years old, and so intelligent that he could repeat with his mouth whatever met his eyes, and record in his heart whatever struck his ears. Then Are was commanded to learn by heart the genealogies of the emperors, and likewise the words of former ages. Nevertheless time elapsed and the age changed, and the thing was not yet carried out.

Prostrate, I consider how Her Majesty the Empress, having obtained Unity,[12] illumines the empire. Being versed in the Triad,[13] she nourishes the people. Ruling from the Purple Palace, her virtue reaches to the utmost limits of the horses' hoof-marks. Dwelling amid the Somber Retinue, her influence illumines the furthest distance attained to by vessels' prows. The sun rises, and the brightness is increased; the clouds disperse, neither is there smoke. The chroniclers never cease recording the good omens of connected stalks and double rice-ears. Never for a single moon is the treasury without the tribute of continuous beacon-fires and repeated interpretations. In fame she must be pronounced superior to Bum-Mei, in virtue more eminent than Ten-Itsu.[14]

Regretting the errors in the old words, and wishing to correct the misstatements in the former chronicles, on the eighteenth day of the ninth moon of the fourth year of Wa-do, she commanded me, Yasumaro, to select and record the old words learned by heart by Hiyeda no Are according to the Imperial Decree, and dutifully to lift them up to Her.

In reverent obedience to the contents of the Decree, I have made a careful choice. But in high antiquity both speech and thought were so simple, that it would be difficult to arrange phrases and compose sentences in [Chinese] characters. To relate everything in an ideographic transcription would entail an inadequate expression of the meaning. To write according to the phonetic method would make the story of events unduly lengthy. For this reason have I sometimes in the same sentence used the phonetic and ideographic systems conjointly, and have sometimes in one matter used the ideographic record exclusively. Moreover, where the drift of the words was obscure, I have by comments elucidated their meaning. But need it be said that I have nowhere commented on what was easy? Again, in such cases as calling the surname *Kusaka*, and

---

[10] *The Yellow Emperor* was a legendary ancient Chinese ruler; the *king of Chou* was Wen Wang, the founder of the Chou dynasty in China. Here the Chinese literary and historical background of early Japan becomes explicit.

[11] *the Two Essences:* yin and yang.

[12] *obtained Unity:* gotten the throne.

[13] *Triad:* heaven, humanity, and earth.

[14] *Bum-mei, Ten-itsu:* ancient Chinese rulers.

the personal name written with the character *Tarashi,* I have followed usage without alteration. Altogether the things recorded commence with the separation of Heaven and Earth, and conclude with the august reign at Woharida.[15] So from the Deity Master-of-the-August-Center-of-Heaven[16] down to His Augustness Prince-Wave-Limit-Brave-Cormorant-Thatch Meeting-Incompletely makes the First Volume. From the Heavenly Sovereign Kamu-Yamato-Ihare-Biko down to the august reign of Homuda makes the

Second Volume. From the Emperor Oho-Sazaki down to the great palace of Woharida makes the Third Volume. Altogether I have written three volumes, which I reverently and respectfully present. I, Yasumaro, with true trembling and true reverence, bow my head, and bow my head again.

Reverently presented by the Court Noble Futo no Yasumaro, an Officer of the Upper Division of the Fifth Rank and of the Fifth Order of Merit, on the 28th day of the first moon of the fifth year of Wa-do.[17]

---

[15] *reign at Wohadira:* of the Empress Suiko, who died in 628 C.E.
[16] The first god.

[17] March 10, 712 C.E.

The Creation of Japan*

In chapter 1 of the Kojiki, the spontaneous birth of the first gods is described. Although the narration starts at "the beginning of heaven and earth," the myths of the Kojiki (and the Nihongi as well) are much more stories of the creation of Japan than full-fledged stories of the creation of the world. The reader notices, for example, no mention of the making of humanity in general or of animals. At

the end of chapter 2, the key gods Izanagi (the Male-Who-Invites) and Izanami (the Female-Who-Invites) come into being, and they begin to create islands. Chapters 4 and 5 tell the story of the births of their first children, and we can see a concern for proper male-female relationship here. In chapter 11, the sun goddess Amaterasu is given the rule of heavenly deities. In chapter 33, the culmination of these myths is reached when the grandson of Amaterasu descends from heaven to rule the land that was to become Japan.

---

* *Kojiki,* chapters 1–5, 11, 33

CHAPTER 1 THE BEGINNING OF HEAVEN AND EARTH

The names of the Deities that were born in the Plain of High Heaven when the Heaven and Earth began were the Deity Master-of-the-August-Center-of-Heaven, next the High-August-Producing-Wondrous-Deity, then the Divine-Producing-Wondrous Deity. These three Deities were all Deities born alone, and hid their persons. The names of the Deities that were born next from a thing that sprouted up like

a reed-shoot when the earth, young and like floating oil, drifted about medusa-like, were the Pleasant-Reed-Shoot-Prince-Elder-Deity and the heavenly-Eternally-Standing-Deity. These two Deities were likewise born alone, and hid their persons.

The five Deities in the above list are separate Heavenly Deities.

CHAPTER 2 THE SEVEN DIVINE GENERATIONS

The names of the Deities that were born next were the Earthly-Eternally-Standing-Deity, next the Luxuriant-Integrating-Master-Deity. These two Deities were likewise Deities born alone, and hid their persons. The names of the Deities that were born next were the Deity Mud-Earth-Lord, next his younger sister the Deity Mud-Earth-Lady; next the Germ-Integrating-Deity, next his younger sister the Life-Integrating-Deity; next the Deity Elder-of-the-Great-Place, next his younger sister the Deity Elder-Lady-of-the-Great-Place; next the Deity Perfect-Exterior, next his younger sister the Deity Oh-Awful-Lady; next the Deity the Male-Who-Invites, next his younger sister the Deity the Female-Who-Invites. From the Earthly-Eternally-Standing Deity down to the Deity the Female-Who-Invites in the previous list are what are termed the Seven Divine Generations. (The two solitary Deities above [mentioned] are each called one generation. Of the succeeding ten Deities each pair of deities is called a generation).

CHAPTER 3 THE ISLAND OF ONOGORO

Then all the Heavenly Deities commanded the two Deities His Augustness the Male-Who-Invites and Her Augustness the Female-Who-Invites, ordering them to "make, consolidate, and give birth to this drifting land." Granting to them a heavenly jewelled spear, they charged them thus. So the two Deities, standing upon the Floating Bridge of Heaven, pushed down the jewelled spear and stirred with it. When they had stirred the brine till it went curdle-curdle, and drew [the spear] up, the brine that dripped down from the end of the spear was piled up and became an island. This is the Island of Onogoro.

CHAPTER 4 COURTSHIP OF THE DEITIES, THE MALE-WHO-INVITES AND THE FEMALE-WHO-INVITES

Having descended from Heaven onto this island, they saw to the erection of an heavenly august pillar, and they saw to the erection of a hall of eight fathoms. Then he asked the Female-Who-Invites, "In what form is your body made?" She responded, saying, "My body is formed with one part not fully formed." Then the Male-Who-Invites said, "My body is formed with one part more than fully formed. Therefore, would it not be good to take that part of my body which is more than fully formed and insert it into that part of your body which is less than fully formed, and procreate the land?" The Female-Who-Invites responded, "That would be good." Then the Male-Who-Invites said, "Let us walk in a circle about this heavenly pillar, meet, and have intercourse." Then she said, "You go around from the right, and I will go around from the left." When they agreed and went around, and the Female-Who-Invites said first, "What a charming and lovable male!" Then the Male-Who-Invites said, "What a charming and lovable female!" When each had finished talking, he said to his wife, "It is not fitting that the woman speak first." But they still began procreating, and she gave birth to a leech-child. This child they placed in a boat of reeds, and let it float away. Next they gave birth to the Island of Aha. He also is not reckoned among their children.

CHAPTER 5 BIRTH OF THE EIGHT ISLANDS

Then the two Deities took counsel, saying: "The children to whom we have now given birth are not good. It will be best to announce this in the august place of the Heavenly Deities." They ascended to Heaven and enquired of Their Augustnesses the Heavenly Deities. Then the Heavenly Deities commanded and found out by grand divination, and ordered them, saying: "They were not good because the woman spoke first. Descend back again and amend your words." So descending back, they again went round the heavenly august pillar as before. Then his Augustness the Male-Who-Invites spoke first:

"Ah! what a charming and lovely maiden!" Afterwards his younger sister Her Augustness the Female-Who-Invites spoke: "Ah! what a charming and lovely youth!" When these words were said, they had intercourse as before, and procreated the Island of Ahaji, Ho-no-sa-wake. Next they gave birth to the Island of Futa-na in Iyo. This island has one body and four faces, and each face has a name. So the Land of Iyo is called Lovely Princess; the Land of Sanuki is called Prince Good-Boiled-Rice; the Land of Aha is called the Princess-of-Great-Food; the Land of Tosa is called Brave-Good-Youth. . . .

CHAPTER 11 THE INVESTITURE OF THE THREE DEITIES, THE ILLUSTRIOUS AUGUST CHILDREN

At this time His Augustness the Male-Who-Invites greatly rejoiced, saying, "I, begetting child after child, have finally gotten three illustrious children." Then jinglingly taking off and shaking the jewel-string forming his august necklace, he bestowed it on the Heaven-Shining-Great-August-Deity, saying: "Augustness, rule the Plain-of-High-Heaven." With this

charge he bestowed it on her. Now the name of this august necklace was the August-Storehouse-Shelf-Deity. Next he said to His Augustness Moon-Night-Possessor: "Rule the Dominion of the Night." Thus he charged him. Next he said to His-Brave-Swift-Impetuous-Male-Augustness, "Rule the Sea-Plain."

CHAPTER 33 THE AUGUST DESCENT FROM HEAVEN OF HIS AUGUSTNESS THE AUGUST GRANDCHILD

Then the Heaven-Shining-Great-August-Deity and the High-Integrating-Deity commanded and charged the Heir Apparent His Augustness Truly-Conqueror-I-Conquer-Swift-Heavenly-Great-Great-Ears [saying: "The Brave-Awful-Possessing-Male-Deity] says that he has now finished pacifying the Central Land of Reed-Plains. In accordance with our gracious charge, descend to, dwell in, and rule over it." Then the Heir Apparent His Augustness Truly-Conqueror-I-Conquer-Swift-Heavenly-Great-Ears replied, saying: "While I have been getting ready to descend, there has been born [to me] a child

whose name is His Augustness Heaven-Plenty-Earth-Plenty-Heaven's-Sun-Height-Prince-Rice-ear-Ruddy-Plenty. This child should be sent down. [As for this august child, he was augustly joined to Her Augustness Myriad-Looms-Luxuriant-Dragon-fly-Island-Princess, daughter of the High-Integrating-Deity, and begot children: His Augustness-Heavenly Rice-ear-Ruddy, and next His Augustness Prince-Rice-ear-Ruddy-Plenty].

Therefore, in accordance with these words, they laid their command on His Augustness Prince Rice-ear-Ruddy-Plenty, charging him with these words, "This Luxuriant Reed-Plain-Land-of-Fresh-Rice-ears is the land over which you shall rule." So [he replied]: "I will descend from Heaven according to your commands." So when His Augustness Prince Rice-ear-Ruddy-Plenty was about to descend from Heaven, there was at the eight-forking road of Heaven a Deity whose refulgence reached upwards to the Plain of High Heaven and downwards to the Central Land of Reed-Plains. So then the Heaven-Shining-Great-August-Deity and the High-Integrating Deity commanded and charged the Heavenly-Alarming-Female-Deity [saying]: "Though you are a delicate female, you are a Deity who conquers in facing Deities. So be the one to go and ask thus, 'This being the road by which our august child is about to descend from Heaven, who is it that is there'?" So to this gracious question he replied, saying, "I am an Earthly Deity named the Deity Prince of Saruta. The reason for my coming here is that, having heard of the [intended] descent of the august child of the Heavenly Deities, I have come humbly to meet him and respectfully offer myself as His Augustness's vanguard." Then joining to him His Augustness Heavenly-Beckoning-Ancestor-Lord, His Augustness Grand-Jewel, Her Augustness Heavenly-Alarming-Female, Her Augustness I-shi-ko-ri-do-me, and His Augustness Jewel-Ancestor, in all five chiefs of companies, they sent him down from Heaven.

Thereupon they joined to him the eight-feet [long] curved jewels and mirror that had allured [the Heaven-Shining-Great-August-Deity from the Rock-Dwelling], and also the Herb-Quelling-Great-Sword, and likewise the Deity Thought-Includer, the Hand-Strength-Male-Deity, and the Deity Heavenly-Rock-Door-Opener of Eternal Night, and charged him, "Regard this mirror exactly as if it were our august spirit, and reverence it as if reverencing us." Next they said, "Let the Deity Thought-Includer take in hand our affairs, and carry on the government." These two Deities are worshipped at the temple of Isuzu. The next, the Deity of Luxuriant-Food, is the Deity dwelling in the outer temple of Watarahi. The next, the Deity Heavenly-Rock-Door-Opener, another name for whom is the Wondrous-Rock-True-Gate-Deity, and another name for whom is the Luxuriant-Rock-True-Gate-Deity—this Deity of the August Gate. The next, the Deity Hand-Strength-Male, dwells in Sanagata. Now His Augustness the Heavenly-Beckoning-Ancestor-Lord [is the Ancestor of the Nakatomi Chieftains], His Augustness Grand Jewel [is the ancestor of the Imibe Headmen]; Her Augustness the Heavenly-Alarming-Female [is the ancestress of the Duchesses of Saru]; Her Augustness I-shi-ko-ri-do-me [is the ancestress of the Mirror-Making Chieftains]; His Augustness-Jewel Ancestor [is the ancestor of the Jewel-Ancestor Chieftains.]

The Shrine at Ise*

The Shrine at Ise is the most important Shinto shrine standing today. The following is a description of the initiation of the shrine as well as its connection between the emperor and Amaterasu, to whom the shrine is dedicated.

25th year, Spring, and month, 8th day. The Emperor commanded the five officers, Takenu

Kaha-wake, ancestor of the Abe no Omi; Hiko-kuni-fuku, ancestor of the Imperial Chieftains; O-kashima, ancestor of the Nakatome Deity Chieftains; and Tochine, ancestor of the Mono-nobe Deity chieftains . . . saying: "The sagacity of Our predecessor on the throne, the Emperor Mimaki-iri-hiko-inie, was displayed in wisdom; he was reverential, intelligent, and capable. He was profoundly unassuming, and his disposition was to cherish self-abnegation. He adjusted the machinery of government, and did solemn wor-

---

* *Nihongi*, chapter 5

ship to the Gods of Heaven and Earth. He practiced self-restraint and was watchful of his personal conduct. Every day he was heedful for that
day. Thus the welfare of the people was sufficient, and the Empire was at peace. And now,
under Our reign, will there be any remissness in
the worship of the Gods of Heaven and Earth?'

3rd month, 10th day. The Great Goddess
Amaterasu was taken from [the princess] Toyo-
suki-iri-hime, and entrusted to [the princess]
Yamato-hime no Mikoto. Now Yamato-hime
sought for a place where she might enshrine the
Great Goddess. So she proceeded to Sasahata in
Uda. Then turning back from there, she entered

the land of Omi, and went round eastwards to
Mino, and so she arrived in the province of Ise.

Now the Great Goddess Amaterasu instructed
Yamato-hime, saying: "The province of Ise, of
the divine wind, is the land in which the waves
from the eternal world reside, the successive
waves. It is a secluded and pleasant land. In this
land I wish to reside." In compliance, therefore,
with the instruction of the Great Goddess, a
shrine was erected to her in the province of Ise.
Accordingly an Abstinence Palace was built at
Kawakami in Isuzu. This was called the Palace of
Ise. It was there that the Great Goddess Ame-
terasu first descended from Heaven.

Emperor Yuryaku and the Story of the Woman Akawi-ko*

Most of the Kojiki *is made up of legendary stories
about the Japanese emperors told to extol their
greatness. This bittersweet story of the woman
Akawi-ko and the emperor Yuryaku, with the poetic songs which conclude it, is indicative of Japanese literary style. In this chapter, the old woman
Akawi-ko comes before Emperor Yuryaku to prove
her faithfulness to a command he had given her
many years before.*

Once when the Heavenly Sovereign, going out
for amusement, reached the River Miwa, there
was a girl whose appearance was very beautiful
washing clothes by the river-side. The Heavenly
Sovereign asked the girl, "Whose child are you?"
She replied, "My name is Akawi-ko of the Hiketa
Tribe." Then he said to her, "Do not marry a
husband. I will send for you," and [with these
words] he returned to the palace. Then eighty
years passed while she reverently awaited the
Heavenly Sovereign's commands. Then Akawi-
ko thought: "While looking for the [Imperial]
commands, I have already passed many years,
and as my face and form are lean and withered,

there is no longer any hope. Nevertheless, if I do
not show [the Heavenly Sovereign] how truly I
have waited, my disappointment will be unbear-
able." She caused merchandise to be carried on
tables holding a hundred items, and came forth
and presented [these gifts as] tribute. Then the
Heavenly Sovereign, who had quite forgotten
what he had formerly commanded, asked Akawi-
ko, saying: "What old woman are you, and why
have you come here?" Then Akawi-ko replied,
saying: "Having in such and such a month of
such and such a year received the Heavenly
Sovereign's commands, I have been reverently
awaiting the great command until this day, and
eighty years have past by. Now my appearance is
quite decrepit, and there is no longer any hope.
Nevertheless I have come forth in order to show
and declare my faithfulness." Then the Heavenly
Sovereign was greatly startled [and exclaimed],
"I had quite forgotten the former circumstance;
and you meanwhile, ever faithfully awaiting my
commands, have vainly let pass by the years of
your prime. This is very pitiful." In his heart
he wished to marry her, but shrank from her
extreme age, and could not make the marriage;
but he conferred on her an august Song. That
Song said:

---

* *Kojiki*, chapter 154

"How awful is the sacred oak-tree, the oak-tree of the august dwelling! Maiden of the oak-plain!"

Again he sang,

"The younger chestnut orchard plain of Hiketa: would I had slept with her in her youth! Oh! how old she has become!"

Then the tears that Akawi-ko wept drenched the red-dyed sleeve that she had on. In reply to the great august Song, she sang, saying:

"Left over from the piling up of the jewel-wall piled up round the august dwelling,—to whom shall the person of the Deity's temple go?"

Again she sang,

"Oh! how enviable is she who is in her bloom like the flowering lotus—the lotus of the inlet, of the inlet of Kusaka."

Then the old woman was sent back plentifully endowed. So these four Songs are Quiet Songs.

SELECTIONS FROM THE *NORITO*

Festival of the Gates*

Here is a ritual prayer to specific Kami to protect the emperor's palace from evil spirits.

I humbly speak your names: Kusi-iha-mato,
Toyo-iha-mato-no-mikoto,
Because you swell massively imbedded like
    sacred massed rocks
In the inner and outer gates of the four
    quarters.
Because if from the four quarters and the four
    corners
There should come the unfriendly and unruly
    deity called Ame-no-maga-tu-hi,

You are not bewitched and do not speak con-
    sent to his evil words—
If he goes from above, you guard above.
If he goes from below, you guard below,
And lie in wait to protect and to drive away
And to repulse him with words;
Because you open the gates in the morning and
    close the gates in the evening;
You inquire and know the names
Of those who go in and those who go out;
And if there be any fault or error,
In the manner of [the rectifying deities] Kamu-
    naho-bi and Oho-naho-bi
You behold it rectified and hear it rectified,
And cause [the court attendants] to serve tran-
    quilly and peacefully.
Therefore [I speak] your names . . .
And fulfill your praises. Thus I humbly speak.

---

* *Norito*

Ritual Prayer for Forgiveness and Purification of Governing Officials*

Here is a prayer for the purification of the government. The ritual actions accompanying the prayer can often be seen in its text.

He says [referring to the sovereign, in whose behalf a priest of the Nakatomi clan or a diviner of the Urabe clan recites]:

Hear all of you assembled: imperial and royal princes, nobles and officials.

Hear all of you assembled that on the occasion of the great exorcism of the sixth month of the current year, various offences and defilements incurred by the functionaries of the government offices, including those attendants who wear the scarf, the sash, the quiver and the sword, as well as those attendants of the attendants, will be cleansed and purified. Thus He speaks.

"Hear all of you assembled that the ancestral kami of the sovereign dwelling in the Plain of High Heaven commanded the gathering of the 800 myriads of kami for consultation, and then declared, 'Our august grandchild is commissioned to rule and pacify the country of the Plentiful Reed Plains of the Fresh Ears of Grain [Japan].' Following this commission, the unruly kami [of the land of Japan] were either pacified or expelled, and even the rocks, trees, and leaves which had formerly spoken were silenced, and thus enabling the august grandchild (Ninigi) to descend from the heavenly rock-seat, dividing the myriad layers of heavenly clouds, and reach the entrusted lands.

"Thus pacified, the land became the Great Yamato or the country of the Sun-seen-on-high, where the palace pillars were deeply grounded in the rock below and the palace beams were built to reach the Plain of High Heaven for the dwelling of the august grandchild, who, living in the shadow of heaven and sun, ruled the peaceful nation. With the increase of the descendants of the heavenly kami, however, various offences were committed by them. Among them, the offences of destroying the divisions of the rice fields, covering up the irrigation ditches, opening the irrigation sluices, sowing the seeds over the seeds planted by others, planting pointed rods in the rice fields, flaying living animals or flaying them backwards, emptying excrements in improper areas, and the like, are called the 'offences to heaven,' whereas the offences of cutting the living or the dead skin, suffering from white leprosy or skin excrescences, violating one's own mother or daughter, step-daughter or mother-in-law, cohabiting with animals, allowing the defilements by creeping insects, the thunder or the birds, killing the animals of others, invoking evils on others by means of witchcraft, and the like, are called the 'offences to earth,' and are differentiated from the 'offences to heaven.'

"When these offences are committed, the chief of the Nakatomi priestly clan is commanded, in accordance with the ritual performed in the heavenly palace [of the Sun Goddess], to cut off the bottom and the ends of a sacred tree and place them in abundance as offerings on divine seats, and also to cut off the bottom and ends of sacred sedge reeds and slice them into thin pieces, and then to recite the potent words of the heavenly ritual prayers. When this ritual is performed properly, the heavenly kami will hear the words of petition by opening up the heavenly rock door and by dividing the myriad layers of heavenly clouds, while [at the same time] the earthly kami will hear the words of petition by climbing up to the peaks of high and low mountains and by pushing aside the mists of the high and the low mountains.

"When the heavenly and the earthly kami thus hear the ritual prayers, all the offences will be gone from the court of the august grandchild as well as from the four quarters of the land under the heaven, just as the winds of morning and

---

* *Norito*

evening blow away the morning and evening mists, as the anchored large ship is untied and is pushed out into the ocean, or as the dense bushes are cut off at the bottom by sharp sickles. Indeed, all offences and defilements will be purified and will be carried to the ocean from the peaks of the high and low mountains by the princess whose name is 'Descent into the Current,' the kami dwelling in the currents of the rapid stream which surges down the hillside.

"When the offences are thus taken to the ocean, the princess named 'Swift Opening,' the kami who lives in the meeting place of eight hundred currents of the brine, will swallow them up.

"When the offences are thus swallowed up, the kami who dwells at the breath-blowing-gate called the 'Lord Breath-blowing-gate' will blow them away into the netherworld.

"When the offences are thus blown away, the princess named 'Swift Wanderer,' the kami who dwells in the netherworld, will wander away with them and lose them.

"And when the offences are thus lost, it is announced that from this day onward there is no offence remaining among the officials of the sovereign's court and in the four quarters of the land under heaven, while the horses with their ears turned toward the Plain of High Heaven stand listening.

"Hear all of you assembled that all the offences have been cleansed and purified on the great exorcism celebrated in the dusk on the last day of the sixth month of the current year.

"Oh, you diviners of the four provinces, leave here carrying the offences to the great rivers, and cast them away by the rite of purification." Thus he speaks.

GLOSSARY

kami [KAH-mee] gods or spirits, and their sacred power.

Kojiki [koh-JEE-kee] the *Record of Ancient Matters,* the first of the eighth-century C.E. books telling the mythology of Japan.

Nihongi [nih-HAWN-gee] the *Chronicles of Japan,* the second book on Japanese myth, written shortly after the *Kojiki.*

QUESTIONS FOR STUDY AND DISCUSSION

1. Describe the basic structure of Shinto polytheism as reflected in Shinto mythology.

2. Why, in your view, do the Japanese myths place so much emphasis on the creation of Japan instead of on the creation of the world?

3. Compare the status of the emperor in Confucianism and Shinto.

4. To what degree does the *Kojiki* reflect the traditional interpersonal customs of Japan?

5. How might the Emperor's renunciation of divine standing have altered the reading of these texts and their influence in contemporary Japan?

SUGGESTIONS FOR FURTHER READING

W. G. Aston, *Nihongi: Chronicles of Japan from the Earliest Times to A.D. 697.* London: Kegan Paul, 1896.

B. H. Chamberlain, *Translation of* Ko-ji-ki. 1st ed., Tokyo: Asiatic Society of Japan, 1906; 2nd ed., Kobe: Thompson, 1932. The standard translation of the *Kojiki*.

Wm. Theodore de Bary, *Sources of Japanese Tradition*. New York: Columbia University Press, 1958. Contains fresh translations of many important Shinto texts, and a treatment of how early texts were used in Japanese history.

H. B. Earhart, *Japanese Religion: Unity and Diversity,* 3rd ed. Belmont, CA: Wadsworth, 1982. An excellent treatment of Shinto in the context of Japanese religions.

D. Philippi, *The* Kojiki. Tokyo: Princeton University Press and University of Tokyo Press, 1968. Has full and helpful introduction and notes.

Index

Abhidhamma, **113**

Adi Granth
  origin and development, 138–139
  structure, 137–138
  use, 139–140

Agama
  origin, development and use, 117–118
  structure, 117–118

Agni, 24, 26, 32, 37, 45, 46, 47, 49, 50, 51

Ahimsa, 117, 123, 127, **134**

Ahura, 158, 159, 160, 161, 162, 163, 164,
  166, 167, 168

Alms
  in Buddhism, 111
  in Hinduism, 38, 40, 42, 43
  in Jainism, 129, 130
  in Sikhism, 142, 148

Analects, 5, 7, 8
  origin and development, 173–174
  structure, 173
  use, 174–175

Angas, 118, 126, **134**

Aranyakas, 24, 25, 27, **66**

Arhat, **134**

Asceticism
  in Buddhism, 83, 88, 101
  in Hinduism, 25, 39, 40, 42
  in Jainism, 126

Atman, 27, 32, **66**

Avesta
  origin and development, 158–159
  structure, 157–158
  use, 159–160

Bhagavad-Gita, **66**
  introduction to, 53
  selections from, 53–63

Benevolence, 7, 178, 183, 186, 188, 198

Bibliolatry, **20**, 77

Bibliomancy, 10, **20**

Birth
  in Buddhism, 79, 82, 83, 90, 102, 112
  in Hinduism, 30, 32, 33, 34, 41, 42, 56,
    57, 64
  in Jainism, 119, 123, 124, 128
  in Shinto, 224, 225, 227, 228, 229
  in Sikhism, 152, 153, 154
  in Taoism, 219
  in Zoroastrianism, 162

Bodhisattva, **113**

Book of Poetry, 183, 185, 186

Brahman, 27, 31, 32, 33, 40, 42, 43, 45, 51,
  53, **66,** 79

Brahmanas, 24, 25, 27, 28, **66**

Buddha, 7, 71, 73–79, 83, 84, 89, 93, 94,
  97, 98, 100, 101, 105–107, 110–113,
  195

Buddhism, 5, 7, 8, 9, 16, 17, 18, 119, 172,
  195
  general desciption of, 71
  scripture in, 71–77
  scripture selections from, 77–113

Canon, 8, **20**
  in Buddhism, 71, 73, 74, 76, 110, 113,
    114
  in Confucianism, 171, 172, 173, 174,
    175, 198
  in Hindusim, 24, 29
  in Jainism, 118, 134
  in Taoism, 201, 202, 220
  in Zoroastrianism, 159

Caste
  in Buddhism, 111
  in Hinduism, 17, 26–29, 36–38, 41–42,
    44, 53–55, 61
  in Sikhism, 138

Chaur, **154**

Child, children
  in Buddhism, 80,

(Note: boldface entries indicate pages where subjects are defined in a glossary section)

in Confucianism, 174, 180, 183, 188
in Hinduism, 34, 35, 40, 41, 42
in Jainism, 123
in Shinto, 223, 227, 228, 229, 230, 231
in Sikhism, 153
in Taoism, 205, 210, 211
Ching, **198**
Chung-tzu, **198**
Classic of Changes, 172, 189, **198**
Classic of Rites, 172–173, 179, 185, 193
Commentary, **20**, 28, 75, 172, 173, 185, 186
Confession, 73, 102, 119, 141, 158
Confucianism
    general description of, 171
    scripture in, 171–175
    scripture selections from, 175–198
Confucius, 170–177, 180–183, 185, 187,
    198
Creation, 17. *See also* Earth; World
    in Hinduism, 24, 28, 30, 31, 32, 36
    in Jainism, 122, 123, 128
    in Shinto, 224, 225, 227
    in Sikhism, 140, 146, 152, 154
    in Zoroastrianism, 158, 161, 163, 166

Dasam Granth, 138, 139, 140, **154**
    selections from, 152–154
Death, 13. *See also* Funeral
    in Buddhism, 75, 82–84, 88, 90, 91, 103,
        106, 111, 112
    in Confucianism, 172, 173, 178, 188, 191
    in Hinduism, 31, 33, 34, 39, 42, 43, 44,
        46, 51, 52, 53, 56, 58, 61, 65
    in Jainism, 119, 120, 123, 124, 128, 129
    in Sikhism, 139, 144, 145, 152
    in Taoism, 200, 202, 205, 208, 211, 212,
        213
    in Zoroastrianism, 167–168
Dhamma, 73, 75, 98, 102, 103, 104, **113**
Dharma-Shastras, **66**
Divination, 5, 10, 130, 172, 189, 229

Earth. *See also* Creation, World
    in Buddhism, 79, 80, 84, 89, 98, 102, 108,
        110
    in Confucianism, 194
    in Hinduism, 26, 30, 32, 33, 34, 37, 38,
        45, 47, 50, 51, 52, 54, 57, 60, 63
    in Jainism, 124, 128, 129, 130

in Shinto, 225, 227
in Sikhism, 145, 146
in Taoism, 202, 203, 204, 210, 211
in Zoroastrianism, 160, 162, 163, 164,
    167, 168
Eightfold Path, 88, 89, 101
Evil, 10, 17
    in Buddhism, 80, 81, 90, 98, 99, 104,
        111, 112, 113
    in Confucianism, 173, 183, 184, 189,
        190, 193, 194
    in Hinduism, 33, 38, 48, 49, 53, 54, 55,
        56, 57, 64
    in Jainism, 123
    in Shinto, 225, 232
    in Sikhism, 140, 149, 154
    in Taoism, 203, 207, 210, 211, 212–213,
        217, 219,
    in Zoroastrianism, 158, 160, 163, 164, 166

Fasting, 82, 121
Filiality, 171, 173, 180, 181, 198
Five Classics, 172
Forgiveness, 42, 149, 233
Four Books, 172–174, 185
Four Noble Truths, 88–89, 101–102, 109
Fravashi, 161, 165, **168**
Funeral. *See also* Death
    in Buddhism, 85, 86
    in Confucianism, 178
    in Hinduism, 50
    in Sikhism, 137
    in Zoroastrianism, 167–168

Gathas, 158, 159, 165, **168**
Genre, 19, **20**
God, gods
    in Buddhism, 81, 84, 89, 90, 94, 97–98,
        101–102, 111
    in Hinduism, 23–28, 30–33, 36–39, 42,
        43, 45–47, 49–52, 58–60, 63, 64,
        65, 66
    in Jainism, 119, 120–123, 128
    in Shinto, 223–224, 227, 234
    in Sikhism, 138–155
    in Taoism, 212, 213, 216, 217
    in Zoroastrianism, 160
Good, goodness
    in Buddhism, 76, 78, 80, 82, 83, 89, 90,

Good, goodness (*continued*)
93, 95–97, 99, 100, 101, 103, 104,
106, 110, 111
in Confucianism, 173, 175, 176, 177, 178,
180, 181, 182, 183, 184, 186, 187,
188, 189, 190, 193, 194
in Hinduism, 23, 33, 39, 40, 44, 45, 47,
48, 49, 50, 54, 62, 64, 65
in Jainism, 122, 129
in Taoism, 202, 203, 211, 212, 216, 217,
219
in Shinto, 223, 226, 228, 229
in Sikhism, 140, 142, 143, 148, 150, 151,
154
in Zoroastrianism, 158, 160, 161, 162,
163, 164, 165, 166, 167
Government
in Buddhism, 100
in Confucianism, 172–174, 182, 185–188
in Hinduism, 26
in Shinto, 224, 230
in Taoism, 208–210
Granthi, 138, 140, **154**
Great Learning, 173, 174, 185, 187
Guru
in Hinduism, 28, 40
in Sikhism, 138, 139, 140, 145, 148, 151,
152, 154
Gutka, **154**

Haoma, 158
Heaven, heavens
in Buddhism, 79, 80, 81, 82, 85, 89, 111,
113
in Confucianism, 182, 194, 198
in Hinduism, 31, 33, 37, 40, 42, 44, 50,
51, 55, 56, 57, 58, 60
in Sikhism, 138, 146
in Taoism, 202, 203, 204, 207, 211
in Zoroastrianism, 163, 168
Hell, hells
in Buddhism, 97
in Hinduism, 42, 50, 54, 61, 65
in Jainism, 122, 124
in Sikhism, 153
Henotheism, **66**
Hinduism
general description of, 23
scriptures in, 5, 8, 9, 10, 15, 16, 17, 18,
23–30

scripture selections from, 30–66
other views of, 137, 138, 140, 147
Householder, 40–42, 97, 98, 122
Hsiao, **198**
Hymn, hymns
in Hinduism, 24, 30, 32, 33, 45, 47–49,
58
in Sikhism, 137, 138, 150–153
in Zoroastrianism, 158, 159, 161, 162

Icon, **20**, 139
Indra, 24, 26, 32, 33, 37, 47, 48, 49, 51,
58, 142

Jainism, 8, 16, 17, 117, 119
general description of, 117
scriptures in, 8, 16, 17, 117–119
scripture selections from, 119–134
Janam-sakhis, **154**
Japji, 137, 140, 145, **154**
Jatakas, 74, 77, **113**
Jina, 119, 122, 126, 127, **134**
Judgment, 62, 165, 212

Kami, 223, **234**
Kojiki, 223, 224, 227, 231, **234**

Lao Tzu, 201, 202
Law
in Buddhism, 93, 94, 97, 99, 104, 106
in Confucianism, 172, 179, 185, 192
in Hinduism, 24, 26, 27, 28, 30, 40, 42,
43
in Jainism, 122,
in Sikhism, 144
in Zoroastrianism, 158, 161, 163
Love
in Buddhism, 80, 98, 100, 110
in Confucianism, 171, 172, 177, 178,
182, 183, 184, 185, 198
in Hinduism, 48, 49, 50, 51, 53
in Jainism, 120, 123, 126, 129, 130
in Sikhism, 141, 143, 144, 145, 147, 148,
149, 150, 151, 153, 154
in Zoroastrianism, 166

Mahala, **154**
Mahavira, 117–123, 127, 128
Mahayana, **114**
Mantra, 29, 46, 47, 51, **67**, 91

Marriage, 41, 48, 50, 102, 137, 167, 212, 231

Mencius, 173, 183, 184, 188

Monk, monks, 7, 9, 17,
  in Buddhism, 73, 75–77, 88–89, 93–94, 96–99, 101–108
  in Jainism, 118–119, 124, 125, 127, 129, 130

Muhammad, 153

Mul Mantra, **154**

Muslims, 137

Nanak, 137–139, 141–147, 148–149, 150–152, 154

Narrative, 19, **20**, 28, 53, 224

Nihongi, 223, 224, 227, 230, **234**

Nun, nuns
  in Buddhism, 71, 73, 76, 94, 96, 102, 105–106
  in Jainism, 118–119, 125, 127, 129

Om, 34, 39, 40, 51, 52, 58, **67**

Oral tradition, 6, 11, 13, **20**, 76, 158

Pandit, **67**

Parinibbana, **114**

Prakaranas, **134**

Prayer, 33, 44, 67, 77, 113, 139, 145, 149, 158, 160, 161, 192, 232

Priest, priests
  in Hinduism, 24, 27, 32, 45, 49, 52, 62
  in Taoism, 200
  in Zoroastrianism, 158, 159

Prophet, 128, 157, 158

Propriety, 171, 178, 180, 181, 182, 185, 188, 198

Puranas, 24, 26, 28, 143, 144, 145, 146

Quran, 5, 143

Rags, **154**

Rebirth
  in Hinduism, 23, 29, 40, 45, 57, 60
  in Buddhism, 80, 83, 89, 111
  in Sikhism, 138

Reincarnation, 50, 112, 117, 123, 125, 138

Relic, 110

Rishis, 24, **67**

Sacrifice, 5, 7, 11,
  in Buddhism, 78

  in Confucianism, 172, 176, 178, 182, 190–193
  Hinduism, 24, 25, 26, 27, 36, 37, 38, 39, 44, 45, 50, 51, 52, 53, 57, 58, 60, 61, 63, 66
  in Sikhism, 143
  in Zoroastrianism, 158, 159, 161

Samhitas, 24, 29, **67**

Scripture, **20**

Shaoshyant, **168**

Shinto, 16, 223, 224, 230

Shiva, 18, 26, 28, 33, 65, 142

Shruti, 8, 23, 24, 25, 27, **67**

Siddhanta, **134**

Sikhism, 7, 8, 16
  general description, 137
  scriptures in, 137–140
  scripture selections from, 140–134

Skandhas, 83, 89, 90, 91, 97

Smriti, 23, 24, 25, 26, 27, **67**

Soma, 25, 27, 47

Superior man, 208

Sutta, **114**

Sutta Pitaka, 73, 76, 96

Tao, 6, 7, 8, 13, 18, 173, 182, **198**, 201–209, 211, 216–220

Taoism, 5, 7, 8, 10, 16, 17, 18
  general description, 201
  scripture in, 201–203
  scripture selections from, 203–219

Tao Te Ching, 6, 7, 8, 13, 201, 202, 203, 205, 206, 209, 220

Tao Tsang, 201, 220

Tathagata, 84, 85, 88, 93, 94, 101, 105, 106, **114**

Te, 202, 220

Theravada, **114**

Tipitaka, 71, 73, **114**

Tirthankara, 120, 123, **134**

Upanishads, 5, 24–25, 27–30, **67**

Vak lao, 140, **155**

Vedas, 5, 11, 14, 24–29, 34, 41–42, 47, 51–52, **67**, 142, 145–146, 151, 153

Vendidad, **168**

Vinaya, **114**

Vinaya Pitaka, 73, 76, 101, 102

Visparad, **168**

war, 26, 35, 53, 54–56, 107, 113, 191, 209, 217
Wen-yen, **198**
Wife. *See also* Woman
  in Buddhism, 78, 98, 103
  in Confucianism, 179, 180, 190
  in Hinduism, 25, 31, 41, 42, 43, 44, 48, 49, 50
  in Taoism, 210, 211, 213
  in Shinto, 228
Wine, 38, 149, 150, 176, 181, 188, 189
Woman, women. *See also* Wife
  in Buddhism, 79, 80, 84, 90, 95, 103, 105, 106, 111
  in Confucianism, 177, 190, 198
  in Hinduism, 31, 41–44, 48, 49, 50, 51, 54
  in Jainism, 117–119, 124–125, 129–130
  in Shinto, 224, 228, 229, 231, 232
  in Taoism, 217, 218
World. *See also* Creation; Earth
  in Buddhism, 71, 79, 80, 81, 82, 83, 84, 85, 88, 89, 93, 94, 97, 98, 99, 100, 101, 102, 107, 109, 110, 111, 113
  in Hindusim, 23, 24, 25, 27, 30, 31, 32, 33, 34, 38, 39, 40, 43, 44, 47, 48, 49, 50, 52, 55, 57, 58, 61, 65, 66
  in Jainism, 119, 120, 122, 123, 124, 126, 128, 134
  in Taoism, 201, 204, 205, 206, 207, 208, 209, 217, 218, 219
  in Sikhism, 137, 139, 140, 141, 143–147, 152, 153, 154
  in Shinto, 223, 224, 227, 231
  in Zoroastrianism, 157, 161, 162, 163, 164, 165, 166, 167, 168

Yashts, **168**
Yasna, 157, 158, 159, 160, 162, 163, 165–**168**

Zarathushtra, 157, 158, 159, 160, 161, 162, 163, 166, 167
Zoroastrianism
  general description, 157
  scripture in, 157–160
  scripture selections from, 160–168